U.S.-Mexican
Industrial Integration

U.S.-Mexican Industrial Integration

The Road to Free Trade

EDITED BY
Sidney Weintraub

with Luis Rubio F.
and Alan D. Jones

Westview Press

BOULDER • SAN FRANCISCO • OXFORD

Copyright © 1991 by Westview Press, Inc.

Published in 1991 in the United States of America by Westview Press, Inc., 5500 Central Avenue, Boulder, Colorado 80301, and in the United Kingdom by Westview Press, 36 Lonsdale Road, Summertown, Oxford OX2 7EW

Library of Congress Cataloging-in-Publication Data
U.S.-Mexican industrial integration / edited by Sidney Weintraub, Luis
  Rubio F., and Alan D. Jones.
    p. cm.
  ISBN 0-8133-1129-2
    1. United States—Foreign economic relations—Mexico. 2. Mexico—
Foreign economic relations—United States. 3. United States—
Industries. 4. Mexico—Industries. 5. North America—Economic
integration. I. Weintraub, Sidney, 1922–   . II. Rubio F., Luis
III. Jones, Alan D. (Alan Dennis), 1952–   .
HF1456.5.M6U19   1991
337.72073—dc20   90-44541
                                                                     CIP

Printed and bound in the United States of America

The paper used in this publication meets the requirements of the American National Standard for Permanence of Paper for Printed Library Materials Z39.48-1984.

10   9   8   7   6   5   4   3   2   1

Contents

v

Acknowledgments

We gratefully acknowledge the invaluable cooperation of many individuals and organizations on this project.

Without the assistance of the Houston Advanced Research Center's Center for Growth Studies this project would not have been possible. HARC, a Texas research consortium, sponsored a December 1989 conference on industrial linkages between Mexico and the United States that involved government officials, business leaders, and scholars from across the United States and Mexico. This binational conference, which led to the production of this volume, was the first to assess economic cooperation and industrial integration between the two nations from the perspective of six specific industries: automobiles, computers, food processing, petrochemicals, pharmaceuticals, and textiles and apparel. Most of the authors come from the industries themselves. A seventh section has been added to the volume analyzing the environmental impact of industrial integration.

The conference timing was excellent, coming shortly before the joint announcement of Presidents Carlos Salinas de Gortari and George Bush of their intention not only to negotiate a free trade agreement, but also to place top priority on such negotiations. The conference also came at a time when policymakers began discussing the U.S.-Mexican trade relationship in the context of achieving cost-effective production strategies that will allow the two nations to compete effectively with Japan, other Asian countries, and Europe.

In addition to the assistance we received from HARC, we also received valuable help from the Centro de Investigación para el Desarrollo and the Consejo Nacional de Población, both of Mexico City.

We are also grateful to the Hewlett Foundation, the Commission for the Study of International Migration and Cooperative Economic Development, the National Science Foundation, the U.S. Department of Commerce's Economic Development Administration, the Alfred P. Sloan Foundation, the Program for U.S.-Mexico Policy Studies of the Lyndon B. Johnson School of Public Affairs at the University of Texas at

Austin, Arthur Andersen & Co., the law firm of Vinson & Elkins, the Harris and Eliza Kempner Fund, and Council of the Americas, which provided either financial assistance or advice, or both.

We would also like to thank Lisa Chernin of the Windmill Company and Marykay Scott, Spencer Carr, and Lynn Arts of Westview Press for their valuable assistance.

Sidney Weintraub

Special Acknowledgment

This book would never have been completed without the contribution of Jan Rich of the Lyndon B. Johnson School of Public Affairs at the University of Texas at Austin. Her main contribution was to put much murky English into readable form and to translate chapters originally in Spanish into English. She was in frequent contact with authors to get their acceptances of editing changes—a sometimes frustrating task. She obtained permission to use copyrighted material where this was necessary. In sum, she was the perfect research associate.

S.W.

ONE

Economic Outlook in the 1990s

Economic Outlook in the 1990s: Mexico[1]

Rogelio Ramírez de la O

Mexico is at a turning point in its development strategy following decades of substantial government intervention in the economic system which, not surprisingly, culminated in the 1982 crisis. During the administration of President Miguel de la Madrid (1983–1988), the government launched many economic reforms that changed the development strategy. The new strategy is not free from contradictions, such as the generation of current account deficits combined with the maintenance of restrictions and a complex set of regulations on foreign direct investment; or the liberalization of foreign trade combined with failure to introduce new labor legislation enabling Mexican industry to compete internationally. Economic reform, once set in motion, calls for ever expanding reform, particularly when the economy needs foreign resources; Mexico's laws and institutions are not yet sufficiently open to foreign equity capital. But even with an open trade and investment regime, which Mexico does not yet have, the challenges involved in overcoming the crisis of the 1980s are still enormous.

Distortions and Crisis

During the 1920s and 1930s, following the Revolution, Mexico underwent a period of reconstruction. This period provided the government with an opportunity to forge a new political alliance among the various revolutionary factions. Central to the new regime was the strong presence of the state in the economy and the pursuit of the public interest as defined in Article 27 of the new Constitution.

The 1930s saw the first wave of economic nationalism and state intervention focused around the new regime. This was preceded by the

3

founding of the Partido Nacional Revolucionario (PNR), which later was transformed into the Partido Revolucionario Institucional (PRI). The PRI was organized along corporatist lines and became the self-appointed heir to the Revolution. From that point the management of the economy and the promotion of economic development would be linked to single political party rule.

Such a monolithic system created its own informal balance. The Alemán administration (1946–1952) saw correctly that a strong private sector was necessary for post-war industrialization. This was based on import substituting industrialization (ISI) and on large external economies facilitated by public investment in infrastructure. A notion of complementarity between public and private investment was used, with no limits placed on foreign participation in private enterprise other than those explicit in the Constitution.

The one-party, strong presidential rule, and the corporatist structures were, however, to become a problem later on. The Constitution proved to be easily amended on instructions from the executive. Interest groups within the system lobbied for new legislation that was invariably presented by the incumbent president as revolutionary changes justified by popular nationalist sentiment.

Amendments to the Constitution and new laws introduced during the four decades following World War II had a number of related aims: the protection of national capitalist groups from foreign competition; the securing of greater government control over economic activities; justification for the creation of new state enterprises; the granting of greater benefits to organized labor (i.e., unions that were part of the system); and ultimately the consolidation of political and economic control over the country by the interests that controlled the PRI.

The result of this was a gradual asphyxiation of the country's productive forces. The farming system became a fiefdom of political groups, and by the mid-1960s a decline in agricultural output was evident. The industrial sector also showed symptoms of the decline typical of the stage of ISI in which progress is impeded by inappropriate economies of scale, lack of competition and technology, and huge capital shortfalls. In 1973, Mexico enacted legislation to restrict the free use of foreign technology and to limit foreign investment to a maximum of 49 percent in any one company.

Moreover, labor unions obtained growing benefits and a steady increase in real wages. This was justified by growing productivity in the 1950s and 1960s but could no longer be justified in the 1970s and early 1980s. Union power was considerable in most sectors in which government monopolies or similar situations enabled management to negotiate with a single union leadership for an entire industry, such as in oil and electricity. The unions became de facto co-owners and co-managers alongside the government in many of these fast-growing state enterprises.

Economic Policy

The economic policy of the 1950s through the early 1970s became increasingly sophisticated with the growth of financial markets. This growth was influenced by a world economy undergoing one of its longest periods of stability and growth since World War II.

Macroeconomic policy generally reflected the government's interest in achieving both a high growth rate and price stability. During the 1930s and 1940s, the intermediate macroeconomic targets were not very clear—the foreign exchange gains from exports were large during the war and the excessive expansion that followed caused an external crisis in 1954. Following the devaluation of the peso that year, and with the world economy under a fixed exchange-rate system, the government adopted the nominal exchange rate as its intermediate macroeconomic target.

Between 1955 and 1970, Mexico was able to maintain unchanged the nominal exchange rate while the economy was growing at an impressive rate of 6.7 percent annually. This was made possible by productivity gains arising from public investment in infrastructure, the early stage of ISI, and a favorable external environment of low inflation. The government successfully used interest rates and credit tightening to implement its monetary policy, but this success was also dependent on a rigorous control of public finances. Fiscal policy was thus dictated by the medium-term objective of financial stability, and therefore it was used in the short term to check any excessive expansion in aggregate demand. Also instrumental in the success of this model was Mexico's capacity to attract foreign venture capital—to be distinguished from foreign debt—which, at that time, financed most of the current account deficit of 2.5 percent of gross domestic product (GDP).

An import license system was used to grant protection to domestic producers from foreign competition but also to prevent a rapid deterioration of the trade balance. Import restriction also affected output, since Mexico remained dependent on foreign supplies of intermediate and capital goods. Price controls were often used as a quid pro quo for trade protection and to guarantee the availability of low-priced basic goods for a growing urban work force. In summary, the policy contained many ad hoc instruments and measures of direct control, but even so fiscal policy was the principal basis of financial stability. A sound fiscal policy facilitated the task of monetary policy which was focused on a nominal exchange rate target. As long as fiscal policy remained sound and the balance of payments did not deteriorate badly, the fiscal-monetary policy mix provided a good macroeconomic background. Table 1.1 summarizes some of the features of this period of stable growth.

It is difficult to identify the specific causes that triggered the collapse of this model. The first signs of deterioration were evident in the mid-1960s, especially in farming, but a pre-condition for the loss of stability was the abandoning of the macroeconomic rule of maintaining public finances in equilibrium. This happened only in the 1970s and was accompanied by greater state intervention in the economy and deteriorating business confidence.

The government's nationalistic rhetoric became louder in the 1970s, accompanied by high current account deficits and growing foreign indebtedness. State investments no longer created the external economies expected of them, owing largely to their increased diversification into manufacturing and services and errors in the planning of large state concerns. The understanding between the government and the business sector that had been a feature of the regime until 1970 was sacrificed to the government's efforts to regain urban political support, especially among the young, by attacking the interests of privileged groups.

When this process fell apart in 1976 and Mexico had to seek International Monetary Fund (IMF) assistance, the problem was diagnosed as one of regaining macroeconomic equilibrium, at most requiring a short recession and adjustment of relative prices. Such an adjustment was initiated in 1977 and was on the verge of completion when Mexico suddenly found itself rich again with the discovery and

TABLE 1.1 Indicators of Growth and Stability, 1955–1970 (percentages)

Indicator	Percentage
Real annual GDP growth	6.9
Population growth rate	3.3
Real per capita income growth	3.6
Annual inflation	4.5
Annual import growth	7.4
Annual export growth	5.0
Current account balance/percentage of GDP	-2.5
Real annual growth in minimum wages	5.5

Source: Author's compilation.

rapid exploitation of vast oil reserves at a happy moment of world scarcity. Oil and foreign debt were the tools of the high growth achieved during 1978–1981, but this growth had even less healthy bases than that of the early 1970s. When oil prices fell in 1981 and foreign credit dried up, the economy collapsed again.

The crisis so frequently referred to is the period of flat growth and lack of material opportunities for the mass of the population that followed 1982. It was also a period of collective reflection and an opportunity to tackle some problems at their roots. Tables 1.2 and 1.3 show relevant macroeconomic indicators during the period leading up to the crisis. The earlier GDP growth of 5.8 percent annually turned flat, and per capita income plummeted 14.8 percent over the entire period. The contrast between yearly payments on the foreign debt of $482 million (11.3 percent of exports of goods and services in 1972) and $11.3 billion (38.9 percent in 1982) is also relevant, as it reflects the efforts the economy would have to make in adjusting itself while servicing a huge foreign debt.

Adjustment and Economic Reform (1983–1988)

It is unclear whether the new government of President de la Madrid understood the depth of the required economic reform. Most public statements made at that time suggested that it did not, but rather that it believed a three-year conventional macroeconomic adjustment would be enough to correct the imbalances. The government carried out a campaign of moral renovation and some constitutional reforms, but there was no clear indication of any attempt to change the structure of political and economic power or the relationship between the state and the different interests. The resulting mix of this program was a strong macroeconomic adjustment aimed at correcting long-existing imbalances, carried out in a political vacuum and consequently lacking popular support.

This poor mix could be explained by the thesis that the Mexican government was not ready in 1983 to embark on wide reforms, owing to internal divisions within the PRI over the direction of such reforms. Such divisions probably reflected what was happening in the country at large, where strong right-wing and left-wing groups had emerged. Since the government was not prepared to outline a reform program, the macroeconomic adjustment would lack the necessary structural changes and would eventually lose public credibility and support.

Some groups within the government and in the private sector pressed for structural changes and some of these were started after an initial dragging of feet on the part of the authorities, such as cutbacks in the

TABLE 1.2 Macroeconomic Performance 1972–1988
(Annual percent except as noted)

Indicator	Period of Growth and Distortions 1972–1982	Period of Adjustment 1983–1988
Real GDP growth	5.8	0.1
Real per capita income growth	2.8	-2.4
Annual consumer price inflation	22.7	92.9
GDP price deflator (annual average)	23.6	88.1
Annual real exchange rate change	3.1	1.2
Current import growth	18.2	19.6
Current export growth	29.0	-0.7

Source: Banco de México, various reports.

TABLE 1.3 Macroeconomic Performance 1972–1988
(millions of U.S. dollars except as noted)

Indicator	1972	1982	1983	1988
Current account deficit	-1,006	-6,221	5,418	-2,901
Factor payment outflows	626	11,405	10,714	10,403
Foreign investment remitted profits	144	526	184	512
Interest on foreign debt	482	10,879	10,103	8,800
Inflows of foreign direct investment	156	1,657	461	2,590
Inflows of foreign credit to public sector	149	5,259	4,291	946
Inflows of foreign credit to private sector	460	2,223	-2,309	-3,428
Stock of foreign debt ($ billions)	5.5	87.6	93.8	103
Fiscal deficit as percentage of GDP	-3.5	-16.9	-8.6	-12.3
Flow of banking system obligations as a percentage of GDP, excluding foreign liabilities	5.7	16.1	13.2	6.9

Source: Banco de México, various reports.

bureaucracy and the sale of some state enterprises. These, together with trade liberalization, supported the government's plans for gradual change, but seen in perspective, represent the seed of a structural reform which only later took a more concrete form. This reform was oriented toward opening the economy and, by implication, transforming the country's political structure.

This change of direction took place in the midst of a confusing economic program in which policy goals were almost never reached while the government continued to proclaim them as top priorities. The most obvious examples were inflation and the public sector deficit. But rather than being a change of direction imposed by a new government, we argue that this change was endogenous in that it was a result of disenchantment of the same domestic forces with the old model of state intervention and protection against foreign competition and capital. The government found itself in the middle of a struggle between the old vested interests of the system and new groups that were aware of the increasing internationalization of economic forces and the consequent need to become internationally competitive. Even though the de la Madrid administration showed an understanding of these issues, I believe it lacked the coherence and internal consensus to impose the necessary radical reforms.

The administration often referred to gradual changes instead of radical reforms and proclaimed that the change of direction in its policy was only a change of tactics. The opportunity to carry out a radical reform at the point of crisis was thus lost, but in the end the government could not prevent the transformation of the economy and of the private sector, which underwent a significant adjustment and reoriented its operations to become more competitive. After five years of partly failed economic programs and gradual changes, the government still faced the problem of high inflation and was more willing to effect radical reforms. But this new attitude would materialize only in the following administration of President Carlos Salinas de Gortari.

Macroeconomic Performance

The linchpin of the macroeconomic program started in 1983 was the regaining of external equilibrium in order to correct a current account deficit of $12.5 billion in 1981 and $4.9 billion in 1982. The program was supported by the IMF through an extended credit facility loan of $3.8 billion and fresh bank loans of $3 billion that the government did not fully use. Both the Mexican government and the IMF believed Mexico could start to grow again by 1985 and did not foresee that the economic contraction would be as far-reaching as it actually was.

Both the government and the IMF underestimated the exchange rate depreciation required to stop capital flight and to turn around the heavy deficit on the current account of the balance of payments. Between 1981 and 1983, the real exchange rate, according to the Bank of Mexico's definition, depreciated by 48.9 percent—far more than was anticipated in the IMF adjustment program and more than the deterioration in the terms of trade during those years (-20.5 percent) would suggest.

This explains why Mexico started its economic program in 1983 with an overshooting of the current account target and of the programmed increased in international reserves, higher inflation, and a greater economic contraction than envisaged, as shown in Table 1.4.

An extremely weak peso coincided with the rapid economic recovery in the United States. Mexican firms, the largest of which had exported in the past as a supplement to domestic sales, switched quickly to exports and produced a current balance which made it unnecessary for Mexico to use the full amount of the commercial bank credit negotiated earlier. This boosted external confidence in Mexico, but the crucial question of regaining domestic credibility and delivering long-required economic reform remained unresolved. Economic agents remained skeptical of the ultimate success of the government's economic program and therefore postponed their repatriation of capital from abroad despite high real interest rates for peso assets. The negative capital account thus reflected the current account surplus in the balance of payments, but to the extent that the latter was achieved with no economic growth, capital exports reflected lack of confidence and insufficient domestic investment rather than greater export competitiveness.

Capital outflows increased as oil prices fell in 1985 and 1986. Outflows were large also at the end of 1987, when the Mexican stock exchange collapsed. The negative capital account was not corrected until 1988 when the exchange rate was fixed and policy announcements were clear, but this still necessitated an extremely high real rate of interest, as shown in Table 1.5.

TABLE 1.4 IMF Program Targets and Actual Outcomes, 1983–1985

	1983		1984		1985	
	Target	*Actual*	*Target*	*Actual*	*Target*	*Actual*
Inflation (percentage, December annual)	55.0	101.9	35.0	65.5	20.0	57.7
Public sector deficit (percentage of GDP)	8.5	8.6	5.5	8.5	3.5	9.6
Change in international reserves (billions U.S. $)	2.0	3.1	2.0	3.2	2.0	-2.6

Source: International Monetary Fund, various reports.

TABLE 1.5 Real Ex-Post Interest Rates of 28-Day Mexican Treasury Certificates and Capital Account Net-of-Term Loans to Government and Banks, 1983–1988 (millions of U.S. dollars)

Year (Months)	Interest Rate (percent)	Capital Account[a]
1983 (January-June)	-189.3	-248
1983 (July-December)	-34.7	-4,069
1984 (January-June)	45.0	-1,562
1984 (July-December)	30.7	-1,159
1985 (January-June)	38.4	-261
1985 (July-December)	-8.7	-1,422
1986 (January-June)	-12.7	874
1986 (July-December)	57.4	-222
1987 (January-June)	26.1	-1,213
1987 (July-December)	36.4	-4,906
1988 (January-June)	42.8	-1,435
1988 (July-December)	19.3	-3,359
1989 (January-June)	57.1	-1,183

[a] Negative signs indicate negative capital flow.

Source: Banco de México, various reports.

The high interest rates, combined with volatile oil prices, put such pressure on public finances that the government was never able to deliver the promised reductions in the fiscal deficit. It nonetheless tried to minimize the inflationary impact of these two variables by reducing non-interest public expenditure, hitting public investment in particular. Although there were no massive layoffs of public employees, their average real wages fell along with wages in the rest of the economy, as shown in Table 1.6.

Thus, despite the significant reduction in public expenditures, fiscal policy lacked credibility until the government changed its strategy. In 1987, it adopted as a fiscal policy target a primary budget surplus, which excluded all interest payments and transfers to state governments.

Later, in December 1987, the government reduced the 1988 budget that had been approved only a few weeks earlier and announced policies, which if implemented, would have permitted a gradual reduction in interest rates. But even then the credibility of fiscal policy was not easily regained as the foreign debt remained high and many of the cuts in public expenditure were regarded as temporary.

TABLE 1.6 Real Public Sector Revenues and Expenditures, 1983, 1988 (percentage of GDP)

	1983	1988	Real Change[a] 1983-1989 (percent)
Public sector deficit[b]	-8.6	-11.7	31.1
Public revenues	32.9	28.7	-16.5
Oil	14.2	9.8	51.4
Public expenditures	41.0	39.0	-12.3
Program expenditures	25.7	18.0	-30.8
Current	17.7	11.8	-19.9
Wages	6.7	5.1	-17.6
Investment	7.5	3.7	-45.9
Interest	12.4	16.6	23.4
Foreign	4.6	3.6	-27.9
Domestic	7.7	13.1	56.8

[a] Deflated with consumer price indices.

[b] The public sector deficit is obtained from the flows of financing granted to the public sector. This does not usually coincide with the deficit resulting from the difference of revenues and expenditures. In addition to this difference, the deficit is increased by the cost of financial intermediation, i.e., the cost of subsidized credit. The public sector deficit shown here is the official figure used for all purposes.

Source: Banco de México, various reports.

Perhaps the clearest signal the government gave was on trade policy, where a wide-ranging import liberalization was announced in 1985, following by the signing of the protocol to join the General Agreement on Tariffs and Trade (GATT) in 1986. Table 1.7 shows the rapid fall in the number of import tariff codes subject to prior license. Moreover, the differences between minimum and maximum tariffs were reduced, and by 1988 the maximum rate on imports was 20 percent, while many items restricted in the recent past could be freely imported.

That trade liberalization took the lead over macroeconomic reform is no coincidence and its relevance in signaling a change of regime should not be exaggerated. First of all, the recession of 1983 and the collapse of public and private investment made it clear that exports would be the only way to maintain employment, and this made a liberalization of imports imperative. The devaluation of the real exchange rate supported this policy and also gave additional protection against imports. The success of the largest exporters in

TABLE 1.7 Import Tariff Structure (number of tariff items)

Type	1982	1985	1987
Total	8,008	8,091	8,446
Controlled by prior license	8,008	839	329
Subject to tariff	—	7,252	8,117

Source: Sixth Presidential Report to Congress, 1988.

maintaining strong cash flows and repaying their foreign debt became a celebrated event. First, exporters who were in a privileged position required competitive supplies. Second, the United States was absorbing growing imports from virtually all developing countries. Third, with a recession in the domestic market and the peso undervalued, import liberalization would not hurt the balance of the current account, allowing the government to claim success on this policy. Actually, imports began to jump only in 1988, when the exchange rate lost its cushion of undervaluation and the fall in inflation encouraged greater private expenditure.

The Real Sector

Despite the buoyancy of the foreign trade sector, GDP recorded hardly any growth and the fluctuations in activity were remarkable. Table 1.8 shows annual changes in GDP, industrial and manufacturing output, manufacturing employment, and imports and exports for the period.

Thus, while exports of manufactured goods recorded annual growth rates of 28.6 percent on average, the export sector was too small to boost the rate of growth of GDP or even that of manufacturing output. Nevertheless, there were activities which recorded significant expansion, including machinery, electronics, petrochemicals, and metals. Other industries showing rapid growth during the upward part of the cycle included automobiles, cement, and paper.

By contrast, industries which suffered falls or stagnated included woven fibers, plastics, structural metallic products, household electric appliances, and non-durable consumer goods.

This uneven distribution of growth is not surprising, given the strong incentive to export and the collapse of the domestic market. In evaluating export performance, we must take into account that the main export drive originates in industries which exhibit a linkage with foreign ownership or with rapid technological change, such as machinery and electronics. Firms with foreign capital or technology

TABLE 1.8 Indicators of the Real Sector, 1983–1989
(annual percentage changes)

Year	Real GDP	Industrial Output	Manufacturing Output	Manufacturing Employment	Imports of Goods[a]	Exports of Goods[a]
1983	-4.2	-8.9	-7.5	-9.6	-40.7	6.2
1984	3.6	6.5	5.3	-1.1	31.6	8.4
1985	2.6	5.2	7.0	2.3	19.6	-9.6
1986	-4.0	-4.8	-3.4	-4.0	-15.1	-26.7
1987	1.5	4.1	3.9	1.7	6.9	28.9
1988	1.1	1.3	2.3	2.1	54.7	0.0
1989	2.9[b]	5.9[c]	8.3	na[e]	31.1[d]	8.1[d]

[a] Imports and exports in current US dollars.
[b] Through the third quarter.
[c] Through June.
[d] Through July.
[e] Not available.

Source: Banco de México, various reports.

were the top exporters of manufactures, and some of them planned expansions even in the midst of general uncertainty.

Initially, the general rule for exporters was to undergo large reductions in the size of the industrial plant and in employment as well as in the product base. Firms tended to concentrate on fewer and more standardized products once imports were liberalized. A pattern of specialization emerged that in the future would permit an expansion of the industrial plant. The automotive industry exhibited this pattern most clearly, as this industry—owing to its international linkages—adapted rapidly to a changing environment, especially when the changes were in line with its worldwide pattern of sourcing and specialization (see Table 1.9). Most automotive firms reduced their size and the variety of products they manufactured, enabling them to achieve longer production runs. They also exported more, and, at the same time, imported more. Nevertheless, large expansions were delayed, and today this industry cannot maintain exports if the domestic market grows too rapidly. The culmination of this process of specialization would be to make new investments in order to provide for growing exports and specialization while servicing the growing domestic market, which began to recover in 1988. Only new investment can validate the economic reforms and the policy of import

TABLE 1.9 Cumulative Growth of Selected Industries, 1983–1988

Sector	Percent
High growth	
Automobile engines, parts, bodies	47.6
Machinery	42.9
Electronics	9.4
Petrochemicals	83.7
Metals	60.4
In-bond food processing	122.5
In-bond textiles	138.7
Negative or no growth	
Woven fibers	-28.4
Plastics	-26.2
Structural metal products	-33.9
Household electric appliances	-40.0
Non-durable consumer goods	3.2
Meat and dairy products	0.9
Footwear	-19.9
Soaps, detergents	-1.9

Source: Banco de México, various reports.

liberalization, and in the modern export sector this means direct foreign investment.

Other firms unable to export tried to maintain their share of the weak domestic market. Price controls were removed in 1983, enabling many of them to rebuild their profit rates, but greater competition among them and low real wages were deterrents. With the opening to imports and the erosion of the exchange rate undervaluation, these firms faced the need to become more efficient and to increase services and quality. At times, they lost market share to competitors. The final pattern of adjustment in the non-tradables sector is not clear, but certainly greater efficiency and lower profit margins will be preconditions to survival in a more competitive environment. Mergers and acquisitions of weak firms by stronger ones are frequent in these sectors.

Table 1.10 shows a crude measurement of the index of average labor productivity in the manufacturing sector, estimated by dividing the index of output by the index of employment. This suggests remarkable gains in productivity which should, however, be interpreted cautiously as the aggregation may result from opposite changes across industries

TABLE 1.10 Productivity in the Manufacturing Industry 1983–1988 (1983=100)

Indicator	1983	1984	1985	1986	1987	1988
Index of output in manufactures	100	105.3	112.7	108.9	113.1	116.5
Personnel employed in manufactures	100	98.9	101.3	97.2	98.8	100.9
Index of productivity	100	106.4	111.3	112.0	114.4	115.4

Source: Banco de México, various reports.

and thus be deceptive on the degree of change in both industries recording positive and negative changes. It may also be influenced by the fact that rigid labor laws prevented many firms from shedding workers, which weakened their capacity to adjust to a new reality.

The New Policy Regime: Outlook and Risks

In 1987, Mexico obtained a new package of foreign finance from official sources and commercial banks on the ground of the previous year's abrupt fall in oil prices. A large amount of these resources was disbursed in 1987 and this, combined with continuing high inflation, caused undue monetary expansion and ultimately a crisis in October 1987.

This crisis was peculiar because no underlying problem appeared to have justified the panic in the financial markets and the capital flight which obliged the Bank of Mexico to withdraw from the foreign exchange market. Only two months earlier, President de la Madrid had delivered an optimistic and confident annual report to Congress. The Bank of Mexico only acknowledged one year later, in its annual report on the economy, that this crisis was provoked by a change in expectations, while the capital flight was attributed initially to the accelerated prepayments of foreign private debt.

Nevertheless, the fact was that inflation remained high, rising from 105.7 percent at an annual rate in December 1986 to 133.9 percent in August 1987. Although the public sector was recording a primary budget surplus of 6.9 percent of GDP, this was insufficient to instill confidence in government policy.

Moreover, the government and its fiscal policy failed to convince economic agents that inflation would be stopped. The 1988 budget finalized during the autumn of 1987 contained provisions for increased program spending of 121.8 percent, more than doubling the 1987 figure, which contained an overshooting of 17.7 trillion pesos over the original budget of 86.2 trillion pesos. This amounted to 4.5 percent of nominal GDP and 3.7 percent of the actual GDP. The increase in interest payments in the 1988 budget was 128.3 percent over 1987 payments and the public sector borrowing requirement (PSBR) was budgeted at 18.5 percent of GDP compared with 17.4 percent of GDP in 1987.

This seems quite enough to qualify the fiscal policy as one incapable of reducing or contributing to a reduction in inflation during the last year of the administration. The crisis of October 1987, therefore, shook the government's lenient stance towards inflation, obliging it to make significant amendments amounting to a new budget, even though the original one had just been approved by a lenient Congress. The amendments contained a reduction in program spending over the original budget of 6.8 percent, of interest payments of 23.8 percent, and of transfers to state entities of 10.9 percent. The PSBR was put at 10 percent of GDP. These percentages, while significant, nevertheless represented very little to informed economic agents in the light of the systematic budget overshootings of the past. This was so even after the government announced several measures to meet such targets, such as reducing the numbers of telephone lines for the bureaucracy and restricting the making of photocopies in government offices. The amendments to the revenue budget included 50 percent to 85 percent price increases in public sector goods and services. Combined with a general price and wage freeze, these produced a strong budget position.

If fiscal policy lacked credibility and the announced corrections in public expenditure and revenue were not perceived as dramatic, the opposite was true of monetary policy. The government announced a fixed exchange rate for two months and introduced savage credit cuts on outstanding bank lending. The fixed exchange-rate rule was renewed in subsequent agreements among government, business, and labor. These agreements also included small increases in minimum wages and in private sector prices. During 1988, only a 3 percent wage increase was granted over the general increase in January. The labor movement's cooperation was secured by the fixed exchange rate rule that appeared to guarantee workers against unexpected inflation, and by the private sector's commitment to maintain nominal (controlled) prices.

Inflationary expectations thus began to change as a result of the new rule, reinforced by the much publicized political accord among government, labor, and business. Price increases decelerated markedly, aided by further reductions in import tariffs and the removal of more important license requirements. The fall in expected inflation allowed the authorities to effect massive cuts in budgeted public expenditures without affecting real expenditures. The result was that for the first time during the de la Madrid administration, actual expenditures were below that budgeted. Expenditures on programs, for example, was 11.7 trillion pesos below the revised allocation of 83.4 trillion pesos, and the PSBR was lowered to 11.7 percent of GDP, despite higher-than-budgeted nominal (and real) interest payments on the domestic debt.

Monetary-led deflation in 1988 thus created the opportunity for fiscal policy to regain credibility. This was largely a one-time effect, however, as the 1989 budget could not repeat the same generous nominal increases as those budgeted for 1988. Thus, for 1989 the budget contained only a 16.6 percent increase in expenditures on programs, a fall of 19.5 percent in debt interest payments (domestic and foreign), and a 29.2 percent increase in taxes. The programmed PSBR was 6.4 percent of GDP, which meant that fiscal policy would soon take center stage again. The result of this budget was a 3.2 percent increase in expenditures, 8.1 percent in taxes, a fall in interest of 17.8 percent, and a 6.3 percent PSBR. On the whole, this was a very good outcome. Nevertheless, the government could not maintain a fixed exchange rate, and the rate had to be devalued as of January 1, 1989 by one peso daily or 16 percent annually.

The potential of monetary policy has not been exhausted, but the absence of a fixed exchange-rate rule prevented a reduction in nominal interest rates. Following the stringent restrictions on credit in early 1988, the monetary authorities relaxed their controls somewhat, and bank credit to the private sector began to rise in real terms. This made the regulating role of monetary policy more difficult. Now, while monetary policy is still the preferred short-term policy, any change in economic conditions or in expectations will be reflected in interest rates.

To summarize the core of my argument: there was a change of regime in 1988 which obliged the government to fight inflation even at the expense of hard-won international reserves. This change moved the central focus of policy away from the external balance and to inflation, and assigned the leading role to monetary policy in the short run. It also established a strong primary budgetary surplus as an intermediate target of fiscal policy. Given the insufficient credibility of fiscal policy, peso interest rates have remained high in real terms, dominated by expectations in financial markets. Today it is the credibility of the exchange rate, the austere fiscal policy, and potential external shocks which determine expectations.

Macroeconomic Strategies and Risks in the New Policy Regime

When we discuss the outlook for macroeconomic policy and its possible outcomes in terms of growth and inflation, we assume that the shift in the policy regime, which adopted the fight against inflation as its top priority, will remain valid over the medium term. This seems a safe assumption not only in view of government policy announcements, but also because domestic expectations are evolving in a way that makes any departure from established policy politically dangerous for the government. Also, a low inflation rate is a sine qua non of any consolidation of the new economic model which sees the Mexican economy being increasingly open to trade and investment. The other reasons that make low inflation necessary under this model will now be discussed.

Under the new model, the exchange rate regains its character as the intermediate target of monetary policy. As long as Mexico's inflation rate exceeds those of her trading partners and the nominal rate remains fixed, the peso real exchange rate will appreciate, in turn helping to reduce inflationary pressures. The appreciation of the real exchange rate will have two other effects: the current account balance will deteriorate; and real yields of peso financial assets measured in dollars will show a similar appreciation, increasing the scope for capital inflows.

Therefore, in the new regime, the economy must again, as in the 1950s and 1960s, run a current account deficit and regain access to foreign capital. Since voluntary bank credit will not be open to Mexico for some years to come, the only capital that can be counted on is foreign direct investment (FDI) and repatriated Mexican capital. Both inflows will depend on the government showing an unequivocal commitment to maintaining open trade and investment policies and to the integration of Mexico into the global economy. A deterioration in the current account of the balance of payments is a highly probable risk of the new economic program. Table 1.11 shows the deterioration that took place in 1988 and 1989.

This occurred despite low economic growth in 1988 of 1.1 percent in GDP, which recovered to about 3 percent in 1989, such that the prospects of an even greater deficit in the future are related to the permanent recovery in economic activity, given that higher domestic demand will pull more imports and may discourage export growth. Table 1.12 shows the continued rise in imports and how their growth has surpassed the growth of GDP and of exports since the end of 1987.

To consider the likelihood that the real exchange rate (pesos to the U.S. dollar) exerts an independent influence on the volume of foreign trade, we estimated one equation for imports and another for exports of manufactures for the period January 1986 through July 1989. In the import equation, domestic demand as represented by GDP levels (Y) and

TABLE 1.11 Current Account and Trade Balances 1986–1989
(millions of U.S. dollars)

Monthly Current Avg.	Acct.	Exports of Goods		Imports of Goods			Non-Oil Current Account
		Oil	Non-oil	Consumer Goods	Inter-mediate	Capital	
1986	-139.4	525.6	810.3	70.5	636.0	246.2	-665.0
1987	330.5	·719.2	1002.2	64.0	735.4	219.2	-388.7
1988	-241.8	559.1	1162.4	160.1	1079.2	335.9	800.8
1989	-333.7	647.8	1274.1	260.3	1252.4	350.9	
Jan.		612.9	1154.3	187.1	1663.0	325.5	
Feb.		560.7	1167.6	212.8	1155.4	330.5	
March		679.6	1300.4	260.9	1239.3	319.8	-2655.3[a]
April		692.5	1242.6	258.1	1285.5	381.2	
May		681.6	1340.7	300.0	1309.8	347.7	
June		659.3	1438.9	343.0	1361.6	400.8	-3233.3[a]

[a] Total of each quarter.

Source: Banco de México, *Indicadores Económicos*, October 1989.

the real exchange rate (TC) explain the variations in total imports. Total imports are monthly values deflated by the import price index of the Bank of Mexico, while the real exchange rate is measured by the ratio of the U.S. consumer price index to the Mexican consumer price index, multiplied by the ratio of the nominal exchange rate to the exchange rate of the base period. Given the slow response of trade volumes to changes in the real exchange rate, we included in the equation both the current values of the exchange rate and those of one, two, and three months behind. All values are expressed in natural logarithms (L).

The results of this estimation are as follows ("t" values in parentheses):

$$LM = 10.26^{**} + 1.04 LY^{**} - 1.04 LTC^{**} + 0.39 LTC_{t-1} - 1.01 LTC_{t-2}^{*} + 0.8 LTC_{t-3}$$
$$\quad (5.8) \qquad (3.6) \qquad (-3.4) \qquad (0.9) \qquad (-2.2) \qquad (0.3)$$
$$R = .94 \qquad\qquad F = 117.6 \qquad\qquad D.W. = 1.57$$

* significant at the 95 percent confidence level; ** at 99 percent

As would be expected in economic theory, the growth in GDP (Y) raises imports, in this case, by a factor of 1.04 times. There is a negative relationship between the real exchange rate and imports, especially with the current value of TC, and its two-month lagged value, which denotes a relatively fast import response or even market anticipation of the exchange rate and the consequent decision to place orders for imports. It is sufficiently clear that imports fall with the real depreciation of the peso exchange rate and rise with its appreciation.

Nevertheless, the major determinant of import growth appears to be the growth in GDP. Although the growth in imports during the period analyzed should also be attributed to the fact that liberalization of trade occurred in several stages, the effects of such liberalization were already present in 1986. Even though trade liberalization was accelerated in December 1987 in support of the anti-inflation program, its effect on trade volumes is mainly a one-time effect.

Exports of manufactures are expressed in current dollar values deflated by the price index for non-oil exports of the Bank of Mexico. The real exchange rate is the same estimate as in the import equation (thus the sign of its coefficient should be positive in the export equation) and foreign demand is approximated by the GDP of the United States (USY) in constant terms. In this equation we had to include a dummy variable (D) to distinguish the period January 1986 to July 1987, when domestic economic conditions began to change and the economy became less able to generate current surpluses owing to rapid domestic growth and to a stronger peso exchange rate. Thus, during that period economic policy was aimed at responding to the lower export revenues following the fall in oil prices via a rapidly depreciating exchange rate. After July 1987, however, the effect of oil prices already had been transmitted onto the economy, international reserves had accumulated, and domestic demand began to rise, accompanied by the strengthening of the peso exchange rate. The coefficient of the dummy variables in the equation below thus represents the difference between the coefficients of two equations corresponding to two groups of observations: those until July 1987 and those from August 1987 onward. The fact that the dummy coefficients are significant means that the difference in export performance between the two periods is significant.

The export equation contains, in addition to USY and TC, a variable denoting the level of capacity use (CU). This is measured as the ratio of current level of the index of industrial output to the level in July 1985, which is a base period, when industrial output reached a peak. If exports of manufactures are constrained by insufficient domestic industrial capacity, CU would have a negative sign in the equation.

The results of this estimate are as follows ("t" values in parentheses):

(2) LXN $=-44.4^{**} + 5.78$LUSY$^{**}+ 1.68$LCU$^* + 1.98$LTC$^* + 1.01$LTC$_{t-3}^* +$
        (-5.5)   (3.2)   (2.5)   (2.5)   (1.7)
    $+44.$OD$^{**} - 4.49$DLUSY$^* - 1.31$DLCU$^* - 2.30$DLTC$^{**} - 0.86$DLTC$_{t-3}^*$
        (4.0)   (-1.9)   (-1.4)   (-2.7)   (-1.3)
R = 0.84   F = 16.9   D.W. = 1.50
* significant at the 95 percent level of confidence; ** at 99 percent

This equation explains rather satisfactorily the changes in the level of manufactured exports during a period when changes in policy and in economic activity were quite significant. The coefficient of CU (although less significant than those of the other two variables) is positive in the equation and therefore suggests that there was not constraint on capacity during the period, but the same is not true of the dummy DLCU. The coefficient of this dummy suggests that there was a significant difference in the constraint represented by existing industrial capacity and that in the second group of observations. From August 1987 onward, the greater use of domestic capacity is no longer associated with export growth.

The same difference applies to the coefficient of the variable that denotes foreign demand (USY) and its dummy (DUSY), which indicates a significant reduction in the second period in the response of Mexican exports to increases in foreign demand. This means that from August 1987 onward, the increase in Mexican exports of manufactures was only 1.29 times the increase in GDP in the United States, while in the first period it had been 5.78 times. The difference is so significant that it leaves no room for doubt that we are observing two different export curves.

This is further confirmed by the significance of the dummies for the current exchange rate (DTC) and the exchange rate lagged three months (DTC$_{t-3}$). The equations for the two groups of observations can be obtained by subtracting the values of the dummy coefficients from those of the reference group. Such equations are:

(3) Exports of the first period, January 1986 through July 1987:
X1= -44.4 + 5.78LUSY + 1.68LCU + 1.98LTC + 1.01LTC$_{t-3}$

(4) Exports of the second period, August 1989 through July 1989:
X2= -0.4 + 1.29LUSY + 0.37LCU - 0.32LTC + 0.15LTC$_{t-3}$

The difference established is that during the first period, exports of manufactures were supported by foreign demand growth, greater use of domestic industrial capacity (since capacity use was very low at the beginning of 1986), and the depreciation of the real exchange rate of the peso.

During the second period, exports continued to be supported by foreign demand, but they increased at a much lower rate in proportion to the increase in demand, and they were not supported by the greater use of industrial capacity, and they were supported by the exchange rate only to a small degree. It is sufficiently clear that export growth during the second period decelerated quite significantly. In fact, export growth during the first period of 18 months was 65.7 percent in current dollars (2.4 percent in constant terms per month); whereas in the second period of 24 months was 30.1 percent in dollars (0.6 percent in constant terms per month).

Changes in output and in the current account in recent years can be observed in Table 1.12.

The appreciation of the real exchange rate also affects national income and demand via the terms of trade. And here the more rapid increase in domestic expenditure than in output during 1988 and 1989 lends further support to the notion that price disinflation is associated in Mexico with a pickup in demand levels owing to the strong exchange rate.

Domestic Economic Activity

Output is likely to increase, with a time lag, as demand-depleted inventories recover. But output will not recover evenly among the different sectors because of their different situations. The varying performance of industries over the past six years suggests that their idle capacity levels differ. Many firms that performed badly did not invest at the rate necessary to renovate worn-out equipment or to keep up with technological change.

With a strong exchange rate and reasonable tariffs, imports will replace domestic production in some industries that have difficulty in meeting demand because of insufficient capacity or lack of competitiveness in price and quality. At the same time, exports should continue growing in those industries that have proved capable of penetrating foreign markets.

The pattern of trade will change, with consumer goods for a time recording the highest growth, until domestic demand finds its new level and the selection process between domestic and imported goods is completed for the market as a whole. From then on, import levels may stabilize somewhat, but the new mix in the typical consumption basket and in the vector of intermediate demand will be different from the present one. This would entail a negative import substitution process, the reverse of what we observed during the 1940s and 1950s, but will not represent in itself any weakness in the new growth model; it will

TABLE 1.12 Output, Demand, and Current Account by Quarter 1986–1989 (1985=100)

Indicator	1986				1987				1988				1989	
	1	2	3	4	1	2	3	4	1	2	3	4	1	2
Volume index GDP	97.3	98.1	93.6	98.6	96.4	97.8	97.8	104.8	99.2	98.9	98.6	105.3	1,101.1	1,102.7
Imports of goods	86.6	91.1	80.5	80.7	74.0	84.5	94.8	99.5	106.0	127.8	142.1	148.3	137.9	157.0
Exports of manufactures	115.8	134.3	133.6	170.3	162.1	187.2	180.2	195.0	181.7	205.4	206.5	199.4	192.7	220.3
Domestic expenditures	92.7	106.4	104.2	115.8	115.2	115.7	112.1	117.8	123.3	118.1	112.9	115.8	119.8	121.1
Current account (billions of current U.S.$)	-0.5	-0.9	0.7	0.4	1.4	1.4	0.5	0.6	-0.3	-1.5	-1.8	-0.8	-0.8	-1.2
Non-oil current account (billions of current U.S.$)	-2.1	-2.2	-2.2	-1.3	-0.6	-0.8	-1.0	-1.4	-1.1	-2.1	-3.1	-3.3	-2.7	-3.2

Source: Banco de México, Indicadores Económicos, October 1989, and our own estimate on constant-price imports and exports.

merely reflect the reallocation of expenditures between imports and domestically produced goods under a new exchange rate and trade regime.

Because we lack analytical and empirical tools to measure the final effects on trade and economic activity, it is impossible to predict the effect of these changes on the rate of industrial employment. The implication is that any employment forecasts must be regarded with suspicion as is also the case with import forecasts, and macroeconomic plans based on employment levels should therefore be abandoned. The recent U.S. experience of rapid employment growth during recovery, mainly in services, contrasted with that of Western Europe, where unemployment has remained high despite a milder recovery. Some increase in unemployment should be expected in the short run, brought about by the restructuring of many industries in response to the new trade regime.

It is possible, given the strength of the economy in the services sector, that some initial recovery would pull workers toward services, where average productivity is likely to be lower than in the industrial sector. This would conform with the deteriorating educational background of the labor force, which follows a 22 percent reduction in real public expenditure per student between 1980 and 1988. The Mexican government would be well advised to revise its labor laws to facilitate the growth in services, especially in small firms that have been responsible for a large part of the employment increase in these sectors. The government should also consider apprenticeship plans for young workers in industrial activities. The training provided would redress some of the negative effects of the falling quality of education. Part-time and job-sharing plans, especially in services, would be a way of increasing employment. An open trade policy will require a supply of well-trained workers for those industries participating successfully in the global economy. Since these industries are located in specific regions, a successful employment policy would require special educational funding for technical schools in identified growth areas.

Potential Growth

Table 1.13 shows the poor record of GDP and gross fixed investment over the last six years and the recovery observed in 1989. Given this record, I doubt growth can be maintained at high rates in the medium term (1990–1992) unless there are sufficient foreign resources available to Mexico. Even so, we do not know the likely strength of the recovery in domestic demand arising from new opportunities created by economic reforms and the expected greater interplay of Mexico and the world

TABLE 1.13 Annual Growth Rates of GDP and Investment, 1980–1989 (percentages)

Period	GDP	Gross Fixed Investment
1950s	6.1	12.8
1960s	7.2	16.4
1970s	6.5	10.0
1980–1982	5.5	4.1
1983–1988	0.1	-2.6
1989	2.9[a]	8.0[a]

[a] Through the third quarter

Source: Banco de México, various reports.

economy. A strong increase in demand could cause growth to exceed any moderate rate in the 4 percent range estimated by the government. But I doubt that long-term rates higher than 5 percent could be sustained without inflation or high external deficits, assuming oil prices recover only gradually throughout the decade.

I see two main limitations on higher growth. One is the insufficient infrastructure, which will take years to restore to a state similar to that before the debt crisis. The country will, in fact, need a steady expansion of such infrastructure, requiring high rates of investment that will be difficult to achieve. And even if investments in this area are substantial, the time lag before output growth is generated will be considerable.

The second limitation is the quality of the future labor force, which will be less educated and will have experienced a lower level of child nutrition because of the fall in real wages. Those who will enter the labor force in 1998 were born in 1980 and brought up during the crisis years. It will be difficult to incorporate this labor into fast-growing global industries and the potential for output growth will consequently be inhibited.

Projections of population and labor force growth made by Moreno and Nuñez (1986) suggest the population and labor force growth outlined in Table 1.14.

The number of new jobs created will most likely be insufficient to meet the new demand for jobs, even assuming high rates of economic growth. Resulting levels of unemployment and underemployment are likely to be only partially offset by government policy. It seems probable, therefore, that Mexico will remain an exporter of labor for

TABLE 1.14 Population and Labor Force Growth (millions of inhabitants)

Year	Population	Working-age Population	New Job Demand Over Preceding Period
1980	69.6	27.7	
1990	84.5	38.3	11.6
1995	92.2	45.5	7.2
2000	100.1	52.2	6.7
2010	114.5	62.5	10.3

Source: Lorenzo Moreno and Leopoldo Nuñez Mexico, *Proyecciones en Población Urbana y Rural 1980-2000*, Académia Mexicana de Investigación en Demografía Médica, México, 1986. Reprinted by permission.

many years to come and that new employment will be biased towards low-productivity services.

The Potential of Mexico-U.S. Trade

Table 1.15 shows Mexico's share in U.S. imports and exports, and Table 1.16 shows the value of U.S.-Mexico trade in four benchmark years, according to U.S. trade statistics. Mexican imports rose 19.5 times in nominal value between 1960 and 1987, while Mexican exports rose much faster, 45.6 times. Discounting tariff categories 2 through 4, which include oil, the rise in Mexican exports was only 37.3 times, which is a rate of growth still higher than that reported for U.S. exports to Mexico.

The differential in growth rates of imports and exports was not as large in the 15 years to 1975. After that date, U. S. exports grew 178 percent while Mexican exports jumped 463 percent. If categories 2 through 4 are eliminated, the jump was 441 percent. As a percentage of total U.S. trade, the Mexican share rose in 1987 to 5 percent of total imports and 5.7 percent of total exports, as shown in Table 1.15.

TABLE 1.15 Mexico's Share in U. S. Import and Export Trade, 1960–1987 (percentages)

Share	1960	1975	1983	1987
Share of U.S. Imports	1.9	3.4	6.6	5.0
Share of U.S. Exports	2.6	4.7	4.5	5.7

Source: U. S. Department of Commerce, various reports.

TABLE 1.16 Bilateral Trade Between Mexico and the United States: 1960, 1975, 1983, 1987 (millions of U.S. dollars)

SITC Sec.	Description	1960		1975		1983		1987		Percent of Total Trade			
		Import	Export	Import	Export	Import	Export	Import	Export	1960	1975	1983	1987
0,1	Food and beverages	35	245	513	893	1,425	1,652	673	2,343	24.0	16.2	12.1	13.7
2-4	Animal, vegetable, mineral raw materials	32	12	578	617	1,143	8,827	1,642	4,137	3.8	13.8	39.0	44.2
5	Chemicals	103	9	503	92	1,068	352	1,439	507	9.6	6.9	5.6	6.3
6	Manufactured goods (textiles, wood, cork, paper, minerals, metals)	152	153	521	435	910	1,183	1,509	2,007	26.1	11.0	8.2	9.3
7	Machinery and transport equipment	347	1	2,430	1,005	3,516	3,574	6,928	8,727	29.8	39.7	27.8	18.2
8	Miscellaneous	53	25	329	393	575	760	1,292	1,777	6.7	8.3	5.2	5.9
9	Not classified	na	na	186	163	118	428	562	773	na	4.0	2.1	2.4
	Total	722	445	5,060	3,598	8,758	16,776	14,058	20,271	100.0	100.0	100.0	100.0

Note: Imports are to Mexico from the United States and exports are those of Mexico destined for the United States.

Source: U. S. Department of Commerce, U.S. General Imports, World Area by Commodity Grouping, and U.S. Exports, World Area by Commodity Grouping, 1970–1987.

The low growth of U.S. exports in the 1975–1983 period, 7.1 percent annually, is attributable to the collapse of Mexico's economy in 1982. During the next period, 1983–1987, U.S. export growth rose by 12.6 percent annually, also explained by the trough of 1983. Growth in Mexican exports shows a similar disparity: 21.2 percent annually in the period 1975–1983 and 4.8 percent in the 1983–1987 period, explained by the weakened oil prices since 1985.

Another explanation for the changes in relative growth rates of trade is the changing composition of trade, as indicated in Table 1.16. Until 1960, the bulk of Mexican exports consisted of food and light manufactures, in Section 6 of the Standard International Trade Classification (SITC), classified by the main material used in their production as distinct from machinery and miscellaneous manufactures. In 1987, by contrast, the important categories were raw materials (oil) and machinery. For Mexican exports, the highest real growth before 1983 was in raw materials, but after 1983 it was in machinery and miscellaneous manufactures. For U. S. exports to Mexico, machinery has always been the most important category. Before 1983, the highest growth was in chemicals. After 1983, it was in miscellaneous manufactures and machinery.

That is, the center of growth of Mexico-U.S. trade now lies in manufactured goods and precisely in those categories of machinery and miscellaneous manufactures where internationalization of production has been the strongest over the last two decades. Machinery exports in 1987 represented 43 percent of Mexican exports to the United States and 49.3 percent of U.S. exports to Mexico. These compare with a nil share of Mexican exports in 1960 and 28 percent in 1975.

In the most recent period of 1983–1987, when Mexico underwent a severe economic adjustment, U.S. exports to this country rose 53.9 percent in real terms, or 11.4 percent annually, while Mexican exports grew only 4 percent annually, although some individual industries surpassed these rates. For U.S. exports to Mexico, miscellaneous manufactures rose 21.1 percent annually in real terms, followed by machinery, up 17.2 percent. For Mexican exports to the United States, machinery jumped 24 percent annually, followed by miscellaneous manufactures, up 22.7 percent.

A more disaggregated analysis of trade shows that Sections 7 and 8 of the SITC record the greatest increase in activity. In Section 7 the highest growth in Mexican exports is in road vehicles and components (56.7 percent annually), as shown in Table 1.17. High growth was also recorded by industrial machinery, office data processing equipment, and metalworking machinery. The automotive industry, electrical machinery, telecommunications, and power generating machinery are

TABLE 1.17 U. S.-Mexico Trade in Machinery and Equipment
(Section 7 of SITC)

Item	Description	1987 (millions of U.S. dollars)		Real Growth 1983–1987 (percent)	
		Exports	Imports	Exports	Imports
71	Power-generating machinery	1213.7	621.1	99.7	72.6
72	Specialized machinery	64.0	478.0	-20.8	62.4
73	Metal-working machinery	6.7	176.1	150.0	80.5
74	Industrial machinery	425.4	767.7	381.4	82.6
75	Office and data processing machinery	489.1	506.0	166.4	113.1
76	Telecommunications equip.	1774.1	642.4	59.8	72.0
77	Electrical machinery	2816.8	2180.6	123.3	111.4
78	Road vehicles	1938.3	1359.6	502.8	137.3
79	Transport equipment	29.0	197.0	-5.9	-29.6

Note: Imports are to Mexico from the United States and exports are from Mexico destined for the United States.

Source: U. S. Department of Commerce, FT 455 and FT 155, *Exports and Imports by Country and Commodity*.

the largest categories of Section 7 Mexican exports to the United States, with a total of $7.7 billion.

U. S. exports to Mexico recorded the highest rates of growth in road vehicles, office data processing equipment, and electrical machinery, as Table 1.17 indicates. Such intra-industry trade, i.e., in the same SITC sections, suggests that Mexico is becoming specialized in certain classes of equipment and that this specialization allows longer production runs and more exports but at the same time leads it to import other classes of equipment.

In Section 8 of the SITC, the highest growth in Mexican exports was in furniture, 33 percent annually, followed by professional and scientific equipment, 28.9 percent, but the amounts of these exports are in comparative terms smaller than those of machinery (see Table 1.18).

This brief analysis of the growth and composition of Mexico-U.S. trade and the sectors of most dynamic growth, especially in Mexican exports, emphasizes that most of the recent expansion of bilateral trade is related to those industries that are engaged in the process of internationalization of production. Therefore, trade has been linked to the operation of multinational corporations and industrial specialization.

TABLE 1.18 U. S.-Mexico Trade in Miscellaneous Manufactures
(Section 8 of SITC)

Item	Description	1987 (millions of U.S. dollars)		Real Growth 1983–1987 (percent)	
		Exports	Imports	Exports	Imports
81	Plumbing fixtures	63.2	27.0	92.0	385.4
82	Furniture	309.1	90.2	213.3	143.2
83	Personal goods	27.8	5.4	53.4	83.7
84	Clothing	433.3	213.6	122.8	71.8
85	Footwear	104.6	6.7	74.8	299.4
87	Scientific instruments	280.7	396.7	176.4	146.8
88	Optical goods	45.1	60.4	34.3	40.3
89	Miscellaneous	513.7	491.7	109.1	118.7

Note: Imports are to Mexico from the United States and exports are from Mexico to the United States.

Source: U.S. Department of Commerce, FT 455 and FT 155, *Exports and Imports by Country and Commodity*.

Trade has followed direct foreign investment, and the opening up of the economy to trade flows must lead producers to specialize and increase exports. Although the concept that trade and investment are related is hardly new in economic literature, its implications in the field of public policy have not been sufficiently understood. Many countries liberalize trade but fail to liberalize investment and, meanwhile, continue to have separate policy departments for trade and industrial development.

A brief commentary on Mexican regulations on foreign direct investment is appropriate here. The 1972 law on foreign investment prohibited foreign ownership of more than 49 percent in any Mexican company, as well as totally restricting ownership of many industries, like primary petrochemicals, which were reserved exclusively for the state. The law also imposed rules for exclusive Mexican ownership in other areas, such as in road transport and radio broadcasting, and a minimum of 60 percent Mexican ownership in some others, as in auto parts.

This law has been applied since 1973 with great discretionary power on the part of the government, since it contained many conceptual loopholes and lent itself to different interpretations, depending on the occasion. The end result was that it offered a poor legal framework for the promotion of foreign investment in Mexico, and its application coincided with the worst economic crisis of the post-war period. Both these factors scared away foreign investors.

In 1989, under the new government of President Carlos Salinas, regulations interpreting this law were issued for the first time, replacing directives that had previously clarified some aspects of the law. Under these new regulations, complete foreign ownership was possible in those areas not specifically restricted either in the Constitution or in secondary law. But the regulations remain restrictive, since they impose additional requirements on those investments which are now free of the stipulated maximum of 49 percent for foreign ownership. For example, these investments must not exceed $100 million, must be located out of the three largest cities, and must produce a positive foreign exchange balance during the first three years of operation.

The regulations certainly signify to those who know Mexico and its legal system well that the Mexican government wanted to send a message to foreign investors that the 1972 law was being made more flexible. Legal flexibility, however, is not something likely to calm foreign investors' fears about potential government actions that could change the business climate. Some industrial sectors reserved exclusively for the Mexican state, such as electricity, railways, petrochemicals, will need massive investment that the public sector will not be able to finance, and a patching up of the legal framework will be a way of concealing the opening of such sectors to private capital. For example, instead of allowing the entry of foreign capital to those industries, a complicated system of trusts and equity participation with no vote was designed for foreign investors. In the final analysis, the merits of the new legal framework are to be seen in the amount of foreign investment flowing into the country.

Further research is needed on Mexico-U.S. bilateral trade and on the effects of trade and investment policies on sectoral developments. This research should ideally be policy-oriented. Another area in which more research is needed is the potential of industrial complementarity or integration of production processes between Mexican and U.S. industries, bearing in mind that in future years a large part of the modern industrial apparatus of Mexico will be dependent on U.S. markets, while many U.S. firms would very likely be involved in manufacturing operations in Mexico.

Notes

1. I acknowledge and appreciate the comments received from Professor Sidney Weintraub and Alan Jones, which helped me to improve this paper.

Any remaining errors are my own responsibility. A primary source for this chapter was Lorenzo Moreno and Nuñez Leopoldo, *México: Proyecciones de Población Urbana y Rural 1989-2000*, México: Académia Mexicana de Investigación en Demografía Médica, 1986.

Economic Outlook in the 1990s: The United States

Clark W. Reynolds

Current prospects for the United States economy are mixed. Recent forecasts range from slow growth at best (2 percent to 3 percent per year), to recession at worst. A weakened domestic economy might well contribute to a collapse in security markets, some reversal in foreign lending, and the onset of stagflation. Whatever the outcome, the nation must deal at last with its combined fiscal deficit and foreign imbalance, while simultaneously undergoing major economic restructuring and social rehabilitation. This is a difficult time in which to address the U.S.-Mexico industrial relationship.

Beginning with a sharp adjustment to the oil shocks of the 1970s, the 1980s saw recovery and steady growth in demand, outstripping a somewhat slower supply response, financed by an increased flow of foreign savings. The world's largest economy found itself increasingly internationalized, as consumers shifted to imports from domestic manufactures, financial markets went global, and investment became increasingly dependent on capital inflows from abroad. Those who had prophesied that U.S. living levels would come down in the 1980s as a consequence of the competitive forces of increased international exchange were surprised to find the economy so resilient. Some believed that with increased shifting of global goods and factor markets, the U.S. would experience a reduction in the competitive edge of its own labor and capital. There was concern that domestic wages and incomes, high by world standards, would fall prey to the inroads of international competition. Dollar incomes, in terms of global purchasing power, might decline.

Instead, as U.S. interest rates rose, savings flowed in from an increasingly integrated international financial market, causing the value of the dollar to rise rather than fall. Debt service and capital flight from Mexico and other developing countries contributed to the inflow of savings. After a brief recession at the beginning of the 1980s, the U.S. experienced its longest period of sustained growth in the postwar era. The boom was driven by increased defense outlays, consumer demand, and an unprecedented fiscal deficit caused by Reagan's neo-Keynesian tax cuts. The rising gap between domestic supply and demand was sustained by increased imports, with the current account deficit covered by foreign borrowing. In addition, U.S. consumers increasingly demanded attractive foreign goods.

Unfortunately, the growth of the 1980s was not accompanied by major new investments in plant and equipment. Despite an enormous tax cut at the beginning of the decade, savings, other than those used to purchase consumer durables, did not respond and the windfall income was used to fuel a consumption boom. The financial system itself contributed to the short-term churning of the securities market, as junk bonds tempted portfolio managers with high yields that required increasing attention to short-term cash flow maximization at the expense of long-term planning and investment. Those firms that did attempt to accumulate net worth to support long-term expansion faced the threat of hostile takeovers, in which raiders tempted shareholders with immediate capital gains at the expense of future growth.

As a result of the lack of investment, productivity growth lagged, infrastructure deteriorated in major urban areas, and roads, bridges, and port facilities fell into disrepair, while airports failed to expand and power-generating capacity stagnated. Despite the facade of economic boom over the past decade, a coming down was already being experienced by many households and businesses in major regions of the United States, extending well beyond the troubled inner cities. Sharp declines in real wages were occurring, particularly at the low end of the labor market, where most job growth was concentrated, real incomes were falling for the majority of single-parent households, which represented a rising share of the population, and key industries were barely breaking even, if not sustaining losses.

Today the handwriting is on the wall. The U.S. economy faces a structural challenge of major proportions. Its productive plant must adjust, at every level, to compete in an increasingly global market. The fiscal constraints of Gramm-Rudman, and an administration firmly opposed to increased taxation, call into question the nation's ability to upgrade the education and skills of U.S. labor to deal with the challenges of better-trained competitors abroad. Major social groups are dropping out of the race, with some of their most ambitious members falling prey to the inducements of easy money, power, and prestige in the streets from crime and drug trafficking, set against the dismal alternative of low-paid service employment.

The economy, society, and intervening fiscal regime are out of balance. A large external deficit would be less onerous if foreign borrowing were being used to increase real investment in physical and human capital, infrastructure, research and development, to reduce these structural imbalances. In some cases foreign firms are setting up plants and increasing the productivity of existing U.S. industry through greater participation in ownership. But the majority of foreign capital is simply purchasing domestic assets or financing the fiscal deficit rather than contributing to the future growth of the economy and its eventual ability to repay.

This lack of productive investment might be explained, if not justified, if the U.S. economy were truly senile, with no scope for innovation and growth. In fact, however, the U.S. has never enjoyed greater productive potential, particularly for competition on the frontier of the international market. There have already been great accomplishments from the application of techniques which make use of new information technologies for networking in production, inventory control, distribution, marketing, and management. The challenges of international competition are leading to growing flexibility of American enterprise. As some segments of U.S. industry come down, others are rising, in a symbiotic process described by Joseph Schumpeter as creative destruction. The networking of foreign capital, entrepreneurship, labor, and output at all stages are key elements in the innovation-based development of the future.

The pattern of development of the 1980s was uneven, not only for output, with emphasis on defense and services and a growing imported component of manufactures, but in terms of income distribution and social participation. After experiencing rising real wages from the late 1960s to the mid-1970s, Blacks, Hispanics, and other minorities, as well as the youth of America, are suffering from significant declines in wage income over the period since 1975. This is taking place despite shifts in the demand for labor in the direction of low-skilled service and assembly activities over high-skilled manufacturing. The changing structure of the job market in the United States reflects a disproportionately rapid growth in the supply of those with inadequate educational and technical skills. As the supply of labor at the low end outstrips demand, productivity and real wages decline. The net effect is one of rapid labor absorption but at a significant cost in terms of slow average productivity growth in the United States, compared with its partners in the Organization for Economic Cooperation and Development (OECD).

In addition, there has been a fiscal shift from attention to social services and income support for the poor to entitlements for middle-class households and the affluent who have weighed in with much political clout over the past ten years, during a time of general dissatisfaction with government's role in the economy. The 1980s have been characterized as a time of hard hearts and soft heads from the viewpoint of the relationship between economic policy and social equity.[1] From the viewpoint of efficiency and international competitiveness, many (and not only the Japanese) have attacked the United States as pursuing a short-sighted, bottom-line orientation on the production side, asset manipulation rather than productive portfolio management on the financial side, and consumerism rather than savings on the expenditure side. Whatever the particular viewpoint expressed, there is a general concern that the economy is no longer healthy, that the role of the state in the equity-efficiency tradeoff must be reconsidered, and that there are no panaceas.

As baby boomers mature in the 1990s, those in the bulge of the U.S. population pyramid will be entering their peak earning years. There is a question as to whether or not they will be living in an increasingly unstable and insecure two-tier economy, in which youth, many women, minorities, and a rising tide of immigrants compete for positions at the low end of the job market, while professionals, managers, technically skilled personnel, and other property owners comprise a new upper class. The generation of the 1990s will be saving and paying taxes to support the changes on which they must depend for their ultimate security and sustenance in the next century. Indeed, the savings of baby boomers may be jeopardized if social conditions are not improved. Decisions being made today will influence these trends in important ways. There is a major question as to whether increased international economic linkages, which involve global decision-making and the competition from lower cost foreign inputs, can be made consistent with domestic economic, social, and political goals, including improved income, well-being, and democracy for all. The approach to increased U.S.-Mexico economic relations must be viewed in this light.

Implications for U.S.-Mexico Industrial Integration

There is great disparity between the two economies, with Mexico's GNP less than 4 percent of the U.S. GNP. But this gap is more a reflection of productivity differentials than of population size. Mexico's labor force is one-fifth that of the U.S. and its population one-third. The figures indicate that greater economic integration must be viewed more in terms of dynamic than static effects, although an immediate impact is already being felt in specific industries, regions, and income groups. If new linkages were to lead to any significant convergence in per capita income levels, the consequences for North American production and productivity could be monumental. The gains would be due as much to the upward shift in output per worker in Mexico, and the ability of the United States to benefit from a restructuring of its production from lower to higher productivity activities, as to sector-specific productivity growth.

Over the period of Mexico's miracle from 1940 to 1970, there was a gradual but perceptible convergence in total productivity and output per capita between the two countries, due in particular to the shift factor of Mexican employment from lower to higher productivity occupations and from rural subsistence agriculture to commercial agriculture and urban employment.[2] A rapid rate of investment in those years for both raw materials and primary product exports and import-substituting industrialization permitted this diffusion of growth on a regional and sectoral basis. While real wages increased, the gains were registered more in terms of increases in family income over time than in the growth of real wages for particular occupations and skills, particularly at the low end. The convergence continued with debt-financed growth of the early 1970s and the stimulus of the oil boom and further indebtedness in the latter part of the decade through 1981, as Mexico's output per worker and per capita outstripped that of the United States by a significant margin. From 1978 through 1981, Mexico's economy grew by more than one-third in real terms.

However the crisis of 1982 brought the growth process to a sudden halt, first introducing a period of adjustment and stagflation, as per capita output fell precipitously, followed by the recent success in price stabilization but without any significant growth in per capita income. In other words, as the United States experienced its deficit-financed growth of the 1980s, Mexico languished, and the two economies diverged sharply in terms of productivity and output per capita for the first time since 1940. Real wage dispersion was even greater, as Mexico's real wages fell much more sharply than those in the United States for low-skilled labor, and for higher skilled labor Mexican wages fell while those in the United States increased. The growing gap between the two countries gave rise to even greater pressures for migration and trade in those goods and services embodying low-wage labor, while for the first time there began to be evidence of a brain-drain from Mexico to the United States in the early-to-mid-1980s.

The experience was sobering for Mexico, in that the old model of import-substituting industrialization, driven by the state and financed by the rental income from raw materials and primary product exports, was no longer functioning. The virtual one-party political system, which had depended so heavily on its ability to deliver growth and improvement at livable levels, at least for given households over time, despite the maintenance of a badly skewed distribution of income, found itself increasingly vulnerable. Inside and outside of the principal party there were calls for reform and a search for a new development model. Under the pressure of the 1982 crisis, Mexico for the first time since the temporary alliance of World War II, began to consider and implement policies favoring explicit economic linkages with the United States, legitimizing through official action what had until then been a process of silent integration.

The macroeconomic scenario for a broader North American economy, in which Mexico were to become an increasingly full partner, is one in which a model of dynamic diffusion of development rather than static comparative advantage is most appropriate. At present, the six-to-one disparity in average productivity levels, much greater between the highest and lowest productivity regions, between the two countries leads to major migratory pressures from the south to the north, and the potential for capital flows from north to south. However, the political climate and atmosphere of economic uncertainty, as well as the overhang of debt obligations and risk attached to reconversion of pesos into dollars, limits the southward investment flow, while U.S. migration policy introduces major costs and risks to labor flows northward.

The burgeoning *maquila* industry gives evidence of pressures in both directions, labor north and capital south, with legal measures giving a measure of security to those assembly plants which employ Mexican labor to process imported intermediate goods to supply U.S. markets. However the low value added per worker in *maquilas* gives little indication of the potential for productivity and income convergence from a more comprehensive pattern of economic integration.

Comprehensive research on the costs and benefits of economic integration between the two economies has yet to be done in either country. Some early and relatively primitive estimates of the implications of increased exchange in the area of migration, however, indicate that there are enormous efficiency costs to the barriers between the two countries. Estimates of the efficiency gains from an open labor market relative to a closed border indicate, notwithstanding the unrealistic nature of such an opening, given the clear political and social costs involved, static efficiency gains amounting to 2 percent of the combined GNP of the two countries. The present value of such gains accumulated for another generation amounts to almost $1 trillion dollars.[3] Evidence indicates that in key sectors, such as food products and petrochemicals, there are major gains to be realized from a matching of capacity on one side of the border with demand on the other, and that the flows of goods and services will increase in both directions. Often the obstacles to such gains from exchange reflect policies that are more concerned with static costs and benefits, in terms of net sectoral trade balances, than in terms of the dynamic gains from gross trade and production.

Clearly a more reasonable alternative to the free movement of labor from south to north would be a combination of measures, reflecting greater movement of capital and technology in both directions, as well as more integration of production and marketing along the lines of dynamic comparative advantage.[4] However, there is as yet no accepted technical method of forecasting dynamic comparative advantage, despite the ability of economists to define it and provide historical evidence of its significance. Externalities, increasing returns, learning-by-doing, and the evolution of tastes make the prediction of such a process more an art than a science.

Yet this is by no means a justification for lack of attention to industrial policy, or whatever other term may be more politically acceptable. Policymakers link the provision of public goods and services to their vision of the economy, since the appropriate mix of such activities depends on the direction the economy is expected to take. Decisions about public contributions to infrastructure and investments in human capital at the local, state, and federal level, as well as policies affecting health, safety, transportation, other public services, and the environment, all reflect a sense of direction in the economy. They also reflect the education and skill requirements for a particular trajectory of economic change. De facto industrial policies are present in even the most laissez-faire, market-driven systems, as is evidenced by the central role of U.S. defense policies and government procurement and contracting in the postwar period. Japan and the Asian newly industrializing countries, as well as Europe, evidence considerable benefits from a cooperative role between the state and the private sector in the pursuit of dynamic comparative advantage in which flexibility is the key. Thus, experiments that succeed are allowed to continue while those that fail are forced to adjust.

A vision of a more interactive U.S.-Mexican economy, driven by potential gains from productivity and income convergence between the two systems, production economies of scale, and access to a wider range of skills, resources, and technology from common development, calls for a much more comprehensive approach to policy coordination than has characterized relations between the two countries since World War II. In effect, we are talking about a new alliance, one which respects the sovereignty, distinct political nature, social structure, and aspirations of the two countries.

As investors from Europe, Japan, and other regions join in the process of North American development and become increasingly active in the U.S. economy, they may be expected to play an increasing role in the U.S.-Mexico process of interdependence. This is even more likely in the case of Canada, which has entered into a full economic partnership with the United States. The role of Mexico in the North American system must be consistent with the goals of the U.S.-Canadian Free Trade Agreement.

Some of the implications of this macroeconomic scenario are worth mentioning. In terms of monetary policy, interest rates and the capital market, there is little evidence that the U.S. will be able to reduce the cost of capital in the near-to-medium-run, given the failure to come to grips with fiscal measures that might better deal with the government deficit. Until the Middle East military buildup, the peace dividend from improved East-West relations might have provided some scope for budgetary adjustment. On the other hand any effort to take the social security surplus off-budget and use it, as would make eminently good sense, for more explicit development-enhancing expenditures in physical and human capital, including renovation and enhancement of the nation's infrastructure, would more than consume the gains from reduced defense outlays.

Indeed, attention to the capital requirements of restructuring and growth, as well as for research and development, will shift the demand for investment at least as much as the supply of savings might increase from the maturation of the baby boomers and the increased accumulation from their stage in the life-cycle. Sustained high interest rates in the United States, relative to Japan and Europe, are bound to increase the influence of foreign savings in the North American development process, particularly if Japanese savers are willing to tolerate below-equilibrium yields on their securities, a process which is already beginning to face greater resistance. In addition, the misuse of U.S. financial savings for the churning and proliferation of junk bonds and other high risk securities shows that savings are present for potential investments in more truly productive ventures. These investments could be reflected in the convergence of production, marketing, and productivity growth between the United States and Mexico. VITRO, a Mexican company, has already acquired Anchor Glass, making use of junk bonds as well as commercial bank lending in

the United States and its own Mexican equity. The company contended
that the bonds would be more productively invested in such a venture
than in the kind of asset swaps that are proliferating in the United
States.

On the trade front, the question is whether the United States will
continue to approach its deficit with symptomatic relief, such as
jawboning the Japanese and pressuring for dollar devaluation, rather
than through attention to its internal structural deficit, which forces a
trade imbalance. The United States also needs to stress industrial
research and development that can produce a more competitive product
mix. This is not to say that there are not major legal and institutional
obstacles to market penetration in Japan and other trade surplus
markets that must be reduced if the spirit of the General Agreement on
Tariffs and Trade is to prevail. Similarly, political pressures in the
United States tend to favor costly nontariff barriers and voluntary
quotas with enormous efficiency cost to consumers and a distorting effect
on income through the rents they create for both exporters and import-
competing activities.

This problem is not likely to go away in the short run. Indeed, things
may get worse before they get better, as both Japan and Europe gird up
for skirmishes with the United States that could begin to develop the
potential for a trade cold war. It is appropriate at such a time for the
North American economies to develop their own economic system,
which takes advantage of regional contiguity, leading to trade creation
through the elimination of barriers, rather than diversion. Since so
much trade is affected by non-tariff barriers, however, some diversion
is likely, leading to rents for North American partners of the United
States that will arise from operating within the regional umbrella,
GATT ideals notwithstanding. This is implicit in the recent U.S.-
Mexican negotiations in which Mexico was granted an increase in the
voluntary steel export quota to the United States, clearly at the
expense of other steel exporting countries.

What must be avoided in such a process is the temptation to create a
new regionwide protection mechanism that would take the earlier
import-substituting industry model of Mexico and extend it to the North
American economy as a whole. There are clearly possibilities for such
an outcome if a boomer mentality arises for regional relations and if
other trading blocs exhibit their own restrictive tendencies. It is
essential that the approach to North American interrelationship be
viewed as a step in the direction of enhanced global free trade rather
than as a regression to regionalism and balkanization of the
international system.

Fortunately, the new interdependencies among firms and industries and within the capital market, as well as the related technological linkages, are giving rise to a new set of clients of globalism who exert considerable influence at the highest political levels. In addition, the ideologies of nationalism and state-centralist control of command economies are collapsing. In their place a new pragmatism may emerge in which consistency can be achieved between the efficiency gains from increased international exchange and the social demands for more equity and democratization. In terms of migration pressures, driven by growing labor market interdependence between the United States and Mexico, it is evident that increased economic linkages will call for a more bilateral approach to such issues, notwithstanding the need by both the United States and Mexico to establish national policies on migration problems that are more encompassing than the issues affecting the two countries.

The gains from such an exchange arising from the diffusion of employment and productivity, either from Mexicans moving north or U.S. capital and production moving south, can be considerable. But there are bound to be dislocation costs for labor and capital on both sides of the border if present barriers to exchange are dramatically lowered. The success of the U.S. political economic system has depended on both the generation of productivity growth and its sharing between labor and capital. Recent research[5] indicates that freer movement of unskilled labor between Mexico and the United States would lead to considerable gains for U.S. capital and the majority of its workers—all but the bottom 10 percent in the lowest skill levels—as well as for the great majority of Mexican workers in the lowest earning levels. But there would be static losses to Mexican property owners as real wages rose in Mexico, and to the minority of its upper income workers as the price of wage goods and personal services rose.

Clearly, the analysis of Heckscher, Ohlin, and Samuelson shows that increased trade might well lead to convergence in wages and profit rates, but that the owners of abundant factors—unskilled labor in Mexico and capital in the U.S.—would tend to gain at the expense of the scarce factors, calling for some compensation for the losers if equity and political balance were to be maintained. Such considerations would challenge the U.S. social pact, as reflected in the Full Employment Act of 1946 and in legislation preserving the right of labor to organize and bargain collectively for improved wages and working conditions. However, as U.S. security interests are increasingly perceived to be linked with social conditions in Mexico, measures that permit growth in productivity and employment in Mexico will become an ever more important element in the national policy of both countries.

In terms of environmental policy, growing interrelations between the two countries will also play a crucial role. The United States places increasing demands on industry to avoid polluting the environment or introducing dangerous substances into the consumption stream. Occupational health and safety measures are also raising the cost of production in the United States, as in other advanced industrial countries. Market forces are growing for producers to shift polluting activities to those regions where there is less legal or de facto opposition to their environmental effects.

In some cases, such emissions from smelters, coal-burning power plants, and other sources of acid rain, the negative factors cross borders, offsetting the private benefits from production relocation in neighboring countries to avoid one's own national regulations. Not surprisingly, the first binational accords in North America on environmental matters have reflected such transnational realities, since both partners benefit from an agreement. However, as Mexico and the United States become more integrated economically, there will have to be a greater degree of cooperation in the implementation and enforcement of common environmental, health, and welfare measures to avoid dumping of polluting activities south of the border and to prevent asymmetries in the treatment of labor.

Fiscal harmonization is also high on the agenda, if true linkage is to be achieved between the two economies. There is much to be done in this regard. For example, the United States has quite separate fiscal regimes in each of the states, whereas Mexico tends to apply national tax policies throughout the country, with some regions favored by special exemptions and subsidies. Mexico has instituted a national value-added tax, while the United States has relied on more traditional measures, and there are considerable asymmetries in the tax structure that could complicate and even distort the pattern of binational investment. By the same token, greater economic integration would call for more comprehensive approaches to the treatment of peso/dollar relations, reflecting the growing existence of a potential currency area and the profound impact of U.S. monetary policy on Mexico as well as the vulnerability of Mexican exchange rate policy to the permeability of trade and capital markets.

The world is exhibiting an astounding pace of change in some of the countries and regions long considered impervious to reform. This is a time when events seem to be outpacing analysis, much less rational policymaking. The political economy textbooks written a few months ago are already out of date. The next decade will be a time when North America emerges from the wings to stage center. There is immense scope for economic and social development from proper management of the U.S.-Mexico relationship on a bilateral, and eventually trilateral basis, with Canada becoming actively involved. But at this moment in U. S. development, the primary initiative is most likely to come from its partners.

Notes

1. Blinder, A. S., *Hard Heads Soft Hearts: Tough Minded Economics for a Just Society*, Addison-Wesley, 1987.

2. Reynolds, C. W., "A Shift-Share Analysis of Regional and Sectoral Productivity Growth in Contemporary Mexico," International Institute for Applied Systems Analysis, Laxenburg, Austria, Research Report RR-80-41, November, 1980. (Reprinted by U.S. Department of Commerce, National Technical Information Service (NTIS), PB81-159865.)

3. Reynolds, C. W., and McCleery, R., "The Political Economy of Immigration Law: Impact of Simpson-Rodino on the United States and Mexico," *Journal of Economic Perspectives*, Vol. 2, No. 3, Summer 1988.

4. See No. 3, also, Weintraub, S., *A Marriage of Convenience: Relations Between Mexico and the United States*, Twentieth Century Fund Report, Oxford University Press, 1990.

5. See No. 3.

TWO

Industrial Integration Policy

Industrial Integration Policy: U.S. Perspective

Sidney Weintraub

The essays in this volume were commissioned to highlight the importance of the separate governmental and private strategies in Mexico and the United States in shaping the nations' combined industrial development. The deeper thesis of this collection of studies is that the industrial strategies in the two countries are not completely separable, that the border dividing them is becoming less a barrier than an annoying and sometimes costly fact of economic life. This reality is what stimulated the two presidents to support a free trade agreement.

This essay focuses on U.S. industrial practice as it affects Mexico, but it should be read in conjunction with the essay by Luis Rubio F., which analyzes the same phenomenon from the Mexican side.

Industrial relations between the two countries are influenced by their proximity, the legal and regulatory framework under which companies must operate, and the growth prospects of the two economies. They are determined as well by the regional and global strategy of multinational corporations. Thus, this essay will address the dynamic created by U.S.-based corporations that have established production relationships with subsidiary or affiliated firms in Mexico. Much—perhaps the majority—of non-oil trade between the two countries now takes place within these companies. This interchange of goods is increasingly in intermediate products. Under these circumstances, when related parties rely on each other's products for their own production, the distinction between imports and exports loses much of its validity. What moves across the border is called international trade because there is a border, but the process is not significantly different from shipments of industrial inputs between plants in the United States. Free trade, when it comes, is designed to make this point explicit.

The border is inconvenient because it involves extra costs. It hinders transportation because of restrictive regulations in each country, customs delays, and import duties. There are also quantitative import restrictions imposed by each country. Because of these growing cross-border industrial alliances, the pressure to reduce the costs of separate sovereign policies is growing. That is what happened between Canada and the United States when the free trade agreement between them went into effect on January 1, 1989.

The first discussion in this essay centers on the influence of Mexican policies on the industrial relationship between the two countries. Official U.S. policy also has an impact on the relationship, and this will be covered briefly. Corporate strategies in various industries will be dissected, drawing on other papers in this volume, particularly those covering the U.S. industries. The final section will analyze the results of these combined influences on the bilateral industrial relationship.

Influence of Mexican Industrial Policy

Mexican industrial policy after World War II until the mid-1980s relied heavily on restriction and regulation—that is, on ways to diminish the influence of markets in the conviction that these led to unsatisfactory outcomes. The main elements of the post-war policy were the following:

1. Almost indiscriminate protection against imports, through a licensing system that favored firms producing in Mexico, including those controlled by foreigners.
2. Discretionary control of foreign direct investment, limiting its sectoral distribution and equity participation.
3. Reserving the commanding heights of the economy, defined partly in the constitution but also determined somewhat arbitrarily by government ownership through the parastatals.
4. Forcing producers to purchase an increasing share of industrial inputs from Mexican sources (domestic content provisions).
5. Using the power of government procurement to favor Mexican-owned industries.

The results of these combined policy measures were mixed. A domestic industry was established, but for the most part it was unable to compete in world markets. Industry had a captive domestic market, and consumer prices therefore were high. This clearly did not translate into efficiency. By emphasizing government control in various sectors, many white elephants were financed, such as in the steel industry, to cite just one example, and much waste and corruption was tolerated. By forcing foreign investors into certain sectors, Mexico unwittingly gave U.S. multinationals a dominating position in such industries as food processing, chemicals, machinery, electronic equipment, and transportation. These industries have turned out to be among Mexico's leading export earners. Mexican policy thus achieved the foreign investment mix it sought, but then was discomfited by the result.

Mexico decreed that final assemblers in the automotive industry must export products of equivalent value to their imports, and this influenced the nature of foreign investment. The extent of foreign equity was constrained generally, and this led to many affiliations with Mexican producers. Inputs had to be purchased locally up to specified minimum percentages, and this forced many local-foreign partnerships.

The purpose of Mexican industrial policy was, in large part, to increase Mexico's industrial independence. What happened instead was that the programs encouraged complex linkages with foreign industries. Since U.S. investors make up more than 60 percent of foreign direct investors in Mexico, these affiliations were predominantly with U.S. companies.[1] What occurred was a mutual, even if asymmetrical, dependency of companies on either side of the border.

The underlying policies are changing, but the past has left a legacy. Most import licenses have been replaced by moderate tariffs of up to 20 percent and averaging about 10 percent.[2] Most industries must now compete with imports.[3] Regulations promulgated in May 1989 have eased requirements for foreign investment, although many restrictions remain.[4] Domestic content provisions are slowly losing their force, although they persist in such key industries as automobiles and computers. Many parastatals were closed, such as the Fundidora steel plant in Monterrey, or sold, such as the airlines, hotels, and the telephone company. The scope for private initiative in the petrochemical industry was expanded by removing many products from the basic category reserved for the state.

The salience of the industrial linkages between affiliated companies in Mexico and the United States is best viewed through the prism of the economic policy changes undertaken since the collapse of oil prices in 1981. In that year, petroleum exports were 75 percent of Mexico's total. In 1989, they were 35 percent.[5] Put differently, non-oil exports in 1989 were almost twice oil exports. The crisis in the Persian Gulf raised the oil component of total exports in 1990. Linkages between U.S. and Mexican producers show up primarily in manufactures, which made up 55 percent of all Mexican exports in 1989. The most dynamic Mexican exports in recent years have been in precisely those industries with close links to U.S. producers, particularly automotive parts. Mexican economic recovery is now clearly dependent on export performance in manufacturing and the main market is with affiliated companies in the United States.

The *maquiladora* plants represent a special case of industrial linkage—and in a strict sense, do not represent linkages of the type discussed.[6] As with relationships generally between U.S. and Mexican producers, the *maquiladora* plants make a virtue of sharing production between the two countries. However, *maquiladora* plants use few Mexican material inputs. The value added in these plants in Mexico comes almost exclusively from labor and utilities, whereas industry generally provides both material and labor inputs.

Evidence overwhelmingly suggests that the main driving force behind the extent of U.S. foreign direct investment in Mexico has been the health of the Mexican economy. Thus, despite Mexican restrictions on foreign equity holdings and sectors in which non-Mexicans could invest, foreign direct investment was substantial during years of high Mexican growth and declined when growth slowed. Thus, flows of direct investment into Mexico exceeded $2 billion a year in 1980 and 1981, years of high growth in the Mexican economy, and declined to less than $500 million each year between 1983 and 1985, when the economy declined or stagnated.[7] Direct investment flows have grown since then to more than $3 billion in 1987, $2.6 billion in 1988, and $2.2 billion in 1989, but these were heavily influenced by debt-equity swaps. They occurred in part because the foreign investor could buy pesos cheaply to make the investment.

However, while the amount of foreign direct investment was largely a function of Mexican economic growth and the cheapness of the peso, its distribution was determined largely by the combination of official Mexican and private multinational corporate policies. These policies had unforeseen consequences. They increased cross-border industrial linkages, and they have now made Mexican economic recovery highly dependent on maximum exploitation of these affiliations. Mexican economic health, therefore, is now more dependent than ever on the foreign scene because of the salience of manufactures in total exports, on U.S. economic growth, and on the degree of openness of the U.S. market.

Influence of U.S. Industrial Policy

Mexico had a conscious post-war industrial policy, and the United States did not. Mexican authorities chose industries to support—automotive, petrochemical, steel, among others. Mexico made them part of the public sector or otherwise subsidized them, used the government's procurement potential to support them—the domestic pharmaceutical industry is an example of this—and protected them zealously against import competition. It is this set of measures that is now changing.

The United States did all these same things: it subsidized industries such as in defense and agriculture (to the extent it can be called an industry), protected domestic production, and supported national production through official procurement, but not as thoroughly or systematically. Mexico was deliberately protectionist; the government consciously distorted price signals from the market through its regulatory actions. The United States, by contrast, tended to act in response to special interest pressures in the cases of textiles and apparel, automobiles, and steel, just to cite a few.

However, coordinated or not, with or without planning, U.S. policy actions did influence industrial linkages with Mexico. As steel prices rose because of import protection, steel users looked for ways to economize, thereby stimulating the growth of U.S. automotive investment in Mexico, where labor was cheap. The use of product-by-product quotas to limit textile and apparel imports from competitive producers in Asia encouraged the search by U.S. producers and importers for new sources and separate quotas for these products, and Mexico was one of the beneficiaries. The U.S. government put considerable pressure on Mexico to protect the intellectual property of the foreign pharmaceutical industry. The system under which U.S. import duties are charged only on the value added outside the country for many products using U.S. inputs was a major stimulus for the growth of the *maquiladora* industry.

Official inaction by the United States also had considerable impact on the direction of the multinationals' investment. Official U.S. policy deplored the use of performance requirements in the Mexican automotive industry (that is, domestic content provisions and the requirement that the industry's imports into Mexico be matched by exports, generally bound for the United States), but tolerated them even as U.S. companies moved production in response to the Mexican strictures.

Above all, what has permitted the cross-border trade in intermediate products to flourish has been the relatively low U.S. nominal and effective tariffs, the result of successive rounds of trade negotiations in the General Agreement on Tariffs and Trade (GATT). The benefits of this tariff structure were extended to Mexico under the most-favored-nation clause. Mexico did not reciprocate with lower import restrictions, at least not before 1986, when Mexico's entry into the GATT coincided with the big push toward import liberalization. Intermediate products could thus move into the United States from Mexican and other sources at little cost. Absent this, the relative advantage gained from cheap Mexican labor could have been nullified.

Perhaps the greatest danger to deepening the industrial integration is that U.S. protectionism will nullify the implicit bargain under which production is taking place. The United States already limits some imports from Mexico; steel and textile products are examples, although these imports are controlled on a worldwide basis. Efforts are made regularly by producers without links in Mexico to use U.S. fair trade laws relating to dumping and subsidies to control the level of competing Mexican imports. U.S. labor unions have regularly voiced objections to the system of imposing duty only on the foreign value added in *maquiladora* production. U.S. labor unions also oppose free trade with Mexico.

Mexico has several defenses against this growing U.S. protectionist tendency. The most important is probably the national U.S. interest in having a stable, relatively prosperous Mexico. A wealthier Mexico would be a better market. A Mexico with high economic growth and opportunity is necessary to retain potential migrants at home. In addition, the cross-border alliances between Mexican producers and powerful industrialists in the United States are a potent force in keeping open the U.S. market.[8] A free trade agreement would permit these linkages to develop to their logical limits.

Not just a changed, more protectionist U.S. policy can alter the direction of industrial interpenetration of the two countries. It is not foreordained that Mexico will pursue its industrial opening to its logical conclusion. Mexico can reverse course and return to a policy of development from within, not necessarily to the status quo ante, but to something more akin to it than to free trade. But this would be costly. Even more germane, such a policy reversal would require overcoming the vested interests that have been developed in industrial integration with the United States.

The more the industries in the two countries cooperate in production and mutual sales, the more difficult it will be to change course. A major safeguard against increased protectionism in either country is that powerful economic interests in each of them now have a stake in the freest possible trade.

Corporate Strategies

Several attributes attracted U.S. multinationals into Mexico. The most important is low labor costs, about a seventh to a tenth of comparable costs in the United States after including fringe benefits. It is no accident that the explosion in *maquiladoras* occurred in this decade after the substantial devaluation of the peso reduced the dollar cost of Mexican workers.

But cheaper labor is far from the whole explanation, particularly in industries in which wage costs make up a relatively small proportion of total costs. U.S. and other foreign automotive companies established themselves in Mexico to be in a position to exploit the national market. The same is true in many of the other industries covered in this book, such as computers and pharmaceuticals.

Perhaps the most important explanatory feature is that Mexico is close enough to the United States to permit scale production and relatively inexpensive transportation of the intermediate products back and forth. Mexico became a center of engine production for U.S. multinationals largely for this reason. This production permitted the U.S. companies to comply with the Mexican policy of requiring exports more or less equal in value to their imports and to produce these exports at a competitive cost. The automotive multinationals thus mandated certain products for manufacture in Mexico as part of their global strategy.

An earlier point merits repetition: these investments have been made and the industrial linkages have been established. They exist in many industries and it would be costly to sever them, certainly in the automotive industry. The two automotive papers, written by Marc E. Maartens from the U.S. vantage and by Florencio López-de-Silanes from the Mexican perspective make clear how much cooperation exists between the two countries in this industry. Maartens points out that in the 1980s, the Mexican government promoted an aggressive export program leading to new export-oriented, state-of-the-art engine plants that produce their output primarily for the United States. For 1989, the Mexican automotive industry exported about one-third its total vehicle output of more than 600,000 vehicles.

López-de-Silanes expands on this theme. He notes that Volkswagen's recent shift of operations from the United States to Mexico contributed to an increased flow of units into the North American market. He also points out that the Mexican engine export take-off of 1982-1984 is one of the best examples of silent industrial integration between Mexico and the United States. This was triggered by General Motors' and Chrysler's new engine plants in Saltillo and Ford's plant in Chihuahua. Most of this production flowed into the U.S. multinationals' small-car plants in the United States and Canada. López-de-Silanes also notes that between 1982 and 1989, Mexican auto parts exports multiplied fivefold, and nearly 80 percent of the production was for the U.S.-Canadian region.

But Maartens warns that to continue attracting new state-of-the-art vehicle assembly plants that provide export production, Mexico must overcome the barrier of the global automotive industry's near-term excess capacity.

Donald Lyman's discussion of the computer industry stresses that U.S.-Mexican integration was driven more by Mexican regulation than market forces. He concludes, on the whole, that Mexican policy thus far has succeeded, in that production of mini- and microcomputers and of peripherals has increased in recent years, as have exports of computer systems and peripherals. Lyman brings out the importance of intermediate imports from parent companies for the Mexican computer industry.

Lyman also raises questions about the long-term development of a competitive computer industry in Mexico. He questions whether Mexico is doing enough to develop the skilled manpower necessary to remain competitive in this rapidly changing industry. He notes that the industry trend is toward multinational sourcing, and states that it is not clear that Mexico would necessarily remain a desirable production source without further development of its professional base.

These observations drive Lyman's recommendations. He advocates additional, phased-in deregulation of the Mexican computer industry; upgrading of Mexico's scientific and technological structure; and, above all, relying less on the future of regulation to force industry development and more on developing Mexico's areas of comparative advantage through analysis of market forces in this sector.

Robert Sherwood emphasizes the research-intensive nature of the U.S. pharmaceutical industry. He says that about 15 percent of sales revenue in 1987 was devoted to research and development. The U.S. industry, he notes, thinks globally and has established distribution facilities quite widely. Unlike many other industries studied in this volume, Sherwood asserts that Mexico's proximity to the United States is unimportant to the pharmaceutical industry. The U.S. industry operates in Mexico largely through wholly owned subsidiaries that mostly process imported raw materials. Some limited joint ventures established recently between U.S. and Mexican laboratories resulted from Mexican government policy—not the preference of U.S. pharmaceutical companies, he notes.

Sherwood criticizes two Mexican policy measures in this industry— the call for Mexicanization of the industry under the 1973 foreign investment law and the weakening of intellectual property protection under a 1976 law. Both measures have since been relaxed, as Sherwood notes. His main recommendation is that the Mexican government increase protection of intellectual property, which he believes would foster pharmaceutical research in Mexico. Protection of intellectual property undoubtedly will be an issue in free trade negotiations between the two countries.

In his paper on the Mexican pharmaceutical industry, Enrique Gruner agrees with Sherwood that Mexican government policy helped shape the pharmaceutical relationship between the two countries. Gruner's stress, however, is on the oligopolistic nature of this industry, one dominated by vertically integrated multinationals, which severely limits the establishment of sourcing industries in Mexico. He concludes that Mexican import liberalization would not foster competition, but rather would further concentrate the industrial processes of the multinationals themselves. Gruner also enters a mild dissent to Sherwood's emphasis on Mexico's failure to protect intellectual property. Gruner argues that Mexico was sometimes accused of pirating when domestic technologies evolved in a process replicated in many countries around the world.

Rina Quijada concentrates on the primary petrochemical industry in the United States: the olefins (ethylene, propylene, and butadiene), and the aromatics (benzene, toluene, and xylenes), which are the building blocks for thousands of petrochemical products. Forty-seven companies—located principally in Texas and Louisiana—produce primary petrochemicals in the United States. Of these, five account for 51 percent of annual production. While not a government monopoly, as is Petróleos Mexicanos (Pemex) for the production of so-called basic petrochemicals in Mexico, the U.S. primary petrochemical industry is oligopolistic. This may be inevitable because, as the study points out, large capital investment is needed for the production of primary petrochemicals (as contrasted with production of secondary products, where there is greater ease of entry).

Because Pemex alone can produce basic petrochemicals in Mexico, direct investment still seems distant for U.S. companies, Quijada concludes. She believes that the primary U.S. contribution to Mexico's basic petrochemical program, at least for the near term, will be through licensing technology and know-how.

Benito Bucay F. makes some points in his discussion of the Mexican petrochemical industry as it relates to its U.S. counterpart that merit highlighting. He emphasizes that the two countries have a great potential for joint development because of the physical proximity of the two industries and the availability of natural resources. He also stresses that more than half the U.S. industry is located in Texas and Louisiana. The Mexican plants producing primary (basic) petrochemicals are generally newer than their U.S. counterparts, an important feature in an industry marked by a high entry cost. Bucay believes that an excess of primary products will emerge in the United States in the 1990s, whereas Mexico is likely to have a surplus of secondary petrochemical production. This combination, coupled with proximity, should make the situation ideal for bilateral understandings in this industry.

Stephen L. Lande points out that the mill sector of the U.S. textile industry competes effectively on world markets, unlike the apparel sector, in which more and more lines of production are moving offshore, including the production of U.S. companies. The United States regulates the flow of textile and apparel imports under the Multifiber Arrangement (MFA); imports of these products from Mexico are limited under a bilateral agreement concluded pursuant to the MFA. Lande states that U.S. textile product import restrictions are more severe for Asian suppliers (Hong Kong, South Korea, Japan, and Taiwan) than for Mexico. Mexico benefits from the severe restrictions imposed on imports from more competitive suppliers. But, because import quotas are based on historical market shares, Mexico, as a relative newcomer, suffers in quota size.

Lande's recommendations are made in the context of the political sensitivities of this industry in the United States. He concludes that special treatment for textile and apparel imports from Mexico is unlikely to be significant in the absence of an overall free trade agreement that subsumes this industry. A free trade agreement will not be in place in any event for a number of years, and the next major opportunity to address this industry will come in 1991, when the current bilateral textile agreement comes up for renewal.

Ovidio Botella C., Enrique García C., and José Giral B. make an interesting observation related to Lande's comments, namely, that Mexican protectionism is diminishing precisely when U.S. protectionism is growing. They conclude that the health of the Mexican industry will depend increasingly on exports, particularly of apparel to the U.S. and Canadian markets; and that Mexican reliance on *maquiladora* plants in this sector is less than ideal because the plants add little Mexican value but do use up valuable quotas based on total U.S. textile and apparel imports, that is, the quotas include both the value of U.S. inputs and Mexican value added.

Lloyd E. Slater points out that the U.S. food industry is huge, contributing about 10 percent to the GDP. Less than 4 percent of production is exported, but this conceals the large sales by U.S. food conglomerates from foreign plants. There is also substantial foreign investment in the U.S. food industry, indeed more than the counterpart U.S. foreign investment. The United States has a trade deficit in processed food because exports are dominated by low value-added products (fats and oils, meat, poultry, and breakfast cereals), whereas imports tend to have higher value added (confections, cheese, cookies, alcoholic beverages). Some features of the U.S. food industry highlighted by Slater are the growth of multiproduct multinationals, greater consumer consciousness of diet and nutrition, and changes in food processing and marketing technology (the presence of microwave ovens, ability to bulk ship liquids without spoilage, and the introduction of versatile plastic packaging).

Slater points out that Mexico is an important food supplier to the United States, largely of fresh fruits, vegetables, and beer. He notes that Mexican firms process more than 85 percent of U.S. frozen food product imports. The food trade has become a truly binational effort; many large U.S. food companies have established operations in Mexico, and about half the Arizona distributorships for fruits and vegetables are controlled by Mexican producers.

José Carlos Alvarez Rivero and Herbert Weinstein believe that ethnic Mexican processed foods can generate a commercial boom in the United States, given the large number of Mexicans living in cities like Los Angeles, Houston, and Chicago. The purchasing power of this market should not be ignored by food companies, who can reach potential consumers with relatively modest advertising expenditures, the authors say.

Roberto A. Sánchez notes that the border region is already a booming, binational economic center, but he cautions that increased development is straining the urban infrastructure, which could pose an obstacle to future border industrialization and economic growth. He says the region suffers from a water shortage and existing supplies are increasingly threatened by municipal sewage. C. Richard Bath points out that border industrial development has generated a new environmental issue—toxic waste disposal. Relatively recent Mexican regulations governing the disposal of hazardous wastes could stimulate the growth of the Mexican waste management industry, Bath concludes.

The precise nature and extent of future industrial links between the two countries will depend on the growth rates of the two economies.

Clark Reynolds sees large gains from U.S.-Mexican economic integration, which he hopes will eventually cover more than trade and investment—i.e., that it should deal with currencies, labor, and microeconomic policies. He is most critical of U.S. economic policy during the 1980s, a time in which too little attention was placed on raising productivity.

Rogelio Ramírez de la O analyzes Mexican economic policy in its various phases: from the 1930s to the administration of President Miguel de la Madrid (1982–1988), a period characterized by extensive government intervention in the economy. He looks at the reforms initiated under President de la Madrid, which involved opening the economy to imports, undervaluation of the exchange rate (which stimulated exports), high real interest rates for peso instruments, and for a time, sharp reductions in the public sector deficit. He also analyzes current policy, a period in which inflation control is the dominant government priority. Ramírez notes that there are risks in the current policy: deterioration in the balance of payments during the phase of economic recovery, and the decline of infrastructure as a result of the collapse of public investment since the onset of the economic crisis in 1982. He concludes by noting that in future years the Mexican industrial apparatus will be heavily dependent on U.S. markets, and many U.S. firms will be increasingly engaged in manufacturing operations in Mexico.

Conclusions

The evolution of their respective policies has made both Mexico and the United States increasingly dependent on each other. Mexico was always highly reliant on the United States as a source of finance, technology, inputs for its industry, and as an outlet for its exports. This reliance was constrained to some extent by Mexico's policy of development from within. This did not reduce Mexico's need for imported intermediate products, but it did limit the urgency of Mexico's non-oil exports. The collapse of the oil market and the subsequent economic reforms during the 1980s have brought Mexico front and center into the world economy and emphasized the need for a competitive manufacturing sector.

The United States, because of the size of its economy, also tended to look mostly inward. However, in recent years, foreign goods have increasingly penetrated the U.S. market and highlighted the importance of raising U.S. competitiveness both in its own market and in foreign markets. The United States can look inward once again—increase its protectionism—only at a high cost to its income. The need for industrial competitiveness is recognized in the United States, as it now is in Mexico.

The studies in this volume look at one aspect of this need for competitiveness, how it can be augmented by bilateral cooperation. This can take many forms, as is evident from the different industry studies. It can involve joint production, as is the case already in the automotive industry and may expand to the petrochemical industry. Cooperation can result in U.S. help in technological upgrading, which is what Mexico seeks in the computer industry; or mutual research, which is not now the case but which Mexico seeks in the pharmaceutical industry. Or it can produce trade in different food products in which each country has a natural advantage.

The studies lead to varying conclusions in several industrial sectors:

1. In the automotive industry, because of sunk investments, mutual dependence is already extensive.
2. U.S. investment is more modest in the Mexican petrochemical industry, but considerable potential exists for greater cooperation.
3. Future cooperation in the computer industry depends on professional and technological upgrading in Mexico.
4. The food industry is marked by binational investment, some in each direction, and increasing trade.
5. The textile industry is a particularly good example of the mixture of cooperation and conflict, the latter due primarily to concern over labor displacement in the United States.
6. Perhaps the most difficult of all the industries studied is pharmaceuticals, because of its domination by large, vertically integrated multinationals and its important social role in both societies.
7. Renewable natural resources must be preserved so that binational development can continue.

Transcending these particular industry studies, what emerges from the research is that national policies do matter in shaping decisions of private companies. Mexico is now largely open to U.S. investment and imports, which places much of the initiative in the hands of the private actors. The United States is still largely an open market for trade and investment, but there are substantial pressures for trade restrictions. The best interests of the two countries require that protectionism be resisted and that instead the tendency toward industrial cooperation in trade and production be fostered.

Notes

1. American Embassy, Mexico City, "Foreign Investment Climate Report," August 1990.

2. Ignacio Trigueros, "A Free Trade Agreement between Mexico and the United States?" in Jeffrey J. Schott, ed., *Free Trade Areas and U.S. Trade Policy* (Washington, D.C.: Institute for International Economics, 1989), p. 259.

3. Mexico has not liberalized all imports. Industries that still require import permits (automotive and some agricultural products) still represent some 20 percent, by value, of imports. See *ibid*.

4. *Diario Oficial*, May 16, 1989.

5. Banco de México, *Indicadores económicos*.

6. It is not always self-evident when a producing plant is a *maquiladora* or not, and companies may switch back and forth. By maquiladora I have in mind only those plants that import U.S. intermediate products in bond, add further value in Mexico, and then send the transformed product back to the United States to take advantage of the U.S. tariff provisions that require payment of the duty only on the value added in Mexico.

7. Banco de México, *Indicadores económicos*.

8. This theme is developed in I.M. Destler and John S. Odell, *Anti-Protection: Changing Forces in United States Trade Politics* (Washington, D.C.: Institute for International Economics, 1987).

Industrial Integration Policy: Mexican Perspective

Luis Rubio F.

The economic relationship between Mexico and the United States is complex and extremely diverse. Not only the obvious characterizes the relationship. Besides huge and ever-growing flows of people, money, and goods, these two countries share problems that include issues as varied as sewage, drinking water, salinity in rivers that cross both nations, narcotics, smuggling, and many other legal and illegal transactions. All of these are big and small traits of this relationship. Yet, they tell only part of the story. The two countries are also experiencing a process of gradual integration that is taking place as a result of both deep market and social forces, and, more recently, by government design.

Mexico and the United States are clearly in the process of economic integration. Yet, the process is not conflict-free. An increasing share of Mexico's economy is in ever closer contact with the United States. Though Mexico's weight is small relative to the U.S. economy, co-production operations and joint ventures have increasingly linked critical productive processes to the point where several major U.S. industrial sectors are heavily linked to Mexico. Yet, in spite of these trends, Mexico's economy has tended to become increasingly more open while the U.S. economy has moved in the opposite direction. Mexican exporters and investors increasingly experience hindrances to doing business in the United States in a way that reminds Mexicans of the complaints Americans used to voice about Mexico. In a similar context, Canada decided to go for an all out free trade agreement, principally as a means to do away with growing United States protectionism. Mexico has since decided to do the same.

Why Economic Reform?

In 1985, Mexico began a process of economic restructuring with profound implications for the country's industry as well as for the economic relationship between Mexico and the United States. Up to 1985, Mexico had pursued a policy of industrialization by substitution of imports which had essentially consisted of manufacturing in Mexico all sorts of goods. Firms imported machinery and raw materials and produced goods for the domestic market. Over the years, the domestic government developed a policy frame that restricted imports, fostered firms while heavily regulating foreign investment, and induced investment in priority sectors through direct and indirect subsidies. This led to the growth of a burdensome bureaucracy entrusted with the responsibility to control foreign trade, investment and, in general, economic activity through endless discretionary decision making processes that became a source of enormous political power. As the policy of industrialization by substitution of imports collapsed in the 1970s, Mexico's governments attempted to avoid harsh policy decisions that eventually materialized in the reform initiated in the mid-1980s.

During the decades that substitution of imports lasted, industrial ties with the United States were restricted, usually limited to the purchase of raw materials and machinery, as well as technology, but maintaining a distant customer-to-supplier relationship, rather than one of partnership. In many cases, foreign investors joined with Mexican firms in the development of joint ventures, but these were geared to the domestic market. As a result, during the period characterized by substitution of imports—roughly from 1940 through 1985—Mexico's economic ties with the United States were heavily biased toward industrial imports. Funds to carry out the import substitution policy came basically from exports of agricultural products and, eventually, from oil exports. Foreign investment financed the current account deficits that existed during those years, thus contributing to a balanced evolution of the balance of payments as well as of the government's fiscal accounts. Late in the 1960s, Mexico's agricultural exports began to diminish as a result of the demands of a growing population as well as declining productivity. These circumstances destroyed half the equation of Mexico's successful industrialization, thus placing the whole scheme at risk. At stake was a GDP growth of 6.6 percent on average for 40 years, as well as the welfare of an increasingly urban population.

In the 1970s, the government decided to avoid the dilemma that was frustrating the country's industrial policy. Foreign credit became widely available as a result of the recycling of petrodollars. For the Mexican government, the availability of foreign financing served two goals. One was that no choices had to be made regarding economic policy. As perceived by the government, foreign credit would serve the same purpose as exports, in that imports of industrial goods remained easily available. The other goal that foreign credit served was to finance government projects in sectors such as steel, petrochemicals, and fertilizers. Hence, most foreign credit was channelled to goods, imports for industry, and to development of government-owned basic industries. As foreign debt piled up, the scheme became untenable and Mexico entered into a profound recession with three-digit inflation from which it is only now beginning to recover.

In 1985, the government finally decided to begin a process of economic liberalization. The reform implemented since then consists of a series of actions in various realms: liberalization of imports, privatization of government-owned industries, deregulation of industry at large, liberalization of foreign investment and of the financial sector, and so on. Much of the reform was made possible by a deep change in the government's perception of the importance of international trade and economic reform for the development of the country. Though opposition from the protectionist-minded bureaucrats as well as from the governing party structure was (and is) large and well organized, liberalization eventually won, and those fostering it consolidated their positions in the administration that began its term in December 1988.

The rationale for liberalization and deregulation is both economic and political. The current economic team has a profound conviction in the benefits to be derived from freer trade for the economy and for the development of the country. But the political rationale is not any less persuasive: a stronger economy would lead to a politically stronger polity. Hence, freer trade is seen as a vehicle for economic recovery as well as for political consolidation. At this stage, much of the reform process is in place, but much more remains to be implemented, particularly in the area of regulations. Though a modernization of the regulatory framework affecting the economy is currently in process, its success remains to be seen, as it often depends upon ministries other than those fostering the deregulation process. Furthermore, most of these changes would take place in areas that have traditionally given those ministries, such as communications, and their bureaucracy enormous discretionary power. Hence, the issue today is whether all regulations and institutions will be equally modernized or whether many critical issues will remain unresolved, thus reducing the overall competitive potential of the economy or, more appropriately, hindering it from being as competitive as it might otherwise be. Therefore, the foremost issue of the Mexican economy in the next two or three years will be precisely the scope and depth of changes in regulations. Many of these changes will have a profound impact on industrial integration across the Mexico-U.S. border. Nevertheless, what has already been done has radically altered the economic relationship between both nations.

Conflict and Cooperation in U.S. Industry

From 1940 through 1980, Mexico developed a series of policies that constituted the equivalent of an industrial policy. Though no general, clear-cut, across-the-board policy ever took shape, a series of specific policies forced Mexican industry to develop along lines that led to heavy concentration of firms in some sectors, while virtually no investment flowed to others. In spite of the lack of a broad, coherent policy, sectoral decrees and subsidies guided the industrial development, assuring high profit margins for individual firms.

Whereas Mexican industry developed under the auspices of the government, U.S. firms developed in the context of a competitive and basically open market. Government actions and decisions, however, guided the U.S. firms in their development, much as in the Mexican context. Though often implicit, regulations, tariffs, voluntary restraint agreements, antitrust actions, and other barriers to trade de facto constituted an industrial policy. Yet, without any doubt, U.S. firms developed in a widely open environment compared with Mexican enterprises. Both nations, however, ended by developing an industry geared toward their own domestic markets. Though qualitatively and quantitatively very different, both face a conceptually similar challenge in the world context.

As long as the policy of import substitution was in place, few and relatively minor contacts developed among firms across the border. Normal business transactions, some partnerships, and exports to Mexico were the typical relationships. Mexico began to export some industrial goods in the 1970s, but remained largely an importer. Hence, save for relatively few trade disputes—some of them rather noisy—the economic relationship was a quiet one.

With Mexico's policy of liberalization of imports, a fundamental shift in priorities has taken place. First, Mexico has increasingly developed a manufacturing export base that sometimes competes with U.S. firms. In most cases, however, Mexican exports have become part of a pattern of integration among firms, in which specialization in the manufacture of goods has become the rule. Most of these cases have to do with multinational companies that have integrated their manufacturing processes across the border, but many Mexican firms have done so as well. Also, Mexican firms have begun to penetrate the U.S. market both through exports as well as through acquisitions. The same goes for a large sector of industry, the *maquilas* or in-bond plants, which are scattered all along the border. These are largely U.S.-owned and were conceived as export bases; they do not represent a transformation of the old industrialization by substitution of imports. Yet, they do confirm the existence of a process of industrial integration that is largely based on cooperation rather than conflict.

Though patterns of integration vary substantially, the trend is clearly toward closer ties across the border. So far, most of the explanation for these developments can be found in two simple circumstances. One is geographic closeness, together with dramatic wage differentials, which makes Mexico an attractive base for assembly plants and other labor-intensive segments of the industrial process. The other circumstance is the idle capacity of firms on Mexican soil—both Mexican and multinational—that came about because of the recession that started in 1982. Spare capacity in Mexico served the needs of a rapidly growing market in the United States; many firms restructured their operations so as to participate in the northern market. Today, those plants have become fully integrated.

As various nations around the world reach agreements to cooperate and exchange access to their markets in order to take advantage of each country's strengths, such as cheap labor, technology, or capital, economic blocs will begin to take shape. That is the case of Europe with Spain and Portugal and of Japan with Malaysia and South Korea. Over the next few years it will become evident that Canada and the United States will not be able to enhance their competitiveness without Mexico, at least in some sectors. Hence, regardless of current or past industrial policies, industrial integration appears to be an ongoing process. However, the consolidation of this pattern of cooperation will depend upon the depth and speed of the economic reforms in Mexico. This entails not only a successful process of domestic deregulation and liberalization, but a reformulation of the nation's laws affecting the economic activity, particularly those related to foreign investment. Even though virtually all of the protectionist framework that characterized Mexico's international trade has been dismantled over the last three years, Mexican institutions and laws have lagged, hindering an easier and more rapid pace of change. Despite the rhetoric, both the United States and Mexico are likely to benefit from closer economic ties; for these to develop at the required pace, however, Mexico will have to continue pursuing its liberalization program, including foreign investment, in an increasingly competitive arena.

In fact, Mexico and the United States have been advancing in the process of ordering and formalizing the trend toward integration both by removing obstacles as well as by fostering negotiations on trade, investment, and sectoral linkages. Hence, the governments of both nations recognize the trend and are working to enhance the process while attempting to avoid any potential negative consequences. The process is, thus, well underway not only as a matter or course, but also by design.

Mexican Industrial Policy Today

Since there was no formal industrial policy, the elimination of many of the key policies and regulations that guided industrial development —such as import controls, subsidies, priority sectors and sectoral decrees —has amounted to the elimination of the whole concept of industrial policy. Firms were suddenly forced to act in a quasi-market environment with almost fully open borders.

Thus, Mexican firms today are beginning to guide themselves by fundamental concepts, such as comparative advantage, rather than government policy, for their development. This has entailed a dramatic shift in criteria, priorities, and thrust, and many companies are unlikely to succeed in the new environment. But those that do survive are likely to thrive, as several cases already exemplify. The liberalization of imports has also created a new environment in which domestic firms operate in a milieu characterized by competition from foreign firms in both the world markets (through exports) as well as in the domestic market (from imports). Furthermore, deregulation of foreign investment has also changed the structure of firms, and has altered joint ventures. In many cases, new deals are taking shape, while in others old partnerships are being dismantled.

For Mexican firms, this process of change has entailed a radical transformation of their structure, regulations, and operating environment. Each industrial sector, as the six that were chosen for this conference exemplify, is facing the new environment in a different way. Some have witnessed the elimination of virtually all barriers and restrictions, while others are still heavily regulated. All, however, have been subjected to the forces of competition.

Six Changing Industries in Mexico

Six industrial sectors were chosen to analyze how both countries are facing each other in the industrial arena. Each has a different history and is characterized by a contrasting structure. Some sectors are characterized by heavy concentration of large firms with typical vertical integration processes, while others tend to exemplify more competitive structures. Yet, while the typical world patterns of integration and concentration might be present in Mexico, some fundamental differences are remarkable. This stems from one essential point: because the Mexican government has monopolized several basic industries for decades, many firms have not been able to duplicate what their counterparts are doing in other nations. In one instance of the sample chosen—the petrochemical industry—vertical integration has had an absolute limitation because the government has a monopoly on basic petrochemical production. Hence, though the industry is, in general, not unlike its counterparts in other countries, in Mexico it has a fundamental difference in its structure.

The sectors that were chosen tell a similar story: all are experiencing increasing links across the border, most of them complementary rather than competitive. Some have advanced their process of integration to extraordinary degrees, as in the case of the automotive and computer industries. Others, such as the food industry, have lagged. Yet, there is a growing export-oriented sector in agriculture that is fully integrated with the food giants in the United States. Hence, although with natural differences, most industrial sectors are following a similar pattern. Textiles are just beginning to move in both directions, mainly through the *maquila* plants, but this is one area where import restrictions on the U.S. side alter the overall pattern. In pharmaceuticals, integration has been slow, largely due to old conflicts in patents and property rights; however, as these are finally settled, opportunities for joint production are likely to materialize in the future.

Each sector is characterized by its own particular traits. Yet, all of them provide ample evidence that the border is increasingly becoming not much more than an administrative barrier, albeit a cumbersome one, to industrial processes. Mexico has yet to obtain the advantages and the political benefits of such a process in terms of GDP growth, but the pattern is there for all to see.

As world competition grows and as trading blocs further enhance the competitiveness of some countries, notably in Europe and Asia, the three North American nations will increasingly have to rely on each other. Critical industries, such as automobiles, will not advance on the road to competitiveness without a labor-intensive nation such as Mexico, much like South Korea or Malaysia have complemented the Japanese, and Spain, Portugal, and Greece have strengthened the Northern Europeans. Hence, whether by design or by circumstance, closer integration is almost a foreordained conclusion. But without a proper legal framework, such a process will be extremely conflictual and will carry a permanent risk of derailing.

While cooperation is not likely to characterize all industrial sectors, this appears to be the obvious way for Mexican and multinational firms in Mexico for the next several years.   As cooperation and comparative advantages become more obvious, a process of specialization is likely to take shape, not only on a firm-by-firm basis as is currently the case, but also on a sector-by-sector basis. At this time, most Mexican firms are making the best use of their spare capacity and are basing their decisions on joint production or integration, which is the most efficient way in the short term.   Over the years, however, as new investment pours into each industry, the pattern is likely to change.   New investment will look for specific comparative advantages, thus strengthening bilateral links and fostering specialization in industrial sectors across the border.   In both instances the conclusion cannot be but the obvious: industrial integration has only one possible future course—more of it.

THREE

Automobiles

Automobiles: U.S. Perspective

Marc E. Maartens

This is a view of the Mexican automotive industry from both the U.S. and global perspective. It analyzes the U.S. government's role in shaping industry products, the Mexican government's influence over the industry's investment plans, and the extent to which the U.S. and Mexican automotive industries have already integrated, and it makes recommendations for future integration.

The automotive sector is rapidly evolving into a worldwide, competitive industry that is concentrated in regional production centers and markets. Vehicles are designed or produced in one region or country and sold in another. The industry calls this globalization of the market. A relatively small group of producers with headquarters in the United States, Western Europe, and Japan dominate this global marketplace.

Table 3.1 shows that the world's production of cars, trucks, and buses totaled about 46 million vehicles annually in the 1980s. Although production figures seem high, the automotive industry is growing more slowly now than it did in previous decades. After the 1930s, automotive production grew by leaps and bounds until the 1970s and 1980s, when growth moderated to about 30 percent in each decade, or about 2.7 percent growth compounded annually. For the first half of the 1990s, approximately 2.5 percent annual growth is projected; slower growth in the United States and Western Europe will be offset by greater growth in the rest of the world.

The North American region contributed only about 14 million vehicles out of the 46 million produced annually in the 1980s, as shown in Table 3.2. Both the Asia-Pacific and the European regions outproduce North America, and the products of both these regions have

TABLE 3.1 World Motor Vehicle Production

Year	Total World Production (units)	Percent increase over previous period
1900	9,500	
1910	255,000	2584
1920	2,400,000	841
1930	4,100,000	71
1940	4,900,000	20
1950	10,600,000	116
1960	16,500,000	56
1970	29,400,000	78
1980	38,500,000	31
1981	37,200,000	−3
1982	36,100,000	−3
1983	39,800,000	10
1984	42,100,000	6
1985	44,800,000	6
1986	45,300,000	1
1987	45,900,000	1
1988	48,200,000	5
1989	48,900,000	1
1990-95 trendline	50,000,000	2.5[a]

[a]Compound annual rate.

Sources: Motor Vehicle Manufacturing Association (actual) and Marc E. Maartens Associates (estimates).

achieved substantial market penetration in the United States and Canada.

Table 3.3 shows the extent to which the United States and Canada have penetrated the global market for vehicle production. From the 1950s to the 1980s, the U.S. and Canadian market share dropped from over 75 percent to 23 percent as the Asia-Pacific and European producers made important progress in product and quality. At the same time and for similar reasons, foreign vehicles obtained a 30 percent market share in the United States, giving the United States a vehicle trade deficit of about $45 billion annually.

To a large extent, industry trends are shaped by a car-driving public that wants technological advances: smoother rides, fuel-efficient engines, digital instrument clusters, more comfortable seats, better metal fit, and so forth. Technological advances in manufacturing processes provide these performance improvements and luxuries. New

TABLE 3.2 World Motor Vehicle Production by Region (millions of units)

Year	North America	Europe	Asia Pacific	Latin America	All Other	Total
1980	9.9	15.4	11.3	1.5	0.4	38.5
1981	9.9	14.4	11.5	1.0	0.4	37.2
1982	8.7	14.8	11.0	1.0	0.6	36.1
1983	11.0	15.7	11.5	1.0	0.6	39.8
1984	13.1	15.3	11.9	1.0	0.8	42.1
1985	14.0	16.0	12.9	1.1	0.8	44.8
1986	13.5	16.7	13.1	1.2	0.8	45.3
1987	13.0	17.5	13.5	1.1	0.8	45.9
1988	13.6	18.2	14.2	1.3	0.9	48.2
1989	13.4	19.0	14.5	1.1	0.9	48.9
1990s (trend)	14.0	19.0	15.0	1.0	1.0	50.0

Sources: Motor Vehicle Manufacturers Association (actual) and Marc E. Maartens Associates (estimates).

robotized, world-class facilities are being constructed in the United States, Western Europe and the Asia-Pacific areas, making older plants obsolete. Just-in-time delivery practices avoid large plant inventories and related storage areas on the plant floor.

To attract these new state-of-the-art vehicle assembly plants, Mexico must overcome the barrier of the global industry's near-term excess capacity. That excess capacity is evident in the United States as well as other countries. Overcapacity, now running at 20 percent across

TABLE 3.3 U.S. and Canadian Vehicle Production as Percent of World Production

Year	Percent of World Total	
	United States	United States and Canada
1950	76	80
1960	48	50
1970	28	33
1980	21	24
1985	26	31
1988	23	27
1989	22	26

Sources: Motor Vehicle Manufacturers Association and Marc E. Maartens Associates, Inc.

Europe, is likely to increase dramatically after the production boom of the past five years. Changing technologies squeeze more product out of existing modern plants. And better-built cars and trucks have a longer useful life.

Competition among the surviving global companies is going to be stiff in the 1990s, and this will affect Mexico's vehicle production. The surviving Big 12 automotive manufacturers are the Big Three of the United States (General Motors, Ford, and Chrysler); the Big Four of Western Europe (Volkswagen, Renault, Fiat, and Mercedes); and the Big Five of the Asia-Pacific region (Toyota, Nissan, Honda, Mazda, and Mitsubishi). Many smaller European or Asian producers already have been swallowed by a member of the Big 12. The financial press is full of speculation as to which of the smaller and even medium-sized companies will next be absorbed. This affects Mexico to the extent that funds spent on acquisitions are not available for new plant construction in Mexico.

The surviving manufacturers on each side of the border are prominent in the global market. The American Big Three (Chrysler, Ford, and General Motors) wholly own their Mexican counterparts. For the past few years and within prevailing Mexican government regulations, their U.S. domestic divisions have run these operations as if Mexico already were part of a trade arrangement similar to the U.S.-Canada Auto Pact. Japan's Nissan and Germany's Volkswagen (VW) also operate in Mexico, completing the Mexican Big Five.

Mexican Automotive Development

From the 1920s through the 1960s, the Mexican market, like markets in many countries, was best characterized as local. Vehicles were assembled from imported components and sold in Mexico. The styles and types were similar to those produced in the United States. In the 1960s, import-substituting assembly operations with local content were encouraged by Mexican government regulations calling for locally cast and machined engines and other components. This resulted in partially frozen vehicle models. It was no longer economically feasible to follow source design, such as on current U.S.-type vehicles, as readily as during the prior assembly stage. To a significant extent, the market stagnated at a given technology.

In the 1980s, the Mexican government promoted an aggressive export program, leading the U.S. Big Three to establish several modern, state-of-the-art engine plants and one world-class vehicle assembly plant (Ford at Hermosillo), which thrust Mexican automotive products onto the world market. Such construction programs must continue and the parts-supplier industry must be encouraged to initiate similar programs if Mexico wants to secure and increase its participation in the emerging, regional vehicle market and strengthen its foreign-exchange earnings.

At the same time, the Mexican automotive industry has become two-tiered. At one level, the Big Five continues operating low-level technology engine and vehicle assembly plants that supply the local market. These vehicles, produced mostly in Central Mexico, meet local standards of emission, safety, and damageability. At the second level, new export-oriented, state-of-the-art engine plants are producing their output primarily for the United States. In the past few years, the Big Five also began exporting vehicles.

The Motor Vehicle Manufacturers Association statistics classify Mexico as a member of the North American production region. Typically, in the 1980s, about 11 million of the world's annual vehicle production were produced in the United States. Almost 2 million were produced annually in Canada, and about half were exported to the United States. Mexico produced about 500,000 each year, as shown in Table 3.4. Cumulative production and scrapping of vehicles gives the following ratios of persons per registered vehicle for 1988: 1.4 for the United States, 1.7 for Canada, and 11 for Mexico.

In comparison with Latin American markets in the 1980s, as shown in Table 3.5, Mexico's annual production volumes were outranked by

TABLE 3.4 Vehicle Production for the North American Region
(millions of units)

Year	Canada	Mexico	USA	Total
1980	1.4	0.5	8.0	9.9
1981	1.3	0.6	8.0	9.9
1982	1.2	0.5	7.0	8.7
1983	1.5	0.3	9.2	11.0
1984	1.8	0.4	10.9	13.1
1985	1.9	0.4	11.7	14.0
1986	1.9	0.3	11.3	13.5
1987	1.7	0.4	10.9	13.0
1988	2.0	0.5[a]	11.2	13.7
1989 (est.)	2.0	0.6[b]	11.0	13.6
1990s (trend)	2.0	0.6	11.4	14.0

[a] Includes 0.1 exports.
[b] Includes 0.2 exports.

Sources: Motor Vehicle Manufacturers Association (actual) and Marc E. Maartens Associates (estimates).

TABLE 3.5 Vehicle Production in Selected Countries (millions of units)

Year	Argentina	Brazil	Korea	Mexico	Spain
1960	0.1	0.2	a	a	a
1970	0.2	0.4	a	0.2	0.5
1980	0.3	1.2	0.1	0.5	1.2
1981	0.2	0.8	0.1	0.6	1.0
1982	0.1	0.9	0.2	0.5	1.1
1983	0.2	0.9	0.2	0.3	1.3
1984	0.2	0.9	0.3	0.4	1.3
1985	0.1	1.0	0.4	0.4	1.4
1986	0.2	1.0	0.6	0.3	1.5
1987	0.2	0.9	1.0	0.4	1.7
1988	0.2	1.1	1.1	0.5	1.9
1989	0.1	1.0	1.1	0.6	2.0

[a] Less than 0.1.

Sources: Motor Vehicle Manufacturers Association (actual) and Marc E. Maartens Associates (estimates).

Brazil's approximately 1 million units, but were greater than Argentina's roughly 200,000 units.

Mexico's domestic market, after peaking in 1981 at about 600,000 units, leveled off at about 400,000. Growth came at first through substantial expansion of the domestic market and later through export. For 1989, the industry's export volume was about 200,000—one-third of Mexico's estimated total vehicle output of 600,000 vehicles.

Whether a market of locally made, low-priced vehicles for the lower-income groups of the population can be developed in the 1990s as the Mexican government desires depends on many factors. The availability of credit and the gradation of sales taxes are financial constraints for the consumer. And the producer needs to consider the availability of products and the economic viability of facilities dedicated to that market sector. These considerations must be weighed against the objective of maintaining a foreign-exchange/trade-balance equilibrium. So far only Volkswagen produces this kind of vehicle in Mexico.

Taxes

The automotive industry is as concerned about tax issues as any other investor in Mexico. Although the Mexican tax structure still contains some measures that reduce Mexican competitiveness as a producer for global markets, recent and pending changes in the laws sponsored by the Mexican government have improved Mexico's competitive position somewhat.

The Mexican corporate income tax rate, formerly 42 percent, has been reduced in recent years to 35 percent, and no longer results in significant amounts of Mexican tax on U.S. investors that cannot be credited against U.S. corporate income taxes. In addition, the Mexican withholding tax on dividends payable to foreign corporate shareholders from taxed profits has been eliminated. What remains is the withholding tax on gross payments for technical assistance, including reimbursement for costs, but it has been reduced from 21 percent to 15 percent.

The tax on royalty payments for the use of patents or trademarks, however, remains at 40 percent. There is a relatively new annual net asset tax, essentially a net worth tax, of 2 percent, which is creditable against the Mexican corporate income tax. It is particularly burdensome on new companies and other companies that do not earn taxable profits. Banks that lend to Mexican companies still suffer a 15 percent withholding tax on interest and other lenders must pay a 35 percent tax. Thus, Mexican companies would find it expensive to obtain funds from foreign lenders that have no income taxes against which to credit this cost.

All of the taxes mentioned above are creditable against U.S. taxes payable by the respective U.S. recipients of earnings or fees from Mexico, except the 2 percent net asset tax, and it is anticipated that the Mexican government will redefine the asset tax so that it will become creditable to the extent that Mexican corporate income taxes are creditable.

Most countries that encourage world commerce and investment enter into tax treaties with their principal trading partners in order to eliminate double taxation. Mexico's competitive position would be further enhanced if it would enter into such treaties.

Mexican Government Objectives and Industry Response

The Mexican government's stated objectives for the automotive industry emphasize foreign-exchange earnings, local and export markets, and global competitiveness. The government is convinced, correctly in my opinion, that it must deregulate the industry to achieve global competitiveness. It also understands that it must attract foreign capital, foster manufacture of non-polluting, safe vehicles, and encourage development of a world-class component parts industry.

A gradual approach to industry deregulation is the best way to achieve the government's desire of global competitiveness in parts and vehicle manufacture. Consider that Mexico must attract new world-class plants, which cost about $1 billion each, and reach payback only after about 15 years. While the industry agrees that investment in world-class technology is essential, given the capital requirements, the industry cannot afford sudden lurches towards a free and open economy after years of tight regulations. Time phasing, graduated and guided liberalization are the watchwords. These require creative responses from the U.S. automotive industry and the U.S. government.

The Mexican government believes that the value of the automotive industry's exports should at least balance the industry's imports. That seems fair and reasonable. But the government's view that any excess export revenue should contribute to the development of non-exporting sectors is controversial. While the industry might consider usage of such excess for its own non-exporting members, it looks with a jaundiced eye on having its surplus used in sectors other than the automotive.

The Mexican government wants to promote growth of both the domestic and export markets. Industry agrees that promotion of the domestic market is the foundation of a healthy industry. It is difficult to promote a global export industry if the domestic market is languishing. Industry also believes that in the present market environment, integrating with the United States means integration with the world. As the United States market allows practically free access to any producer, the Mexican export product must be able to compete with products of U.S., Japanese, or European design or origin. Environmental, fuel economy, safety and damageability standards must be developed and adapted to world-class requirements. Exports to the United States must conform to the U.S. standards. Lack of uniform standards is one of the factors that caused two-tiered development of the Mexican industry.

Logically, the Big Five would be willing to support their Mexican manufacturing and terminal-assembly operations with required investments to foster the growth that the Mexican government wants, should that prove economically attractive. Their labor-intensive *maquiladoras*, however, have a problem. *Maquiladoras* can continue present operations as long as their products or manufacturing processes do not become obsolete through technological advances. As these changes occur, it is not likely that robotized capital-intensive *maquiladoras* would be built in Mexico's border zone rather than near the plants that will demand just-in-time delivery of components.

In the next decade, robotized facilities will spring up in close proximity to assembly plants for just-in-time delivery of output now produced by these satellite *maquiladoras*. Molded-plastic seats, for example, will partially replace cut-and-sew operations now performed by *maquiladoras*.

The Big Five operate and control most of the 50 or so *maquiladoras* producing automotive-component parts in the northern border zone under government regulations separate from the general automotive regulations primarily for export to plants or transplants of their parents.

Industry also believes that adjustment of the socio-economic environment is perhaps the most difficult goal for Mexico to attain. Politics are affecting these issues even more than the other points discussed. A stable and flexible labor force, freedom to price, freedom of product offerings, and freedom to invest all affect the industry's future development or its inability to develop.

The automotive industry does employ about 465,000 people, or 3 percent of Mexico's industrial labor force. Worldwide, the American Big Three have about 1,255,000 employees. In Mexico, the Big Five employ about 40,000 people in their manufacturing and assembly operations, plus about 25,000 in their captive *maquiladoras*. Applying a conventional industry factor of 6, an additional 400,000 people are estimated to be employed by the Mexican automotive supplier and service industry. But even though a substantial number of Mexicans are employed in the industry, strict rules affecting work hours, vacation time, and duration of employment are hampering development of skilled employees. Limited availability of Mexican government-sponsored training programs also restrains the industry.

The 1989 Automotive Decree

Since the 1960s, every Mexican presidential administration has promulgated a new automotive decree. To Mexico's advantage, the decrees followed a consistent and predictable direction. Accordingly, a new decree from the Salinas de Gortari government was promulgated on December 8, 1989, generally effective with the 1991 car-model year. Clarifying rules and regulations to implement this decree were published on November 30, 1990, but require further clarification. The decree initiates time-phased and guided liberalization of the Mexican automotive industry toward international competitiveness. Similarly, a new truck decree and a new *maquiladora* decree foster guided liberalization.

Key points of the new automotive decree are:

1. Importation of built-up vehicles will be permitted.
2. Mandatory inclusion of specific local content has been eliminated. Instead, 36 percent value-added must be furnished by the Mexican automotive supplier industry through application of specific formulas.
3. Restrictions on foreign ownership will be liberalized.

4. International pricing levels, excluding Mexican taxes, will be the benchmark for Mexican-produced vehicles sold in Mexico.

The decree reflects in large measure the objectives outlined in this chapter. To reach global integration smoothly, the industry lobbied for guided liberalization to move step-by-step from the present environment in a time frame covering more than one presidency.

A word of caution: as Mexican policies turn from economic nationalism to a freer economy, promoted by less authoritarian politics, it may not be as certain as in prior decades that the Mexican government can follow an essentially non-varying policy line. But one should accept that risk willingly as the price for greater freedom of action that will be beneficial in the long run. New *maquiladora* decrees and the decrees regulating automotive trade in the border zone also need to reflect this new thinking.

Recommended Government Actions

If both the U.S. and the Mexican governments take actions that will promote, or at least not hinder, the chances to meet these objectives, the industry can be on the threshold of new and dramatic developments in the next two decades. The Mexican government measures should include additional actions to:

1. Eliminate further minimum local content requirements for the supplier and terminal assemblers to avoid restricting vertical integration.
2. Permit *maquiladoras* to sell to the terminal assemblers on an unrestricted basis.
3. Discontinue limitations on foreign exchange generation sources.
4. Permit freedom of pricing.
5. Eliminate product offering restrictions.
6. Permit existing manufacturers and terminal assemblers to import, with full foreign exchange compensation, finished vehicles to satisfy market demands.
7. Prohibit the importation of used built-up vehicles.
8. Widen the scope of international trade agreements, when appropriate.
9. Eliminate requirements for Mexican majority ownership rules for the supplier industry and improve intellectual ownership protection to stimulate foreign investment and technological inflow. A beginning has been made in this matter with the trade and investment agreement recently signed with the United States.

10. Promote a stable and flexible labor environment to increase foreign investors' confidence.
11. Establish competitive sales tax and import duty structure, similar to U.S. levels, to stimulate local demand.
12. Establish a competitive general tax structure to stimulate foreign investment.
13. Improve and make available a wider range of financing instruments for industry and commerce to stimulate investment and demand.
14. Provide adequate fuels on a nationwide basis.
15. Improve transportation, communications, and seaport infrastructure and improve customs service.
16. Simplify administrative requirements.

Industry Agenda

The automotive industry has its own agenda for integration. It is focusing on the following:

1. Integration should provide for free competition for specialized niche products. Product specialization increases the chances for successful integration. Specific components like manual transmissions or specific vehicles would be produced in Mexico for both the domestic and the export markets. To offer the Mexican consumer a full line of finished vehicles, Mexico would let the terminal assemblers import the balance of the country's finished vehicle requirements. Potential export markets would include expansion in the California market because of its geographic proximity.
2. With component product specialization, the Mexican industry would be able to supply parent assembly plants with original equipment parts. More liberal vertical integration would stimulate development of facilities now not contemplated. New perspectives of global sourcing place Mexico in contention for product production in new high-tech plants. Technological demands would increase, but they would force the parent industry to make technological advances available to the Mexican counterpart industry.
3. Linkages between U.S. and Mexican firms would dramatically increase as existing Mexican suppliers required new and advanced technology to compete in the global market. New entries are envisaged. Some observers project that vehicles now produced in Korea, Taiwan, and other Asian locations could in the future be produced in transplants in Mexico. Consider that,

as Table 3.5 shows, Korean production volumes increased from about 200,000 vehicles in 1970 to more than 1 million in 1988. In the same time frame Spanish production increased from about 500,000 to almost 2 million vehicles. This occurred after both countries successfully encouraged producers to install world-class manufacturing and assembly facilities.

Integration

The automotive industries of the United States and Mexico have begun to integrate, and it would be beneficial for both countries if this process were to accelerate over the coming decades. To reach this objective, Mexico must be globally competitive in product, technology, quality, durability, delivery, and price.

Regulatory rules in the United States affect both the Mexican domestic and export markets. For example, Mexico, for economic reasons, does not follow designs that comply with all U.S. rules for damageability, which means that deviations must be engineered and production adjusted to match local parts with imported components. Emission controls determine the type of engines produced, and conforming changes must be made in engine plants. But for exports to the United States, vehicles produced in Mexico must meet U.S. product specifications.

Various protective measures and subsidies distort the free economy on both sides of the border. For example, in the United States a 25 percent tariff on small trucks makes these imports economically difficult. Japanese voluntary export restraints restrict the free flow of Japanese vehicles into the United States. In 1988 and again in 1989, however, U.S. imports of Japanese vehicles actually were less than quota. In Mexico, the more severe prohibition of finished vehicle imports, while protecting the inefficient Mexican industry, limits availability of models.

Regulatory rules in Mexico have a definite impact on the willingness of outsiders to invest. On the global market, the investor has a choice of locale for investments. If other areas in the producing region have more favorable investment climates, these areas will be preferred. So it would be in Mexico's best interest to create a climate as favorable as its economic circumstances permit.

Existing restrictions on product offerings limit manufacturers to government-prescribed model quantities and types, thus hindering the development of a free market economy. Existing performance requirements stipulate local-content levels and types of product. The requirements also link production values to export values to correct trade imbalances that were unfavorable to Mexico for decades.

Mexican law officially restricts vertical integration, which discourages foreign investment in new supplier plants. U.S. manufacturers have freedom of choice in vertical integration. Depending on the economics, they vertically integrate proprietary components such as powertrain production, major stampings, and electronics. But Mexico essentially limits vertical integration to engines, trim, and glass. Mexico further restricts vertical integration by stipulating that suppliers must be 60 percent Mexican owned. But Mexican capital is scarce; so, wisely, the Mexican government now applies this rule with greater flexibility than in prior years, and substantial links exist between the U.S.-Mexican supplier industries channeling technology and products across the border.

Ultimately, liberalization of the foreign ownership rules should benefit Mexico. The major manufacturers and terminal assemblers operate in Mexico under a grandfather clause permitting their foreign parents to completely own Mexican operations. However, the Mexican ownership rule still is onerous enough to discourage not only foreign investments in new supplier plants, but also expansion and modernization of existing inefficient supplier facilities. Existing manufacturers and terminal assemblers are effectively prevented from vertical integration at their own discretion. Procedures for obtaining permission are cumbersome, particularly for technology, software for robots, and intellectual property right transfers. And the outlook for approval, while much improved, is still uncertain. This situation substantially reduces Mexico's attractiveness as a location for new automotive plants.

Trade Agreement

Trade between the United States and Mexico in 1989 amounted to about $50 billion, and the value is expected to grow. The automotive trade balance favors Mexico at about $1 billion per year, a trend that is likely to continue. Two factors combined to create the surplus: the producers increased exports substantially because quality and cost were better than expected, and the domestic market did not expand as strongly as originally projected. Consequently, fewer original equipment parts were imported. Presently contemplated measures should be designed to keep the automotive trade at least in balance as the Mexican economy improves in the 1990s.

A bilateral auto pact, similar to the U.S.-Canadian bilateral auto pact, or a comprehensive free trade agreement, are viable options and would be helpful for strategic planning for increased U.S.-Mexico integration. U.S. and Canadian labor leaders in the automotive sector are sensitive to competition from inexpensive Mexican labor, although much of that opposition is based upon misconceptions. The new Mexican plants are capital intensive and employ little labor. But it will take time to change these perceptions.

In the interim, ad hoc arrangements should be the preferred course of action. Formalization of a tri-country free trade area is now a real possibility. To some extent, however, the industry acts as if such arrangements were already in force. Care should be exercised so that plans and measures now implemented would not impede these more comprehensive formal steps.

In addition to liberalizing the provisions and administration of the automotive decree, global integration would be further stimulated if the administration of Mexico's transfer of technology decree were likewise liberalized. Mexico's vehicle manufacturers and component suppliers must employ global designs and technology in order to participate in global integration programs. The foreign proprietors of such designs and technology must show they are being reasonably compensated when their designs and technology and any related technical assistance furnished are used in Mexico. They want to be protected against unauthorized use in Mexico before entering into technology agreements with Mexican firms. Under the Mexican Technology Decree, however, only transfers and assistance approved by and registered with the Mexican authorities can be compensated and protected in Mexico. Mexican suppliers and vehicle producers are severely handicapped in their competition with global producers and suppliers when the Mexican authorities delay or refuse approval of the technology transfers. The proprietary rights can not be protected without an approved registration under the Mexican decree.

Conclusions

At present the industry is multi-tiered. It certainly would be more efficient if the industry consolidated into a single world competitive level. Because of new decrees and related regulations, this evolution is likely to take place, as it did in Canada. Given the time it takes to plan, construct, and launch the required facilities, it is estimated that this process will stretch over the coming decade and perhaps longer. For the plants built in the import-substituting era, this process will be dramatic. Not all will be able to survive. The *maquiladoras* are safe, as long as their products or manufacturing processes do not become obsolete through technological changes. When that occurs, serious relocation problems will arise. But for the top-level, export-oriented plants already competing in the global market, the transition should not be difficult.

Most observers agree that the industry cannot wait for a formal auto pact or free trade area. Ad hoc arrangements already in place will expand gradually over time, leading to more complete integration of the U.S. automotive industry with its Mexican counterparts. Meanwhile, no steps or measures should be taken by the governments or the industry that could impede execution of a bilateral or trilateral auto pact, or formalization of a free trade area covered by a free trade agreement.

Automobiles: Mexican Perspective

Florencio López-de-Silanes

The automotive industry has a central role within both the U.S. and Mexican industrial sectors. In Mexico, the industry employs about 7 percent of manufacturing labor. The sectoral linkages between the two countries, although influenced by both world trends and country-specific regulations, have constantly increased since the establishment of the first U.S. automobile assembly plant in Mexico. Over the past 30 years, both governments have been concerned about the multiple backward and forward linkages of automobile manufacturing, as well as its influence on output, employment, and trade flows. The binational relationship has been complicated by the oligopolistic structure of the automotive industry, which was formed by multinational corporations, as well as the pronounced economies of scale that characterize the industry's production processes. The decisions that have helped to shape this industry on both sides of the border have been affected by the quest to penetrate and seize automotive markets.

This analysis examines the various aspects of what I call the silent integration of the automotive industry in Mexico and the United States. I also analyze the costs of current regulations on both sides of the border, and the limits that these regulations impose on continuing industrial integration. I believe that, given the trends toward globalization and increased world competition, integration will not only enhance automotive output and employment in both the United States and Mexico, but will also become largely irreversible without incurring major economic losses in either country.

Evolution of the Industry

As the world automotive industry developed, three major technological and organizational transformations shaped its growth in the United States and contributed to its emergence and growth in Mexico. The first significant breakthrough came after nearly 30 years of unit-by-unit production, primarily in Germany and France. In 1908, Ford triggered the transition to a mass production system and increased the U.S. share of world markets to about 90 percent. The second industry breakthrough didn't come until the emergence of the European Economic Community, which was capable of obtaining efficient output scales that would drastically affect the market. Once its mass production system was in full swing, Europe's product differentation provided a primary advantage over the United States. While U.S. companies concentrated on large vehicles, European production supplied a large market demand for a wide variety of small, medium, and luxury cars. By 1960, the European Community was contributing 40 percent of world production and had penetrated almost 10 percent of the North American market. The Big Three (Ford, General Motors, and Chrysler), retaliated with smaller models and recaptured half of their lost domestic market five years later.

The third significant transformation, the total quality and just-in-time processes, moved the industry to flexible manufacturing. In the late 1960s, Japan incorporated these new methods into its production organization, pushing the Japanese automobile industry to world leadership.[1] As a result of these changes and the oil shocks of the 1970s, Japan's share of world production increased from 1.3 percent in 1960 to 26 percent in 1982. That year, the Japanese auto industry was the world's largest, and it captured 23 percent of the North American market. The United States demanded voluntary export restraints to limit Japanese penetration, and by 1989 the Japanese share of the U.S. market had dropped slightly to 20 percent.

The international framework of intense competition and the Japanese attack on U.S. companies in their own territory induced the Big Three to search for low-cost production bases in Third World countries. Thus, they established plants in countries like Korea, Brazil, and Mexico. Since the mid-1970s, General Motors, Ford, and Chrysler also have attempted to regain part of their lost market by establishing associations with Japanese producers.

The rise in gasoline prices in the 1970s meant a shift in market demand away from big engines and backwheel drive vehicles. U.S. companies reacted by restructuring their geographic production. Thus, the new market for smaller engines and frontwheel drive vehicles was supplied from countries like Mexico and Brazil, which offered lower labor costs and attractive investment incentives.

The decade of the 1970s also marked a change in the mass production system. Before this decade, mass production required a constant flow of investment to fund each vehicle model change, making the production of vehicles and auto parts in small runs very difficult. The minimum cost-efficient scales were too high for developing economies, and the consumers in the few countries that ventured into automobile manufacturing paid high prices for home-produced models. In Latin America, only Brazil, Argentina, and Mexico developed a significant automotive sector. In all these economies, producers faced not only the high costs of low-scale production, but also the burden created by strict regulation.

But the advent of the robotic age and production techniques already discussed ushered in production flexibility that reduced the minimum productive scales, which in turn facilitated the ability of developing countries to competitively enter the world auto market. Mexico has been favored by both its location and its comparative advantage in some production processes.

Emergence of a Mexican Industry and Development of a U.S. Link

The Mexican automotive industry developed as part of the general industrialization process in the first half of the twentieth century. Before 1925, Mexicans could only import finished vehicles, but that same year Ford inaugurated its first Mexican assembly plant, taking advantage of large investment subsidies. Because of the Great Depression, assembly operations did not expand much until 1935, when another U.S. company, General Motors, opened a plant. Other foreign and domestic companies, such as Fabricas Automex with a Chrysler concession, followed shortly, as outlined in Table 3.6. By 1940, the Mexican automotive sector employed 1,328 workers, or about 0.5 percent of total labor in transforming industries, as Table 3.7 indicates. Almost 95 percent of the assembly materials used were imported.

World War II brought about industrial recovery in Mexico. By 1960, despite heavy imports, the automotive sector represented about 2 percent of total workers and 2.2 percent of manufacturing GDP (see Table 3.7 and Figure 3.1).

But real development in automotive manufacturing was not forthcoming. In 1960, 53 percent of the domestic demand for passenger cars was supplied by imports, while 80 percent of the value of parts used in domestic assembly also was imported. Exports amounted to only $300,000, while the import bill totaled $83.5 million, creating serious problems in the national trade balance.

The Mexican government's 1962 Automotive Decree established a new regulatory framework aimed at forming a national automotive

TABLE 3.6 Mexican Vehicle Assembly, 1925–1962

Firms Before 1962	Starts	Models Produced	Ownership
Ford	1925	Ford	100% foreign
General Motors	1935	General Motors	100% foreign
Fabricas Automex	1938	Chrysler	100% private, domestic
Promexa	1962	Volkswagen	100% private, domestic
DINA	1951	Renault	100% Mexican government
Willys Mexicana	1946	American Motors	100% private, domestic
Represent. Delta	1955	Mercedes Benz	100% private, domestic
Planta Reo	1955	Toyota	100% private, domestic
Impulsora Mexicana	1967		
Auto. (FANASA)		na[a]	na
Automoviles O'Farril	1937	Hillman	100% private, domestic
Autos Ingleses	1946	Morris	100% private, domestic
Studebaker-Packard	1951	Lark	100% private, domestic
Citroen	na	Citroen	na
Equipos Superiores	na	Austin	na
Autos Internacionales	na	Volvo	na

[a]Not available.

Source: Author's compilation.

industry. Under the decree, automobiles produced were required to have a 60 percent domestic content, called the Grado de Integración Nacional (GIN). Table 3.8 outlines the effects of the decree, which also introduced Mexican majority ownership rules in auto parts manufacturing. Foreign investors were limited to 40 percent ownership for components production. The price controls and production quotas for vehicles of the 1950s remained. These regulations were supplemented by a declared government intention of limiting the number of producers to reach efficient scales.

The government envisioned an industry structure consisting of only four companies, all domestically owned. Thus, Automex was authorized to produce large Chrysler model cars; Promexa and DINA to produce popular small cars (Volkswagen and Renault models); and VAM to produce Jeeps. But U.S. producers strongly opposed the measures, as did the U.S. government, which issued statements protesting the exclusion of U.S. auto makers. The pressure led to the inclusion of Ford and General Motors in the Mexican automotive structure. Nissan also was allowed to enter two years after the decree was released. The seven companies that remained in the market made

TABLE 3.7 Mexican Automotive Employment, 1940–1989

Year	Number of Automotive Workers			Percent of Total Automotive			Percent of Manufacturing		
	Total	Autos[a]	Parts[b]	Autos[a]	Parts[b]	Total Mfg. Workers	Total	Auto[a]	Parts[b]
1940	1,328	na[c]	na	—	—	289,908	0.5	—	—
1945	444	na	na	—	—	475,461	0.1	—	—
1950	3,701	na	na	—	—	698,611	0.5	—	—
1960	16,059	na	na	—	—	791,458	2.0	—	—
1965	34,936	na	na	—	—	1,343,510	2.6	—	—
1970	60,000	23,000	37,000	38.3	61.7	1,726,000	3.5	1.3	2.1
1971	65,000	26,000	39,000	40.0	60.0	1,772,000	3.7	1.5	2.2
1972	69,000	27,000	42,000	39.1	60.9	1,831,000	3.8	1.5	2.3
1973	81,000	34,000	47,000	42.0	58.0	1,925,000	4.2	1.8	2.4
1974	93,000	40,000	53,000	43.0	57.0	1,996,000	4.7	2.0	2.7
1975	97,000	39,000	58,000	40.2	59.8	2,002,000	4.8	1.9	2.9
1976	93,000	37,000	56,000	39.8	60.2	2,046,000	4.5	1.8	2.7
1977	81,000	32,000	49,000	39.5	60.5	2,051,000	3.9	1.6	2.4
1978	93,600	36,400	57,200	38.9	61.1	2,133,000	4.4	1.7	2.7
1979	107,900	42,600	65,300	39.5	60.5	2,291,000	4.7	1.9	2.9
1980	121,200	47,700	73,500	39.4	60.6	2,417,000	5.0	2.0	3.0
1981	135,600	53,900	81,700	39.7	60.3	2,542,000	5.3	2.1	3.2
1982	118,700	48,300	70,400	40.7	59.3	2,485,000	4.8	1.9	2.8
1983	94,300	35,800	58,500	38.0	62.0	2,310,000	4.1	1.5	2.5
1984	108,500	39,100	69,400	36.0	64.0	2,361,000	4.6	1.7	2.9
1985	132,300	45,700	86,600	34.5	65.5	2,487,166	5.3	1.8	3.5
1986	117,700	41,800	75,900	35.5	64.5	2,387,058	4.9	1.8	3.2
1987	123,300	43,700	79,600	35.4	64.6	2,305,936	5.3	1.9	3.5
1988	135,500	46,400	89,100	34.2	65.8	2,354,361	5.8	2.0	3.8
1989[d]	180,000	52,000	128,000	28.9	71.1	2,432,055	7.4	2.1	5.3

[a]Autos include trucks, tractors, and other vehicles.
[b]Parts do not include all components, only those registered as auto parts.
[c]No data available.
[d]Preliminary data.

Sources: Calculated using data from Secretaría de Programación y Presupuesto, Instituto Nacional de Estadística, Geografía e Informatíca, Banco de México, Censos Industriales, several issues.

FIGURE 3.1 Automotive GNP in Mexico (as a percentage of manufacturing GNP)

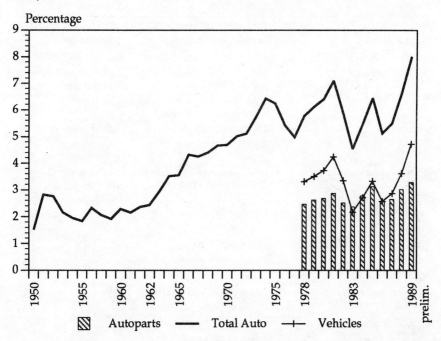

Sources: Calculated with data from Nacional Financiera S.A., Instituto Nacional de Estadística, Geografía e Informática, and Banco de México.

heavy investments in the Mexican automotive industry over the next several years (see Table 3.8). By 1968, the value of their total fixed assets had multiplied 4.5 times.

At the same time, the interrelations between the U.S. and Mexican automotive sectors deepened. To meet the domestic content requirement, U.S. multinationals, led by Ford, linked U.S. component producers with Mexican capital to create auto part companies in Mexico. Tremec and Spicer resulted from these efforts. Other U.S.-based companies like Eaton made direct investments in the Mexican components industry.[2]

Automobile production more than doubled between 1960 and 1968 with an annual growth rate of 20 percent. The increased vehicle production and larger domestic value added for components and parts boosted the Mexican automotive GDP to 4.4 percent of manufacturing GDP. But the sector's significant trade imbalance persisted—the industry was not an exporter. Imports amounted to 32 times the value of exports in 1968 alone.

TABLE 3.8 Changes after 1962 Manufacturing Decree

Firms	Changes	Owner in 1969
Ford	Remains unchanged	100% foreign
General Motors	Remains unchanged	100% foreign
Fabricas Automex	1962: Chrysler gets 33%	
Fabricas Automex	1968: Chrysler increases share to 45%	55% private domestic; 45% foreign
Promexa/VW	1964: Volkswagen gets 100%, changes name to Volkswagen	100% foreign
Nissan	Established in 1964	100% foreign
DINA	Remains unchanged	100% Mexican government
Willys Mexicana/VAM	1963: American Motors gets 40%, becomes VAM	60% Mexican government; 40% foreign
Representaciones Delta	Closes in 1964	
Planta Reo	Closes in 1963	
Impulsora Mexicana Automotriz	Closes in 1969	
Automoviles O'Farril	Bought by Promexa in 1962	
Autos Ingleses	Bought by Promexa in 1962	
Studebaker-Packard	Bought by Ford in 1960–1961	
Citroen	Closes in 1962–1963	
Equipos Superiores	Closes in 1962–1963	
Autos Internacionales	Closes in 1962–1963	

Source: Author's compilation.

U.S. automobile producers strongly resisted the idea of exporting from Mexico because of low-quality, inefficient auto parts production. Car exports from Mexico also ran counter to the interests of the largest multinational producers, particularly in the United States.

Mexico had two possible solutions to the sector's external imbalance: higher exports or higher GIN. After numerous disputes between the foreign and domestic auto makers, the government opted for an export promotion policy. The 1969 and 1970 agreements with auto makers and the subsequent 1972 Automotive Decree formalized a new mechanism under which the growing imports would be balanced by exports containing at least 40 percent auto parts not made by the producers (see Table 3.9 for producers). This policy, however, strongly favored foreign auto producers. For example, under the export requirement Automex faced opposition by Chrysler in the United States. After severe losses in 1972, the Mexican producer sold its shares to its U.S. partner. As a result, private Mexican capital in passenger cars all but vanished.

TABLE 3.9 Ownership Changes after 1972 Decree and 1969–1970 Agreement

Firm	Change	1977 Owner
Ford	Remains unchanged	100% foreign
General Motors	Remains unchanged	100% foreign
Fabricas Automex	1972: Chrysler gets remaining 55%, changes name to Chrysler	100% foreign
Volkswagen	Remains unchanged	100% foreign
Nissan	Remains unchanged	100% foreign
DINA	Remains unchanged	100% Mexican government
Willys Mexicana/ VAM	Remains unchanged	60% Mexican government; 40% foreign

Source: Author's compilation.

Auto producers invested large amounts to increase exports, which jumped from $4.3 million to $26.6 million by 1970 (see Table 3.10). Production increased 18 percent annually between 1968 and 1975. The sector's GDP rose to 6.7 percent of total manufacturing GDP and auto workers represented 4.8 percent of the manufacturing labor force by the end of this period (see Figure 3.1 and Table 3.7). The auto parts industry grew stronger, providing 60 percent of the sector's employment.

About 90 percent of Mexican automotive exports consisted of auto parts as a result of the U.S. companies' decision to begin globalizing their production. Nevertheless, the domestic market growth required component imports, and the sectoral trade deficit was not alleviated by the trade balancing mechanism of 1972. By 1976, more than 20 percent of the national trade deficit could be attributed to the automotive sector.

Silent Integration in the North American Automotive Industry

Integration in the Globalization of Production Processes

The June 1977 Automotive Decree strongly emphasized automotive exports, and embraced measures aimed at avoiding sectoral trade deficits. The decree created a new mechanism, a balance-of-payments restriction that required each auto producer to provide exports to balance its direct and indirect imports as well as all other company-made payments abroad. The decree also included a new GIN calculation that focused on direct component costs rather than

TABLE 3.10 Automotive Trade Balance, 1960–1989 (millions of U.S. dollars)

Yr.	Total	Veh.	Eng.	Parts	Total	Veh.	Parts	Auto Trade Bal.	Exp.	Imp.	Bal.
	Automotive Exports				*Automotive Imports*				*Auto. Trade/ National Trade (percent)*		
1960	0.2	0.0	na[a]	0.2	119.3	86.5	32.7	(119)	0.0	10.1	26.6
1961	0.5	0.0	na	0.5	136.0	93.7	42.3	(136)	0.1	11.9	40.0
1962	0.8	0.0	na	0.7	131.9	93.7	38.2	(131)	0.1	11.5	51.7
1963	0.9	0.3	na	0.6	152.3	109.3	43.1	(151)	0.1	12.3	48.7
1964	0.5	0.1	na	0.4	203.0	153.2	49.8	(202)	0.0	13.6	41.4
1965	0.8	0.1	na	0.8	182.6	131.7	50.9	(182)	0.1	11.7	39.7
1966	1.0	0.0	na	1.0	155.7	104.9	50.8	(155)	0.1	9.7	35.8
1967	2.4	0.1	na	2.3	157.7	115.5	42.2	(155)	0.2	9.1	24.5
1968	4.3	0.0	na	4.3	162.4	96.6	65.8	(158)	0.4	8.5	21.0
1969	17.8	0.5	na	17.3	202.5	151.5	51.0	(185)	1.3	10.2	28.5
1970	26.6	0.2	na	26.4	219.7	166.4	53.3	(193)	2.1	9.4	18.6
1971	45.1	1.5	5.9	37.7	188.2	133.7	54.5	(143)	3.3	8.3	16.1
1972	64.4	5.7	10.5	48.2	278.3	212.5	65.8	(214)	3.9	10.1	19.5
1973	138.1	39.7	21.5	76.9	308.4	206.9	101.5	(170)	6.7	7.9	9.4
1974	156.7	43.4	24.8	88.5	348.2	234.7	113.6	(192)	5.5	5.7	5.8
1975	184.0	9.6	35.4	139.0	807.3	189.6	617.6	(623)	6.0	12.0	17.1
1976	170.9	10.3	54.7	105.9	799.7	186.5	613.2	(629)	4.7	12.7	23.8
1977	140.2	20.3	1.9	117.9	629.9	90.9	539.0	(490)	3.0	11.0	46.4
1978	390.6	108.8	90.4	191.4	1,022.8	243.2	779.6	(632)	6.4	12.9	34.1
1979	446.2	118.2	51.6	276.4	1,477.3	451.5	1,025.8	(1,031)	5.1	12.3	32.6
1980	366.2	128.7	32.7	204.8	1,896.7	657.7	1,239.0	(1,530)	2.4	10.1	41.4
1981	339.5	113.8	61.5	164.2	2,219.4	681.6	1,537.8	(1,880)	1.7	9.3	41.7
1982	403.5	73.5	214.2	115.8	881.6	170.7	710.9	(478)	1.9	6.1	ns[b]
1983	945.4	159.6	602.8	183.1	413.1	36.4	376.7	532	4.4	5.4	3.9
1984	1,415.3	166.1	982.7	266.5	793.5	96.2	697.2	622	5.8	7.1	4.8
1985	1,420.6	148.8	1,039.2	232.6	932.3	171.1	761.2	488	6.6	7.1	5.8
1986	2,044.0	527.6	1,152.7	363.7	571.6	86.7	484.9	1,472	12.8	5.0	32.0
1987	3,028.8	1,317.0	1,290.9	420.9	1,089.4	117.2	972.2	1,939	14.7	8.9	23.0
1988	3,181.1	1,493.6	1,300.4	387.1	1,869.6	194.7	1,675.0	1,311	15.5	9.9	78.6
1989	3,506.0	1,567.0	1,366.0	573.0	2,124.0	161.0	1,963.0	1,382	15.4	9.1	ns[b]

[a]Not available.
[b]Not significant.

Sources: Compiled using Instituto Nacional de Estadística, Geografía e Informática and Secretaría de Comercio y Fomento Industrial data.

production costs, as it had previously. The required GIN coefficient was set at 50 percent for automobiles and 65 percent for trucks. Production quotas and price controls were eliminated. DINA and VAM faced less stringent export requirements, because of their capital structure, and other auto makers were banned from producing heavy trucks and diesel engines.

The U.S. producers unsuccessfully opposed the new regulations. Finally, five months after the decree was issued, General Motors announced projects for *maquiladora* (in-bond plant) expansion as well as new Mexican investment as part of its globalization strategy.[3]

The 1977 Automotive Decree was important because it forced multinational corporations, especially the Big Three, to focus on Mexican export strategies at a crucial moment in the development of global production. Auto producers were required to consider shifting production processes to Mexico in order to meet export requirements and still benefit from investment subsidies. Investment decisions in this industrial sector have significant long-term impacts and require considerable planning time. But by 1983, most of the auto producers had begun large investment programs in Mexico. General Motors opened two plants in Saltillo that produced passenger cars and engines. In 1983, Ford inaugurated its Chihuahua engine plant. Nissan began producing engines and opened a new forge plant in Ciudad Lerma in 1978. Several years later, the Japanese producer expanded into aluminum forging and engine production in Aguacalientes. As a result of financial distress, more ownership changes occurred among the remaining government-owned car makers (see Table 3.11).

The auto parts company growth that generated significant exports was promoted by joint ventures of U.S. auto makers and large Mexican

TABLE 3.11 Ownership Changes after 1977 Decree

Firm	Change	1982 Owner
Ford	Remains unchanged	100% foreign
General Motors	Remains unchanged	100% foreign
Chrysler	Remains unchanged	100% foreign
Volkswagen	Remains unchanged	100% foreign
Nissan	Remains unchanged	100% foreign
DINA/Renault	1978: Renault gets 40% ownership	60% Mexican government; 40% foreign
VAM	1977: government gets 34% more of VAM	94% Mexican government; 6% foreign

Source: Author's compilation.

industrial groups. In 1981, Ford joined with Grupo Alfa to open Nemak, which exports aluminum engine heads. A year later, two other Ford ventures with Grupo Vitro and Grupo Visa created Vitroflex, which produces glass, and Carplastic, which produces plastic boards. General Motors, together with Grupo Condumex, created Condumex Autoparts, which exports harnesses. These joint ventures implied stronger connections between the U.S. and Mexican automotive industries, because one of the primary objectives of these newly created companies was not just to produce for the domestic market, but also to export to North America.

The multinational auto makers benefitted in several ways from such associations. They could produce higher quality products, profiting from the comparative advantage of their Mexican partners. They did not have to risk large amounts of capital and were able to use existing investment subsidies in Mexico. They could meet export requirements and enjoy profits at the same time. And their U.S. plants obtained inputs from strongly competitive sources, thus reducing production costs. In 1986, the four previously mentioned joint U.S.-Mexican ventures were among the nine Mexican auto parts producers exporting more than $10 million each.

The automotive *maquiladoras* also received an economic boost in the 1977 Automotive Decree, which allowed up to 20 percent of the compensating exports of the car producers to accrue through the value added by *maquiladoras*. U.S. auto makers, especially General Motors, increased their involvement in the *maquiladora* industry, particularly in the production of harnesses and electrical components. Between 1979 and 1982, the automotive sector of the *maquiladora* industry had increased its participation in total value added from 5.9 percent to 17 percent. In the same period, employment in these automotive plants more than doubled as a percentage of total *maquiladora* labor, reaching 9.7 percent (see Table 3.12).

The automobile industry in Mexico benefitted significantly from the economic boom during the oil bonanza years between 1977 and 1981. Passenger car production grew at an average of 25 percent per year during the period. Total vehicle production peaked at almost 600,000 units in 1981, while automotive GDP reached 7.1 percent of manufacturing GDP. Similarly, automotive workers represented a record 5.3 percent of total manufacturing labor. Nevertheless, increased production was tied to large trade deficits in the industry. The expansion of the domestic market, combined with the slow adjustment process for new export investments, generated an extraordinary sectoral trade deficit of $1.88 billion in 1981. In 1980–1981, the automotive sector accounted for more than 40 percent of the Mexican trade deficit.

TABLE 3.12 Automotive *Maquiladora* Industry, 1979–1988

		Transportation Equipment			Transportation Equipment/National Total		
Year	Workers	Value Added (millions of U.S. $)	Exported Value (millions of U.S. $)	Value Added/ Export Value (%)	Workers (%)	Value Added (%)	Export Value (%)
1979	5,035	37.4	na[a]	na	4.5	5.9	na
1980	7,500	62.2	na	na	6.3	8.1	na
1981	10,999	125.5	na	na	8.4	13.0	na
1982	12,288	130.7	na	na	9.7	17.0	na
1983	19,048	171.8	na	na	12.8	21.1	na
1984	29,079	222.8	na	na	14.6	19.4	na
1985	39,848	329.5	1,438.8	22.9	18.8	26.0	28.2
1986	48,140	307.9	1,621.8	19.0	19.6	23.8	28.7
1987	59,278	381.6	2,082.2	18.3	19.4	23.9	29.3
1988	83,290	596.3	2,849.8	20.9	21.4	25.5	28.1
1989	87,813	725.1	3,389.3	21.4	20.1	23.8	27.1

[a]Not available.

Source: Compiled using Instituto Nacional de Estadística, Geografía e Informática and Banco de México data.

The 1983 Decree: Solutions to the Automotive Trade Deficit

Mexico's balance-of-payments crisis in 1982 prompted the government to undertake stronger measures to reduce the commercial deficit of the auto industry. Thus, the emphasis of the 1983 Automotive Decree was to reduce imports and increase exports. The decree outlined three policies: limiting the number of lines and models produced; increasing the GIN coefficient for both vehicles and parts; and using a balance-of-payments scheme that did not allow deficits.

By 1987, each manufacturer producing for the domestic market was permitted to produce only one line with up to five different models. Reactions to the new policy varied. Ford and Chrysler adapted by reorienting their production toward lines with more than one variant. They justified additional lines by increasing the percentage of exports. Under the decree, they could supply the domestic market with these lines after reaching a certain export level. General Motors and Nissan responded by eliminating all but one line in 1987. Volkswagen was allowed to have special lines in two out of the three lines that it still produces. The special lines included a sedan that was the least expensive car in the market (now the object of the *auto popular* program) and a van called the Combi that was urgently needed for urban transportation.

As these examples show, the 1983 decree was only partially successful. The measure attempted to increase the scale of production, but by 1988 some models were still produced in no more than 1,000 units. The restrictions outlined in the decree limited manufacturers' capacity to respond to new changes and opportunities in the market, a flexibility clearly important in establishing export growth. Furthermore, economies of scale are not necessarily established by lines, since the model variations within each line can be very large. The restrictions alone could not generate more efficient scales of production for vehicles or components.

Most component companies in Mexico cannot reach production levels high enough to generate benefits from scale economies, even though the concentration of the domestic auto parts industry in Mexico is several times higher than it is in the United States. The 40 largest producers account for nearly two-thirds of the country's auto parts production, which implies that the remaining companies are too small to produce efficiently. And even among the top 40 companies, only a few can compete internationally at efficient scales.

To reduce the flow of imports used in domestic production, the GIN coefficient in 1987 was increased to 60 percent for passenger cars and 70 percent to 80 percent for trucks. As early as 1985, bus and tractor GINs were increased to 90 percent. In auto parts, the GIN required per product line jumped from 50 percent to 60 percent, and each company as a whole was required to have a global GIN of 80 percent.

The automotive industry met the GIN requirements for 1984–1985. But since 1986, auto manufacturers have not always been able to do so, and they sometimes incur penalties. The restriction has been especially binding for the U.S. producers, who have been forced to increase their vehicle exports so that they could lower the GIN requirements on those exported lines. As a whole, the requirement has not generated a significant increase in domestic content, even though it has created higher production costs and consumer prices. This inefficiency was aggravated by an additional compulsory list of domestic auto parts to be included in each vehicle.

The 1983 decree also tightened the balance-of-payments requirement that had been instituted with the 1977 decree. The National Industry of Auto Parts' (INA) required percentage of exports rose from 40 percent to 50 percent. Beginning in 1983, no deficit in the final balance was to be accepted. Reactions varied according to geographic location of the multinationals' headquarters. General Motors, Ford, and Chrysler moved from huge trade deficits in 1982 to significant, growing surpluses. These three corporations can more easily introduce Mexican-made cars into the U.S. market than can Nissan or Volkswagen. Auto parts manufacturers supplying U.S. or Canadian plants also have an important advantage in transport costs. Additionally, the Mexican *maquiladoras* provide a strong advantage to the Big Three, whereas Nissan and Volkswagen barely cover the 20 percent allowance in their balance-of-payments from *maquiladora* products.

The more restrictive GIN and balance-of-payment schemes drove Renault and VAM out of the market. The end result of automotive industry regulation was to eliminate domestic capital in the manufacturing of passenger cars (see Table 3.13).

The 1989 Decree and Other Policy Measures

By the end of 1988, the country had embarked on a path of structural reform and trade liberalization, but the automotive industry remained isolated from these mainstream forces. All the parties involved in the automotive sector participated in a series of meetings that resulted in three 1989 decrees designed to promote industry development, consolidate the progress made over the past 25 years, and increase the sector's participation in the world economy by intensifying competition.

The government was troubled by the high ratio of consumers to registered cars—a ratio that in 1988 was almost nine times higher than

TABLE 3.13 Ownership Changes after 1983 Decree

Firm[a]	Change	1990 Owner
Ford	Remains unchanged	100% foreign
General Motors	Remains unchanged	100% foreign
Chrysler	Remains unchanged	100% foreign
Volkswagen	Remains unchanged	100% foreign
Nissan	Remains unchanged	100% foreign
DINA/Renault--VAM	1983: DINA/Renault merges with VAM. Closes in 1986	

[a]In 1990, vehicles other than passenger cars were mostly supplied by Mexican producers. The producers were: Ford, Chrysler, General Motors for small trucks; DINA for medium trucks; DINA, Fábricas Autotransportes Mexicanos (FAM), Kenworth Mexicana, Trailers de Monterrey for heavy trucks; DINA, FAM, Kenworth, Trailers de Monterrey and Victor Patron for tractors; and DINA, Mexicana de Autobuses, Trailers de Monterrey for buses.

Source: Author's compilation.

in the United States. Therefore, in August 1989 one decree gave certain tax exemptions to popular compact cars. The government was to give up a percentage of its tax revenue and auto makers were to forfeit some sales profit per unit to increase the number of vehicles sold in the domestic market. Volkswagen embraced this scheme with a proposal to make its sedan model an *auto popular*. By year's end, Volkswagen had become the domestic sales leader with a 70 percent increase in sedan production and sales over the 1988 totals. By September 1990, the sedan's monthly sales had quadrupled. The demand growth projected from this strategy calls for both the government and multinationals to take additional actions to implement tax and markup cuts that could enlarge other market segments.

In December 1989, the government issued a new automotive decree setting industry rules. A separate and more profound truck decree established a similar calendar of gradual, guided liberalization for heavy trucks, buses, and tractors. The rules included substantive changes that became effective in November 1990 with the 1991 models. Some of the most significant changes of these two decrees were:

1. Specific domestic content requirements were eliminated for individual automobile, truck, and auto part products. Nevertheless, a local content rule still applies. A total of 36 percent of the National Value Added (NVA) for all auto makers' production processes must come from the NVA of the national auto parts industry or from other domestic suppliers.[4] Clearly, this new rule is more general and less restrictive than the former GIN regulation. It applies to the end production of the auto maker's operations and not to individual products, it is smaller in absolute terms, and it opens the possibility of incorporating domestic suppliers other than the INA. The elimination of mandatory lists of specified domestic auto parts for each vehicle also gives manufacturers more input flexibility.

2. The balance-of-payments scheme for auto makers was replaced with a less restrictive trade-balance mechanism, in which only import-export results are considered. This eliminates the need to compensate for other payments abroad, and provides incentives to increase *maquiladora* exports. It also creates incentives for investment in domestic assets used in production, since it allows partial credit for such operations. Trade surpluses can accumulate beginning with the 1992 car model year. An auto producer can even transfer its trade surplus rights to another producer.

3. Auto makers have some freedom to choose the units they wish to produce in Mexico, and those they wish to import from the same company. Nevertheless, restrictions still exist on the number of imported units. In general, the ability to import built-up vehicles improves the search for efficient production scales in automobiles and parts, and it reduces the number of models relative to the size of the market. Auto parts imports continue free of quantitative restrictions.

4. The industry is generally deregulated. Deregulation includes elimination of limits on lines and models per company, restrictions on the proportion of base vehicles marketed, the compulsory list of domestic auto parts to be included in each vehicle, and mandatory gasoline engines on medium-sized trucks.

5. A schedule will be implemented gradually to allow free entry of producers, as well as imports of heavy trucks, buses, and tractors. This will eliminate one of the most troublesome issues in this market segment—the marked inefficiency of present domestic producers. It also provides more competitive incentives in market structure and pricing behavior.

Other Policies

Several economic policy measures undertaken in the last two years had direct or indirect positive effects on the automotive industry. Macroeconomic policy created a more stable environment for enterprises by providing predictable exchange rates and relatively low inflation. The new administration has improved its public finances and deepened trade reforms by reducing discrepancies in protection rates among industrial sectors. These two actions provide a more certain and increasingly competitive structure that signals a more efficient use of resources.

With the new foreign investment regulation, case-by-case authorization has been replaced with a more general framework of automatic approval, even for cases of 100 percent foreign ownership. Automobile and engine production benefit from such a structure, but auto parts are still restricted to Mexican majority ownership rules. Nevertheless, the new regulation provides an option for a trust or *fideicomiso* through which foreign capital can gain higher equity percentages in auto parts companies.

The privatization of state-owned companies will create positive externalities for all sectors, including automobiles. The government also is selling its ownership in the iron and steel industry, opening opportunities for foreign investment that can provide needed improvements in quality and efficiency. The state is also withdrawing from auto parts and components production. All these measures should significantly increase the competitiveness of domestic auto parts, engines, and automobile production.

In sectors like transportation, excessive or complicated regulations caused less competitive market structures to appear. These, in combination with insufficient investment in infrastructure, resulted in bottlenecks that reduced potential export growth in auto parts and vehicles. The new transportation law eliminates some of these problems, thus enhancing industry competitiveness. In the area of intellectual property, new technology transfer regulations provide increased certainty required within the automotive industry.

Deepened Integration with Exports and Investment

The 1980s brought about structural changes in the Mexican automotive industry. Macroeconomic conditions and sectoral regulations contributed to define separate trends for domestic sales and exports. The period of high inflation and the fall in per capita real income particularly affected domestic automobile sales. From 1981 to 1983, total passenger car sales dropped 43 percent. Nonetheless, the recovery of the economy in 1988–1990 and other policy measures previously mentioned have helped to gain back market penetration. Domestic passenger car and total vehicle sales increased at an average annual rate of more than 25 percent in 1988–1989 (see Figure 3.2).

Exports of automotive products were a major component in preventing industry losses between 1983–1987 and contributed to the sector's improved position over the past two years. Large exports to the United States from the Big Three and the good performance of some auto parts companies allowed the automotive GDP and its labor force to nearly regain their 1981 participation levels in total manufactures by 1988 (see Table 3.7 and Figure 3.1). While 1989 was a record-setting year with 641,000 total vehicles produced, I estimate that production rose to 720,000 units in 1990.

The policies undertaken in the 1969–1982 period to promote automotive industry exports had a fundamental error: they tried to force exports against a stream of incentives in favor of production for the domestic market. These policies lacked efficient and quick mechanisms to avoid import licenses or tariffs on the foreign inputs needed for exports. And, throughout most of those years, the currency was overvalued. An automotive enterprise with some export potential was clearly at a disadvantage when faced with an international competitor.

FIGURE 3.2 Vehicle Production in Mexico 1975–1990

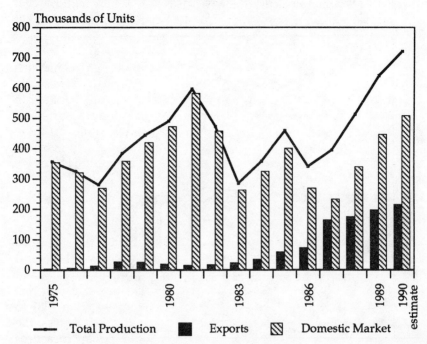

Source: Asociación Mexicana de la Industria Automotriz, several publications.

The trade liberalization program begun in 1983 has eliminated some of this anti-export bias. The present scheme of export incentives allows automotive companies to have access to inputs at international prices.[5] Automotive manufacturers and some large component companies have been among the enterprises favored by special export programs like High Exporting Companies (ALTEX). In 1987–1988, the five automobile multinationals made almost half of all imports through this preferential treatment program.

As a combined result of Mexican trade liberalization and globalization, dramatic changes occurred in the trade balance of the automotive sector. The huge deficits of the early 1980s changed to growing surpluses, as Figure 3.3 indicates. This has come about partly as a result of the fall in imports brought on by low domestic sales in the 1983–1986 period. But exports have played a major role in this trend as well. The multinational auto makers set in motion strong export programs based on new plants.

The export surge can be divided into two periods. The first involved the engine export take-off of 1982–1984, one of the best examples of

FIGURE 3.3 Mexican Automotive Trade 1960–1989

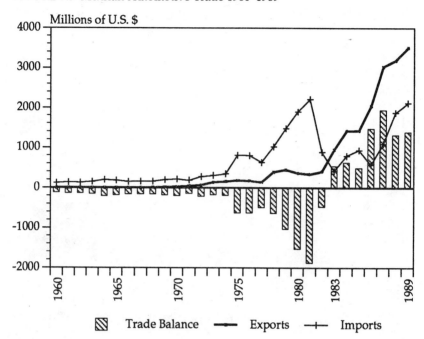

Source: Calculated with data from Instituto de Estadística, Geografía e Informática, Banco de México, and the Secretaría de Comercio y Fomento Industrial.

silent industrial integration between Mexico and the United States. This was triggered by General Motors' and Chrysler's new engine plants in Saltillo and Ford's plant in Chihuahua. Engine exports quadrupled in two years and have continued their steady growth. Most of this production flowed into the U.S. multinationals' small car plants in the United States and Canada.

The second stage in export growth began in 1986, and it involved vehicles. The new high-technology Ford plant in Hermosillo and the greater dynamism of General Motors and Chrysler were crucial to this stage. More recently, Volkswagen's shutdown in the United States and its operational shift to Mexico contributed to an increased flow of units into the North American market. Total units exported jumped from 20,000 to nearly 200,000 between 1983 and 1989. This represents a complete restructuring of the export market of built-up vehicles. In 1983, only 1 percent of these units were shipped to North America, mostly by Volkswagen. By 1989, almost 90 percent of the units exported were directed to the United States or Canada. The Big Three made 85 percent of those. This behavior is suggestive of the increased integration and production specialization among Mexico, the United States, and Canada.

Between 1982 and 1989, exports from the Mexican auto parts industry multiplied five times. The U.S.-Canadian region represents auto parts' main market, absorbing nearly 80 percent of the total in 1989. Parts exports are concentrated among a small number of companies, and joint ventures between U.S. multinationals and Mexican capital contribute significantly.

The *maquiladoras* represent the most recent component of North American automobile integration. The automotive in-bond plants specialize in production of electric and plastic components, seats, and several exterior parts like bumpers, door locks and rims. Their growth exemplifies the use of an efficient combination of inputs from the two countries to achieve cost minimization. From only 7,500 workers and a little more than $62 million of value added in 1980, transportation equipment in-bond plants represented nearly 88,000 workers and $725 million in value added by December 1989. These plants employ one out of five *maquiladora* workers and contribute almost 24 percent of total value added by the entire *maquiladora* industry in Mexico (see Table 3.12). General Motors is the auto maker most involved in *maquiladoras*. Out of its 15 Mexican in-bond plants in 1987, eight were among the 27 largest auto parts producers.

After a sharp fall of domestic car production and imports from the United States during 1981–1986, the recovery of the Mexican market has brought about an upsurge in imports, which regained pre-crisis levels. In 1989, Mexican auto parts imports were nearly 28 percent higher than their historic peak in 1981. Of this amount, about 80 percent comes from U.S. companies (see Table 3.10). The recent automotive decree will generate much higher import values beginning with the 1991 model year, due to built-up car imports and higher percentages of foreign content in domestically produced vehicles.

It is clear that intra-industry trade already characterizes the automotive sectors of the United States and Mexico, and and it is reasonable to expect further increases in two-way trade as industrial integration continues.

The Costs of Regulation and its Limits to Future Integration

The numerous backward and forward linkages and spillover effects of the automotive industry have been a constant incentive to special commercial and industrial policies for this sector. Similarly, the special characteristics of the automotive market structure—the presence of large returns to scale, the crucial role of research and development, the oligopolistic structure of final and intermediate supply, and the multinational label of the companies involved—have drawn the attention of policy makers and economists in both the United States and Mexico. If further integration is to occur, both countries must eliminate additional restrictions on the sector.

Mexican Restrictions

Domestic content requirements protect local intermediate input industries without the use of tariff or import quota restrictions. They have been implemented to prevent large sectoral trade deficits, to create a wider range of manufacturing activities, and to take advantage of spillover effects. Balance-of-payments and trade-balance restrictions are part of the export performance policies intended to resolve major trade disequilibria, but they also protect auto parts and components producers. Variants of these restrictions exist in the automotive sectors of countries like Brazil, Korea, Argentina, and Canada.

The 1990 models still faced the 1983 GIN rules, ranging from 60 percent to 90 percent. They also came under no-deficit rules for the balance of payments for each auto maker. As my previous studies show, as substitutability between domestic and foreign auto parts is reduced, production costs significantly rise for vehicle and parts manufacturing. The 1983 Automotive Decree increased costs by an estimated 8 percent to 25 percent for the entire spectrum of automobile models.[6]

Although the NVA mechanism of the 1989 decree somewhat alleviates this problem, the system is still complex. The decree brings in trade balance results, and makes stipulations as to auto part exports and the import content of these exports. These regulations create distortions in the production process, because factors other than marginal productivity of inputs must be weighed. It is still too early to know how production restructuring will emerge, but some preliminary estimates indicate that production costs will still range from 3 percent to 10 percent higher for domestically produced models, as a result of the 1989 regulations.[7]

The structure of automobile production over the last few years reveals a two-tiered industry with two different and disconnected production processes. Passenger cars for export were produced in large-scale, modern plants, but models destined for the domestic market were assembled in old plants at very low production runs. For several years, only a few hundred units were produced in some models. The protection that auto makers received under rules that prohibited imports of built-up vehicles did not prompt the industry to attain efficient scales at any stage of the production process, from assembly to auto parts production.

The ability of auto makers to import their own vehicles, a measure introduced in the 1989 decree, reduces this distortion by stopping the domestic manufacture of models in inefficient small runs. Nevertheless, some conditions aimed at insuring sufficient domestic production still constrain freedom of operation. The percentage of the trade surplus for each company that can be devoted to vehicle imports begins at 40 percent for 1991, and reaches a maximum of 57 percent from 1994 onward. Auto makers are also constrained by a stipulation that total automobile imports not exceed 20 percent of domestic sales.

Protection to Oligopolistic Multinationals

Existing industry regulations not only affect suppliers, but also consumers, since they create distortions in pricing behavior. The protection extended to the oligopoly of auto makers established in Mexico is costly, given the absence of any national passenger car producer. Automobile producers receive the rents created by commercial protection through tariffs and import limitations. So far, they do not have to face the possible entry of other competitors in any segment of the market. This allows them to strongly exert their oligopolistic power in the domestic market.

Automobile production ranks third after oil and tobacco in an index of import licensing coverage over domestic production. A similar index for all industries substantially decreased from 92.2 percent in June 1985 to 23.2 percent in May 1988. Meanwhile, the auto parts sector became more open to international competition than the average of the economy, obtaining an index of 12.9 percent in 1988. The opposite condition applies to vehicle production, which in 1988 remained closed with 95.1 percent of import licenses over domestic product. If we consider that the new 1989 decree sets a restriction on the percentage of car imports to a maximum of 20 percent of domestic sales by 1993, the protection index would be reduced only to a level of about 65 percent, or 70 percent at most. This structure clearly benefits the auto makers in the markets, since they will continue to face reduced foreign competition while enjoying additional access to competitively priced inputs (see Figure 3.4).

The commercial protection extended to auto makers and the restrictions affecting cost structures create high domestic car prices well

FIGURE 3.4 Import Licensing Coverage Over Product (1986 Mexican production weights)

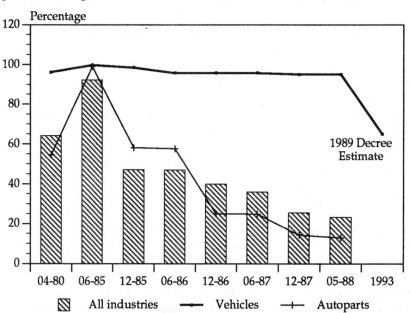

Sources: Compiled using Secretaría de Comercio y Fomento Industrial and World Bank data.

above international levels. The price differential has two components: regulation and taxes. Although tax differences are certainly important, some studies have indicated that, after adjusting the tax differential between Mexico and the United States, the price of Mexican passenger cars was about 40 percent above prices of similar cars in the United States.[8] The 1989 decree attempts to reduce this price discrepancy with watch-over price control mechanisms. A better alternative would be an increasingly open sector that leads to a more competitive structure.

U.S. Restrictions

One of the main challenges in U.S.-Mexican trade relations and industrial integration is to obtain greater and more stable access for Mexican products in the U.S. market. The fact that such access is difficult implies the need to eliminate U.S. discriminatory measures that generate uncertainty for Mexican exporters and investors. The upsurge of neo-protectionist pressures in the U.S. economy has a direct effect on trade flows. Japanese voluntary export restraints on automobiles create uncertainty about the use of such measures against countries that could become large exporters of these products. During the first part of the 1980s, Mexico was one of the main countries to suffer the effects of U.S. countervailing duties. U.S. legislation and procedures on subsidies are stronger than GATT regulations, creating potential limits to trade flows between the two countries.

U.S. trade and industrial policies place both tariff and non-tariff barriers to an expanded automobile trade flow. These restrictions not only deny access to some Mexican automotive products, but also create uncertainty in the exporting process, distorting long-term investment decisions.

Despite the low average tariff rate on automotive products sold in the United States, exporters complain about special protective measures. One example is the 25 percent duty rate paid on small truck imports. In the absence of such measures, Mexican producers could capture a large part of the U.S. demand in this market segment. The potential for product specialization between the two countries is practically eliminated with this prohibitive tariff.

Significant among the non-tariff barriers to the U.S. market is the Corporate Average Fuel Economy Act (CAFE), which affects automotive exports to the United States. The regulation aims to increase fuel efficiency. This act stipulates that all vehicles not containing 75 percent domestic content are to be considered imports. And as imports, they must meet higher fuel efficiency standards. Consequently, U.S. producers have an incentive to reduce Mexican value added in their products. Japanese and European plants in U.S. territory have made additional efforts to increase the U.S. value added in their operations. This measure restricts Mexican access to U.S. auto parts markets as well as to built-up vehicles that must meet stricter fuel efficiency rules.

Future Integration

Since the Automotive Pact of 1965, Canada and the United States have had free trade in automotive products. For 23 years, the Canadians enjoyed some protective measures, including a 60 percent domestic content requirement and a variant of an automobile trade balance. Nevertheless, free trade and stable market access have changed the Canadian automotive structure. Today, the Big Three are responsible for practically all Canadian vehicle production. Almost all exports are directed to the U.S. market, and Canadian demand is largely supplied by U.S. imports. The creation of such an economic bloc using free trade conditions benefits its participating members, but makes it difficult for third countries like Mexico to gain market access. The geographic reorientation of Mexican automotive exports toward North America increases the importance of the rules governing the U.S.-Canadian free trade area.

The implicit formation of strong economic regions will make market access difficult in various parts of the world for both the United States and Mexico. Their ability to compete against these economic blocks will be dependent on their capacity to reduce costs, which will in turn be based on further globalization of production processes. Automotive exports will run into trouble in the European Economic Community, where overcapacity is already adversely affecting market access. Competition is expected to increase in 1992, and a European domestic content requirement could be imposed. The Japanese automobile market is almost impenetrable, and is likely to remain so over the next decade. Market penetration is likely to become more difficult as well in East Asia, where special regional arrangements are forecasted.

The evolution of the automobile industry in Mexico has reached a turning point at which clear, long-term policies are needed. As the Canadian and Spanish auto industries indicate, integration into larger markets restructures production, channels growth through specialization, and brings consumers lower prices and a wider market selection for all members of the region. Integration could have a similar effect on the Mexican and U.S. automotive industries.

Increased intra-industry trade and specialization provide the Mexican automotive industry with a viable alternative. In the medium term, domestic markets cannot offer the scales of production required for cost competitiveness. Additionally, many Mexican component plants have reduced contact with auto makers and find themselves lagging in technology, with few options for modernizing. The world industry trend is to reduce the number of suppliers, since auto makers will demand complete systems rather than separate components. Many parts producers should plan to gain entry into the global supply system through closer integration with the North American market, producing the components in which Mexico enjoys comparative advantage.

U.S. auto makers face increased competition at home and uncertain export possibilities in the near future. To win in both domestic and export markets, the Big Three must move faster in their globalization strategies. Their U.S. and Canadian-based plants need rapid efficiency gains and increased competitiveness to succeed in market penetration. Today, Mexico ranks high on the list of sources to help in providing the necessary conditions to confront world trends.

Tripartite North American Free Trade Agreement

Traditional gains-from-trade literature indicates that differences in endowments and technology benefit countries embarking on freer trade. These gains can be expected in a Mexican-U.S.-Canadian free trade agreement. The enormous differences in production processes and available resources among these three economies are complementary. But additional considerations exist in the automobile sector. Mexico, with a capital scarcity, produces labor-intensive components at a lower cost than they can be produced in the United States. But a good part of the large, intra-industry trade in automotive products for the North American market comes from high technology plants that use skilled labor.

Automobile and auto parts production involve imperfect competition structures and show increasing returns to scale. These two characteristics constitute a source of gains from trade that emerge from product specialization. The integration of the U.S. and Mexican automotive industries gains from both the complementary resources and technology, as well as from a larger market.

Free trade between Mexico and the United States will enhance industrial activity for both countries since it must involve the minimization of non-tariff and tariff barriers to trade flow, the assurance of stable market access, and the establishment of mechanisms to avoid unilateral actions and to settle differences.

Guaranteed fair and stable access to the U.S. market will support the restructuring that Mexican producers need to undergo. This will provide an incentive to further liberalize and deregulate this sector. The Mexican automobile and auto parts industries also will be considered part of the larger North American automotive industry, which will help to avoid discrimination against the use of Mexican products to meet country-specific content requirements. Mexican auto parts producers will also gain an advantage over close competitors in Korea, Taiwan, and Brazil. Closer commercial ties in the sector will encourage foreign investment and technology transfers, which will render auto parts producers more competitive.

U.S. multinational plants already established in Mexico will have the advantage of importing duty free auto parts and vehicle models currently produced at inefficient scales. U.S. and Canadian-based plants will benefit from cheaper access to the electric, metal, glass, and plastic components in which Mexico already has a cost advantage. These plants also will take advantage of new export opportunities provided by access to a growing Mexican market. The new economic zone will allow some products to achieve efficient production scales, reducing imports from third countries, therefore increasing jobs within the region.

Although it is difficult to quantify the increased production and employment that can accrue through free trade in oligopolistic industries with complex regulations, I have estimated trade flows could increase 20 percent to 25 percent over 1989 levels.[9] This estimate does not include Mexican vehicle imports from North America. Such an incorporation would considerably increase the effect on U.S. exports, and, therefore, employment.

Future Policy Considerations

The structural transformation and product specialization resulting from the Canadian-U.S. Automotive Pact should be considered in negotiations for a free trade agreement between the United States and Mexico. The measures undertaken to liberalize and deregulate automobile production in Mexico should take into account the special characteristics of the industry, providing for gradual elimination of barriers while ensuring market access to reduce adjustment costs. Other countries undergoing similar restructuring have used such mechanisms.

If industrial integration is to succeed, market agents in both countries must be given complete information about the rules that will regulate interaction among the players involved. A clear adjustment path must be specified, participants must stick to the rules, and necessary measures and institutions must be established to watch over this process to ensure continuity. This will eliminate uncertainty, allowing economic agents to adjust their medium and long-term decisions to the new growth pattern of the North American automotive industry. Some specific actions include:

1. Eliminate tariff and non-tariff barriers between the countries.
2. Harmonize hidden barriers to market access posed by country-specific content requirements and rules of origin. The target should be gradual phase-out of these measures in favor of a unique regional requirement.
3. Foreign capital should flow gradually into the Mexican auto parts sector through a combination of more flexible foreign investment and vertical integration regulations.
4. Develop a modern iron and steel industry in Mexico to reduce the costs of automobile production. This will lower costs and avoid imports.

5. Harmonize security, quality, and fuel efficiency regulations among the countries to eliminate multi-tiered production structures.
6. Allow for an adjustment period for the 1989 Mexican regulations, and complement them with clear free-entry possibilities for more competitive structures and prices.
7. Provide for gradual liberalization of the used-vehicles market to create required pressure on first and secondary markets to equalize prices in all three countries. Some special considerations must be made for fuel efficiency and pollution.

Conclusion

Although the argument for trade liberalization and deregulation has a very strong domestic rationale, increasing protectionist pressures in the United States and the oligopolistic nature of the automotive industry call for coordination of Mexican deregulation and trade negotiations with the United States. Otherwise, both countries may lose an opportunity to fruitfully integrate supply and demand, which would help to gain stable access for all products. Free trade and industrial integration imply that some segments of the automotive industry will be reallocated. This will not be a painless process, but the automotive sector can benefit from economies of scale and complementary resources, which will smooth the structural adjustment. The potential for trade and output growth as well as the advantage of more integrated and cost-efficient production processes in this industry point to net employment gains in Mexico and the United States.

In the 1990s we will be faced with a rapid evolution of the automotive sector as economic regions are created and strengthened. As design and production processes are improved, the comparative advantage of low-cost labor will be affected. Production is likely to concentrate in a few multinational corporations for which borders have little meaning. Changes in competitive forces will increasingly depend on productivity, quality, and technological improvement. Within this environment, Mexican and U.S. integration will take place. A positive outcome calls for creative strategic action in the North American automobile industry.

Notes

I appreciate the useful comments of Humberto Jasso, Alberto Chong, Robin Lumsdaine, and Boris Simkovich. I am responsible for any errors.

1. A good account of these changes is available in Alan Altschuler, et al, *The Future of the Automobile: The Report of MIT's International Automobile Program* (Cambridge: MIT Press, 1985).

2. Prominent Mexican-owned auto parts producers of those years included Motores y Refacciones and Industria Automotriz.

3. A detailed account of the negotiations between the Mexican government and the multinationals is available in Douglas Bennett and Kenneth E. Sharpe's *Transnational Corporations vs. The State; The Political Economy of the Mexican Auto Industry* (Princeton: Princeton University Press, 1985).

4. Total National Value Added for the auto makers is defined as the sum of the value of total sales in the domestic market, plus the value of its trade balance result. The NVA for the auto parts and components companies is defined as the sum of the sales of parts to the auto makers minus the imports used in those parts, plus the value of exports promoted by the auto maker less the import content of those exports.

5. An account of export incentives is available in Jaime Zabludovsky and Florencio López-de-Silanes, "Trade and Industrial Policy for Structural Adjustment in Mexico," presented at a 1989 symposium, "The Present and Future of the Pacific Basin Economy," sponsored by the Institute of Developing Economies, Tokyo.

6. These results reflect the simulations in a production model that incorporates the regulation of the Mexican automotive industry outlined in Florencio López-de-Silanes' *The Automotive Industry in Mexico: A Model of its Regulations*, (Mexico City: Instituto Technológico Autónoma de México thesis, 1989).

7. The methodology of these calculations conforms to the model specified in No. 6.

8. This is from Frederico Carstens and A. Escalante Mier, *Prices in the Mexican Automobile Sector 1974-1986: An Hedonic Analysis*, (Instituto Technológico Autónoma de México thesis, 1987).

9. This estimate comes from a simulation exercise to measure the growth of automotive trade between Mexico and the United States as a result of the elimination of tariff barriers and domestic regulation. For the exact methodology, see note 6.

FOUR

Petrochemicals

Petrochemicals: Mexican Perspective

Benito Bucay F.

Mexico's petrochemical industry began in 1956, when Pemex, the government-owned oil monopoly, started producing sulfur as a byproduct of gas sweetening operations and initiated small-scale production of DDB (dodecylbenzene, now currently referred to as hard detergent alkylate)[1] by converting a gasoline unit being retired. At that time, the initial surge for development in petrochemicals in the United States[2] was in full swing and many people, insiders and outsiders alike, marvelled at the prospect of a never-ending stream of new products that were bound to appear. Some forecasted that within 20 years the use of oil as a fuel would decline. The world would find it much more valuable as a prime raw material.

About 20 years after the expropriation of the oil companies, some government officials began to worry that Mexico might lose its riches by letting the local petrochemical industry grow unchecked. This resulted in a new law on November 30, 1958, that was was immediately dubbed "the petrochemical law." Very generally, it indicated that primary petrochemicals were those products derived from the first stage of chemical or important physical transformation of refinery products. It also defined secondary petrochemicals as those resulting from subsequent chemical transformation.

The definitions framed the development of the industry afterwards. For example, the law restricted ownership of facilities that made primary products to Pemex, while the manufacture of secondary[3] products was restricted to companies with minimum 60 percent Mexican ownership. These were mostly private companies.

The concepts embodied in the law proved to be far-reaching, well beyond initial intentions. The fast pace of development of the industry in the 1960s and 1970s led to a rather uneven pattern of investment. In the period 1970–1986, production rose by more than 11 percent per year, imports grew by 8 percent and exports by more than 16 percent (from a very small base), which combined into a very healthy 10.5 percent per year for the industry as a whole over that period.[4] There were persistent trade deficits over this time due to the inability of Pemex to fulfill basic demand.

At the same time, two factors combined to create a serious structural problem. The protected economy and the rigidity introduced by the legal separation of primary products and derivatives resulted in small-scale operations that often relied on obsolete technology to meet legal restrictions.

This situation started to change in 1981–1982 when the National Plan for Industrial Development was enacted to stimulate investment in export-oriented facilities. This led to the major complexes now in operation. The net effect today, however, can be summarized simply: the industry has a large, cumbersome structure under which Pemex supplies about 50 percent to 60 percent of the basic building blocks needed; a substantial secondary industry is divided into a highly efficient, modern, fragmented and wide-based derivative industry that seeks to compensate for obsolete and small-scale facilities with a strong push toward productivity and adaptability.

Private Development and Foreign Investment

By 1960, when the regulations to the Petrochemical Law were enacted, there already existed a sizeable range of secondary facilities, mostly owned by large chemical companies such as ICI, Dupont, and Union Carbide. A grandfather clause exempted these foreign-owned operations from Mexicanization, but impeded their future growth unless they allowed Mexican ownership. A system of permits ensued that resulted not only in putting pressure on these companies, but also in creating de facto monopolies for those firms with manufacturing permits. Administration of the law was vested in the Comisión Petroquímica Mexicana made up of representatives from Pemex, the Secretaría de Comercio y Fomento Industrial (SECOFI), and the Secretaría de Energía, Minas e Industria Parastatal (SEMIP).

Through the 1960s, each of the large chemical companies decided to Mexicanize, to avoid foregoing the substantial growth ahead. Two notable cases set the pace. Celanese, having started as a Mexicanized operation, was able to capture growth from the late 1940s on, promptly becoming, and remaining, the largest private chemical company in Mexico. The other, Monsanto, still wholly owned through the 1960s, Mexicanized by merger with a successful local chemical company,

Resistol, in 1971, thus capturing the growth rate enjoyed by the rest of the industry. Other major companies followed suit, and by the end of the 1970s most of the secondary products were made by joint venture companies with substantial Mexican interests. Goodrich merged its chemical operations with Cydsa, a large and efficient Mexican producer of fibers and heavy chemicals.

However, the current opening of the Mexican economy poses a new and fundamental issue for the foreign investor that was not a factor for almost 30 years: investing in Mexico, let alone in a minority position, is no longer necessary if the objective is to gain access to the local market. In addition, the question of how to mesh a partly owned investment along with wholly owned ones into a single global strategy clouds the investment decision.

Despite these concerns, the Mexican petrochemical industry is now a factor to contend with. Today, it represents 2.7 percent of GDP, ahead of the automotive industry and more than twice the size of iron and steel (see Table 4.1); gross fixed investment exceeds $30 billion, and feeds goods and raw materials to 42 different industry sectors. The industry is noted for its capital intensity and low labor demand. Today the industry is populated by a large number of experienced and well-trained engineers, supervisors, and operators with impressive efficiency records. Some companies with newer investments, such as Tereftalatos' TPA, Cydsa's and Primex' PVC resins, and Celanese's (now Hoechst's) Cangrejera complex, are world-class contenders that send more than two-thirds of their output to the export market. See Table 4.5 for a list of the major companies.

Opportunity and Need for Integration

Even under conservative assumptions, the Mexican market for petrochemicals will continue to grow at significant rates and provide ample opportunities for investment. Over the five years 1989–1994,

TABLE 4.1 Share of GNP by Industry Sector

Product	1969	1970	1985	est. 1987
Petrochemicals	0.9	1.1	2.5	2.7
Automotive	0.4	1.1	1.5	1.7
Iron & steel	1.2	1.3	1.0	1.0
Pulp & paper	0.3	0.5	0.8	0.8
Cement	0.2	0.3	0.3	0.4

Source: Secretaría de Energía, Minas e Industria Parastatal, 1988.

demand will increase by about 13 million tons, as the industry continues the trend set by developed countries. Per capita demand today is only 180 kilograms versus about 1,000 kilos in the United States.

More importantly, Mexico and the United States represent a unique combination not present anywhere else in the world. The sharing of a common border and water access, the growing demands and proximity of consuming areas, the availability of natural resources, a combination of both need and technology supply, all point to a situation in which proper integration of the two economies presents great potential for joint development.

The projected growth of the Mexican market offers investment and commercial opportunities for the United States, while the geographic concentration and linkages of the U.S. petrochemical industry (55 percent of the industry is located in Texas and Louisiana), plus the availability of technology are promising sources for everything Mexico needs in this sector. Because they are newer by about seven years on average, many Mexican facilities were built with environmental and health concerns in mind, whereas retrofitting many U.S. facilities is simply too costly.

It is also evident that Mexico, even with ample capital, will be unable to satisfy its future demand. A commercial tie-in with the United States will be of great benefit to both industries, particularly if there is a downturn in the U.S. economy.

This mutual reinforcement is mandatory as Europe 1992 becomes a reality. In contrast to some other U.S. sectors, the chemical industry has less to worry about from competitors in the Pacific Basin than it has from the Europeans. Not only is Europe the birthplace of the chemical industry, but throughout this decade the European industry has undergone a remarkable transformation and restructuring that has strengthened the remaining contenders. Today, four of the five largest companies in the world are European, and only one (Dupont) is U.S.-based. The picture doesn't change much if one looks at the ten largest.

Last, but not least, the rush to specialties makes Mexico more interesting. It is becoming the testing ground for global non-chemical companies like IBM, Ford, General Electric, Xerox, and NEC. The country is awakening to the need for research and for a number of years to come, research and development in Mexico is going to be cheaper than elsewhere. The in-bond industry will evolve and become a multinational, efficient manufacturing area, in effect, a North American tiger, to match the Far Eastern ones.

It would seem, therefore, that working toward a bilateral agreement, sectoral if not broad based, would benefit both partners.

Industry Structure

The 1950s was a decade of rapid growth of petrochemicals in the United States. Processes were developed leading to dramatic improvements in quality and cost of production and pointed to a future in which a barrel of oil would be worth many times more than its fuel value. The Mexican oil industry had been nationalized only 20 years before and some technical people in Pemex, plus a few influential political figures, were concerned that the country's oil wealth might again become private and foreign. As a result, the Petrochemical Law—a law regulating Article 27 of the Mexican Constitution on state ownership of mineral wealth—was enacted in 1958, on the last day of the Ruiz Cortines administration, and its regulations were issued 18 months later.

The law ratified the 1938 expropriation, defined primary petrochemicals, and stipulated that only Pemex or a wholly owned government company could produce, distribute, and market these products. Secondary petrochemicals were defined as those derived from primary petrochemicals, and the 60 percent ownership rule was instituted.

The Comisión Petroquímica Mexicana provided permits to applicants who demonstrated the required equity composition and demonstrated that the project would utilize the most adequate technology for prevailing conditions. Plant location and export plans also were considered.

When these regulations were enacted, many companies—both foreign and Mexican-owned—were already operating and producing secondary products: Goodrich and Monsanto were manufacturing PVC resins; Union Carbide and Monsanto had been making polystyrene; Cydsa (wholly Mexican-owned) had been producing polyester and nylon polymers and fibers. All these companies were exempted under grandfather provisions, but their future growth into new areas depended upon meeting the new requirements.

The first permit granted was to Negromex (40 percent owned by Phillips Petroleum) to manufacture carbon black. Celanese, working through a new subsidiary, received a significant license for a complex that would parallel its remarkable Bishop, Texas unit. By 1963, issuance of petrochemical permits was in full swing.

After a while, this bureaucratic process became badly distorted; paper companies were set up, obtained petrochemical permits to build and then sat on them, using their position to obtain much coveted import licenses. Unplanned trading of permits resulted. There were other distorting elements. The law was used by the government to force majority Mexican ownership. The Foreign Investment Law was enacted a few years later. The vague and non-technical definition of secondary petrochemicals was carried to absurd limits and, in many instances, private companies applied for permits covering products far removed from petroleum, in effect carving out a niche free from competition, and the authorities dutifully obliged.

Looking back to that period, it is easy to see how the combination of loosely worded legislation, non-technical agendas, like the desire to Mexicanize[5] foreign-owned companies, and sheer protectionism resulted in haphazard development of the industry. By the late 1960s, the situation had become so patently absurd that the government opted for listing what products should be considered primary—thus reserved for Pemex—and which ones were legally defined as secondary and therefore had to meet the requirements of the Petrochemicals Law, particularly concerning foreign ownership.

The Period of Accelerated Development

While this was taking place on the legal front, the market was growing very rapidly; all through the decade of the 1960s, consistent 12 percent to 15 percent growth per year was the norm. This factor alone was sufficient to attract investment, but when coupled with low inflation (less than 5 percent per year through that period) and stable currency, the industry proved irresistible.

By the mid-1970s, essentially all the industry was following the 60/40 ownership rule, and the worst predictions from both sides of the controversy never came to pass. Foreign investment did not leave, but, on the contrary, substantial new investment took place. The industry was not taken over by the big foreign multinational companies as some of the fiercest nationalists had prophesied.

However, two structural defects of the industry became entrenched and are still present today. Together they pose serious obstacles for further development as the country opens up to trade and investment. One has to do with evolving technology. The legal battles of the 1960s ended when the product lists were published. The lists, especially for primary products, were cast in concrete. For example, if any product needed an olefin[6] as its raw material, then only Pemex would be allowed to produce it.

At first this was merely a nuisance, but as world technology evolved, particularly after the oil embargo, toward processes in which many steps could be compressed into one to reduce costs and save energy, these restrictions became and still are a major hurdle. Private industry had to depend on obsolete technology as long as it fit the requirements of the law. Pemex was also limited in its use of newer technologies if it meant invading the private field, which was strongly resisted. With Mexico now competing worldwide against fully integrated giants using the most efficient technology, the artificial barrier that the law created has become a major strategic weakness.

The other structural defect results from the fact that the law empowers only Pemex to develop the primary industry. This is a task of such monumental proportions that no country or company in the world, not even the Soviet Union, has a similar charter. The problem was compounded when Mexico, and specifically Pemex, became a major oil producer; the sheer size of the oil industry in value-volume terms dwarfs the petrochemical side of Pemex operations and, naturally, petrochemicals get a low priority.

As a result, except for a few products for a few years, Pemex has never been able to satisfy the needs of the growing secondary industry, and the country is forced to import a significant proportion of its primary product needs. Thus, in the period 1983–1987, $2.2 billion were spent to import primary petrochemicals, which constituted 22 percent of the total needs of the industry, or 35 percent if fertilizer ammonia is excluded. The problem became even more acute starting mid-1987, when a phase of rapidly escalating world prices for primary products began, and will become even more aggravated as plants with new permits start operating. Permits granted in 1987–1988 alone add 25 percent to the total secondary capacity that existed at the beginning of 1987.

The significance of this problem is that any advantage Mexico might have because of its position as a major oil producer is eliminated if the added costs of importing 35 percent of its inputs and re-exporting almost all of that are taken into account. Thus the perception of Mexico's comparative advantage, at least today, is an illusion.

The National Development Plan of 1980:
Subsidies or Cost of Doing Business?

When it became apparent that Mexico was on the threshold of receiving enormous oil riches after the 1979 oil shock, the government issued an ambitious plan that promoted petrochemical development in four regions, later cut to two: Altamira and Coatzacoalcos, both on the Gulf Coast. The plan offered up to a 30 percent reduction in the prices of energy and feedstocks through 1992, to those industries that would build facilities in these two locations.

The image of building world-class, fully competitive facilities proved irresistible for the industry and many companies heeded the call. Construction was barely halfway completed in 1981 when oil prices dropped, debt piled up very fast, and the Mexican debt crisis exploded in the summer of 1982. Private industry had no choice but to complete its half-built facilities or disappear, but the government, both in Pemex and for public works, simply cut investment to the bone.

Industry ended up by investing in infrastructure to the point where fixed investment was 40 percent to 50 percent more than originally planned. In 1987, fiscal stringency dictated the removal of the 30 percent incentives originally granted. Because of the long building period, the incentives paid never amounted to more than one-quarter of what they would have been, and certainly never compensated for the extra investment.

There is, however, a positive side to this story. The facilities built during this phase (like Cydsa's new PVC, Temex' TPA, Negromex' PB Rubber, and Celanese's Cangrejera complex) are among the most modern and efficient in the world, and do assure selected niches of competitiveness which will serve Mexico well for many years. In effect, they are the main reason for the marked improvement in the competitive position of this sector. Secondary petrochemicals represented 88 percent of all the petrochemical exports in 1986, and were the reason for a positive industry trade balance of $360 million, which compares favorably with the negative balance of $590 million in 1982, which had been roughly the same for more than 10 years.

Age is another factor. The average age of the Mexican petrochemical plant is 6.5 years, versus more than 13 for those in the United States and more than 16 for European plants. This makes them more modern and competitive, and also better adapted to environmental and health needs than competitive plants in other parts of the world.

In spite of the criticism, the present position of the primary industry, all of it operated by Pemex, is impressive. It currently encompasses 46 process plants in eight large complexes among which Cangrejera, Morelos and Pajaritos, located on the southernmost part of the Gulf Coast, are the major ones. Table 4.2 gives the principal data on the products covered, and Table 4.3 lists those not covered. Note that in many cases production is well below the 80-plus percent operating rate that is the goal of the industry. Despite this, with the big swing in exports of derivatives that started in 1987, the deficits in national primary production have grown and imports of basics now represent about one-third of total needs.

Most of the technology needed to build the industry was acquired from abroad, although in a few selected areas the Mexican Petroleum Institute[7] has been the source. Major U.S. and European companies, such as Universal Oil Products, Exxon, Gulf, ICI, and Shell, have licensed basic engineering designs, which are then turned into detailed engineering by Mexican engineering firms and local contractors.

By comparing the long list in Table 4.2 with a product list of a typical, world-class producer, the contrast is evident: not only is the Mexican scale of operations smaller, but the diversity is enormous. After the very costly price and volume wars of a few years ago,[8] the European petrochemical industry, and the U.S. industry to a lesser degree, have undergone considerable restructuring. The number of contenders in every product has been reduced, plants have been shut down, and investment reoriented to improving the efficiency of existing units, in some cases with dramatic results.

As examples, the number of European facilities producing PVC (vinyl resins) went from more than 40 in 1979 to 17 in 1987; the number of producers of polystyrene is half today what it was eight years ago. After long years of piling up losses, the European industry has turned around, and 1988 was its best year ever.

Turning to Mexico, the open economy plus the overall push the government is making for efficiency and competitiveness is going to force a similar trend in Pemex. Rather than attempting to become a supplier of everything dubbed a basic product, Pemex will have to decide where it has the best chance and concentrate there, eventually disposing of or shutting down a number of marginal operations.

For example, as a result of decisions made over the past 20 years, I believe that Pemex has a better-than-average-chance of becoming an efficient, large-scale ethylene producer. On the other hand, the same process has resulted in a chronic and severe deficiency of propylene, which would require investments on the order of $1 billion to $2 billion to correct. Neither Pemex nor the country can justify such a major outlay and, therefore, we should look to other strategies.

If this were to happen, we might see in the next few years a different picture in Mexican basic petrochemicals: fewer products and plants, but more efficient ones participating actively in world trade from a fully opened economy.

The Secondary Petrochemical Industry

The haphazard way in which the industry developed during its first two decades led to many businesses being dubbed as petrochemicals when they were not, and many were built under a wing of double protection afforded by the permit system and the non-tariff barriers to trade. However, especially after 1981, a few companies developed to become relatively important contenders in world trade.

TABLE 4.2 1986 Primary Mexican Petrochemicals (thousands of metric tons)

Product	Capacity	Production	Imports	Exports	Consumed
Acetaldehyde	144.0	136.5	57.7	—	194.2
Acrylonitrile	74.0	53.6	55.4	—	109.0
Ammonia	2,891.0	1,948.5	27.0	114.5	1,861.0
Benzene	399.3	221.8	—	—	221.8
Butadiene	55.0	17.9	108.1	—	126.1
Cyclohexane	106.0	39.3	26.6	—	65.9
Vinylchloride	270.0	141.3	133.4	—	274.7
Cumene	40.0	41.9	3.1	—	45.9
Dichloroethane	414.1	270.4	—	—	270.4
DDB	138.1	103.4	8.4	—	111.8
Styrene	180.0	69.4	86.7	—	156.1
Ethane	3,070.6	2,550.4	—	—	2,550.4
Ethylene	918.4	767.2	—	26.0	741.2
Isopropyl alcohol	15.0	11.1	39.1	—	50.1
Methanol	171.5	182.3	7.9	—	190.2
Ethylene Oxide	128.0	114.0	4.92	—	118.2
LDPE	309.0	242.2	84.1	—	326.2
HDPE	100.0	69.1	95.5	—	164.6
Propylene	360.3	231.7	—	—	257.8[a]
Tetramer	116.5	51.0	62.3	—	113.3
Toluene	465.0	238.0	50.5	—	288.5
M/P Xylenes	400.6	231.2	—	—	231.2
Orthoxylene	66.3	41.5	11.6	—	53.1
Paraxylene	280.0	122.5	133.3	—	255.8
HCN	11.3	7.5	—	—	7.5
Heavy alkyl-benzenes	12.4	11.3	—	—	11.3
Heptane	21.0	12.8	—	—	12.8
Hexane	132.8	101.0	—	—	101.0
Total (includes minor products)	11,706.0	8,304.6	1,200.1	190.6	9,314.2

[a] Does not include derivatives

Source: Author's compilation.

As a result, the secondary industry today is really made up of two tiers. This is evident as one looks at the scale of operations, as shown in Table 4.4, which lists many of the present operations in Mexico. The first group consists of modern, efficient, and competitive facilities such as Celanese' acetone and 2-EHA plants, Temex's TPA plant, Cydsa's and Primex's PVC plants in Altamira, and Negromex's PB rubber unit at the

TABLE 4.3 1986 Consumption of Selected Primary Petrochemicals Not Produced by Pemex (thousands of metric tons)

Product	Consumed
Propylene oxide	23.7
Perchloroethylene	16.1
Polypropylene	86.3
Acrylic acid	1.6
Polybutenes	4.4
Chlorinated hydrocarbons (choloroform, methylene chloride, trichloroethane, ethylene, carbon tet)	24.9
Isobutanol	5.1
Nonene	2.3

Source: Secretaría de Energía, Minas e Industria Parastatal, 1987.

same location. Included in the second group are Esquim's alkyl-phenols and Narsa's polystyrene plants. These plants are small and use older technology adapted for a different environment, and are not likely to survive under today's economic policies.

These remarks may paint an unduly negative picture. The fact is that many of the small-scale facilities were forced to adapt, and necessity has provided the push to innovate in both product and process, and developing a specialty is the formula for survival. There may be no other producer of polypropylene fiber in the world today that profitably makes one-million pound lots of very heavy or very light denier fabric, other than a Mexican one that also has to import the base resin.

This is not the case generally, but is frequent enough to predict that within a few years, the industry in Mexico will be split between very few large, efficient, and world-class competitive producers of petrochemical commodities and many (but still fewer than today) small producers of specialties who depend on service as the main tool for survival. The small producers will become a source of technology for other developing countries as well as boutiques or marketing specialists in selected niches.

A Single Petrochemical Industry?

In spite of everything, the fact is that we are talking of two industries in Mexico which, no matter how closely they cooperate with each other, are in a difficult position to face fully integrated world competitors.

TABLE 4.4 Major Secondary Petrochemical Facilities
(thousands of metric tons)

Firm	Product	Capacity
Celanese Mexicana	Polyester polymer/fiber	94
	2-EHA	70
	Acetic acid	182
	Acetic anydride	90
	Acetone	60
	Butyraldehyde	90
	Vinyl acetate	65
Industrias Resistol	Polystyrene	92
	ABS/SAN	28
Cydsa	Acrylic polymer/fiber	90
	PVC resin	160
Christianson	Glycoethers, alkylphenols, ethoxylates	11
Polioles	Ethylene/propylene glycols	65
	Polystyrene	12
	Polyethylene glycols	25
Idesa	Polyethylene glycols	40
	Polystyrene	50
Sintesis	Phthalic anhydride	30
Organicas	Maleic anhydride	7
Tereftalatos	Purified terephthalic	230
Humex	Carbon black	96
	SB rubber	73
Novum	SB, PB rubbers	100
	Carbon black	75
Primex	PVC resin	115
Univex	Caprolactam	75
Petrocel	DMT	270
	TPA	60
Fenoquimia	Phenol	42
	Acetone	25
	ACH/MMA	20
Tetraetilo de Mexico	Tetraethyl lead	14
Fisisa	Acrylic polymer/fiber	40
Nylmex/Fiqusa	Nylon resin/fiber	55
	Polyester resin/fiber	115

Source: Secretaría de Energía, Minas e Industria Parastatal.

Polystyrene is an enlightening example: 85 percent of world production comes from producers integrated back with styrene monomer or further. At the same time, the large world producers use 90 percent of their output to serve their own domestic markets and only 10 percent is exported. In contrast, over 50 percent of Mexican production is exported, while none is integrated because of the duality imposed by the Petrochemical Law. Even if the Pemex supply were to be counted as integrated, still one-third of the monomer has to be imported. This example is repeated in even more dramatic terms in the cases of VCM/PVC and TPA/polyester fibers.

In effect, the mere existence of the barrier imposed by the Petrochemical Law is a major strategic weakness. There are two important trends in Mexico today:

1. The government and Pemex have launched a new program to invite private interests, both Mexican and foreign, to participate in the financing of new expansions in basics. Off-balance sheet schemes are under discussion and the process may result in new production of some basic products.
2. Active discussion is also going on concerning a redefinition of what is a basic petrochemical in the eyes of the law. This has already led to the elimination of many dubious cases and will reduce the Pemex role to that of supplier of basic building blocks (olefins, aromatics, and methanol).[9]

Both of these trends should be seen as worthwhile, but a major issue remains unresolved: given these structural defects plus an open economy, what are the comparative advantages of the Mexican petrochemical industry? Why should it attract investment?

Let us list some factors which may influence the investment decision:

1. Mexico has not only become an open economy, but through modernization and evolution of the *maquiladora* concept, it is also becoming a world manufacturing location, as Taiwan and Singapore are already. Large corporations like IBM, Ford, NEC, or Alcatel have significant operations in Mexico to serve world markets. New market product or raw material testing is cheaper for them in Mexico than in many other locations. For them, manufacturing in Mexico has become almost mandatory.
2. In the United States, much of the growth is taking place on the West Coast, while the manufacturing is done in the East, and the raw materials are in the South. A Mexican petrochemical facility is well located to serve the Western United States.

3. While it is true that there is a serious brain drain of Mexican scientists and engineers, it is also valid that many young technicians remain in Mexico and the restrictions arising from economic conditions have fostered their creativity. This makes for more effective research and development, particularly concerted efforts focused on market needs.

In summary, while it is difficult to see how the industry's structural problem will be corrected, it is also possible to see new roles for the Mexican petrochemical industry as it faces the challenge of a global economy (see Table 4.5).

Relations with U.S. Industry

Most major U.S. chemical companies were involved in the early stages of development of the Mexican industry. Most are still present, although in a minority equity position as required by law. Some of the main cases are outlined in Table 4.6.

One conspicuous absence in this list is Dow Chemical, today the second largest chemical company in the United States. Mostly as a result of the restrictions of the Petrochemical Law, the major U.S. oil companies are absent.

TABLE 4.5 Major Chemical Companies in Mexico

Company	Products	Affiliations
Celanese Mexicana	Nylon, polyester, fiber, solvents	Hoechst/ Celanese
Cydsa	Acrylic fibers, PVC, heavy chemicals	No U.S. affiliation
Dupont, S.A	Explosives, paints, resins, agricultural chemicals	E.I. DuPont De Nemours
Industrias Resistol	Polystyrene, ABS, phenol, acrylic resins, adhesives, sealants	Monsanto
Novum	Pharmaceuticals, rubber, carbon black, fatty acids	Merck Cabot Henkel
Petrocel	DMT, TPA	Hercofina
Polimeros de Mexico	PVC, polystyrene	Rhone Poulenc Hoest.
Polioles	Glycols	BASF
Temex	TPA	Amoco
Union Carbide Mexicana	Silicones, agricultural chemicals, gases	Union Carbide

Source: Author's compilation.

TABLE 4.6 1988 Sales Involving Firms with U.S. Affiliations
(millions of U.S. dollars at average 1988 exchange rate)

Company	U.S. Affiliation	1988
Celanese Mexicana	Hoescht Celanese 40%	700
Industrias Resistol	Monsanto 40%	420
Union Carbide Mexicana	Union Carbide	175
Industrias Oxy	Occidental Petroleum	55
DuPont S.A. & Affiliates	E.I. DuPont de Nemours	500
Petrocel	Hercules 40%	175
Tereftalatos Mexicana	Himont 40%	125
Polycyd	B.F. Goodrich 40%	120

Source: Author's compilation.

All in all, industry figures indicate that of the total sales of the industry, not just petrochemicals but also other organic and inorganic products, U.S.-related corporations represent about 45 percent of the total industry output.

Even more significant, many U.S. companies are involved in licensing product and process technology, and they are involved in some related fields such as safety and environmental engineering.

Existing regulations require that all technology transfer agreements be registered with a branch of SECOFI. The extent of involvement can be surmised from a few figures: out of 6,600 registered contracts in the country, 875 or 13 percent involve the chemical industry, and 258 or 30 percent are those in which a U.S. corporation is the licensor. Even setting aside state-of-the-art issues, the extent of U.S. involvement and participation is significant.

A few conditions could change this situation. Essentially all of the licensing contracts are process rather than product related, and in many cases the licensor is not commercially exploiting the resulting product. However, in those cases where the licensor is oriented towards product marketing, Mexico's open economy now allows the company to do so with much less concern about giving up technology. We therefore should see a reduction in technical know-how transfer and an upswing in development of the Mexican market.

Serious overbuilding in the 1970s, coupled with stagnant markets, led to large losses for the industry,[10] which resulted in closing a large number of plants. A good example is ethylene: in the period 1978–1984, the United States alone shut down 9.6 billion pounds per year in capacity, 25 percent of the peak rate during the period.[11] This was coupled with an intense process of mergers and rationalizations. By

1985, the world industry had stopped the red-ink bath of the previous years and by 1986, the producers that were left made reasonable profits.

Repeated predictions of a slowdown in the U.S. economy made the survivors cautious and no expansion in world capacity occurred. When the U.S economy continued to grow, shortages appeared, which were made even more critical when China opened its economy, leading to an upsurge in world demand. The result was a rapid escalation of prices (a three-to-four-fold increase over a short period of time became the norm) and profits soared, making 1987 and 1988 the best years ever for the industry. In the United States, return on equity for the major companies exceeded 20 percent and in the case of Dow Chemical it reached over 35 percent, both record levels. The year 1989 witnessed the beginning of a down cycle; China had to ration its limited hard currency reserves and U. S. economic growth slowed. The record profits of the previous two years stimulated most companies to bring on new capacity, although mostly by debottlenecking, since few grassroots additions have been made, and prices are coming down rapidly. We should see the world markets stagnant and oversupplied through 1991, although not as seriously as ten years before, with a slow recovery for two more years and a resumption of profitable levels by the middle of the decade. The U.S. industry will be slightly better prepared for the slow growth than before, but the times will be difficult, perhaps more so as European integration becomes a reality in 1992. Recall at this point that the four largest chemical companies in the world are European and that the United States has only two among the top ten.

In summary, I expect a scenario of retrenchment and cost-cutting, difficult but not nearly as bad as the previous experiences.

The U.S. industry has been a net exporter in the past, but this scenario may lead to a reversal. If so, this raises the specter of restrictive U. S. trade actions. This is of particular interest to Mexico. Mexico also has to consider the effects of phasing out of the U.S. general system of preferences.

Outlook for the Mexican Petrochemical Industry

This decade opens for Mexico with two contrasting positions: a continuing shortage in basic petrochemical production and a significant export posture in secondary products such as fibers, plastics and resins, rubber, and surfactants.

The Mexican government has estimated[12] that over the five-year period 1990–1994, an investment of about $6 billion is needed. It is difficult to see how this can be justified.

The Mexican industry, particularly in secondary petrochemicals, is very much dependent on exports to the United States (25 percent to 50 percent in some cases), which could be in jeopardy if there is a slowdown in the U. S. economy and a growth of protectionism.

Mexico is emerging from its debt problems after a long period of limited investment; needed infrastructure is not there and even if the monies were available, rebuilding that infrastructure is going to be a rather slow process.

An open economy with an environment of retrenchment and cost-cutting for the U.S. counterparts will make it more profitable to buy U.S. surplus than to build new plants.

At the same time, the Mexican economy will resume growth following eight years of stagnation. Living standards, which dropped precipitously throughout the period 1982–1990, will begin to pick up and the appetite for consumer and industrial goods should pick up rapidly. It would seem, therefore, that the secondary segment which has been exporting in a significant way will turn inward while importing a good part of the basics.

The overall fit seems very nice if it were not for the fact that this prediction implies significant trade deficits, which may be the major obstacle to achieving such a fit.

Toward a Bilateral Agreement

As we review the outlook for the industry in both countries, it is not too difficult to see the emergence of a unique situation characterized by the following:

1. Excess supply of basic products in the United States.
2. Production deficit of basics in Mexico and surplus in secondary petrochemicals, plus a few of the basics.
3. Next-door neighbors with most of the industry located in the crescent along the Gulf Coast that goes from Baton Rouge to Coatzacoalcos.
4. Large, well-developed pipeline manifold on the U.S. side that allows fast and economic movement of basic products and a large, underdeveloped network on the Mexican side. The proximity of these networks should make connecting them a low-cost project. This combines with a chronic shortage of storage capacity that limits incoming and out-going flows.
5. A slowdown in the U.S. economy and a resumption of significant growth in Mexico, where pent-up demand is large.

Outside of this region, Europe 1992 may challenge both countries and make its trade planning difficult at best.

The conclusion of the above seems obvious: a bilateral trade agreement covering just this sector or covering substantially all trade, including this sector, which would take away all tariff and other restrictions should benefit both countries greatly. International manufacturing in Mexico, a logical step from the *maquiladora* program, would find its sourcing even more dependable and propel Mexico into the position of the Asian newly industrializing countries, to the benefit of all.

In effect, it's going to be very difficult to find two countries and an industry so uniquely positioned and with so much to gain from each other. This uniqueness may also be the base on which to build a strong argument, should this be necessary, if the GATT rules pose a barrier to such a sectoral agreement.

Notes

1. The industry is full of technical abbreviations. Unless the context demands it, we will not describe them because this would be cumbersome.

2. P. H. Spitz, *Petrochemicals - The Rise of an Industry* (New York: J. Wiley & Sons, 1988).

3. See No. 2.

4. *Petrochemicals 1987*, Comisión Petroquímica Mexicana (Mexico City: SEMIP, 1988).

5. We carefully distinguish between nationalization, the process of expropriating assets privately held, regardless of the owner's nationality, and Mexicanization, by which companies become majority owned by Mexican nationals. This does not imply state ownership.

6. One of the three families of petrochemical building blocks. The other two are the natural gas hydrocarbons, particularly methane, and the aromatic hydrocarbons. All the industry's products, from rubber to fibers to plastics to fertilizers, are made from these building blocks.

7. The institute is a separate branch also owned by the government and devoted to research and development and process engineering.

8. J. L. Bower, *When Markets Quake* (Cambridge: Harvard University Press, 1986).

9. This was the case indeed. The lists of both basic as well as regulated secondary petrochemicals have been reduced considerably. As a result, many products once regulated as secondary are now free from regulations or restrictions. The same is true for many processes.

10. See No. 8.

11. F. H. Romanelle, "U. S. Chemicals Industry: A View Towards Commodities," 19th ANIQ Forum, Mexico, 1987.

12. *Petrochemical Development Plan*, SEMIP and PEMEX, 1989.

Petrochemicals: U.S. Perspective

Rina Quijada

The U.S. petrochemical industry began 70 years ago with the production of isopropanol from a propylene-rich stream at Standard Oil Company in its Bayway, New Jersey refinery. From this small beginning, the petrochemical industry in the United States grew to net sales of approximately $100 billion in 1988.[1]

Few generalizations can be made about the industry because of its complexity, the factors shaping its future, and the numerous parties involved in it. I will concentrate on products made directly from hydrocarbons, those commonly known as primary petrochemicals. Primary petrochemicals are the olefins (ethylene, propylene, and butadiene) and the aromatics (benzene, toluene, and xylenes). These are the building blocks for thousands of petrochemical products, including plastics, detergents, and pharmaceuticals. Of the many thousands of petrochemicals that have been developed from the building block petrochemicals, about 14,000 have achieved significant commercial status. These petrochemicals account for about 80 percent of the total tonnage of the U.S. chemical industry.

Historically, the United States has been the world's largest producer of petrochemicals. However, during the last 20 years, the preeminence of the U.S. industry has been eroded by the rebuilding of Western European plants and the diversification by oil-producing nations into petrochemicals. Table 4.7 indicates the production figures for the basic petrochemicals in the United States during the period 1987–1993.

Primary petrochemicals in the United States are produced by 47 companies whose production facilities are located principally in Texas and Louisiana near feedstock and energy sources. The five largest

TABLE 4.7 U.S. Basic Petrochemical Production (thousands of metric tons)

	Ethylene	Propylene	Butadiene	Benzene	Toluene	Mixed Xylenes
1987						
Capacity	16,359	10,179	1,699	7,416	4,351	5,005
Production	15,801	8,517	1,313	5,355	3,860	3,320
Operating rate (%)	97	84	77	72	89	66
1989[a]						
Capacity	17,716	10,603	1,751	8,084	4,433	5,459
Production	17,397	9,300	1,431	6,060	3,960	4,020
Operating rate (%)	98	88	82	75	89	74
1993[a]						
Capacity	22,348	12,970	2,001	8,629	4,433	5,525
Production	19,889	10,765	1,618	7,087	4,100	4,290
Operating rate (%)	89	83	81	82	92	78

[a]Estimated.

Sources: Chemical Market Associates, Inc. *World Light Olefins Analysis 1989;* and *World Benzene Analysis 1989.*

producers account for about 50 percent of total annual production of these primary petrochemicals. The U.S. primary petrochemical sector includes domestic private companies, as well as multinationals with production facilities throughout the world.

Table 4.8 shows foreign-owned U.S. petrochemical companies that have petrochemical interests. In 1987, foreign-affiliated companies

TABLE 4.8 Foreign-Owned U.S. Petroleum Companies

Foreign Investor	U.S. Investment	Percent Ownership
Royal Dutch/Shell	Shell Oil	100
British Petroleum, UK	BP Chemicals America	100
Petroleos de Venezuela	Citgo Petroleum	50
Unocal	Champlin Refining	100
Petrofina-Belgium	American Petrofina	83
Hoechst	Hoechst Celanese	100
BASF	BASF/UTP/GP	41.6

Source: Chemical Market Associates, Inc.

accounted for 17.8 percent of total U.S. reserves of crude petroleum and natural gas and 16.3 percent of production.[2]

The U.S. petrochemical industry is controlled by the private sector. Prices for basic petrochemicals are determined by market forces; there are no tariffs on basic petrochemicals, such as ethylene, propylene, and benzene.

The open-door U.S. investment policy, which allows unrestricted foreign investment in the U.S. chemical industry is, however, not reciprocally available to U.S. investors in all major petrochemical-producing nations. Mexico prohibits private investment in basic petrochemicals, and foreign investment may not be greater than 40 percent in secondary petrochemicals.

The constant appearance of new downstream products and processes in the petrochemical industry has marked the United States as a leader in innovation. The availability of state-of-the-art technology and a large contiguous market make this industry especially important to the United States, as well as to the entire international petrochemical industry. As the world's largest petrochemical producer, the United States has maintained a strong export position in petrochemical products and technology.

The petrochemical industry is dependent on new technology to improve production and reduce costs. Technology improvements are one way of keeping abreast of competition. At present, many firms that once were primarily involved in the commodity side of the petrochemical industry are endeavoring to diversify into the specialty chemical area. These efforts, however, usually involve acquisitions, joint ventures, and other business approaches that do not involve the creation of new companies. As growth of the cyclical commodity side of the business is expected to moderate, the U.S. petrochemical industry will continue to be actively involved in the more profitable, less cyclical specialty chemical businesses.

The major differences between commodity petrochemicals and specialty chemicals are shown in Table 4.9.

I will examine the structure of the basic petrochemical industry in the United States and the present and future relationship between the industries in Mexico and the United States. Strong ties between the petrochemical industries of the two nations can be developed if certain changes occur.

Industry Structure

Of the basic petrochemicals, ethylene, propylene, and benzene are considered the most important. Their growth is representative of the overall performance of the U.S. petrochemical industry. There is little

TABLE 4.9 Commodities versus Specialties

Production	Commodities	Specialties
Volume	Large	Small
Plant/facilities	Capital intensive	Relatively inexpensive
Sales/services	Moderate	High
Technical requirement	Rely on engineering and process research	Rely on innovation and applications research
Labor	Minimal, highly automated	Labor intensive
Cost	High fixed costs	High marketing and service
Return on investment	Moderate	High

Source: Chemical Market Associates, Inc.

debate that the United States is the most influential country in the world in the area of commodity petrochemicals. As a result, the pricing and supply/demand situation in the United States has a definite impact on markets in Western Europe, the Far East, and Latin America.

Before entering into the details of specific products, it is helpful to look at the basic energy/petrochemical relationships. This interface is described in Figure 4.1.

The following general conclusions can be reached from this graphic:

1. The petrochemical industry is heavily dependent on the relationship between crude oil and natural gas.
2. Crude oil is used to produce both gasoline and fuel oil as well as petrochemical feedstocks.
3. Natural gas provides ethane, propane, and butane feedstocks for olefins production, methane for ammonia and methanol production, and fuel for these industries.

Figure 4.2 shows the petrochemical interface between basic petrochemicals and intermediate products, such as cyclohexane and styrene.

In the United States, aromatics are sourced mainly from refinery operations, while ethylene is sourced mainly from natural gas liquids. Significant quantities of propylene are derived from both sources.

Ethylene

The United States accounts for about 31 percent of world ethylene demand and is considered the most influential participant in this

FIGURE 4.1 The Energy/Petrochemical Interface

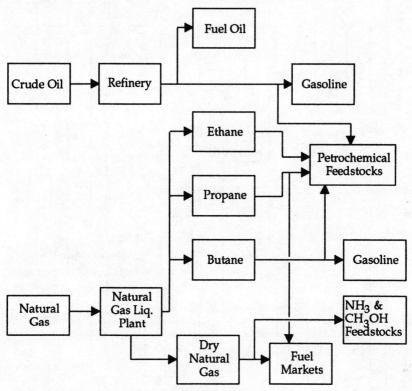

Source: Chemical Market Associates, Inc.

market. Ethylene production in 1988 of 16.8 million tons was a record high for the United States. This production was slightly more than 30 percent of the world's ethylene production. In Table 4.10, the location of the 22 U.S. ethylene producers is clearly shown. The capacities of the top five producers, representing 47 percent of total capacity, are shown in Table 4.11.

U.S. ethylene demand is likely to grow from 16.7 million tons in 1988 to 20 million tons in 1993, an average growth rate of 3.7 percent per year.

Over the last 10 years, the U.S. petrochemical industry has experienced a continuous integration by the major producers. This vertical integration is driven by the desire to achieve economies of scale, value added benefits, and reduced transportation costs. Transportation costs are a particular concern for ethylene and propylene, for which pipelines are required for efficient transportation.

FIGURE 4.2 Petrochemical Interface

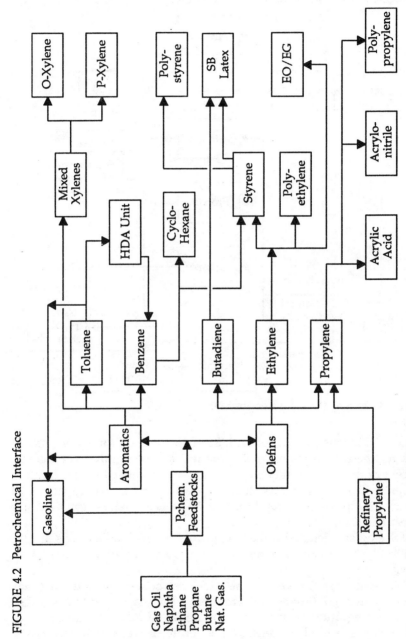

Source: Chemical Market Associates, Inc.

TABLE 4.10 U.S. Ethylene Producing and Consuming Locations

Location	Companies (P=Producing; C=Consuming)
Houston/Cedar Bayou/Deer Park/ Pasadena, TX	Mobil Chem. (P); Occidental (C); Quantum (C); Shell Chem (P); Soltex (C), Ethyl (C); Phillips 66 (C); Chevron (P/C)
Baytown/Channelview/Bayport/Mont Belvieu/Clear Lake/LaPorte, TX	Exxon (P/C); Arco Chem. (C); Lyondell PC (P/C); Hoechst Celan. (C); BF Goodrich (C); DuPont (C); Quantum (C)
Texas City, TX	Amoco Chem (C); Sterling Chem. (C); UCC (P/C)
Beaumont/Orange/Port Arthur/ Pt. Neches, TX	DuPont (P/C); Mobil (P); PD Glycol (C); Chevron (P/C); Quantum (C); Texaco (P/C); Oxy Petrochem. (C); Nova (C)
Bay City/Chocolate Bayou/Sweeney, TX	Oxy Petrochem. (P/C); Hoechst Celan. (C); Amoco Chem. (P); Quantum (C); Phillips 66 (P)
Freeport/Oyster Creek, TX	Dow Chem. (P/C)
Victoria/Pt. Comfort/Seadrift, TX	FPC (C); UCC (P/C); Oxy Petrochem (C); DuPont (C)
Corpus Christi, TX	Oxy Petrochem. (P); Koch (P/C); Occidental (C)
Odessa, TX	Rexene (P/C)
Lake Charles, LA	Oxy Petrochem. (P); PPG Inc. (C); Vista Chem. (P/C); Westlake Poly. (C)
Norco/Taft, LA	Shell Chem. (P); UCC (P/C)
Plaquemine/Carrville/Convent/ Geismar/Donaldsonville, LA	Dow Chem. (P/C); Georgia Gulf (C); GE Plastics (C); Fina (C); Occidental (C); UTP (P); BASF (C); Borden Chem. (C); Shell Chem. (C); Uniroyal (C); Vulcan (C)
Baton Rouge/Addis, LA	Copolymer-DSM (C); Exxon (P/C); FPC (C)
El Dorado/Magnolia, AR	Great Lakes (C); Ethyl (C)
Barnsdall, OK	Petrolite (C)
Clinton, IA	Quantum (P/C)
East Morris, IL	Quantum (P/C)
Tuscola, IL	Quantum (P/C)
Calvert City, KY	BF Goodrich (P/C)
Brandenburg, KY	Olin Corp. (P/C)
Claymont, DE	Sun Ref. (P/C)

Source: Chemical Market Associates, Inc.

TABLE 4.11 Top Five U.S. Ethylene Producers (thousands of metric tons)

Company	Location	Capacity	
		1988	*1993*
Shell	Texas/Louisiana	1,873	2,132
Dow Chemical	Texas/Louisiana	1,830	2,541
Exxon Chemical	Texas/Louisiana	1,520	1,860
Cain Occidental	Texas/Louisiana	1,275	1,520
Union Carbide	Texas/Louisiana	1,275	1,556
Total		7,773	9,609
Total U.S. Capacity		16,826	22,349

Source: Chemical Market Associates, Inc. *World Light Olefins Analysis 1989.*

Table 4.12 lists the major consumers of ethylene in the United States. The list of consumers is similar to the list of major ethylene producers in Table 4.11, and shows the level of integration within the industry. Quantum Chemical, the tenth largest ethylene producer in the United States, has moved to the first position as an ethylene consumer. Dow Chemical is the second-largest consumer and Union Carbide is third largest.

Although ethylene derivatives are not a part of this discussion, it is interesting to note the U.S. ethylene consumption pattern shown in Figure 4.3.

All the ethylene produced in the United States is consumed domestically. Until 1988, the United States had no practical way of exporting or importing ethylene; only derivatives of ethylene are exported. Since then, however, a terminal facility has been installed on the Texas Gulf Coast to permit importing ethylene.

TABLE 4.12 1989 Primary U.S. Ethylene Consumers (thousands of metric tons)

Company	Capacity
Quantum	2,221
Dow Chemical	2,076
Union Carbide	1,991
Cain/Occidental	1,199
Chevron	913
Phillips 66	801
Shell Chemical	762
Exxon	739

Source: Chemical Market Associates, Inc., *World Light Olefins Analysis 1989.*

FIGURE 4.3   1988 U.S. Ethylene Consumption (thousands of metric tons)

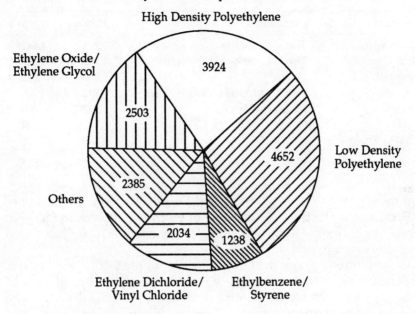

High Density Polyethylene

Ethylene Oxide/
Ethylene Glycol

3924

2503

Low Density
Polyethylene

4652

2385

Others

2034

1238

Ethylene Dichloride/
Vinyl Chloride

Ethylbenzene/
Styrene

Source: Chemical Market Associates, Inc.

The fact that the United States is limited in its olefins export-import capabilities could create a problem for the future of the ethylene industry. Large increments of olefins capacity are being added to the system—about 2.5 million tons of incremental capacity and 4.5 million tons of new plant capacity will be added during the 1989–1993 period. With the probability that capacity will exceed demand, it is likely that operating rates will fall significantly until 1992. As a result, the U.S. ethylene industry may face some near-term difficulty as far as operating rates and profit margins are concerned.

Propylene

In 1988, U.S. propylene demand reached a record 9.1 million tons, 32.5 percent of world propylene demand. Growth in U.S. propylene demand is predicted to average 3.4 percent per year over the 1988–1993 period, compared to an average 4.9 percent per year growth for the entire world. In the United States, propylene consumption is expected to grow most rapidly in the derivatives: polypropylene, cumene, and propylene oxide.

The top five U.S. propylene producers, shown in Table 4.13, account for approximately 50 percent of total installed capacity. In fact, the

TABLE 4.13 Top Five U.S. Propylene Producers

Company	Location	1989	1993
Exxon Chemical	Texas, Louisiana, New Jersey	1,370	1,642
Shell Chemical	Texas, Louisiana, New Jersey	1,183	1,183
Lyondell	Texas	1,020	1,020
Chevron	Texas, California, Pennsylvania	746	791
Amoco	Texas, Indiana	722	805
Total		5,041	5,441
Total U.S. Capacity		10,365	12,970

Source: Chemical Market Associates, Inc. *World Light Olefins Analysis 1989*

top three producers (Exxon, Shell, and Lyondell) operate 33 percent of U.S. capacity. The top U.S. consumer of propylene is Himont, followed closely by Exxon. Almost all the top propylene sellers are associated with an oil company.

A significant share of the U.S. propylene supply (about one-third) is obtained directly from refineries. Refineries are the source of most of Mexico's propylene supply. For the near future, Mexico will continue to rely on some imports of propylene to fill its requirements, but substantial additional quantities will be needed by 1992–1993. Mexico is planning a propane dehydrogenation plant to produce its required propylene. This project at the Morelos complex, in the state of Veracruz, is expected to come on stream by the end of 1993. The rest of the world obtains a greater share of its propylene supply from steam crackers.

As its olefins capacity expands, the United States will move from being a net propylene importer to a significant net exporter in the early 1990s. After 1993, however, the trend should reverse as the United States again becomes a net propylene importer. Figure 4.4 shows the 1988 U.S. propylene end-use pattern. Overall, propylene derivatives demand is expected to grow at about an average 2.7 percent per year in the period 1988–1993. Currently, Canada supplies a significant amount of propylene to the United States.

Benzene

In the United States, benzene demand, including exports, increased from 5.9 million tons in 1987 to 6.4 million tons in 1988. Demand is forecast to increase to 7.4 million tons by 1993. There have been substantial additions to benzene capacity during the past few years, and by 1990 nearly 700,000 tons of capacity were scheduled to be added

FIGURE 4.4 1988 U.S. Propylene Consumption (thousands of metric tons)

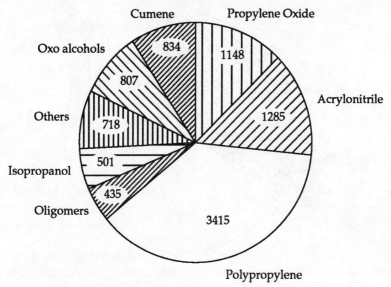

Source: Chemical Market Associates, Inc.

to the system through expansions and debottlenecks, restarts of idle capacity, and even grass roots investments.

Benzene is produced from five sources in the United States: reformate from refinery reformers, pyrolysis gasoline from olefin steam crackers, toluene hydrodealkylation (HDA) units, toluene disproportionation units, and coke oven operations. Reformate is the major source of U.S. benzene, while coke-oven benzene is of minor importance. Benzene supply from reformate is fairly steady each year, as this is one of the cheaper sources of benzene. Some refiners dedicate facilities just for benzene production. The swing supply of benzene is that produced via toluene HDA or toluene disproportionation. Producers have the option to run these units or sell toluene as a gasoline octane component. Benzene produced from toluene for chemical use will continue to grow at a forecast 3 percent per year through 1993. This means that HDA economies will continue to determine benzene pricing.

Benzene content in motor gasoline is an important issue that could affect U.S. benzene availability. The state of California has proposed, through the California Air Resources Board, to limit the permissible level of benzene in gasoline because benzene is a known carcinogen. It is probable that permissible benzene levels can be met by modifications in refinery operations without materially affecting benzene availability. Figure 4.5 shows the U.S. benzene consumption pattern for 1988.

FIGURE 4.5 U.S. Benzene Consumption (thousands of metric tons)

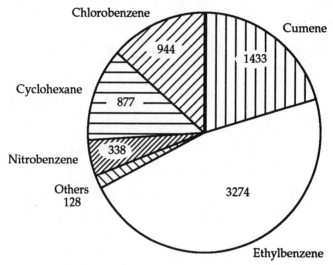

Source: Chemical Market Associates, Inc.

U.S. benzene demand is dominated by consumption for styrene, cumene, and cyclohexane. Styrene requirements represent more than 50 percent of total domestic benzene demand, while consumption for cumene/phenol represents 22 percent of demand, and cyclohexane 14 percent.   The strongest growth in benzene demand will be for cumene/phenol, which is forecast to grow at an average rate of more than 5.5 percent per year from 1988 through 1993. This is due mainly to very strong growth anticipated for polycarbonates, which require phenol as a raw material. Total growth in U.S. domestic demand for benzene for the period 1988–1993 is expected to average around 3 percent per year.

Interaction with the Counterpart Mexican Industry

Trade between the United States and Mexico is important for both countries. The United States is Mexico's largest trading partner. In recent years, about two-thirds of Mexico's trade has been with the United States. In the case of the United States, Mexico is among its five most important trading partners. U.S.-Mexican bilateral trade is affected by a number of trade programs, such as the General System of Preference (GSP) program and the Foreign Trade Zone (FTZ) program.

The GSP, established in Article 5 of the Trade Act of 1974, is a non-reciprocal duty elimination granted by the United States on designated products originating in developing countries. In Table 4.14, basic petrochemicals are listed along with the GSP treatment. Under the GSP program, the single largest group of products imported from Mexico is chemicals and related products.

Total U.S. imports of chemical products from Mexico increased from an estimated $1.1 billion in 1976 to $8.3 billion in 1985, an average annual growth rate of 25 percent, as shown in Table 4.15.

In order to put trade between the United States and Mexico in a world context, the four following 1988 trade grids have been developed to identify the origin and destination of some basic petrochemicals involved in world trade (see Figures 4.6–4.9). For three of the commodities—propylene, butadiene, and styrene—the United States exports to Mexico with Mexico receiving a significant share of the butadiene exports. In contrast, Mexico's exports of these commodities to the United States are quite small. Mexico exports to the United States a small amount of styrene, but imports from the United States a far larger quantity of the chemical. Mexico also exports ethylene to the United States, although the United States receives far more ethylene from Western Europe.

Conclusions

The petrochemical industry has several unique characteristics that should not be overlooked when evaluating the economic relationship between Mexico and the United States.

1. It is a capital-intensive industry, thus strong financial support is required.

TABLE 4.14 1989 U.S. Harmonized Tariff Schedule

	Rates of Duty	
Product	*Most Favored Nation Rate*	*Preferential Rate*
Ethylene	Free	
Propylene	Free	
Butadiene	Free	
BTX	Free	
Styrene	7.5%	Free[a]

[a]Generalized System of Preference, of which Mexico is the leading beneficiary.

Source: Chemical Market Associates, Inc.

TABLE 4.15 U.S. Imports of Chemicals and Related Products from Mexico
1980–1985 (hundreds of thousands of U.S. dollars)

Year	Imports from Mexico		Total U.S. Imports	
	GSP	Total	GSP	Total
1980	62.7	6,862.6	285.6	88,306.9
1981	81.9	7,214.8	406.1	91,094.2
1982	80.7	8,765.9	414.7	75,350.3
1983	130.6	8,883.0	624.9	68,918.1
1984	275.2	8,379.7	813.6	75,056.4
1985	294.0	8,313.8	1,070.2	68,347.5

Source: U.S. Department of Commerce, monthly import data.

2. It is not labor-intensive, thus it has limited direct socioeconomic benefits.
3. It should be located close to its feedstock supply, i.e., natural gas or crude oil.

These characteristics make the petrochemical industry an unlikely candidate for the *maquiladora* program along the U.S.-Mexico border. The *maquiladoras* are best suited for consumer goods production, where the main activity is the assembly of imported parts or equipment, utilizing relatively low-cost labor. In the case of basic petrochemicals, resource availability is a primary consideration in plant location.

Mexico's state oil company, Pemex, plans to spend an estimated $2.5 billion during the next six years to add new petrochemical capacity. Financial limitations of the nation could prompt government decisions favoring more private participation in even the basic petrochemical industry.

Foreign investment in Mexico's secondary petrochemical industry is encouraged under the Petrochemical Development Plan. But, foreign ownership is restricted to 40 percent, while complete private, domestic ownership is permitted. Table 4.16 shows the remaining 19 basic petrochemicals. The most recent reclassification was carried out in order to encourage private investment in the petrochemical industry. The previous list included 34 petrochemicals. All petrochemicals not included are considered secondary, and private ownership is encouraged.

By law, only Pemex can produce basic petrochemicals in Mexico— direct investment still seems to be distant for U.S. companies. This implies that the main contribution of the United States to Mexico's basic petrochemical program will be through licensing technology and know-how, at least for the immediate future.

FIGURE 4.6 1988 Ethylene Trade Grid (thousands of metric tons)

Imports by	Exports by									
	U.S.A.	Canada	Mexico	South America	West Europe	East Europe	Africa/ M. East	Japan	Other Asia	Total
U.S.A.			11	3	25					39
Canada										0
Mexico										0
South America					32		14			46
West Europe						15	218			269
East Europe					44		41			85
Africa/M. East					27					27
Japan					2		17			31
Other Asia					12		175	161		348
Total	0	0	59	3	142	15	465	161	0	845

Source: Chemical Market Associates, Inc.

FIGURE 4.7 1988 Propylene Trade Grid (thousands of metric tons)

Imports by	Exports by									
	U.S.A.	Canada	Mexico	South America	West Europe	East Europe	Africa/ M. East	Japan	Other Asia	Total
U.S.A.		241		44	3					288
Canada	30									30
Mexico	13			1	6					20
South America										0
West Europe	50	2		36		179	14			281
East Europe					2					2
Africa/M. East	7				54					61
Japan									10	10
Other Asia	20			15	54		143	147		379
Total	120	243	0	96	119	179	157	147	10	1071

Source: Chemical Market Associates, Inc.

FIGURE 4.8 1988 Butadiene Trade Grid (thousands of metric tons)

Imports by	Exports by									
	U.S.A.	Canada	Mexico	South America	West Europe	East Europe	Africa/ M. East	Japan	Other Asia	Total
U.S.A.		22		4	232					258
Canada	3									3
Mexico	55				44					99
South America										0
West Europe										0
East Europe					42					42
Africa/M. East					50					50
Japan					83					83
Other Asia										0
Total	58	22	0	4	451	0	0	0	0	535

Source: Chemical Market Associates, Inc.

FIGURE 4.9 1988 Styrene Trade Grid (thousands of metric tons)

Imports by					Exports by					
	U.S.A.	Canada	Mexico	South America	West Europe	East Europe	Africa/ M. East	Japan	Other Asia	Total
U.S.A.		184	1	2	26	1				214
Canada	1									1
Mexico	34									34
South America	79	5			3					87
West Europe	93	40		32		15	30	4	7	221
East Europe	2				31		63			96
Africa/M. East	14				11					25
Japan	25	66					117		10	218
Other Asia	248	119		19	9		85	35		515
Total	496	414	1	53	80	16	295	39	17	1411

Source: Chemical Market Associates, Inc.

TABLE 4.16   Restricted Basic Petrochemicals

Ammonia	Methanol
Benzene	N-Paraffins
Butadiene	O-Xylene
DDB	P-Xylene
Ethane	Pentanes
Methyl tertiary butyl ether	Propylene
Ethylene	Dodecene
Heptene	Toluene
Hexane	M-Xylenes
Carbon black feedstock	

Source: Chemical Market Associates, Inc.

Process technology for petrochemical production is generally freely available for licensing. For example, the Unipol process, developed by a U.S. company, is now licensed throughout the world. This process greatly simplifies the technology and reduces the cost of producing both polyethylene and polypropylene.

Another factor to consider in the U.S.-Mexico relationship is the tariff schedule of the United States. There are no U.S. tariffs on the six primary olefins and aromatics. However, under the Toxic Substances Control Act of 1976, the U.S. Environmental Protection Agency (EPA) is responsible for establishing standards for the use of these chemicals. As of January 1987, U.S. producers of primary olefins and aromatics were required to pay a superfund tax, to be utilized for the cleanup of toxic waste. Mexico is not exempt from paying the superfund tax. The superfund rates are shown in Table 4.17.

Many programs have been developed to improve trade between Mexico and the United States. When considering trade in basic petrochemicals, however, one must be aware that the most important factor in comparing each nation's relative competitiveness is the

TABLE 4.17 Superfund Tax for Imported Products

Petrochemical	Tax Rate (per ton)
Ethylene	$4.87
Propylene	$4.87
Benzene	$4.87
Xylene	$10.13

Source: Chemical Market Associates, Inc.

difference in the cost of feedstocks and fuel. Estimates of the price of natural gas are $2.46 per thousand cubic feet and the price of fuel oil in Mexico is $7.56 per barrel. Comparative U.S. price estimates give Mexican producers an 18 percent price advantage for natural gas and 49 percent advantage for fuel oil. Hence, production costs of basic petrochemicals should be lower in Mexico due to savings realized through lower natural resource costs. This advantage could be an incentive for future petrochemical joint ventures between Mexico and the United States.

If the new projects planned for Mexico's basic petrochemical industry materialize, Mexican import requirements of these products and their derivatives could be reduced in the coming years. Table 4.18 lists new projects scheduled through the first part of the 1990s.

I believe that petrochemical trade between the United States and Mexico will continue to increase on the derivatives side, but decrease in basic petrochemicals.

Because of geographic considerations, the U.S. petrochemical industry has two borders to consider when looking at tariff reduction programs. It may be useful to briefly examine the similarities and differences between Canada and Mexico, shown in Table 4.19.

The Free Trade Agreement between Canada and the United States will, in a few years, eliminate tariffs on most products traded between the two countries. A Mexico-U.S. free trade agreement is still several years away.

Previous experience shows that specific issues will be the key to the success of cooperative programs between Mexico and the United States. Allowing private investment in upstream investments in Mexico will insure the future availability of the basic petrochemicals necessary for the production of value added derivatives. A gradual decrease in government intervention will allow market forces to determine pricing and thereby increase competitiveness in the international market.

TABLE 4.18 Mexico's Major Capacity Additions (thousands of metric tons)

Product	Company	Capacity Change	Date
Ethylene	Pemex, Morelos	500	mid-1989
Propylene[a]	Pemex, Morelos	27	1991
	Pemex, Morelos	350	1993
Benzene	Pemex, Cadeyreta	74	1993

[a]Pemex has two plants producing propylene in Morelos.

Source: Chemical Market Associates, Inc.

TABLE 4.19 Canada and Mexico: Similarities and Differences in the Basic Petrochemical Industry

Canada	Mexico
Energy rich	Energy rich
Bordering nation	Bordering nation
Strong economy	Soft economy
Developed nation	Developing nation
Low government intervention	Strong government intervention
Foreign participation	Only government participation
Active U.S. trading partner	Active U.S. trading partner

Source: Chemical Market Associates, Inc.

In 1989, Mexico's new administration indicated through changes in the foreign investment law the desire to promote foreign investment in the petrochemical industry—except in those sectors reserved for the Mexican government, such as the primary olefins and aromatics. While Mexico has opened the door to foreign investment, the door is not open far enough to attract the large investments required in the petrochemical industry. It is unlikely that foreign ownership limited to 40 percent will be attractive, even considering the availability of potentially lower-cost feedstocks. Petrochemical markets have become global. As a newcomer to international petrochemical trade, Mexico can also profit from the know-how afforded by foreign involvement in management and marketing.

Free trade zones, GSP treatment, participation in the General Agreement on Tariffs and Trade, *maquiladoras*, and a free trade agreement are not the only means by which the commercial cooperation between the two nations can be enhanced. There is solid ground to build on, but it will require major changes on both sides of the border and careful examination of the existing programs to arrive at mutually beneficial programs.

Notes

1. *Chemical and Engineering News*, June 19, 1989, pp. 61-62.
2. U.S. Department of Energy, *Profiles of Foreign Direct Investment in U.S. Energy 1987*, December 31, 1988, p. 12.

FIVE

Pharmaceuticals

Pharmaceuticals: U.S. Perspective

Robert M. Sherwood

This analysis addresses the relationship between the research-intensive pharmaceutical industry of the United States and the emulative pharmaceutical industry of Mexico.

The pharmaceutical industry of the United States is neither labor intensive nor capital intensive. Its main feature is that it is knowledge-intensive. It is research driven, spending about 15 percent of sales on research and development in 1987. This has risen from annual expenditures in the range of 11 percent to 12 percent in the 1970s,[1] which is somewhat higher than the norm for most other industries. While the U.S. market for pharmaceuticals is quite large, the industry generally thinks in world market terms with most of the laboratories depending to a significant extent on foreign sales.[2] Research tends to be conducted in the United States while manufacturing facilities are located both in the United States and abroad. Sales and distribution facilities are even more widely dispersed around the world.

Pharmaceutical research has moved through several phases. From the late 1930s, with perfection of Sir Alexander Fleming's discovery of penicillin, through the post-World War II period, the industry collected samples of microorganisms and tested them for utility in human and animal therapy. Soil samples from around the world were sought, tested and developed into products as one part of this phase. Fermentation technology tended to be the key manufacturing method for producing the medicines.

Gradually, scientific advances led to computer-assisted design of molecules and their production by organic synthesis. The cost of this type of research is high with a tiny success ratio. It is now quite feasible to design a molecule but hard to predict its effect in the human body. More recently, biotechnology has been brought to the service of pharmaceutical research, with artificial methods employed in producing new medicines. This, too, is costly, and success is often elusive. There is a very recent trend to return to nature for the source of beneficial substances. Where primitive peoples have found medicinal benefit from a plant, the beneficial substance can usually be isolated and intensified as the basis for a new medication.

The evolution of the leading pharmaceutical products has been from anti-infectives to more sophisticated chronic treatments for heart disease, ulcers and nervous disorders, known as rich man's diseases. At the same time, the diversity of research has permitted advances in therapies for diseases with small patient populations, including orphan drugs.

Mexico's geographic proximity to the United States is quite unimportant to the pharmaceutical industry. The relationship with Mexico is no different from what it is with many other countries with comparable markets. The Mexican market is served by U.S. companies largely through their affiliates, which are mostly wholly owned subsidiaries. There is little export from Mexico to the United States by either Mexican-owned or foreign-owned companies, and there is relatively little export from the United States to Mexico except for raw materials, chiefly from Puerto Rican basic manufacturing plants. In recent years, a few limited-purpose joint ventures between Mexican and U.S. laboratories have been formed. They are not a preferred way of doing business, but were forced by Mexican government policy. Companies with wholly owned subsidiaries established prior to 1973 were unwilling to divest to a 49 percent position to satisfy subsequent Mexicanization requirements.

The role of the U.S. government, as in most other countries, is in approving the fitness of products before they can be sold to the public. Government purchase of or reimbursement for medicines is a small but growing factor in the U.S. market. Government agencies such as the National Institutes of Health provide significant funding for medical research. The government also grants patents for pharmaceutical innovations. The role of the Mexican government is somewhat different, as will be described.

This chapter examines the structure of the pharmaceutical industry in the United States and the nature of the limited relationship between U.S. and Mexican companies, and identifies trends involving industry on both sides of the border. Two issues involve patent protection for pharmaceutical inventions and trade secret protection for product registration information.

Industry Structure

In recent years, some 680 companies, including foreign-owned firms, have engaged in the manufacture and sale of ethical and proprietary pharmaceuticals in the United States. About 90 percent of U.S. sales of drugs for human consumption are made by members of the Pharmaceutical Manufacturers Association (PMA), which has slightly more than 100 members.[3] The industry is not heavily concentrated. The four largest firms accounted for about 25 percent of prescription sales, the eight largest for about 45 percent and the leading 20 laboratories for about 75 percent in 1986.[4]

There has been a recent rash of mergers among some large companies, including the merger of foreign with U.S. companies. Smith Kline Beckman (U.S.) and Beecham (U.K.) have merged. Johnson & Johnson has entered a joint marketing arrangement with Merck. American Home is acquiring A. H. Robins. Squibb has merged with Bristol-Myers and still more mergers are expected.[5]

The size of the U.S. pharmaceutical industry relative to other industries is shown by the fact that total industry sales worldwide for 1988, at about $41 billion,[6] were smaller than the sales of each of the five top companies on the Fortune 500 list of U.S. companies.[7]

Size of U.S. Market

The size of the pharmaceutical market in the United States can be measured in several ways. Sales at the pharmacy level are not, for the most part, direct resales from pharmaceutical companies, but involve distributors, wholesalers, and other intermediaries. Export sales are not comparable with pharmacy sales, since finished goods are only a tiny fraction of exports. Perhaps the most useful measure of the size of the U.S. market is the domestic sales of PMA member companies, which were about $27 billion in 1987.[8] This is about 65 percent of their total sales, with the balance being foreign sales of about $14 billion. This ratio has been fairly constant for a dozen years or more, fluctuating along with the parity of the U.S. dollar in relation to foreign currencies.

Globalization Patterns

The globalization of the pharmaceutical industry mostly occurred in the 1950s and 1960s. Some companies, principally the European-based laboratories, operated on a worldwide basis before World War II, but for most U.S. companies, the thrust into global markets came after that war. Globalization usually proceeded in phases. First, finished goods were shipped to distributors in a few foreign countries, often in Latin America. Cuba and Mexico were among the first. Then local sales and distribution organizations were developed. Next, as the marketing effort showed promise and as government officials urged local value added, packaging plants were set up. In these facilities, finished goods were packaged from imported tablets, capsules and, sometimes, ointments. It was convenient to meet local health, regulatory, and language objectives this way. The next stage was the formulating plant. Active ingredients, the efficacious molecules, usually in powder form, were imported and compounded, mixed with inert ingredients to facilitate ingestion and absorption, and formulated into tablets, capsules and ointments. For some products this also involved the use of sterile facilities.

Quality control was also an aspect of this stage. These stages were somewhat labor-intensive and welcome in most developing countries. Finally, production of the basic, or active, ingredients was undertaken in the larger countries. This activity was usually more capital intensive, with large fermentation facilities being characteristic of the early offshore plants.

Early examples appeared in Mexico, Brazil and, for some companies in Argentina. Later, European and Asian plants were built. At the time these plants were built in Latin America, some form of patent protection for pharmaceutical inventions was available in most of these countries. Elimination or reduction of such protection came abruptly in Brazil in 1969, in Mexico in 1977, and gradually in Argentina through a series of court decisions during the 1970s.

Role of Knowledge

The knowledge content of this industry's activity tends to originate in the United States. The discovery and design of new molecules is done chiefly in research laboratories located in the United States. Many of the U.S. companies also have research facilities in European countries, and established facilities in Japan after the advent of pharmaceutical patent protection in 1975. Clinical testing of new molecules is also done largely in the United States, but medical research is also conducted in Europe, drawing on research hospitals there for clinical testing. To meet the requirements of health authorities in market countries, it is common to conduct further trial work there. This work tends to be of secondary importance, confirming earlier findings in a broader patient population and also teaching the local doctor/researcher population something about the new molecule.

Marketing is also an important element of the industry's activities. This, too, is a knowledge-intensive activity. Marketing plans are fashioned chiefly in the United States, with directives sent to field locations. It is important that statements made about the preventive and curative abilities of a medicine are carefully controlled and conform to clinical findings and government approvals.

Knowledge is the industry's major export, but the value of this knowledge is not readily measured. It would be reflected to some extent in royalties from subsidiaries to parent companies, but royalty flows are distorted by restrictions on, or denials of, royalty payments by some developing countries. This knowledge value may also be reflected in transfer prices of active ingredients, but these prices are also skewed by government controls on import prices in some countries and companies do not have uniform approaches to transborder pricing.

The exported knowledge, manifested in patent rights, trade secret manufacturing information, trademarks, and commercial information, fuels the overseas activities of U.S. pharmaceutical companies. Many of the active ingredients which serve the world market are manufactured overseas using knowledge generated in the United States. Molecules for some medicines can be manufactured most efficiently in a single plant. These are typically active ingredients with high activity relative to weight. A tiny amount will go a long way when formulated into tablets, capsules, and ointments. Other molecules are more readily made in numerous plants dispersed in proximity to final retail markets. Organically synthesized molecules are typical of this category. The newer biogenetically engineered molecules tend to be made in the United States, but could be produced elsewhere as well.

The manufacture of the basic active ingredients of medicines calls for simple inputs, usually readily available in most places. Such materials as soya flour, bone meal, oxygen, and various inert ingredients are used. The key to manufacturing active ingredients is usually the technique used to induce the growth of microbes or organic substances. Again, this is part of the specialized knowledge of the industry, for which intellectual property protection is vital.

Employment

Again, the relatively small size of the industry is reflected in the number of people employed. PMA member firms employed about 170,000 people in the United States in 1986, ranging from floor sweepers to Ph.Ds. Nearly 40 percent were production workers, about 27 percent were engaged in marketing, about 22 percent did research and development, and about 12 percent were devoted to administration, distribution and other activities.[9] It is clear that the proportion of highly skilled employees is very high compared to most other industries.

Research Expenditures

The PMA calculates that since the early 1940s the industry in the United States has spent over $36 billion on research and development of new products and has discovered over 1,100 new chemical entities.[10] The annual research and development expenditures by PMA member companies was expected to exceed $7 billion in 1989.[11] Their research and development investment has doubled every five years since 1970. The $7 billion expenditure exceeds funding for biomedical research by the National Institutes of Health and is far more productive in terms of new molecules. For 1986, the PMA reported that, of worldwide total research and development expenditures of $4.7 billion, about 18 percent was spent overseas, up from about 8 percent in 1970.[12]

Research targets, shifting over the years, have downgraded anti-infectives. Today treatment for cardiovascular disease draws top attention. New medical problems, chiefly HIV and AIDS, are also drawing considerable attention. The shift in research to chronic therapies has, among other things, increased the cost of research and development, principally because of the extended periods needed for clinical testing. The sharply increased requirements of the 1962 amendments to the Food, Drug and Cosmetic Act have also added to the elapsed time and costs of obtaining new drug approvals. The intensive employment of high technology methods in research, such as the use of theoretical molecules designed with computer assistance, have increased costs as well. The current elapsed time from invention to pharmacy shelf is in the range of seven to ten years[13] at a cost that can reach $125 million (1986 dollars).[14] In 1984, U.S. patent law was amended to extend by up to five years the life of a pharmaceutical patent to compensate for useful patent life lost due to the longer elapsed time for Food and Drug Administration (FDA) review of new products for safety and efficacy.

Protection and Subsidies

The United States grants little or no trade protection to its pharmaceutical industry. Tariffs are nominal to zero. Foreign companies can and do invest in research, manufacturing, marketing, and distribution activities in the United States. They must, as is true also for U.S. laboratories, satisfy FDA requirements, pay taxes, and treat employees in accordance with the law. There are no direct subsidies for

U.S. companies, or foreign companies either. In minor instances, funds from government sources are available for research. A few government procurement programs specify the purchase of U.S.-sourced goods and services, but these are not specifically designed for pharmaceuticals and would be open to foreign companies producing pharmaceutical products in the United States.

Social Importance of the Industry

The social importance of the pharmaceutical industry rests on its contribution to improved human health care. This is true throughout the world. Since World War II, a number of diseases have been eradicated or reduced to minor public health problems through vaccination. Diseases that once killed, such as tuberculosis and typhoid, are now rare or routinely treated. When doctors had only sulfa drugs to rely on, many people languished for extended periods in hospitals and other health care facilities. Today, the adjunctive therapy provided to the health care community by a wide and growing array of medicines has demonstrably reduced health care costs.

The achievements of modern medicine have been so remarkable they are now virtually taken for granted, so much so that the effort and cost of finding and developing new medicines seems to be overlooked in the popular mind. As a norm, the general population has come to assume new medicines will normally be quickly and readily available. This has made it easy to think that new medicines should cost less than they do. Generic medicines, those for which patent protection has expired or is not available, have sometimes been used as a measure of what medicines should cost. Resort to this benchmark ignores the knowledge content of a product since generic medicines, for the most part, usually reflect only direct production costs, which in this industry are relatively small.

There is, to take the analysis deeper, a shadow image of the pharmaceutical industry as a public utility. Although not regulated other than for product safety and efficacy, the public perceives the industry as in some sense responsible for performing a high public service. The industry in many ways plays that role voluntarily, as in the creation of orphan drugs for limited patient populations. This enhances that shadow image. Yet the industry is market driven and unregulated. Negative comment frequently arises from the friction between this shadow image and the market-oriented nature of the industry in the United States.

Frequently, in response to criticism that prices of medicines are too high, industry supporters say the industry must be allowed to recover its research costs. Industry representatives themselves often make this assertion. It carries the connotation that somewhere in the accounting department there is a box of old unpaid bills. It is certainly true that research costs are high in this industry. Yet the fact is that companies price their products in order to obtain funds for future research, which is the life-blood of the industry and the heart of competition. A theory of price limited to recovery of research costs is also misleading because price must cover the costs of failed research and the risks that a proven new medicine may be quickly displaced by a still newer medicine.[15]

Relations with Mexico

Proximity has not generated a unique relationship with Mexico in the pharmaceutical industry. But proximity may have created an interesting situation. Some of the earliest overseas manufacturing plants were built in Mexico by leading U.S. pharmaceutical companies before 1972. These plants were technologically equal to any found in the United States or Europe, although usually smaller. While built to serve the existing and future Mexican market, exports were also projected in their design capacity. The same was also true for plants built in Brazil, where proximity was less a factor.

In the early 1970s, Mexico took two steps that altered the business environment affecting these plants and pharmaceutical activity in general. The foreign investment law of 1973[16] and subsequent implementing decrees and regulations[17] prohibited the construction of wholly foreign-owned pharmaceutical facilities, while grand-fathering existing investment positions. The 1973 law change was foreshadowed by several years of administrative practice which had sought the same objective. Many foreign pharmaceutical laboratories set up their Mexican operations well before 1973 and held 100 percent ownership positions when the law changed.

At one point, this Mexicanization requirement for future activity even reached to the manufacture of a new molecule in an existing facility which was 100 percent foreign owned. Prior approval was required for this new activity, with approval contingent on reduction of foreign ownership of the facility to 49 percent or less. This amounted to a threatened de facto expropriation, which was not warmly received by U.S. companies. They complained that other companies which had not invested in basic plants in Mexico were better off than those which had made such investments.

The second action, which took effect in 1977, was the rather startling amendment of Mexico's Law on Inventions and Trademarks. Among other things, both process and product patent protection were completely eliminated. The patent term was shortened from 15 to 10 years; early lapse of the patent was fostered and non-voluntary disclosure of proprietary knowledge was mandated in conjunction with compelled licenses.

The Mexicanization investment rule and the weakening of protection for intellectual property did not achieve the purposes intended by Mexican officials. No new plants were built; expansion of existing plants was curtailed; modernization was severely limited; no new investment was made by either Mexican or U.S. interests; and research in Mexico did not advance.

Toward the end of President de la Madrid's administration, two steps were taken to partially reverse these earlier actions. First, the foreign investment authorities issued a revised mechanism dealing with plans to manufacture new pharmaceutical molecules in Mexico. The Mexicanization requirement was discarded in favor of an arrangement whereby a foreign company wishing to introduce a new product was given a limited period of time to signal an intent to manufacture locally. This freezes other actions by the government that might otherwise preclude that decision, such as a border closing, as had happened in the past.[18] The second restorative action came in the 1986 amendments to the Law on Inventions and Trademarks, which took effect early in 1987.[19] Among other things, patent protection was restored for the processes by which pharmaceutical products are made and transition arrangements were provided for full product protection in 1997. The term of the patent was extended to 14 years, the pernicious lapse provision was modified, and the mandatory disclosure of proprietary technical knowledge was dropped. Since then patent office authorities have usefully added regulations which provide mechanisms for enforcement of infringement actions and have, moreover, begun to use these mechanisms.[20] U.S. business lawyers have long noted the lack of effective enforcement mechanisms in Mexico, but the new regulations go a great distance to fill this gap.

The case of Pfizer's piroxicam, a non-steroidal, anti-inflammatory drug, illustrates the extreme case under the restrictive policies in force in the early 1980s. This product, which is marketed worldwide under the Pfizer trademark of Feldene, was introduced in Mexico by Pfizer utilizing imported active ingredients. The costs of introducing the product, including Ministry of Health product registration approval, local clinical trial work, advance information communicated to health care professionals, and marketing expenses, ran to about $3.2 million

over a three-year period. Once a franchise for piroxicam was
established, a local company approached the government claiming it
planned to manufacture the molecule locally. This eventually led to a
prohibition against Pfizer imports of its own active ingredient.
Concurrently, Pfizer requested permission to manufacture the active
ingredient locally in its existing basic plant. Permission was granted
but was conditioned on the requirement to reduce Pfizer's ownership of
its local company to 49 percent. Pfizer refused, claiming it was a de
facto expropriation. When its inventory ran out, it was no longer able to
supply the market and lost its franchise. Only then did the local
company and several others actively market their copies of Feldene.
Their local manufacture consisted of a relatively simple finishing step
in a multi-step manufacturing process.[21]

Transborder Ownership

Since the 1973 investment law changes, a limited number of joint
ventures have been formed, usually for a single molecule, where U.S.
firms have taken a 49 percent position. These ventures were forced by
the Mexicanization rules of the early and mid-1980s and are not the
preferred mode of doing business. As a result, some molecules have been
delayed before launch in Mexico. The recent investment rule changes
modify this picture.

Commercial Dealings

There have been scattered instances where U.S. companies have
licensed new products to Mexican companies for co-marketing. For the
most part, there is little commercial interplay between Mexican and
U.S. companies. Some of the basic manufacturing plants owned by the
U.S. companies produce active ingredients for other U.S. and foreign
companies. These active ingredients would be patent protected in the
United States and other developed countries. There may be some
instances where these plants produce active ingredients for Mexican
companies, but the more frequent practice is for the Mexican companies
to secure their active ingredients from pirate sources. These are
producers in countries like Argentina, Finland, Romania, and Bulgaria,
which have little or no pharmaceutical patent protection.

The dealings between U.S. parent companies and their Mexican
subsidiaries do not necessarily, or even frequently, involve direct
exports across the Rio Grande. When active ingredients are not
produced locally by the subsidiary, the ingredients are apt to be
obtained from a non-mainland U.S. source like Ireland or Puerto Rico,

which have attracted many worldscale plants because of favorable tax arrangements.

Technical assistance for the subsidiary is more likely to originate from the United States, although this support may be routed through an offshore company based in Bermuda, Panama, or elsewhere. It is typical to have a technical support agreement registered with the Mexican technology transfer registry. Most of these were first registered in the mid-1970s after passage of the first technology transfer law in 1973. Those agreements were limited to ten years and most of them were renewed for another ten years in the mid-1980s. They typically carried a royalty of 3 percent, although recently the registry has shown a greater degree of flexibility, with some agreements permitting a higher rate. The term of the agreements continues to be fixed for ten years, although here too the registry has shown flexibility in recent years. Administration of the technology transfer controls under the revamped law of 1982 has borne out the promise of its regulations of November 1982, reflecting growing registry appreciation of the realities of arms-length marketplace transactions.[22]

Pharmaceutical goods produced in finished form cannot be imported into Mexico. Thus, there are no such sales from the United States. In the reverse, medicines sold in the United States must be produced in FDA-approved facilities. Although it is possible that some Mexican plants may have secured FDA approval,[23] it is unlikely that many Mexican-made products have been sold in the United States. FDA approvals for foreign plants, where obtained, are for emergency use in the event of catastrophe in a U.S. plant.

The U.S. patent and trademark office has, from time to time, helped the Mexican patent office train patent examiners, but with the elimination of pharmaceutical patents in 1977 this came to a natural end for pharmaceutical examiners.

As protection is restored, cooperation between the two agencies is likely to resume in some fashion. The FDA and Mexican health authorities might be expected to cooperate in matters of common interest. Mexican health authorities could take note of U.S. decisions in approving or disapproving a new molecule, but the faster approval times characteristic of the European health authorities make them the more common point of reference.

Disease patterns in the two countries are different by reason of climate, general sanitation, housing, population, age profiles, diet, and public health resources. Still, there are areas for potential cooperation between the health care authorities of the two neighbors.

Possible Futures

The Research Race

The mounting pressure to conduct research dominates the pharmaceutical industry around the world today. A decreasing number of laboratories remain in the race. Several years ago, industry insiders speculated that only between 17 and 20 companies continued to conduct full-scale research. That number has diminished to perhaps 10 to 15 today. The shrinkage is both cause and effect of the mega-mergers now taking place in the industry. It is not uncommon for these major research-based laboratories to spend half a billion dollars a year on their research and development programs.

At the same time, a counter trend can be discerned. The advent of modern biotechnology, which permits the use of exotic new biological tools, has placed pharmaceutical research within the reach of small, even tiny, venture companies. Supported by venture capital, the newly emergent small company is gradually changing the face of the industry. Even for the major research-based companies, it is not possible to pursue all the leads which science is making available. The small companies can and do pick up the lead, each in its own niche.

In this setting, the large companies can, at any moment, find that a small company has eclipsed their research path. This is forcing the large companies to keep close track of the work of small companies. Technology strategies today call for a mix of internal research with a program of monitoring the advances of the tiny independent companies. For example, it is reported that Dow Chemical allocates a large portion of its research budget each year to acquisition of, or technological cooperation with, small companies.

The Generic Market

In both Mexico and the United States, by far the largest portion of the market is generic.[24] In the United States, only about 25 percent of sales are products which are under cover of a patent. In Mexico, about 12 percent to 15 percent of sales would be under patent cover were there full pharmaceutical patent protection. The balance of the sales is of products that are no longer under patent cover.

The size of the generic market is such that substantial business opportunity exists for non-research based companies, both Mexican and American. Naturally, the originating company has a pre-existing franchise when the patent expires, but there are many possibilities for others to then enter the market as demonstrated by experience in the U.S. market.

With a sizable population that cannot afford medicine at pharmacy prices, Mexico has made the political decision to provide health care, including medicine, at substantial price reductions. The cost to the government is large and growing as austerity grinds an already struggling population into greater distress.

The World Bank is supplementing International Monetary Fund efforts to help Mexico deal with its external debt burden and with structural adjustment. Could the World Bank finance the purchase of public health care medicine as a contribution to building infrastructure? This broadening of the conventional understanding of infrastructure was advocated some years ago, without success. It would be a method of providing useful assistance as Mexico adjusts its intellectual property protection regime. World Bank funds could be utilized by Mexican government health care providers and repaid in later decades out of general revenue when the Mexican economy returns to greater strength, as it surely will.

In Mexico, the government over the last decade has established a list of products from which government health care providers must select medicines for purchase. The list is almost exclusively composed of generic medicines. Mexican firms are given preference in supplying government needs. Since the decline of oil prices and the burden of external debt service has strained the Mexican economy, the ability of the population to purchase medicines privately has declined. This increased demand for government-supplied medicines is forcing the government to seek ever cheaper sources of supply. This in turn makes sales to government less attractive. However, the ratio of private to government markets appears likely to remain at the current two-thirds to one-third parity into the next decade.

Policy Issues

Patent Protection

Without adequate and effective protection for intellectual property, much that would probably otherwise evolve naturally in the relationship between the neighbors is unlikely to happen. There are two aspects to the intellectual property issue. One centers on patents, the other on trade secrets.

At present, full patent protection for pharmaceutical products is denied under Mexican law. This is scheduled to change in 1997. Even if the law changes as scheduled, it will protect only inventions made after the change. Since it takes up to ten years for an invention to reach pharmacy shelves, it will be a long time before patent protection becomes a factor in marketplace activity, unless special transition provisions are put into effect.

Since Mexico has determined that full patent protection benefits Mexico sufficiently to warrant reinstatement, it might be asked what Mexico gains by waiting until 1997. In the meantime, Mexican researchers are discouraged as they consider finding opportunities to enter a dynamic and constantly changing market.

Despite the proven ability of Mexican biotechnology researchers, the phenomenon of tiny companies developing unique new products through biotechnology will not gain prominence or even a foothold in Mexico under current conditions. Nor will technology alliances between U.S. companies and Mexican researchers. In-house research by both Mexican companies and Mexican subsidiaries of U.S. firms will not be done in Mexico. All this is Mexico's loss.

Trade Secrets

Something like two-thirds of all technology that is transferred from one place to another is conveyed by the vehicle of the trade secret.[25] Though not normally visible to the public because there is no public registry involved, the trade secret is the repository for detailed technical knowledge of how things get done. It is the workhorse of technology transfer.

Although Mexico's protection of the trade secret is in its infancy, encouraging signs of growth can be detected both in the 1987 amendments to the Law of Inventions and Trademarks[26] and in recent administrative actions. Trade secret protection is vital between the time a discovery is made and a patent application is filed, as well as in other situations.

A specific trade secret problem that affects the pharmaceutical industry, as well as others, arises when costly proprietary information is submitted to the Mexican regulatory authorities in support of applications to market a new product. Rather than treat this information as a trade secret, other companies are now permitted to benefit from this information, allowing them to register their copies of the new product without undertaking the costly and time-consuming effort needed to develop such information.

Both in bilateral discussions and in the Uruguay round of multilateral trade negotiations in the General Agreement on Tariffs and Trade, officials of the U.S. Trade Representative's office are pressing for improved protection of intellectual property in countries around the world. This gives focus to the policy issue of intellectual property. Because of weak protection for intellectual property, since 1985 Mexico and other countries have suffered the loss of trade benefits that would otherwise be available under the U.S. Generalized System of Preferences (GSP). Trade from Mexico, denied GSP benefits, has been running at an annual level of about $1 billion.[27] This is meant to heighten Mexico's awareness of its weaknesses in protecting intellectual property. One element of that weakness is the lack of product protection for pharmaceutical inventions.

On May 25, 1989, the U.S. Trade Representative, acting under the 1988 Trade Act amendments, placed Mexico on a priority watch list along with seven other countries. The watch list is meant to signal that serious trade action is being contemplated unless weaknesses in intellectual property protection are corrected. Mexican officials were stung by this listing, but continued to confer with trade officials.[28]

On November 1, 1989, the U.S. Trade Representative announced that three of the listed countries were being removed from this priority designation because of progress made by them toward better protection. Mexico was not among them, but some progress in the bilateral talks was apparently achieved because Section 301 action against Mexico was not initiated.

Mexican officials responsible for intellectual property protection policy are coming to recognize more clearly the internal economic development benefits which Mexico will gain from instituting comprehensive protection. In the Uruguay round of trade negotiations and in other settings, Mexican officials have spoken in favor of sound intellectual property protection. They have been criticized by officials of other Latin American governments for taking this position.

Within the next year or two, Mexico may find the political will to amend its intellectual property system, probably in a variety of ways, to institute comprehensive and sound protection. This is likely to include measures affecting the pharmaceutical industry.

The Decline of the Americas

After World War II, Latin America was viewed as a particularly attractive market area by many U.S. industries, including the pharmaceutical companies. Sizable investments were made in support of this view in Brazil, Mexico, and elsewhere. During the 1970s, the landscape changed, as legislative experiments altered the rules of the game for investment, technology, and intellectual property. The crisis of external debt which struck Mexico in early August 1982, and elsewhere within the next few months, has put a long shadow over Latin America. The decline of Latin America in its relative world position may continue even more as Eastern Europe and the Soviet Union open their economies.

Today, serious questions loom as to whether Latin American countries have the determination to restore their attractiveness for their own citizens and for foreign interests. Mexico shows signs of being able to accomplish this.

The decline of the Americas includes the United States. Under many relative measures, the United States is no longer dominant as in the past. This is quietly shifting the paradigm of Mexican-U.S. relations. The United States begins to need Mexico in new ways which Mexico is quicker to perceive than is the United States. Proximity may at last tell its tale as more things happen between the two neighbors.

A Possible Bilateral Pharmaceutical Future

In recent years, research by the pharmaceutical industry has been shifting to emphasis on chronic therapy for the elderly. The greatest return on investment is thought to come from these research targets. As research competition intensifies, the critical mass for a research-based company has risen in just the last few months from the range of $2 billion to $3 billion to over $5 billion in sales. Companies of this size will move ahead of others in the research race.

But as companies reach this size, a blockbuster new product will have less impact than it would have had in the past. Since blockbusters are scarce, research programs may shift direction in pursuit of an array of modest new molecules with therapeutic promise. Yet there are signs that large laboratories require large bureaucracies to function, with a probable cost to creativity. Moreover, science continues to provide more possibilities for applied research and even the largest laboratories are having difficulty keeping up.

At the same time, the major pharmaceutical companies have an advantage in two related fields. First, they have experience in getting new molecules from the laboratory to the market. They can manage the process of clinical trial work and regulatory approval. Second, they have large marketing forces in place and have an advantage in introducing and sustaining new products in markets worldwide.

These trends mean that the major laboratories, while investing more in research, will at the same time increasingly survey a lengthening list of smaller but more creative laboratories for promising new products which can be co-marketed. These small boutique laboratories will pursue niche research.

Except for the problem of intellectual property, there is no reason why Mexican boutique laboratories could not be successful in this new setting.[29] There are able Mexican researchers, undoubtedly of world class, already at work. There are niche areas in which Mexico could excel. These relate to natural substances and botanicals found uniquely in Mexico and to research derived from oil and corn technology.

Conclusions

Without institution of serious intellectual property protection by Mexico, there is probably little that either government can do to alter their pharmaceutical industry relationships. The U.S. patent office may be able to offer assistance to its Mexican counterpart in various ways, ranging from patent examination and training to data bank access.

Mexico's proximity to the United States could offer an advantage in fostering ties between Mexican and U.S. researchers, especially in biotechnology. It could foster ties to sources of U.S. capital, most probably in the large research-based U.S. laboratories. Improved intellectual property protection is a prerequisite.

There is some potential for more joint ventures between U.S. and Mexican companies. A precedent has recently been set by Merck. This company sold all or a controlling interest in its subsidiaries throughout Latin America to local pharmaceutical interests. This included the first such graceful exit from Mexico by an U.S. company.[30] The Merck precedent is being followed by other companies in Brazil and Argentina. Whether this new pattern will be followed by others in Mexico remains to be seen. It would be a relatively negative signal about the future of the foreign pharmaceutical companies in Mexico.

Broadening item 807 of the U.S. Customs treatment of *maquiladora* activity, i.e., payment of U.S. duty only on value added in Mexico, to include pharmaceutical formulation might be an interesting possibility for cross-border ties. It does not stretch concepts too far to describe the compounding of medicine as fitting *maquiladora* criteria.

Without a change in Mexican government policy, little will alter in the near future in the relative positions of industry in the two countries. Institution of pharmaceutical product patent protection in Mexico would, however, open the door to promising new possibilities.

Notes

1. *Statistical Fact Book*, Pharmaceutical Manufacturers Association, August 1988, p. 18.

2. *Statistical Fact Book*, 1988 Supplement, Chapter 1, "The Pharmaceutical Industry in the U.S.," Pharmaceutical Manufacturers Association. Also, *1988 Annual Report*, Pharmaceutical Manufacturers Association, pp. 7-14.

3. Ibid, p. 2.

4. *Statistical Fact Book*, Pharmaceutical Manufacturers Association, August 1988, p. 5.

5. *Wall Street Journal*, June 29, 1989, p. 1.

6. *1988 Annual Report*, Pharmaceutical Manufacturers Association, p. 4.

7. *Fortune Magazine*, April 25, 1988, p. D11.

8. *1988 Annual Report*, Pharmaceutical Manufacturers Association, p. 4.

9. *Statistical Fact Book*, 1988 Supplement, Chapter 1, Pharmaceutical Manufacturers Association, p. 21.

10. *Statistical Fact Book*, 1988 Supplement, Chapter 2, Pharmaceutical Manufacturers Association, p. 1.

11. *Washington Post* advertisement by the Pharmaceutical Manufacturers Association, July 1989. This is probably reliable since companies would be reporting their planned expenditures for the current year rather than estimates for a future year.

12. *Statistical Fact Book*, 1988 Supplement, Chapter 2, Pharmaceutical Manufacturers Association, p. 1.

13. *Statistical Fact Book*, 1988 Supplement, Chapter 2, Pharmaceutical Manufacturers Association, p. 5.

14. See Steven N. Wiggins, *The Cost of Developing a New Drug*, Pharmaceutical Manufacturers Association, 1987, mentioned in *Statistical Fact Book*, 1988 Supplement, Chapter 2, p. 7. To trace the journey from invention to pharmacy shelf see Frank H. Clarke, *How Modern Medicines are Discovered*, Futura Publishing Co., 1973.

15. The classic recent case is the challenge of Zantac (ranitidine) to Tagamet (cimetidine).

16. La Ley Para Promover la Inversión Mexicana y Regular la Inversión Extranjera, *Diario Oficial*, March 9, 1973. This shifted the rules of the game for equity.

17. Resolución General Sobre Nuevos Campos de Actividad Económica y Nuevas Lineas de Productos, *Diario Official*, September 6, 1977, p. 3 ff.

18. The Feldene incident illustrates this situation.

19. Decree of Reforms and Additions to the Law on Inventions and Trademarks, *Diario Oficial*, January 16, 1987.

20. I wish to thank the law firm of Camp & Einstein of San Antonio, Texas, for this information.

21. An illustration of the counterproductive policy of earlier Mexican administrations is found in the story of the barbasco root that Syntex harvested and exported. The government forced Mexicanization, driving Syntex out of Mexico and took over the barbasco business. Syntex research, however, was able to develop a synthetic substitute that replaced the Mexican natural substance. There are other versions of this episode, including one by Gery Gereffi.

22. For an early appraisal of the 1982 law and its regulations see Robert M. Sherwood, "Mexico's New Regulations: A Review of Difficulties with Application and Interpretation of Technology Transfer Controls," pp. 156-162, *les Nouvelles, Journal of the Licensing Executives Society*, Vol. 18, No. 3, September 1983.

23. For example, Pfizer has long maintained FDA approval for its basic manufacturing plant in Brazil but has never shipped product from there to the United States.

24. Within the pharmaceutical industry, the term generic can have two meanings, which causes confusion. In a country which has patent protection for pharmaceutical innovations, the term applies to the original and all copies thereof after the period of patent cover has ended. In a country with weak or non-existent patent protection, the term is often applied to products which copy original new products by taking advantage of the gaps in that patent system usually long before patent cover would expire were such cover available and effective. The term pirate products is sometimes used.

25. Based on preliminary results from a questionnaire being circulated to members of the Licensing Executives Society. See also Joel A. Bleeke and James A. Rahl, "The Value of Territorial and Field-of-Use Restrictions in the International Licensing of Unpatented Know-How: An Empirical Study," *Northwestern Journal of International Law & Business*, 1:450 (1979).

26. See Article 211(ix).

27. This total consists of losses from the statutory general review, the denial of requests for waivers and the annual review. The total varies from year to year, depending on the requests for waivers. Loss of the GSP benefit is, of course, not necessarily equal to loss of that amount of trade.

28. As part of a parallel mechanism, intellectual property is explicitly included in the list of topics to be dealt with under the bilateral Framework Agreement which now facilitates discussion of issues outstanding between Mexico and the United States.

29. Rumors circulate that Mexican researchers are making valuable discoveries of pharmaceutical importance but are bringing them to the United States for patenting and development. Similar departure patterns are discernible for Brazil.

30. There have been 18 exits from Brazil and only one from Mexico during the 1981–1988 period. None of them has been as graceful as the Merck exits in which joint marketing of Merck products by the surviving joint venture firm is undertaken. When a graceful exit is made, the foreign laboratory departs, but its products remain in the local market. The uncertainty is whether future new products will be introduced as originator companies withdraw from the markets. A wise strategy for Latin American countries might be to create conditions favorable to shifting from imitation to co-marketing. This entails favorable protection for innovation and conditions for marketing royalty payments. Co-marketing is emerging in Europe and the United States as a new trend.

Pharmaceuticals: Mexican Perspective

Enrique Gruner Kronheim

The pharmaceutical industry in Mexico has existed for at least 50 years. Many multinational firms became active in the market in the 1920s as representatives and distributors. However, until the 1940s, the majority of physicians still prescribed medicines that were tailored to individual patient's needs. As the pharmaceutical industry grew worldwide—essentially beginning in the 1930s with the development of penicillin, vitamins, hormones, sulfa drugs, etc.—the range of available products increased, and so did the viability of a domestic industry.

The first stage in the development of a domestic industry consisted of an assembly process based on the importation of nearly all inputs, including containers, caps, and medicines themselves. Mexican entrepreneurs dominated the field as representatives for foreign laboratories, mostly of European origin. The development of a global pharmaceutical industry led to the establishment of foreign laboratories in Mexico, many of which were interested not only in the distribution of their own products, but also in the acquisition of botanical raw materials that later became critical in the development of some products. In the early 1940s, several Mexican companies began to synthesize hormones based on Dr. Russell Marker's developments and discoveries in the field of dioscoreas. Mexico then became the source of almost all the steroids consumed on the world market, both as starting materials for further synthesis or as finished drugs.

Until the 1960s, except for the production of steroid hormones and a few relatively simple compounds, the industry consisted mainly of dosage form manufacturing. In the 1960s, the government program of industrialization by import substitution encouraged the development of a Mexican chemical industry to manufacture pharmaceutical drugs.

The first domestic antibiotic factories were born more or less simultaneously with the establishment of foreign companies like Pfizer and Lederle (American Cyanamid).

The relatively young nature of the industry worldwide and the availability of process technologies after World War II made possible the growth of domestic competition, in many instances with the assistance of Italian technologies. The rapid creation of new compounds and products and the obsolescence of older ones allowed nascent industries in Mexico to manufacture products somewhat less advanced than those in the international markets.

The domestic pharmaceutical industry now consists mostly of pharmochemical producers that have developed compounds based on some imported inputs. The domestic manufacturers produce their products using their own technologies, although some companies have simply produced foreign products by acquired process technologies. Mexico has been accused of pirating certain technologies, but the development of domestic technologies in Mexico was actually an evolutionary process that has been repeated in a number of countries around the world.

One example illustrates this parallel development quite clearly. Four major international laboratories own process patents for the manufacture of ampicillin. Each laboratory followed a technological process that added differing amounts of water to the ampicillin molecule. These formulas were virtually identical, but no one disputed the honesty of any of these four established laboratories. Each received separate process and product patents. However, when a Mexican firm developed a fifth way of producing the ampicillin compound, it was automatically accused of piracy.

Industry Structure

Internationally, the pharmaceutical industry is unlike most other industries. It is extremely oligopolistic in nature. Major multinational corporations dominate this highly integrated industry—a fact that differentiates it from most other industrial sectors. Additionally, the fact that the pharmaceutical industry has a direct and inherent relationship with the health of the population also makes it politically sensitive. Mexico's pharmaceutical industry is no exception. The industry structure has conditioned the manner in which it has evolved in Mexico and the industry has been a source of frequent trade-related disputes.

Two factors have, to a large extent, determined the evolution of the Mexican pharmaceutical industry—one relates to the nature of the industry and the second to the Mexican government's industrial policy. On the world market, the industry's extensive vertical integration has meant that most major companies manufacture their own drugs, which are then sold in dosage forms. This structure has significantly limited the access of potential competitors to the industry, because sheer vertical integration considerably limits the ability to develop a sourcing industry. Development is also severely restricted by the effect of patents. Thus, pharmaceutical development does not demonstrate the integration characteristics of the electronics and automotive sectors, in which those industries are closely allied with their worldwide counterparts.

Mexican governmental policy on the pharmaceutical (and chemical) industry has also limited the importation of inputs with the goal of fostering domestic substitution and industrialization of those inputs. Since the 1960s, this policy has led to the growth of a large chemical industry and to the licensing of technologies for drug production. The industry then sells its products to pharmaceutical laboratories, including foreign-owned subsidiaries, whose main activity in the country consists of marketing those products in finished dosage forms under their own brand names. The limited possibility of importing drugs causes the complementary process of production and distribution to flourish. In the case of subsidiaries of foreign laboratories, the system works because the parent companies are vertically integrated and manufacture those same drugs and often assign prices to them which bear no relationship to costs. Therefore, import liberalization would not increase competition, but would further concentrate the industrial processes of major international firms.

The pharmaceutical sector in Mexico is divided into two industries: the pharmaceutical industry itself, which produces and sells dosage forms, and the pharmochemical industry, which produces the basic drugs or active principles.

A total of 335 laboratories produce dosage forms, and 72 of them are foreign-owned subsidiaries of major international pharmaceutical firms, as Table 5.1 indicates. Only one of the laboratories is government-owned, although in the recent past it owned two other laboratories and had a minority participation in other firms. In 1988, total sales of finished drugs at ex-laboratory prices were 2.8 trillion pesos (about $1.25 billion), of which 80 percent went to the private market, while 20 percent were sales to government agencies. Foreign laboratories accounted for 70 percent of total sales and 79 percent of the private market sales, and national firms accounted for 30 percent of total sales and 65 percent of sales to the government market, as Table 5.1 also indicates.

TABLE 5.1 1988 Sales of Finished Pharmaceutical Products in Mexico

Sales	Mexican Pesos (millions)	Percent of Sales
Total sales (335 laboratories)	2,838,561	100.0
Foreign firms (72)	1,995,162	70.3
Mexican firms (263)	843,399	29.7
Private market	2,269,999	80.0
Government market	568,562	20.0
First 50 firms	2,168,067	76.4
39 foreign firms (20 USA)	1,790,535	63.1
11 Mexican firms	377,532	13.3
Next 20 firms	258,432	9.1
9 foreign firms (6 USA)	111,127	3.9
11 Mexican firms	147,305	5.2
Remaining 265 firms	412,062	14.5
22 foreign firms	93,500	3.3
243 Mexican firms	318,562	11.2
Private market		
Foreign firms	1,794,210	63.2
Mexican firms	475,789	16.8
Government market		
Foreign firms	200,952	7.0
Mexican firms	367,610	13.0

Source: Padron de la Industria Farmaceutica, Secretaría de Comercio y Fomento Industrial, 1989.

Major products, both for private and government markets, include anti-infectives (mainly antibiotics), as well as antiarthritics and analgesics. Most of these products were developed in the 1950s and 1960s and, thus, are product-patent free, even in the United States.

Mexico has a total of 90 pharmochemical firms, of which 35 are foreign owned. Total sales during 1988, including exports, amounted to 738 billion pesos ($328 million), of which the foreign-owned companies sold 36 percent.

The overall trade balance of the pharmaceutical sector has remained negative for Mexico during the last 10 years, even though it has diminished from $255 million in 1979 to $124 million in 1988.

The pharmochemical part of the industry imports basic materials (solvents, reagents) and intermediates to convert them to pharmaceutical compounds (active principles). They are sold mainly to local pharmaceutical laboratories and are also exported to other countries. The trade balance of this industry (exports less imports) has become positive, ranging from a deficit of $74 million in 1979 to a surplus of $40 million in 1988. The change came mainly from increased levels of exports, from $39 million to $118 million over the same period, while imports have remained practically unchanged.

The pharmaceutical industry manufactures the finished dosage forms of medicines using both locally acquired active principles and imported products. A small fraction of the imported products consists of finished dosage forms of very special products, such as anti-cancer drugs. The majority of the imports are active principles. The industry exports are finished dosage forms. The trade balance has remained in deficit from 1979 through 1988. The deficits ranged from $181 million in 1979 to $164 million in 1988. However, the negative trade balance during this period varied considerably, increasing to a maximum deficit of $219 million in 1981. This deficit was caused by an increase in imports of active principles, which probably resulted from the overvalued Mexican currency during that period. The actual figures of all the components of the sector's trade balance are shown in Table 5.2.

Integration with Counterpart U.S. Industry

Government policy in the pharmaceutical sector has aimed to satisfy three goals: 1) make available finished dosage forms in sufficient quality to satisfy the population's needs at a reasonable price; 2) to rationalize the industry by eliminating duplication and unnecessary products; and 3) to strengthen the country's independence by substituting for imports and promoting drug exports.

These goals have guided the development of the industry and of its specific components, such as the issuing of import permits. These policies did promote industry growth in general, but they also hindered a broader cross-national integration of the production processes. The industry structure and the existing installed capacity of U.S. pharmaceutical firms make it impossible for the industry to think about integration along traditional lines. U.S. firms could supply the Mexican market from their existing facilities, making the whole Mexican industry redundant. Thus, Mexican firms must think about potential avenues for joint production that would not entail the disappearance of the whole sector while satisfying the main aims of the Mexican government policy in this sector (see Table 5.3).

In the recent past, individual companies have made some efforts to integrate their markets across the border. In some products, such as ampicillin and amoxicillin, these processes have had major significance. They have enabled Mexico to become an important source

TABLE 5.2 Trade Balance (millions of U.S. dollars)

Item	1979	1980	1981	1982	1983	1984	1985	1986	1987	1988
Imports										
Finished medicines	6	23	23	9	7	6	9	5	7	11
Active drugs	201	203	256	208	120	143	196	130	148	193
Raw materials	113	91	57	47	49	49	71	74	80	78
Total imports	320	317	336	264	176	198	276	209	235	282
Exports										
Finished medicines	26	35	60	57	46	42	46	77	63	40
Active drugs	39	59	66	40	64	50	57	74	87	118
Total exports	65	94	126	97	110	92	103	151	150	158
Total trade balance	-255	-223	-210	-167	-66	-106	-173	-58	-85	-124
Pharmaceutical balance	-181	-191	-219	-160	-81	-107	-159	-58	-92	-164
Pharmochemical balance	-74	-32	9	-7	15	1	-14	0	7	40

Sources: Padron de la Industria Farmaceutica, Secretaría de Comercio y Fomento Industrial, 1989.

TABLE 5.3 Total Pharmaceutical Market 1988 (private and government).

First 10	800,596	Range 67,000 to 94,000 (28.2 percent)
Second 10	534,567	Range 43,000 to 66,000 (18.8 percent)
Third 10	378,446	Range 33,000 to 42,000 (13.3 percent)
Fourth 10	264,922	Range 23,000 to 32,000 (9.3 percent)
Fifth 10	189,536	Range 17,000 to 21,000 (6.7 percent)
Final 20	258,432	Range 10,000 to 17,000 (9.1 percent)
Total		2,838,561 million pesos

Source: Padron de la Industria Farmaceutical, Secretaría de Comercio y Fomento Industrial, 1989.

of these drugs for several markets. Industrywide, however, these incipient examples are marginal. They do, nevertheless, illustrate a potential avenue for long-term development.

The problems of integration are further aggravated by the reluctance of multinational firms to invest in Third World countries because of what they believe to be hostile government policies to the industry as a whole. While this perception may have some merit, the fact of the matter is that lack of investment by major multinationals strengthens the development of an isolated industry, creating a vicious cycle (see Tables 5.4 and 5.5). A stronger direct participation by multinationals in the production processes would breed intra-industry cooperation and would consolidate the basis for potential cross-national integration. Furthermore, direct manufacturing would reduce production costs, and would also eliminate one of the main sources of trade-related conflict between Mexico and the United States, namely, intellectual industrial property. The lack of access to the technologies and patents owned by multinational firms has been the main reason why the domestic industry has had to develop its own production technology and processes. Hence, the future of the industry will depend, to a large extent, on the evolution of these factors.

The Future

Whether domestic or foreign, the pharmaceutical industry is basically a commercial operation, and it requires technological skills which can either be acquired or developed. Few Mexican pharmochemical firms license their technologies from multinational pharmaceutical firms, largely because these multinationals are unwilling to release their technologies. Thus, at the outset, domestic pharmochemical firms often acquire their technology from so-called

TABLE 5.4 Nationality of Leading Worldwide Pharmaceutical Companies

Top 50 Companies (76.4 percent of total sales)	
Number/Country	Percent of Sales
20 USA	32.3
11 Mexican	13.3
7 German	14.1
3 Swiss	7.1
3 French	4.4
3 British	2.4
2 Italian	1.9
1 Swedish	0.9
Second Tier of 20 Companies (9.1 percent of total sales)	
11 Mexican	5.2
6 USA	2.6
2 Dutch	0.8
1 German	0.5

Source: Padron de la Industria Farmaceutica, Secretaría de Comercio y Fomento Industrial, 1988.

pirate companies in Italy, Spain, Hungary, and other countries. Over the years, many of the Mexican firms have been able to develop their own technologies and to use them to compete both on the domestic and international markets. Most of these Mexican manufacturing processes are for traditional or generic products that are patent-free, and that constitute more than 90 percent of the medicines used in Mexico.

The great dividing point in the Mexican pharmochemical industry is between firms that pirate their technologies and those that have developed their own processes. Those that develop their own processes can master the production of fine chemicals, and, at least theoretically, can compete head-on with multinational firms in world markets. Those companies dependent on pirate technologies cannot produce such reliable chemicals, and remain essentially merchants of pharmochemical products. Roughly 40 percent of the Mexican pharmochemical industry consists of firms that develop their own technologies.

The future of the pharmochemical industry in Mexico will depend upon both technological breakthroughs worldwide as well as on the potential for market expansion. Biotechnological developments are

TABLE 5.5 U.S. Companies Operating in Mexico

Abbott[a]	Pfizer[a]
Baxter	Rorer
Bristol[a]	Robbins
Carter Wallace	Schering Corp.[a]
Cyanamid[a]	Searle
Cilag (J + J)	SKF[a]
Gelcaps	Squibb
ICN	Sterling-Sidney Ross
Janssen[a]	Syntex[a]
Lilly	Upjohn[a]
Mead-Johnson[a]	U.S.V.-Grossman
Miles[a]	Warner Lambert
Norwide-Eaton	Wyeth

[a] These companies also have pharmochemical activities.

Source: Author's compilation.

expected to bring on a new cycle of technological innovation in the industry. Market expansion can come only from exports. As a result, the Mexican pharmochemical industry faces a clear-cut dilemma: it can either isolate itself within a protected domestic market or seek to integrate into that portion of the international arena in which industrialized nations' patents do not restrict it. On the domestic level, this dilemma is further complicated by a need to offer the Mexican population both traditional and modern products that are priced affordably.

Given the unsustainable nature of a completely isolated industry, there is a need to develop strategies that could offer alternatives for attaining both the national goals as well as integration into world markets. Integration will occur in part as a byproduct of the increasing activity of multinational firms in the domestic market under new and less restrictive foreign investment regulations. Also, a new law for product patents that becomes effective in 1997 will restrict domestic manufacturing of products that do not have licensing agreements. The resulting environment will either foster joint ventures, specialization agreements and production for third parties of products such as generics, or it will kill the industry as a result of market restrictions and imports. In theory, this is the same dilemma that other Mexican industries face under changing trade laws, but the politically sensitive nature of the pharmaceutical industry will undoubtedly force active government participation in the organization and composition of the industry as a whole.

Greater access to foreign markets and gradual integration of the production processes in this industry would reduce trade conflicts arising from the special nature of this sector, while at the same time allowing for the development of a competitive and complementary industry in Mexico. This kind of evolution would foster creativity and innovation in an industry that has made significant technological advances. Furthermore, it would constitute a sound basis for free trade in which the pharmaceutical industries of both the United States and Mexico would be competitive but healthy and thriving.

SIX

Textiles

Textiles: Mexican Perspective

Ovidio Botella C., Enrique García C., José Giral B.

The United States plays a large role in the Mexican textile and clothing trade both as an export market and as a supplier to Mexican factories. The dynamics of this relationship are changing, however, as U.S. protectionism grows and Mexican protectionism diminishes.

Mexican protectionism has inhibited the growth of domestic competition, which has in turn given the domestic market characteristics that vary drastically from the U.S. market. Certain sectors of the Mexican textile industry are highly concentrated, and, although Mexico can boast of state-of-the-art technology in the production of some manmade fibers, Mexico's technology lags behind that in other countries in the production of cotton and certain other fibers. A lack of competition has particularly affected retail sales techniques, which are less aggressive than in the United States.

With the opening of Mexican markets, these industry characteristics will change. The industry must improve its competitive position both to retain its domestic market and to expand into the world market. Clothing exports, which already provide a significant portion of the revenue in textiles, should play a substantial role in any future market strategy.

Textiles have provided some clear benefits to the Mexican and international economies. The industry provides a number of much-needed jobs for unskilled labor in Mexico, although the number of these jobs is likely to drop as the industry continues to modernize its equipment. Because Mexican labor is relatively inexpensive, foreign corporations with textile investments in Mexico have also profited. But the contribution of textiles fluctuates considerably with the ups and downs in the Mexican economy. Currently, the industry contributes 6.8 percent of the manufacturing sector's GDP and 2 percent of the national

GDP. As Table 6.1 indicates, the industry's percentage of GDP dropped dramatically in 1982 and 1983 with the onset of the nation's economic crisis, and fell again in 1986.

Table 6.2 indicates the Mexican textile industry is sensitive to consumer income fluctuations. The industry was progressing quite successfully until the beginning of the 1980s, when per capita consumption of textiles dropped from 6.47 kilograms to 5.51 kilograms, in response to the drop in per capita income. The United States, by comparison, has maintained fiber consumption of about 20.2 kilograms per person.

In the textile industry, the link between product demand and final consumer demand is a tenuous one because textiles serve both as intermediate and final products. In any industry, costs and relative cost advantages stem from the value added to individual sectors. The textile industry is highly integrated with a progressive chain of added values. Thus, the competitive advantage of the end product can be seriously affected by intermediate stages of production.

The textile industry can be broken down into five integral parts. The first is the fibers production sector, which can be separated into subcategories for natural and manmade products. Natural fibers include cotton, wool, jute, and hard fibers. Manmade or synthetic fibers can be divided into cellulosic and non-cellulosic fibers. The creation of fibers adds 15 percent of value to the raw inputs of the industry.

Spinning is the second productive sector of the textile industry. This sector includes the preparation, opening, carding, drawing, and spinning of fibers. This sector adds another 15 percent value to textile products.

TABLE 6.1 Key Indicators for the Mexican Textile Industry
(millions of U.S. dollars)

Indicator	1980	1981	1982	1983	1984	1985	1986	1987	1988
GDP growth rate (%)	8.3	8.8	-0.6	-4.2	3.6	2.6	-4.0	1.4	1.1
Weave/spin soft fibers	1,810	1,882	1,723	1,691	1,709	1,789	1,667	1,694	1,788
Weave/spin hard fibers	261	264	268	248	220	197	225	205	226
Other textiles	608	641	609	588	592	633	611	637	656
Clothing	1,899	1,996	1,890	1,846	1,837	1,844	1,737	1,620	1,561
Industry	4,578	4,783	4,490	4,373	4,358	4,463	4,240	4,156	4,231

Sources: Compiled using Asociación Nacional de Industrias Químicas and Canaintex data.

TABLE 6.2 Basic Economic Indicators for Mexico

Indicator	1980	1981	1982	1983	1984	1985	1986	1987	1988
Population (thousands)	69,383	71,249	73,122	74,980	76,791	78,524	80,300	81,748	82,839
GDP (U.S. current $, millions)	166,700	238,960	171,270	145,130	171,300	177,360	127,140	141,940	176,700
GDP per capita (current U.S. $)	2,090	2,250	2,270	2,240	2,040	2,080	1,860	1,830	1,760
Textile GDP (%)	2.4	2.3	2.2	2.2	2.1	2.1	2.1	2.0	2.0
Fiber consumed (tons)	449,176	437,570	388,703	362,210	381,462	443,306	390,658	434,265	456,456
Fiber consumed (kg/capita)	6.47	6.14	5.32	4.83	4.97	5.65	4.86	5.31	5.51

Sources: Compiled using Banco de México, Asociación Nacional de Industrias Químicas, Canaintex, and World Bank data.

The third sector is fabric manufacturing, which can be divided into weaving, knitting, and tufting. This sector also includes the manufacture of non-woven fabrics. This part of the productive cycle adds another 20 percent to the product value.

Fabric finishing is the fourth productive sector, which can be separated into dyeing, printing and the actual product finishing. This generates another 15 percent in product value.

The final sector is clothing manufacturing, which is divided into cutting and sewing. This portion of the textile industry adds the greatest value—35 percent.

The end uses of textiles can be divided into six general categories: clothing; household uses; carpets; industrial applications; tire manufacture; and other miscellaneous uses. Each productive sector generates products that have many end users. A 1988 survey of the *Economist Intelligence Unit* indicated that in the Western European industrial textile market, medical hygiene captured a 22 percent share, packaging 20 percent, and ropes, nets, etc. a 15 percent share. But some of the less-penetrated areas, notably filter cloth and military and protection products suggest some future market possibilities. The *Economist* survey indicated that filter cloth captured only three percent of the industrial textile market, military products and protection products two percent each, and composites one percent.[1]

Worldwide, the textile industry has been a labor intensive one, a factor which is paralleled in the Mexican market. Textiles provide 770,000 relatively low-skilled jobs in Mexico. The majority of the jobs, 77.5 percent, are generated in the clothing sector, which includes about 35,000 *maquiladora* jobs. One of the most attractive pulls to foreign corporations in the *maquiladora* industry is inexpensive labor. Overall, Mexico's labor costs in the textile industry were only 83 cents per hour in early 1987, according to Werner International. This represented less than a tenth of the labor cost in the U.S. textile industry. Labor costs were lower than in Hong Kong and South Korea. However, despite lower labor costs, hours of operation in the Mexican textile industry are less than working hours in the Far East.

Outside of clothing, few jobs are generated in Mexican textiles. Spinning provides 10 percent of the jobs, weaving 8 percent, fibers 2.5 percent and finishing 2 percent.

Technology

Changes in technology have revolutionized the methods used throughout the world for processing fibers as well as fiber composition. These technological developments increasingly call for more sophisticated and expensive processing equipment that has begun to cut down on the amount of labor needed in fiber processing. The labor saving comes from improvements in mechanical efficiency. These improvements also allow Mexico to respond to changing market demands without drastic increases in unit costs.

The Mexican textile industry reflects both traditional processing methods as well as more modern ones. In general, manmade fibers are manufactured with equipment and technology equivalent to those used in developed nations, except for some lines of extrusion/spinning of polyester and nylon. The cotton spinning process also boasts the latest technology, but most manufacturing plants are too small to be cost-efficient. As a rule of thumb, equipment suppliers use a 15,000-spindle plant as the minimum size to provide a cost-efficient operation. Table 6.3 gives an overview of the equipment used in the Mexican textile industry. Table 6.4 indicates how much machinery has been imported since 1980 to meet the industry's needs.

Despite its name, the wool spinning process uses primarily manmade fibers, particularly acrylics. Wool production is a very small part of the Mexican textile industry. Raw wool inputs come from Australia and New Zealand, and wool tops come from Argentina and Uruguay. Although wool production is only a marginal part of textile production in Mexico, intensive investments in this sector in the late 1970s provided machinery, technology, and large plants equivalent to those found in the world market.

The weaving and knitting processes also use technology and equipment equivalent to the technology and equipment used in more developed nations. About 45,000 relatively new looms exist in Mexico, making the nation competitive on world markets. In knitting, with the exception of large diameter, circular looms and full-fashion looms, the machinery and technology are competitive with those in developed nations. The knitting sector is highly sensitive to fashion changes, and it must react quickly to these changes to remain competitive.

The machinery and technology used in the carpet industry is also comparable to those used around the world. The majority of Mexican carpeting—95 percent—is made by the tufting process, which is also used in the United States. This is a sector in which plant size is relatively large, but the sector is nevertheless marked by a low level of capacity utilization.

The weakest links in the Mexican textile productive chain are the dyeing and finishing sectors. They have rather old machines—the average age of dyeing and finishing equipment is about 20 years. This sector is in a weak competitive position, which explains why Mexican fabric exports are generally in raw form. The obsolescent machinery restricts fabric width and uses the batch process instead of the continuous process. The result is high production costs because so many chemicals are wasted and energy is used inefficiently. On the other hand, the printing machinery is newer—only about 10 years old. Nevertheless, the printing machinery can handle only about 20 percent of fabric output.

TABLE 6.3 Units of Operating Machinery

Sector	1984	1985	1986	1987	1988
Spinning					
Spindlers	3,293,117	3,427,373	3,494,476	3,570,242	3,586,126
Rotors	29,993	33,273	34,694	39,638	45,782
Total	3,323,110	3,460,646	3,529,170	3,609,880	3,631,908
Texturized	898	900	941	941	947
Weaving	40,319	46,698	43,832	44,857	45,161
Knitting					
Flat knitting	4,451	4,561	4,303	4,348	4,432
Full fashion	184	181	162	161	159
Cir.: large/med.	6,611	6,585	6,059	6,151	6,299
Socks	7,968	7,945	7,873	7,921	7,993
Stockings	4,112	4,169	4,332	4,330	4,431
Raschel	938	947	1,086	1,081	1,090
Tricot	1,065	1,024	1,052	1,065	1,088
Total	25,329	25,412	24,867	25,057	25,492
Narrow fabrics					
Braid	12,329	12,341	12,451	12,703	12,939
Laces	3,097	3,185	3,417	3,533	3,533
Total	15,426	15,526	15,868	16,236	16,472
Tufting	133	133	110	113	113
Spindlers and rotors					
Cotton	1,765,154	2,401,865	2,403,689	2,470,400	2,452,240
Wool	166,794	115,045	114,434	116,949	119,097
Manmade fiber	1,361,169	910,463	976,353	982,893	1,014,789
Total	3,293,117	3,427,373	3,494,476	3,570,242	3,586,126
Looms					
Cotton	13,150	18,116	17,458	18,393	18,559
Wool	1,393	920	1,110	1,086	1,079
Manmade fiber	25,776	27,662	25,264	25,378	25,523
Total	40,319	46,698	43,832	4,857	45,161

Source: Canaintex, 1989.

TABLE 6.4 Textile Machinery Imports (thousands of U.S. dollars)

Type	1980	1981	1982	1983	1984	1985	1986	1987	1988
Preparatory	12,222	9,975	948	1,474	3,195	209	12,309	14,451	26,358
Ring-frames	32,283	33,529	18,340	814	208	10,337	11,359	9,882	18,507
Winders	22,826	24,964	19,194	1,250	1,770	6,319	3,785	5,441	2,476
Twisters	14,634	21,930	8,682	544	720	1,131	4,049	1,568	5,039
Weaving machines	50,966	71,649	54,529	6,838	5,685	24,293	34,791	8,200	69,235
Knitting machines	44,393	36,858	28,985	2,441	5,270	16,209	11,592	12,395	30,554
Dyeing/finishing	31,878	36,128	26,380	2,773	10,824	5,650	11,693	8,700	16,261
Other	78,940	105,528	52,446	6,258	26,971	35,068	10,221	5,089	11,243
Total	288,142	340,561	209,504	22,392	54,643	99,216	99,799	65,726	179,673

Source: Canaintex, 1989.

At the end of the textile chain is clothing, which contributes almost as much to the gross domestic product as the processes of spinning and weaving of soft fibers. Clothing production is a relatively easy process, but one that is labor intensive. Its costs are divided almost equally between raw material inputs (fabrics, threads and accessories) and the cost of labor for cutting and sewing. Because it is labor intensive, the manufacture of clothing has a strong cost-competitive position because Mexico's wages are relatively low. Although sewing machine speeds have steadily increased, this provides only a slight cost reduction.

Because of rising competition from textile imports, mostly from developing countries, developed countries are responding by combining technological innovation with increased market awareness. The main source of technological innovation is in machinery and equipment, thus making machinery age a good indicator of the technological level that the textile industry has reached in any country. Textile companies are investing heavily in these areas and their investments, particularly in processing speed, are transforming textile and clothing production.

Mexico has one of the largest installations of spinning and weaving machinery in the Americas. Its industry has also been upgrading over the past 10 years at a rate faster than the world average in short and long staple and open-end rotors.

The level of technology can vary substantially according to each sector of Mexico's textile industry. Mexico had 2.2 percent of the world's short staple spindles in 1985 but only 0.5 percent of the more advanced open rotors.

Advances in machine speed are increasing productivity in the manufacture of staple yarn. The rotor spinning technology is the most significant innovation in this area, although newer technologies, such as open end, air jet, and friction spinning processes are now challenging the rotor spinning process. For filament yarn, texturizing speeds are increasing.

In weaving, Mexico's cotton processing machinery compares well with international weaving industry standards. Wool processing also fares well against the standard technology used in developed nations, although in wool weaving the rate of equipment replacement has fallen behind the world average. Mexico has 1.6 percent of the world's shuttle looms and 2.7 percent of the shuttleless looms.

The speed increases in the weaving process come from the development of three types of shuttleless looms: projectile, rapier, and air and water jet looms. The knitting sector has also developed new high-speed machines with outputs that are three times faster than those of older machines. Cheaper synthetic fibers and low-fault rates also contribute to the high output. The carpet industry increased its speed through the tufting process.

Production of non-woven fabric—those made directly from fibers rather than from yarn—has also had a significant impact on the Mexican textile industry. In the United States and other developed nations, demand for this type of textile has grown steadily since the early 1970s. There are three processes of non-woven fabric production: dry laid, wet laid, and spunbonded. The newest one, spunbonded, is growing while the other processes are declining in use. A 1988 survey of the *Economist Intelligence Unit* predicted that the market share for dry laid would decline from 50 percent in 1985 to 45 percent in 1990, wet laid from 12 percent to 10 percent in the same period, while spunbonded would grow from 38 percent to 45 percent. These figures included needlefelt for carpets.[2]

Important innovations have also taken place in finishing and dyeing techniques, in the developing of new dyes, creation of new finishes like permanent press, and in continuous and semi-continuous processes. Significant advances have also taken place in the pre-assembly stage with the use of new cutting devices involving numerical control and laser or water jet technologies.

Fiber Consumption

Mexico's consumption habits are, to some extent, a reflection of consumption habits in developed countries. Like U.S. consumers, Mexico's consumers are influenced by the development of new products, relative prices, and changes in technology.

But some anomalies exist in Mexico's consumption habits. Third World countries generally consume substantially fewer manmade fibers than do developed nations. In Mexico, however, manmade fibers represent an unusually high proportion of the total—62.3 percent. This anomaly may be explained by Mexico's proximity to the United States, or the explanation could lie in Mexico's internal per capita income disparities, which permit a relatively high proportion of the population to have the purchasing habits of a population in a more developed country. Tables 6.5 and 6.6 demonstrate Mexico's consumption of imported and domestic fibers.

As we can see in Tables 6.7 and 6.8, cotton and polyester are the most utilized fibers, followed by acrylics. Cotton leads the market despite the losses it has suffered in market share. Its strength lies in its low price, which results from oversupply. But cotton is also popular because people like the feel of the fiber, its absorbency, and its ability to accept flame retardant finishes.

TABLE 6.5 Ratio of Imported Fibers to Consumption (percentages)

Fiber	1980	1981	1982	1983	1984	1985	1986	1987	1988
Cotton	0.0	0.0	0.0	0.9	0.0	11.1	18.6	0.0	3.3
Wool	100.0	100.0	100.0	100.0	100.0	100.0	100.0	100.0	100.0
Natural	4.2	4.9	4.6	4.6	4.4	16.2	22.4	3.9	7.0
Rayon yarn	2.9	2.2	0.3	2.0	0.7	1.0	1.8	1.6	0.9
Rayon staple[a]	27.5	29.6	49.5	100.0	100.0	100.0	100.0	100.0	100.0
Acetate yarn	0.5	0.6	0.0	0.0	0.0	0.0	0.0	0.0	1.3
Acetate staple & tow	0.0	0.0	0.0	0.0	0.0	0.1	0.1	0.0	0.4
Cellulosics	12.2	16.0	19.4	16.9	26.7	32.9	27.4	31.1	53.1
Nylon yarn	12.2	5.8	3.2	0.8	0.9	1.6	3.0	2.6	2.6
Nylon staple	14.7	13.5	30.3	4.3	9.9	10.7	12.4	18.7	23.4
Polyester yarn	3.1	2.3	1.6	0.3	0.7	0.7	0.8	1.0	3.7
Polyester staple	3.5	3.8	3.4	1.9	0.2	1.0	4.6	1.8	6.5
PPP yarn & staple[b]	1.6	8.8	2.2	5.4	4.2	22.6	52.6	49.0	28.2
Acrylic staple[c]	3.3	1.7	0.5	0.1	0.1	0.3	0.1	0.9	0.8
Non-Cellulosics	4.6	3.3	2.4	0.8	0.6	1.3	3.6	2.9	4.4
Total Synthetic	5.6	4.7	4.3	2.0	2.5	3.8	5.4	4.6	7.0
OVERALL TOTAL	5.0	4.8	4.4	2.9	3.2	8.2	11.7	4.4	7.0

[a]No production in Mexico since 1983. Imports come from the United States.
[b]Polypropylene staple imports in recent years are for non-woven use.
[c]Mexico exports acrylic staple to the United States.

Source: Canaintex, 1989.

TABLE 6.6 U.S. Manmade Fiber Imports for Mexican Consumption (tons and percent imports to consumption)

Product	1987		1988	
Cellulosic yarn, monofil and strips	269	1.5%	335	1.8%
Non-cellulosic yarn, monofil and strips	8,504	6.8%	8,090	7.0%
Non-cellulosic staple and tow	8,972	4.3%	3,169	1.5%
Total	17,744	5.0%	11,594	3.3%

Source: Textile Organon, 1989.

Acrylics also perform well in the Mexican market, particularly when compared to polyester. Wool remains a relatively little-used fiber in Mexico.

Over the years, the market share of natural and manmade fibers as well as the share of synthetics and cellulosic fibers have changed dramatically. Availability and the price of raw materials are the principal factors in the changing market.

Domestic Markets

The Mexican textile industry traditionally focused its commercialization on the domestic market, which flourished under the protectionism of the post-World War II import-substitution industrialization approach that preceded President Miguel de la Madrid. Today, in light of the shrinkage and opening of the Mexican economy, the textile industry must improve its competitive position both to preserve its domestic market and to expand into foreign markets.

Currently, there is little sense of competition in domestic retailing, where margins and credit costs are high. The credit cost reflects another major problem of the industry; the high cost of finance affects all links in the textile production chain.

More than 50 percent of textiles are sold in small stores grouped in specific clusters in the big cities. Lagunilla and Correo Mayor are frontrunners in Mexico City. Palacio de Hierro and Liverpool lead in department store retailing. In discount store sales, Aurrera's Suburbia, Comercial Mexicana and Fabricas de Francia are leaders, and all but Aurrera are Mexican owned. Aurrera has 50 percent U.S. ownership.

In general, Mexico has no aggressive bargain sales, as does the United States, and no distinct fashion seasons. These differences are exacerbated by poor inventory control and a lack of an organized supply system.

TABLE 6.7 Fiber Consumption in Mexico (tons)

Fiber	1980	1981	1982	1983	1984	1985	1986	1987	1988
Cotton	169,800	163,240	138,920	121,200	137,310	149,730	138,690	149,500	158,400
Wool	7,474	8,321	6,658	4,699	6,367	9,162	6,919	6,085	6,315
Natural	177,274	171,561	145,578	125,899	143,677	158,892	145,609	155,585	164,715
% Share	39.5	39.2	37.5	34.8	37.7	35.8	37.3	35.8	36.1
Rayon yarn	5,454	5,397	4,379	2,969	1,932	2,310	2,296	2,407	2,149
Rayon staple	14,908	14,992	10,441	2,795	4,603	7,280	4,902	5,346	8,018
Acetate yarn	9,184	8,373	6,547	5,780	5,803	7,012	6,564	5,617	5,414
Acetate staple/tow	5,785	6,610	5,298	5,313	4,926	5,590	4,277	3,937	3,974
Cellulosic	35,331	35,373	26,665	16,857	17,263	22,192	18,039	17,306	19,555
% Share	7.9	8.1	6.9	4.7	4.5	5.0	4.6	4.0	4.3
Nylon yarn	33,936	30,907	29,936	25,423	25,293	28,801	23,283	23,867	22,861
Nylon staple	2,345	4,509	4,066	2,744	3,046	3,417	2,307	2,405	1,920
Polyester yard	89,179	78,058	71,927	67,767	70,794	80,497	59,458	66,505	61,922
Polyester staple	44,082	47,770	46,549	57,619	55,955	68,675	66,043	83,946	93,407
PPP yarn & staple	5,852	5,920	4,323	4,406	4,307	5,547	6,948	7,411	6,391
Acrylic staple	61,177	63,474	59,659	61,496	61,128	75,285	68,971	77,241	85,685
Non-cellulosic	236,571	230,638	216,460	219,455	220,522	262,222	227,010	261,375	272,186
% Share	52.7	52.7	55.7	60.6	57.8	59.2	58.1	60.2	59.6
Total Synthetic	271,902	259,400	243,125	236,312	237,785	284,414	245,049	278,680	291,741
OVERALL TOTAL	449,176	437,570	388,703	362,210	381,462	443,306	390,658	434,265	456,456
Change Rate		-2.6	-11.2	-6.8	5.3	16.2	-11.9	11.2	5.1

Sources: Compiled using Asociación Nacional de Industrias Químicas and Canaintex data.

TABLE 6.8 Fiber Consumption In Mexico (percentages)

Fiber	1980	1981	1982	1983	1984	1985	1986	1987	1988
Cotton	37.8	37.3	35.7	33.5	36.0	33.8	35.5	34.4	37.7
Wool	1.7	1.9	1.7	1.3	1.7	2.1	1.8	1.4	1.4
Natural	39.5	39.2	37.5	34.8	37.7	35.8	37.3	35.8	36.1
Rayon yarn	1.2	1.2	1.1	0.8	0.5	0.5	0.6	0.6	0.5
Rayon staple	3.3	3.4	2.7	0.8	1.2	1.6	1.3	1.2	1.8
Acetate yarn	2.0	1.9	1.7	1.6	1.5	1.6	1.7	1.3	1.2
Acetate staple & tow	1.3	1.5	1.4	1.5	1.3	1.3	1.1	0.9	0.9
Cellulosics	7.9	8.1	6.9	4.7	4.5	5.0	4.6	4.0	4.3
Nylon yarn	7.6	7.1	7.7	7.0	6.6	6.5	6.0	5.5	5.0
Nylon staple	0.5	1.0	1.0	0.8	0.8	0.8	0.6	0.6	0.4
Polyester yarn	19.9	17.8	18.5	18.7	18.6	18.2	15.2	15.3	13.6
Polyester staple	9.8	10.9	12.0	15.9	14.7	15.5	16.9	19.3	20.5
PPP yarn & staple	1.3	1.4	1.1	1.2	1.1	1.3	1.8	1.7	1.4
Acrylic staple	13.6	14.5	15.3	17.0	16.0	17.0	17.7	17.8	18.8
Non-cellulosics	52.7	52.7	55.7	60.6	57.8	59.2	58.1	60.2	59.6
Total synthetic	60.5	60.8	62.5	65.2	62.3	64.2	62.7	64.2	63.9
OVERALL TOTAL	100.0	100.0	100.0	100.0	100.0	100.0	100.0	100.0	100.0

Sources: Compiled using Asociación Nacional de Industrias Químicas and Canaintex data.

Productivity and quality grew steadily in textiles through the mid-1970s, but lost momentum as the 1980s neared. From 1977 through 1981, the growing middle class in Mexico demanded increasing supplies of textiles, and to supply this demand the industry sacrificed quality and productivity in exchange for sheer growth.

The domestic market grew until 1982 without serious competition. Quality continued to decline and protectionism created a pyramiding of costs. Historically, manmade fibers were priced higher in Mexico than in other countries, despite Mexico's competitive advantages in low costs for energy and raw materials manufactured from petrochemicals. Table 6.9 gives an example of the cost problem associated with protectionism.

Export Markets

The United States dominates the Mexican textile and clothing foreign trade, not only as an export market, but also as a supplier. More than three-fourths of Mexico's textile exports go to the U.S. market. The United States supplies 90 percent of Mexico's textile imports. Unlike Brazil, Mexico runs a trade deficit with the United States in textile trade, reflecting, in part, the importance of the *maquiladora* operation. Mexico's second largest textile supplier is Japan, with less than 4 percent of the total.

By contrast, Mexico has a strong surplus with the United States in its clothing trade—more than 98 percent of all Mexican clothing exports go to the United States. Tables 6.10 and 6.11 provide data on this

TABLE 6.9 Mexico-U.S. Textile Cost Ratios

Material	Ratio	Comment
Raw materials	0.70 to 1.15	Pemex subsidies represented 30 percent
Fibers	1.20 to 1.50	Basic quality comparable. No new products.
Yarns	1.25 to 1.60	Little innovation.
Fabrics	1.40 to 2.00	Adequate.
Finishing	1.50 to 2.50	Poor quality, obsolete products.
Cutting and sewing	0.30 to 0.50	Labor costs 0.1 corrected by inefficiency.
Retail margins	1.60 to 3.00	Lack of competition and market demand.
Final prices of garments or linen	1.15 to 2.50	

Sources: Compiled using DuPont, Akra, Celanese, and Cydsa data.

TABLE 6.10 U.S. General Imports of Manmade Fiber Apparel
(millions of square yards equivalent and percentage)

Indicator	1985		1986		1987	
From Mexico	81	2.7%	75	2.2%	91	2.7%
U.S. Total	3,011	100.0%	3,419	100.0%	3,389	100.0%

Source: Organization for Economic Cooperation and Development, *Foreign Trade by Commodities*, 1989.

trade. But Mexico also imports a substantial amount of clothing from the United States.

Aside from the U.S. market, Mexican exports failed to grow in the early 1980s. In 1983, for example, Mexico exported only 3 percent of its production. The Mexican textile industry failed to become an earner of foreign exchange in part because it relied on business from U.S. firms seeking to contract out the more labor-intensive parts of the production process. The *maquiladora* industries in northern border areas were the main beneficiaries of this business. Table 6.12 shows how *maquiladoras* have boosted Mexican textile volumes, and Table 6.13 lists key indicators of the *maquiladora* sector of the textile industry.

The *maquila* factories assemble garments from fabric already cut in the United States. After assembly, the garments return to the United States, but special arrangements exist under which U.S. import duty is paid only on the value added (item 807 of the old U.S. tariff code).

While this generates employment for Northern Mexico, it creates disadvantages for the Mexican economy. First, by the nature of the operation, value added to the garments is limited, thus making only a limited contribution to the Mexican economy. Second, for certain products this type of trade uses up trade quotas, which effectively

TABLE 6.11 Mexico's Textile and Clothing Trade with the United States
(millions of U.S. dollars)

	Exports		*Imports*		*Balance*	
	1985	1986	1985	1986	1985	1986
Textile	84.4	171.3	170.2	191.4	(85.8)	(20.2)
Clothing	291.7	321.9	157.2	182.3	134.5	139.6
Total	376.1	493.2	327.4	373.7	48.7	¯119.5

Source: Organization for Economic Cooperation and Development, *Foreign Trade by Commodities*, 1988.

TABLE 6.12 Textile Volume Output Index (1980 base)

Textile Type	1980	1981	1982	1983	1984	1985	1986	1987
Syn. res., plas. & fiber	100.0	104.5	102.3	112.5	128.4	133.4	131.7	149.7
Spin & weave: woft fibers	100.0	104.0	94.6	90.4	92.9	98.2	90.7	90.9
Spin & weave: hard fibers	100.0	100.5	92.0	87.9	76.5	64.1	75.8	68.5
Clothing & other textiles	100.0	101.9	94.8	90.6	92.5	101.3	93.3	93.3
Textile maquilas	100.0	96.2	95.8	127.9	154.7	176.7	204.4	235.8
Clothing	100.0	102.8	96.9	91.0	93.4	98.4	92.6	92.0
General index	100.0	107.0	103.7	95.8	101.0	108.3	104.6	108.7
Res. & fiber gral. index	1.0	-2.3	-1.4	17.4	27.1	23.2	25.9	37.7
Textile & cloth. gral. index	1.0	-3.9	-6.6	-5.0	-7.5	-9.1	-11.5	15.4
Maquila gral. index	1.0	-10.1	-7.6	33.5	53.2	63.2	95.4	116.9

Source: Banco de México, various reports.

TABLE 6.13 Textiles and Clothing, *Maquiladora* Industry
(millions of U.S. dollars)

Indicator	1985	1986	1987	1988
Exported goods	377	360	410	468
Imported raw materials	289	277	308	340
Added value	87	84	101	128
Percent	23.2	23.2	24.8	27.3
Jobs			31,554	34,706

Source: Banco de México, various reports.

applies quantitative restrictions on products with low added value. If these quotas were applied to the exporting of domestic production, the value added would be higher and thus of greater benefit in alleviating Mexico's debt problem. A third disadvantage is the lack of linkages between the *maquila* factories and the rest of the textile industry. This lowers product and export marketing experience, which might otherwise make the integrated sector more competitive in U.S. and European Economic Community markets.

The government did consider these disadvantages in initiating its export promotion program, *Programa de Fomento Integral de Exportaciones* (Profiex), in 1985. Profiex allowed for temporary imports of raw materials, equipment, and tools to be used in export production. The program offered drawback incentives—the refund of import duties on materials subsequently exported as finished products. The program also provided for the establishment of foreign trade consortia with the participation of foreign countries. Additionally, restrictions were placed on the expansion of *maquiladoras*. The *maquiladoras* were authorized to generate products in which Mexico had unfilled Multi-Fiber Arrangement (MFA) quotas as well as products in which national inputs were fully utilized.

Mexico's second largest market is Canada, which absorbs just over 5 percent of textile exports, followed by the United Kingdom and Italy, which each account for 4.2 percent. Germany receives 3.5 percent of Mexican textile exports. From 1981 through 1986, manmade fibers accounted for 68 percent of textile exports, followed by fabrics at 6 percent, and carpets and clothing at 5 percent each.

Mexico's textile exports to countries of the Organization for Economic Cooperation and Development (OECD) more than doubled in dollar value in 1986, after developing unevenly over the two previous years. In 1986, textile exports were up 116 percent over the 1980 total. In the clothing sector, however, growth was less spectacular: the 1986 total was only 22 percent higher than it had been in 1980. Nevertheless, clothing exports represent a value nearly 1.5 times the value of all other textile exports. In addition to these textiles, Mexico also exports raw cotton. In 1987–1988, a total of 78,200 tons of cotton were exported.

Mexico's textile relationship with the United States may change in the future with two new agreements. In November 1987, Mexico ratified a new trade framework agreement with the United States covering a variety of issues. Under the agreement, both sides were committed to textile talks within 90 days, based on a request from either side. A more specific agreement relating to textiles and clothing was signed in January 1988, under which Mexico agreed to lift import restrictions on U.S. fabrics and yarn, to allow imports of certain quantities of finished clothing from the United States, and to allow textile producers to establish factories in the *maquiladora* zones to process cut fabric for re-entry into the United States.

For Mexico to achieve more substantial export growth, the nation may have to diversify into other geographic areas. Despite recent agreements with Mexico, a mood of protectionism is growing in the United States. Dwindling U.S. interest in Northern Mexican processing in recent years may go even further if the dollar should decline. The weaker U.S. currency has made U.S. domestic clothing production more competitive. The industry already had competitive advantages of quick response and reliability, and good control over product supply and quality. Tables 6.14 and 6.15 summarize Mexico's competitive position in textiles.

Mexico may find additional investments from the Far East. Japan is already taking an active interest in Mexican industries by granting them new loans and by its involvement in the automotive industry. Japan is attracted to cheap currency purchases in Mexico as well as access to the U.S. market. Such market access may provide a sufficient incentive to attract the Far Eastern majors in textiles and clothing.

Concentration

As in the rest of the world, the Mexican manmade fiber industry is dominated by a small number of large companies. Eight Mexican companies account for the majority of the manmade fiber production and, as Table 6.16 indicates, most of this production takes place in the states of Jalisco, Nuevo León, México and Querétaro. The amount of foreign participation in fiber production varies by the type of fiber and industry sector.

TABLE 6.14 Mexican Textile Industry Competitive Position by Product Cost and Marketing

Process	Product	Cost	Marketing
Natural fibers			
Cotton	Equivalent	Weak	Weak
Wool	Equivalent	Equivalent	Weak
Synthetic fibers			
Nylon	Weak	Equivalent	Equivalent
Polyester yarn	Strong	Strong	Equivalent
Polyester staple	Equivalent	Strong	Equivalent
Acrylic	Strong	Strong	Equivalent
Spinning			
Cotton	Weak	Equivalent	Equivalent
Wool	Weak	Strong	Weak
Manmade fibers	Equivalent	Equivalent	Equivalent
Fabrics			
Weaving	Equivalent	Equivalent	Weak
Knitting	Weak	Equivalent	Weak
Carpet	Equivalent	Equivalent	Weak
Finishing			
Dyeing	Weak	Weak	Weak
Printing	Equivalent	Weak	Weak
Finishing	Weak	Weak	Weak
Clothing	Equivalent	Equivalent	Weak

Source: Authors' compilation.

Mexican law reserves the manufacture of all petrochemical raw materials for Pemex, the government's oil and petrochemicals company. For example, Pemex manufactures all acrylonitriles and the basic monomers for nylon and polyester. Polymerized fibers must be made using 60 percent Mexican capital. The main independent plants that manufacture DMT-PTA are Petrocel and Tereftalatos, which both have foreign participation. The U.S. firm of Hercofina has 40 percent ownership in Petrocel, and Amoco has an interest in Tereftalatos Mexicanos. Both plants also have technology contracts.

Cicloamidas supplies several nylon spinners and has technology licenses. Most others are fully integrated. Cydsa leads in acrylics, Celanese leads in nylon and polyester, followed by Akra (Alfa). Akra also has a "Lycra" joint venture with Dupont (see Table 6.17).

In the weaving sector, most of the companies are Mexican owned, as Table 6.18 indicates. However, exceptions exist. Textiles Morelos is

TABLE 6.15 Mexican Textile Industry Competitive Position by Sector

Item	Strengths	Weaknesses	Position
Cotton	Domestic crops	Prices; inventory cost; sanitary regulations	Weak
Manmade fibers	Wages; petrochemical and energy costs	Interest cost; underutilization	Strong
Spinning	Wages; energy, manufacturing, wool & acrylic yarn costs	Interest cost; cotton yarn quality; poor quality stds.; operation intensity; productivity	Equivalent
Weaving	Wages; energy costs	Interest cost; underutilization; productivity	Equivalent
Knitting	Wages; energy and manufacturing costs	Interest cost; raw materials; underutilization	Weak
Finishing & dyeing	Wages; energy costs	Technology; scale; investment; import taxes; quality; vertical integration	Weak
Clothing	Wages; manufacturing costs; quality	Raw materials, marketing	Equivalent

Source: Authors' compilation.

TABLE 6.16 Fiber Production by Location

Location	Percent
Jalisco	25
Nuevo León	22
State of México	21
Querétaro	16
Mexico City	9
Veracruz	Remainder
Michoacán	Remainder
Tlaxcala	Remainder

Sources: Compiled using Secretaría de Energía, Minas e Industria Parastatal and Comisión Petroquímica Mexicana data.

completely owned by Burlington, a U.S. corporation. American Textile is 80 percent Mexican owned, but the remaining 20 percent is owned by an American firm, Gilford. Most of this production is centered in the states of Puebla, Tlaxcala, Jalisco and Nuevo León, although plants exist in other locations.

There are a handful of old firms like Guindy, Kallach, Saba, and Chedraui that each control several thousand looms. They produce mostly cotton and polyester fabrics of inferior quality at a high production cost. In the production of nylon and polyester fibers and yarns, the Guindy group is integrated with Kimex. Saba is integrated within polyester fibers and yarns, and has acquired 25 percent of Celanese. In acrylics, Kallach is integrated with Finacril.

Many small weavers and knitters also exist. They use new looms for tricot and raschel, but also use older technology involving large, circular looms.

TABLE 6.17 Producer Affiliations and Capital Ownership

Mexican Firm	Capital Ownership	Percent
Celanese	Hoescht (Germany)	40
Akra (Fibras Químicas)	Akzo NV. (Netherlands)	40
Akra (Nylon de México)	E.I. DuPont De Nemours (United States)	40

Note: Does not include licensing and royalty agreements.

Source: Textile Organon, 1989.

TABLE 6.18 Private Versus Government Ownership (percentages)

Type of Material	Mexican Government	Private Mexican	Private Foreign
Raw materials	60	25	15
Fibers	3	75	22
Yarns		90	10
Weaving		100	
Clothing		100	
Commercialization		95	5

Source: Authors' compilation.

In carpeting, three firms control 90 percent of national carpet production. These are the Alfa Group, which controls Terza, Luxor-Mohawk, which was recently acquired from Mohasco by Cigarrera La Moderna Group, and Nobilis Lee, which is completely owned by Burlington. To penetrate the export market, carpeting manufacturers need to change their fiber mix to make it more responsive to market demand.

Unlike carpeting, the clothing sector is highly fragmented, with many small companies of less than 10 employees. These firms, mostly Mexican owned as Table 6.18 again indicates, are spread throughout the country, although concentrations exist in the large cities, particularly Mexico City and some locations in the northern border area. The *Cámara Nacional de la Industria del Vestido* (National Clothing Industry Chamber) had a membership of about 3,700 companies in 1988. Another 7,000 firms do not belong to the Chamber.

Fisisa and Kimex have always been independent. They manufacture the three major synthetics, with the exception of Kimex, which does not manufacture acrylics. These two firms use a minimum of licensed technologies.

Overall, as Table 6.19 indicates, cellulosic fiber production has increased sharply since 1980, whereas synthetic non-cellulosic fiber and synthetic fiber production have grown slowly but steadily. Besides, the overall tonnage produced in cellulosic fibers is significantly lower than for non-cellulosic fibers.

Celanese's performance varies by fiber, as Table 6.19 also indicates. In rayon staple and acetate yarn, Celanese's production has dropped steadily since 1980, and the firm ceased production of rayon staple in 1982. However, the firm is holding steady in acetate staple.

TABLE 6.19 Fiber Production in Mexico by Company and Fiber Type (tons)

Fiber	Firm	1980	1981	1982	1983	1984	1985	1986	1987
Rayon yarn	Celanese, Cydsa	6,104	6,240	5,307	4,588	3,099	3,074	3,138	3,349
Rayon staple	Celanese	10,808	10,552	5,294					
Acetate yarn	Celanese	9,136	8,327	6,547	5,786	5,828	7,028	6,834	5,903
Acetate staple & tow	Celanese	8,476	8,661	7,506	6,726	6,133	7,506	6,645	8,325
Nylon yarn	Akra, Celanese, Fisisa, Kimex	29,800	29,122	29,211	27,975	28,157	28,445	25,615	26,606
Nylon staple	Akra, Celanese	2,000	3,901	2,833	4,532	4,672	3,731	5,171	4,424
Polyester yarn	Akra, Celanese, Fisisa, Kimex, Inpetmex	86,415	78,573	73,296	81,000	93,821	98,401	84,122	92,510
Polyester staple	Akra, Celanes, Fisisa, Kimex	42,526	47,571	49,762	69,878	71,733	75,491	73,549	95,735
PPP yarn & staple	Corp. Tex. Mex., Lanera Moderna, Polifil, Politap	8,012	8,490	7,225	8,337	7,900	8,801	7,903	8,993
Acrylic staple	Celanese, Cydsa, Finacril, Fisisa	59,623	62,771	62,643	70,300	74,380	82,896	96,424	107,662
Cellulosic		34,524	33,780	24,654	17,100	15,060	17,608	16,617	17,577
Non-cellulosic		228,376	230,428	224,970	262,022	280,663	297,765	292,784	335,930
TOTAL SYNTHETIC		262,900	264,208	249,624	279,122	295,723	315,373	309,401	353,507

Source: Asociación Nacional de Industrias Químicas, 1988.

Production of polyester staples more than doubled in Mexico from 1980 through 1987, and acrylic staple production is up from 59,623 tons in 1980 to 107,662 tons in 1987.

Although problems existed in the 1970s with manmade fiber quality and cost, today these fibers are much more competitive, with the exception of some nylon fibers, which still struggle with problems in dyeing affinity and tensile stress. About 50 percent of yarn production is integrated with fiber production. The other half, which is generally owned exclusively by Mexican firms, originated with the old cotton yarn facilities.

Adequate supplies of cotton are hard to obtain for two reasons. First, although cotton is not subject to import permits, agricultural officials sometimes block its importation through the use of sanitation regulations. Second, problems exist in the quality standards for cotton.

International Integration

Worldwide, the textile industry has reached a level of diseconomies of scale. During the 1960s in Mexico, it was difficult to justify the installation of state-of-the-art technology for the manufacture of polymer, fiber spinning, or a fully integrated weaving mill. But during the 1970s, the textile market grew faster than did technology, and new, large plants were installed in Mexico.

However, in the industrialized countries, the large, integrated mills began to suffer. Burlington, which owns one of the two largest U.S. mills, underwent a restructuring in 1987. In 1988, the company underwent heavy layoffs, shutdowns, and plans to divest some of its assets. J.P. Stevens, another large U.S. textile concern, is rapidly reorienting much of its production and technology.

The issue of vertical integration is the source of much concern among Mexican industrialists. Industry trends point to specialization with the support of sophisticated logistics such as "just in time" or "quick reaction" that allow quick market response, which helps to lower inventories. Our experience in Mexican textiles is that some forms of vertical integration, such as in the dyeing and carpet sectors, are higher than in other parts of the world. In the case of Mexico, this integration has led to underutilization. In spite of the valid reasons not to integrate in other countries, Mexico should integrate, at least partially. Such integration is needed because the industry carries low levels of inventories because it lacks economic resources and cannot provide reliable quality or prompt delivery to other countries.

In the case of Mexico, an analysis of five textile mills registered only half the productivity of similar mills in Germany, Japan, and the

United States. The problem of Mexican yields did not originate with the machinery itself, which is similar to machinery used elsewhere. The textile industry's statistics indicate that Mexican spinning and weaving mills operate fewer hours per year than do mills in other parts of the world, notably in Turkey and Korea. This indicates that lack of productivity is not linked to technology issues, training, or basic quality, but rather, to problems of low utilization of installed capacity and short operating hours.

Machine downtime lowers efficiency, sometimes by up to 50 percent. This downtime is not limited just to spinning and weaving mills, but rather affects the entire Mexican textile industry. Lack of adequate supervision, poor yarn quality standards, low quality in raw materials, and poor operator training and motivation are contributing factors to this downtime. A shortage of materials, tooling or spare parts, as well as deficient production programming also contribute to downtime.

Aside from the *maquiladoras*, the textile industry in Mexico is, for the most part, domestically owned and operated. Mexico's fiber industry has about 22 percent U.S. equity ownership. Foreign ownership dominates the *maquiladoras,* and the plants themselves contribute little to the Mexican economy: the value added by *maquiladora* textile plants averages 25 percent of the total value of the finished product. On the other hand, the foreign firms do take care of the design, pattern making, cutting, material procurement, and marketing. The *maquiladora* industry is unprofitable not only for the Mexican economy, and perhaps for the U.S. labor force. U.S. unions complain that the *maquila* industry allows U.S. firms to save about $15,000 for each job created in a *maquila* factory.

In 1987, about 250 textile and clothing companies existed in the *maquila* sector, which provided about 30,000 jobs and sales of $410 million. The value added by this industry represented $101 million, as Table 6.13 indicates.

Mexican firms have some technology contracts with U.S. companies, particularly for petrochemical raw materials. These include Petrocel with Hercofina, and Tereftalatos Mexicanos with Amoco. Materials imported from the United States include acrylonitrile, paraxylene, and cyclohexane. National production of acrylonitrile, for example, is only 50 percent of consumption, as Tables 6.20 and 6.21 demonstrate.

Government policy in Mexico during most of the 1980s has been directed at coping with the country's foreign debt burden. This problem was exacerbated by Mexico's substantial reliance on oil exports that experienced sharply dropping prices in the early 1980s. Government attention turned to developing exports in the industrial sector to earn foreign exchange to pay interest on the debt.

TABLE 6.20 Ratio of Imported Raw Material to Consumption (percentages)

Product	1980	1981	1982	1983	1984	1985	1986	1987
Acrylonitrile	13.6	26.7	25.3	36.7	40.8	50.6	51.1	53.2
Ciclohexane	20.3	15.2	32.7	8.7	45.6	50.9	39.8	22.2
Paraxylene	70.7	79.4	79.4	52.2	47.7	62.0	58.0	38.8
Ethylene Glycol	19.2	0.3	0.1	0.1	0.3	7.2	5.1	22.4

Source: Asociación Nacional de Industrias Químicas, 1988.

The government also aimed to decentralize employment and population. Of the 400 or so firms in the cotton sector, about three-fourths are in Puebla, the Federal District, and the state of Mexico; about 30 percent of the 1,600 firms in the manmade fibers sector are in the same locations.

The economic restructuring adopted at the beginning of the de la Madrid administration under the National Development Plan was aimed at meeting the needs of domestic consumption, increasing employment, and providing a mechanism for growth without inflation. The plan also promoted geographic decentralization and recognized that currency devaluations are only a temporary solution to a long-term problem. De la Madrid recognized that to become more competitive Mexico needed structural change.

Future Integration Needs

The Mexican textile industry must promote export sales, giving priority to the clothing sector, particularly for the U.S. and Canadian markets. This strategy, which takes advantage of two close, large markets, will increase both direct exports and enhance the other productive sectors in the textile chain. Stressing clothing exports would represent a striking change from the current export strategy, which focuses on the sale of raw fabric, even though the clothing sector contributes significantly to GDP. Increasing the clothing sales volume will also lower the cost of capital by allowing for more efficient use of productive capacity, particularly in the areas of manmade fibers, weaving, and knitting. Mexico must make the best competitive use of its large installations of spinning and weaving equipment.

The Mexican textile industry also faces a challenge in its dependency on the *maquiladora* industry, which adds insufficient value to many textile products, even though it uses up trade quotas. The quotas should be applied to the exporting of domestic production to enhance the value

TABLE 6.21 Raw Material Imports (tons)

Product	1980	1981	1982	1983	1984	1985	1986	1987
Acrylonitrile	8,556	19,688	17,837	32,107	34,071	49,884	56,000	65,590
Ciclohexane	10,136	7,898	16,946	4,676	23,360	33,159	26,000	14,789
Paraxylene	94,479	147,997	139,272	126,198	124,604	179,223	169,000	118,738
Ethylene glycol	13,148	182	63	70	240	6,211	4,164	20,380

Source: Asociación Nacional de Industrias Químicas, 1988.

added. Additionally, linkages need to be established between the *maquila* factories and the other textile sectors.

A second challenge in the promotion of exports stems from the growing protectionism in the United States and the decline in the dollar. This means that although Mexico should promote textile sales to its northern neighbor, at the same time the industry can benefit from a closer trade relationship with selected European countries.

To promote an export strategy, Mexico must make several improvements in its productive process. First, the industry must improve the quality of cotton yarn, which represents a significant demand on the export market. Second, the Mexican textile industry must improve some lines of extrusion in polyester, especially nylon. Third, the industry must restructure the dyeing and finishing sectors, focusing on new investments in the acquisition of the latest equipment and technology. Fourth, Mexico must focus on enhancing its lobbying efforts in trade agreements to improve the quotas necessary for increasing exports.

In terms of textile productivity, Mexico faces another difficult challenge. Machine downtime and labor practices are resulting in low utilization of installed capacity. These are structural issues that the industry as a whole must address to remain competitive.

Notes

1.   Anson, Robin and Paul Simpson. "World Textile Trade and Production Trends," *The Economic Intelligence Unit*, Special Report No. 1108, June 1988, pp. 66-126.

2.   See note 1.

Textiles: U.S. Perspective

Stephen L. Lande

The United States and Mexico face several obstacles to integrating their textile industries, but these obstacles can be diminished through joint ventures involving U.S. investment in Mexico and a firm resolve from the Mexican government to gain guaranteed access to U.S. textile markets. Mexico faces import limitations that are biting into some categories of Mexican exports—an issue that Mexican trade negotiators must take up with their U.S. counterparts. Since 1958, the United States has limited imports of textile mill products and apparel under a combination of multilateral and bilateral agreements. The United States currently has 40 such bilateral agreements and applies unilateral restraints against others under the terms of the fourth renewal of the Multi-Fiber Arrangement (MFA) and U.S. domestic law. The United States also has fairly high duties on textile products.

The United States and Mexico recently completed negotiations to improve Mexican access to U.S. markets, but these negotiations were more successful for the fast-growing *maquiladora* segment than for Mexican national products. This is partly due to the fact that the United States wants to maintain preferential access for apparel exports from the Caribbean and Central America, and it also stemmed from U.S. State Department frustration with certain aspects of Mexico's foreign policy.

But for Mexico, the more important obstacle to increasing its exports to the United States is the lack of competitiveness of its textile sector. The fear of new import restrictions aggravates the domestic problem by discouraging new export capacity.

It is easier for Mexico to gain access to U.S. markets for its *maquiladora* products, but should Mexico pay for increased access to textile markets by limiting exports of non-*maquiladora* textiles and apparel? U.S. companies profit more from *maquiladora* products than do Mexican producers because Mexico is limited to a small gain from the value added to such products in Mexico. Both U.S. apparel and mill manufacturers benefit from the special tariff regime in chapter 98 of the Harmonized System, under which U.S. fabric parts are cut in U.S. facilities for assembly in Mexico and Caribbean Basin nations. These products are then returned to the United States with no import duty assessed on the U.S. content.

U.S. apparel manufacturers are split between those who rely on Mexico for their garments and those who rely on domestic or third-country production. Those manufacturers who rely on both the Far East and Mexico will support special treatment only if it is not predicated on rollbacks from other sources. The AFL-CIO, largely under pressure from the International Ladies Garment Workers Union, is concerned with the number of jobs both in the apparel sector and in the mills. Thus, the AFL-CIO opposes favorable treatment for Mexican exports unless these exports are offset by reductions from third countries. The mills place a much higher priority on maintaining the current system of import controls under the MFA and want to move toward a system of global import restraints. In this effort, the unions and mills constitute a textile industry coalition, and they would not risk their amicable relations over an issue like special access for Mexico. They advocate special treatment only in the context of a rollback from other suppliers.

I will analyze both the Mexican and U.S. textile sectors, as well as the political issues that affect textile integration. Finally, I will make some recommendations for achieving a more complete integration of the U.S. and Mexican textile sectors.

The U.S. Industry

Any analysis of the U.S. textile industry must begin with the premise that it is divided into two distinct sectors with completely different characteristics. The mill sector, which produces yarns, fabrics, and made-up goods, is approaching a world-class competitive level because manufacturers have made large equipment and technology investments. But U.S. domestic apparel production has been marred by little productive growth or investment, employment declines and continuing losses of market share to foreign imports. Although productivity in the apparel sector can be improved, the basic procedures are still labor intensive, which gives Third World countries a distinct comparative advantage. To illustrate the different competitive levels between mill and apparel sectors, we should note that imports of textile mill products account for less than 10 percent of

U.S. consumption, compared with apparel imports, which account for almost one-third of U.S. consumption.

Although the mill sector of the U.S. textile industry can compete effectively on world markets, the industry argues that the prevalence of unfair trade practices in many countries, particularly subsidization and dumping, require continued import protection. Opponents of continued protection argue that sheltering an otherwise competitive U.S. industry assures oligopoly profits and less efficient production.

Several factors point to increased competitiveness in the U.S. textile mill sector. For example, U.S. mills rely almost exclusively on domestic raw materials, particularly cotton and manmade fibers. Until 1986, U.S. prices for cotton were higher than world market prices. Changes in the U.S. Department of Agriculture's cotton loan and price support program that year significantly lowered U.S. cotton prices. U.S. mills are now able to buy cotton at prices roughly equivalent to world market prices. Conversely, future changes in U.S. agricultural policy could result in U.S. mills again facing non-competitive prices for cotton. The mill sector has also maintained a respectable investment rate over the past few years. Capital expenditures in the textile mill industry from 1984–1986 were 14.8 percent higher than during 1981–1983. The investment rate climbed even more dramatically in 1987, rising 17.4 percent over the previous year.

The recent growth in investment in mills is most impressive when compared to investment in overall manufacturing and in non-durable goods. Overall, manufacturing and non-durable goods investment grew 19.7 percent in the period 1984–1986, and 12.7 percent from 1981 through 1983. However, 1987 growth was only 2.2 percent for overall manufacturing and -3.8 percent for non-durable goods.

From 1977 to 1987, the mill sector increased productivity by an average of 3.9 percent annually, mostly as a result of investments in weaving mills. Productivity in overall manufacturing increased at an average annual rate of 3.1 percent.

A jump in shipments and sales and declining employment contributed to the productivity increase in the mill sector. From 1977 through 1981, shipments increased by 24 percent as employment declined by 10 percent. From 1982–1986, shipments increased by another 5 percent and employment dropped 5 percent. However, since remaining employees increased working hours, their nominal wages rose 20 percent over the period. From 1984–1986, sales in the mill sector rose 9 percent compared to a 5.3 percent increase for overall manufacturing. In 1982, the industry had a capacity utilization rate of only 65 percent. By 1986, capacity utilization increased to 79 percent.

The mill industry's competitiveness against imports may also increase as it becomes more concentrated. The degree of concentration in the industry may increase because it is still relatively low compared to other U.S. industries. In 1986, the four largest companies in four subsectors of the industry accounted for 22 percent to 41 percent of shipments, far below the average in other sectors of U.S. industry.

Concentration has increased with recent acquisitions and buyouts, some involving vertical integration with apparel producers. For example, Westpoint Pepperell, a leading fabric producer, has purchased Cluett, Peabody Co., a diversified apparel producer. Others involve horizontal combinations among different mills. Fieldcrest purchased its competitor, Cannon. Some takeovers involved companies interested in diversifying into the sector. There have also been managerial buyouts to re-establish a company's independence.

The mills, in conjunction with apparel manufacturers and retailers, have taken steps to improve market response. Customers criticized U.S. mills for lack of responsiveness in a 1987 American International Trade Commission report, *U.S. Global Competitiveness: The U.S. Textile Mill Industry*. U.S. apparel manufacturers complained about product delivery times and a lack of manufacturing flexibility in the industry, particularly relating to small orders and to fabric style and quality. Customers also complained that the mill sector was not pricing its products competitively.

To meet these concerns, a new program called Quick Response was implemented by the mills, apparel manufacturers, and retailers, which established better cooperation and communications. The program aims to cut the production cycle in half, thus reducing inventories and carrying costs at each stage of the manufacturing operation. To carry out the program, the cooperating entities are adopting electronic data interchange, merchandise bar coding, and a more precise delivery system modeled after the Japanese just-in-time system. A K-Mart official said his firm will spend more than $1 billion on electronic data exchange equipment between 1988 and 1993. According to an American Textile Manufacturers Institute report, a jeans manufacturer reduced the production cycle from four to three weeks by using an electronic data exchange. Denim fabric inventories were reduced for both the manufacturer and the mill.

Flexibility is key to a quick response program. Producers must be able to make product variations quickly when needed and must also be willing to run small lots. The program appears to have been successful in meeting the demand for smaller runs; one mill reported that its average dye lot dropped from 120,000 yards to 12,000 yards between 1981–1987.

The mills are sponsoring a "Buy America" public media campaign with the cooperation of retailers and apparel manufacturers. Interestingly, in this campaign the mills do not count as domestic production any portion of apparel assembled outside the United States, even though these items frequently contain a high percentage of U.S.-manufactured components.

Improved International Trade Outlook

In general, textile mill products are not seriously affected by imports, especially when compared to the heavy impact of imports in the apparel sector. In fact, several lines of U.S. production encounter relatively little competition from foreign suppliers. In 1986, import penetration of less than 5 percent was recorded for carpets and rugs, most knit fabrics, non-woven fabrics, and spun yarn other than wool. Sectors encountering the most foreign competition were cotton, manmade fiber weaving, and circular knit fabrics. Import penetration in cotton averaged 29 percent and in manmade fiber weaving averaged 8 percent. Growth in these sectors, along with the spun yarn sector, dropped when Mexican producers lost market share to imports from their most important customers, U.S. producers of garments and textile mill products. Imports are more likely than domestic production to incorporate foreign fabrics and yarns.

Recent developments in the U.S. foreign trade picture are helping the domestic industry improve its competitive position vis-à-vis foreign producers. U.S. mills are still reaping the benefits of the dollar devaluation in the second Reagan term, although there was concern over the later resurgence in the dollar. Rising labor and currency pressure in the Far East and the uncertain situation in China have reduced competitive pressure somewhat. The shift in market share for apparel imports from the Far East to Mexico and the Caribbean assists U.S. textile mills, since apparel imports from these areas are much more likely to be assembled from U.S.-formed fabric than are imports from the Far East. This shift in market share should continue to the benefit of U.S. mills as the United States maintains tight limits on the growth of Far Eastern imports and special access for apparel produced from U.S.-formed fabric in the Caribbean Basin and Mexico.

Exports are a relatively insignificant part of the U.S. industry, accounting for less than 4 percent of production. Major exports are broadwoven cotton and manmade fiber fabrics, with Canada and Mexico being the major markets. Cut components exported to Mexico for the *maquiladora* industry may not qualify as exports of mill products, even though they are becoming increasingly important to the profitability of the industry.

The apparel sector is not undergoing a resurgence comparable to that of the mills. More apparel than mill production is moving overseas. The import penetration ratio for apparel has increased significantly, while import penetration for mill products has increased only slightly.

Generally, mill owners have large, fixed investments and are not prone to change location. Apparel production is less tied by fixed investment, since sewing and other portable equipment can be easily moved. The fact that much apparel production is located in urban areas with a transient labor force results in less social pressure to maintain specific production locations.

In the mill sector, U.S. firms have been largely successful in maintaining their U.S. market share against imports, except in the case of some lighter fabrics. Instead, foreign mills have relied on increasing exports of apparel and home furnishings. In apparel, most domestic producers supplement their lines with imports. Many domestic apparel manufacturers have moved all production overseas or maintain only minimal local production. In many cases, manufacturers producing domestic apparel find their competitors to be other U.S. apparel companies, large retailers, and independent middlemen who import directly.

The competitive picture is further complicated when one takes into account the competition between U.S., Far Eastern, and third country producers. Currently, there are three major sources of imports subject to limitations under the MFA. I will not discuss unrestricted imports from Western Europe or Canada.

The most competitive U.S. apparel imports continue to be those produced from Far Eastern fabric. Most of these imports come directly from the big four Far Eastern producers, China, Hong Kong, Korea, and Taiwan. To avoid quota controls, higher wages, and appreciating currencies, other locations are being used to produce or assemble apparel from fabric and components produced in these countries. Thus the share of total U.S. apparel imports from the Big Four has declined to less than 50 percent in 1989. However, a large portion of the increase in the share of the U.S. market held by Asian, non-traditional new suppliers (Bangladesh, United Arab Emirates, and Mauritius), and the Caribbean Basin incorporate inputs from the Big Four. Often the new apparel factories in these countries are controlled by Hong Kong and Taiwanese and to a lesser extent Korean interests. In fact, Mexico is one the few sources of assembled garments from third country inputs that does not have a large Far Eastern presence.

Apparel assembled in Mexico and the Caribbean from components cut in the United States is another import. Most of the components are produced from U.S.-formed fabric, but some are produced from fabric formed in third countries that is simply cut into components in the United States to qualify for reduced duty entry into the United States. Under chapter 98 of the Harmonized System, products assembled from components cut in the United States pay duty only on the non-U.S. value added when returned to the United States. The overseas production facilities are usually either owned by U.S. apparel manufacturers or produced under commitments to U.S. apparel manufacturers and middlemen. Chapter 98 imports usually benefit apparel companies' bottom lines by allowing them a larger profit margin through savings on labor costs and import duties. To the extent that apparel firms own facilities for cutting fabrics in the United States, they have an additional inducement to import under chapter 98.

A third type of import comes from restricted countries other than the Big Four using local components. India and Brazil are the major sources of these products. Mexico is not now a major source of imports from its own inputs, with the exception of acrylic yarns and small amounts of apparel, although the situation may be changing. This indigenous production is not an important factor in the U.S. market.

Given this competitive environment, it is not surprising that, despite a continuing program of U.S. import restrictions, more and more apparel producers are moving offshore. The reduction in the share of the U.S. market held by domestic producers reflects, in part, the inability to induce workers to stay or to enter the apparel industry. In 1978 this sector provided 1.3 million jobs, but by 1988 the total had dropped to 1.1 million. Average hourly earnings for apparel and related production are $6.10, compared to an average of $10.17 for manufacturing overall and $9.42 per hour for nondurable goods manufacturing. Increasingly, apparel manufacturers compete with the expanding service sector for low-wage, unskilled, entry-level workers. Even if wages for apparel work are slightly higher, employees have shown a preference for service enterprises, given the less than ideal working conditions in apparel production. Apparel companies, particularly sewing operations, justify their decisions to move operations offshore by citing the shortage of U.S. operators.

Domestic U.S. apparel producers are looking to technological innovations to improve their competitive position. Through technology, the industry hopes to reduce the need for labor and to improve conditions in the work place. Increasingly, cutting rooms are using computerized grading and marking systems, laser technology, and automated spreading machines. For sewing, manufacturers are investing in programmable, automatic sewing machines that facilitate tacking, pattern sewing, runstitching, pocket setting and welting, and belt loop attachment. These machines can impose a stitch pattern on parts designed to receive the pattern. Manufacturers are also investing in edge-guided, automatic sewing machines, where the sewing cycle is controlled by the shape of parts being sewn; they are also purchasing de-skilling equipment that transfers the control of some sewing machine functions from the operator to the machine.

Computer-aided design and manufacturing systems ultimately will integrate all aspects of apparel manufacturing, from preseason planning and line preparation through shipping. In cutting, this will facilitate pattern design and grading, marker making, cut planning, and coordination of fabric inspection, and will enhance spreading, cutting, and bundling. Sewing transfer systems will move component parts and subassemblies in and out of manufacturing cells, and eventually into finishing and shipping.

Although they sound impressive, these innovations have not been applied to a sufficient proportion of U.S. production because profit margins in this sector are not high. In fact, the need for such capital investments will force some inefficient units to close and will cause others to downsize their operations. Foreign competitors may invest more since they are in a stronger capital position. U.S. producers remain at a competitive disadvantage due to their labor costs, outmoded facilities, and other production rigidities.

Some factors do favor domestic production. A study commissioned by the American Apparel Manufacturers Association (AAMA) identified production factors that influence decisions to produce apparel in the United States, in the Far East, or from components in the Caribbean or Mexico. These include degree of labor content, product complexity, type and origin of raw materials, and production process characteristics, which include product lines, labeling, production runs, and predictability.

In the area of labor costs, Mexico and various Caribbean nations are making gains over traditional Far Eastern suppliers as wage pressure in the Far East continues to intensify. But Mexico still faces labor competition from countries like China, Indonesia, Thailand, and Bangladesh. Mexican and Caribbean assembly operations are preferred over U.S. and traditional Far Eastern production when the labor content of products is high compared to the product's value. U.S. and Mexican-Caribbean assembly is preferred over Far Eastern production when the product's bulk is large compared to value.

Mexican and Caribbean apparel manufacturers are not considered as technically proficient as their U.S. and Far Eastern counterparts. Thus, production involving close tolerance operations is more likely to be performed domestically or in the Far East. A product involving a large number of special production steps is more likely to be produced with high quality machines in the United States. When transportation time is a strong factor, production is more likely to be domestic with Mexico and the Caribbean a second choice.

Complex raw materials are most likely to come from the United States or the Far Eastern newly industrializing countries. In fact, the AAMA study indicates that garments requiring costly fabric or trim are more likely to be produced in the Far East than domestically. Special or exotic trim is more readily available in the United States, and thus garments requiring those items are likely to be domestically produced. Of course, garments requiring Far Eastern fabric or yarn are more likely to be produced in those countries, while those requiring U.S. fabric or yarn will be domestically produced.

Decisions on production location partly depend on the size of the purchasing firm, as well as whether the production is controlled by the buyer or manufacturer. For example, manufacturers prefer the United States for production needing frequent style changes, while buyers prefer offshore assembly or Far Eastern production. Manufacturers prefer the United States for production of items requiring a large number of sizes or a wide variety of colors per style, while buyers feel they have more control when such production is carried out in the Far East. Buyers prefer domestic sources for production requiring short runs, while manufacturers prefer foreign assembly operations. When close coordination is required, domestic production operates most efficiently. Far Eastern and foreign assembly operations are preferred for production involving long, costly changeovers, while domestic sourcing is preferred for short, inexpensive changeovers. Finally, small buyers prefer private label programs produced in the United States or in foreign assembly locations, while large buyers prefer Far Eastern sourcing or foreign assembly.

As for predictability, programs with a short lead time are more likely to be produced in the United States. This is particularly true if the fabric is not on hand and production is to order. In addition to U.S. production, foreign assembly is likely to be used for short lead times when the fabric is on hand.

Table 6.22 demonstrates the lack of success of U.S. import restrictions in limiting the import share of the U.S. market. It shows the continual growth in import/production ratios for specific categories in 1967, 1973, and 1987. All categories showed impressive increases. The growth in the market ratio for sweaters has been most impressive, increasing from 32 percent in 1967 to 194 percent in 1987.

TABLE 6.22 Apparel Import-Production Ratios by Apparel Lines

	Import-Production Ratio		
Apparel Lines	*1967*	*1973*	*1987*
Sweaters	32	75	194
Women & girls' slacks and shorts	18	41	81
Brassieres	10	26	80
Women and girls' suits	1	4	59
Men & boys' suits	1	34	56
Men & boys' trousers, slacks & shorts	6	9	51
Sleepwear	5	4	34
Underwear	1	2	19

Source: American Apparel Manufacturers Association, *1989 Focus.*

The figures in Table 6.23 overstate import penetration because they do not differentiate between regular imports and imports of goods that have been assembled outside the United States from U.S. components. Unfortunately, current U.S. statistics do not differentiate between components produced from fabrics cut and formed in the United States and fabrics cut in the United States but formed in third countries. U.S. components account for at least 60 percent of the final value of these imports and often the percentage of U.S. components is significantly higher. Imports of apparel assembled from U.S. components are growing at a faster rate than regular imports. These imports accounted for 12 percent of total U.S. apparel imports in the first nine months of

TABLE 6.23 U.S. General Imports with U.S. Components Assembled Abroad; Heading 9802.00.80 (percentages)

	Year	
Apparel Product	*1988*	*1989*
Brassieres	74.57	76.73
Men & boys' trousers, slacks, etc.	28.52	28.96
Underwear	26.41	30.92
Sleepwear	25.55	24.74
Women & girls' trousers, slacks, etc.	10.60	14.00
Knit Shirts	6.25	6.78
Women & girls' woven blouses	10.53	8.28
Dresses	10.04	9.23

Source: International Development Systems, Inc., 1990.

1988. By contrast, they accounted for only 8 percent of total imports in 1984, and averaged less than 5 percent between 1966 and 1972. Imports containing U.S. components make up a significant percentage of specific categories of imports.

U.S. Import Restrictions

The U.S. government contends that it regulates the flow of textile and apparel imports to prevent market disruption. Import regulations are administered under the MFA, which was extended for a fourth time in 1986 and will continue through July 1991.

The MFA is an exception to the most-favored-nation principle of the General Agreement on Tariffs and Trade (GATT) in that it permits country-specific import restrictions. The MFA also allows a country to limit imports without having to compensate trading partners whose exports are restricted. In addition, it is easier to make a case for market disruption under the MFA than it is to prove serious injury under GATT rules.

Import levels are negotiated under article 4 of the MFA or through requests for consultations under article 3. If the consultations do not result in an article 4 agreement or a withdrawal of the call, the importing country can impose limits unilaterally, provided they are not below actual import levels during any 12 of the previous 14 months. The MFA provides for a 6 percent annual growth in restricted import categories, with the exception of wool categories, in which minimum annual growth is only 1 percent.

Countries that take exception to an import barrier can appeal to an international monitoring group known as the Textile Surveillance Board, although the appeal procedure is not considered an effective counter to unilateral decisions by developed countries.

At first glance, the impressive growth of imports, particularly in apparel, appears to justify the U.S. industry's position that restrictions should be tightened because U.S. administration of the MFA is not effective and has not prevented a sharp increase in U.S. apparel imports from developing nations. For example, the real growth rate of U.S. apparel imports between 1974, the first year of the MFA, and 1986 exceeded the growth rate for all manufactured imports from developing countries. The domestic industry argues that for most of the 1980s, substantial disruption of the U.S. market has resulted from an extraordinary and unprecedented influx of imports.

According to the AAMA study, import penetration in the U.S. market increased from 8 percent in 1973 to 25 percent in 1986. Imports, not adjusted for inflation, from developing countries increased from $2.5

billion in 1973 to $16.2 billion in 1986, an average annual growth rate of 16.9 percent. In terms of value, the direct import of textile mill products combined with the fabric equivalent of finished apparel imports represented a market penetration of 52 percent in 1986.

Textile imports from developing countries are increasing their penetration of the U.S. market faster than they are increasing their penetration of the European Community (EC) and Japanese markets. The annual growth rate of such imports was almost 40 percent higher in the United States than in the EC in 1986. Looking specifically at apparel imports, the differences are even greater, with U.S. per capita imports twice the EC's level and almost quadruple the Japanese level.

No other class of manufactured imports into the United States has been subject to such stringent restrictions for as long as have textile mill products and apparel. Why then has the import penetration increased, especially for apparel? The domestic industry argues that the liberal way in which the United States administers textile quotas does not limit imports. The absence of global quotas, the lack of effective rules against circumvention, the delay in imposing restraints, and the generous levels at which they are imposed, all combine to assure that the textile restraint program is ineffective. Others believe that over time, market forces, not import restrictions, determine trade flows. Import restriction can retard increases but cannot permanently depress imports. The third argument is that without quotas, import penetration would be even higher and the very existence of the U.S. industry would be in jeopardy. The final argument is that the main beneficiaries of the MFA are the Big Four suppliers. The program not only protected their market share for direct imports, but allowed indirect exports of their products through finishing and assembling components in third countries. Countries with large national textile and apparel industries, such as India and Brazil, may have suffered the most since they could not take advantage of their newly developing comparative advantage.

While apparel imports into the United States have grown much more quickly than imports of textile mill products, there is no evidence that import restrictions on textile mill products are stricter than those on apparel. Import growth between the two sectors varies because U.S. mills have reached world competitive levels, while U.S. apparel manufacturers have not.

Despite the impressive growth of imports into the U.S. market, developing countries and apparel importers and retailers still contend that the MFA provides textiles exporters few safeguards against restrictive action by the United States and other developed country textile importers. They say:

1. The product coverage of the MFA has increased over time, despite objections from exporting countries. The coverage has increased for textile and apparel products of cotton in the Short Term Cotton Textiles Arrangement of 1960, to products of wool and manmade fiber in the MFA of 1974, and for textiles of previously uncontrolled vegetable fiber including linen, ramie, and silk blends after the fourth MFA renewal in 1986.

2. The MFA does not provide an effective way for a developing country to challenge an importing country's claim of market disruption. Once the claim is advanced, the importing country has the right to unilaterally impose quantitative limitations at low levels unless a bilateral limitation is negotiated. The exporting country is under great pressure to agree to such a limitation in order to avoid an even lower unilaterally imposed limitation.

3. The right of exporters to appeal to the surveillance board is not considered an effective deterrent to unreasonable import restrictions. The surveillance board does not often challenge a finding of market disruption. The appeal can usually be exercised only after the restrictions are in place and even if successful, the importing country does not have to remove the restraint permanently, but can simply liberalize the restraint or delay its imposition. Countries are dissuaded from appealing to the board by the leverage importing countries hold over them. Importing countries can limit other categories of textile and apparel imports from the appealing country and can apply pressure in non-textile areas.

4. The MFA does not allow restrictions to be imposed at levels lower than imports during any 12 of a previous 14-month period. This level is usually less than the rate of imports at the time the restraint is imposed, since imports are usually growing and thus their most recent shipment level is much higher than during any 12 of the most recent 14-month period.

5. The threat of low-level imports being imposed in a called category forces exporting countries to enter into a bilateral agreements in order to avoid more severe unilateral restraints. Exporting countries are often forced to agree to limitations in categories not subject to the call as a condition for gaining higher levels than otherwise would be the case.

6. The MFA discourages orders and investments even in products not subject to restraints. Untimely limitations can prevent fulfillment of orders and discourages investors who fear that

they will be limited below levels required to recoup their investment with a fair profit.

7. The fourth MFA permits the United States and other importers that have unilaterally imposed quotas under article 3 to extend the quotas unilaterally for a second year in some cases.

8. There is no effective, guaranteed minimum annual growth rate for imports subject to limitation since exceptions to the minimum 6 percent annual growth rate are allowed. For example, the United States has routinely denied the 6 percent growth rate to the large Far Eastern exporters.

In addition to its system of bilateral agreements and unilateral restraints under the MFA, the United States maintains high duties on most textile and apparel imports. The trade-weighted average U.S. rate on dutiable imports is less than 4 percent. For apparel, the trade-weighted average duty rate is 17.5 percent and for fabrics 10.5 percent.

The future of the MFA is unclear. Negotiations on textiles in the Uruguay Round focused on proposals to terminate the MFA and bring textiles under improved GATT rules. The U.S. and EC position has been to condition their acceptance of this proposal on strengthening GATT rules to assure an end to unfair trade practices in this sector and an orderly phasing out of the MFA into the twenty-first century. Mexico must analyze the agreement that emerges from the Uruguay Round with particular attention to the interim regime, GATT rule modifications affecting textiles, and Mexico's trade behavior when subject to U.S. trade remedy laws.

U.S. Import Restrictions on Mexico

The United States contends that Mexico has been treated generously under the U.S. textile program. The level of restraint on Mexican exports to the United States generally has no serious restrictive effect since shipments are well below the restraint levels, generous growth is provided when agreements are renewed, and the United States has provided particularly generous levels for *maquiladora* exports.

Trade specialists dispute whether countries like Mexico gained or lost under the U.S. handling of the MFA. Those who believe that Mexico has benefited from the MFA argue that Mexico would not have been able to increase its share of the U.S. market if the more competitive Far Eastern countries were not limited by restrictive quotas. In 1988, Mexico was the seventh largest foreign supplier to the U.S. market by value and the fifth largest by volume. By contrast, when the long-term cotton arrangement preceding the MFA was put into place in 1964, Mexico was not a factor in U.S. apparel imports and was only a small supplier of fabric. Conversely, it is argued that Japan and the Far Eastern newly industrializing nations have been able to artificially maintain market share through the MFA. Holding back more competitive new suppliers through quota restraints has reserved large market shares for these suppliers and protected them from being displaced by more competitive imports from other sources, such as Mexico. The more rapid expansion of Mexico's quotas has had only a minor effect on this distribution, since Mexico is starting from such a low base.

My conclusion is that neither side is correct. The U.S. administration of the MFA for the moment plays neither a positive nor a negative role in Mexico's ability to export to the United States. Mexican supply problems, specifically the absence of many world class producers, have been the major restrictive influence on Mexican ability to export to the United States. This has come about because Mexican textile mills and apparel producers had a lucrative protected market and did not have to export. This situation is now changing with the liberalization of the Mexican market, which is forcing Mexican producers to become more competitive. There is a possibility that the liberalized Mexican investment regime will attract investors into this sector, allowing the creation of a world-class industry. If Mexico does become significantly more competitive, then the U.S. administration of the MFA will become an important factor in the ability of Mexico to export to the United States. In fact, a U.S. commitment to provide liberal access for Mexican exports at much higher levels than currently in effect will actually encourage this type of investment flow.

The United States argues that it was particularly generous to Mexico in the most recent four-year renewal of the bilateral agreement, which began on January 1, 1988 and expires on January 1, 1992. This bilateral agreement provided for quota levels 15 percent above the levels in previous agreements. The United States agreed to large increases for acrylic yarn, a category previously embargoed. The United States also granted generous quota treatment to categories consisting of a large percentage of U.S.-assembled components under a special regime. As with previous bilateral arrangements, a six percent annual growth rate was provided for all categories except wool, in which the standard one percent growth rate applied.

The United States maintains a stricter regime toward the larger Far Eastern suppliers, Hong Kong, Korea, and Taiwan and to a certain extent, the People's Republic of China. Hardly any growth is provided at the time agreements are renewed with these suppliers. This restrictive policy is resulting in smaller suppliers, including Mexico and

Caribbean countries, gaining a larger share of the U.S. market at the expense of the traditional suppliers.

The most significant new provisions of the current bilateral agreement were those establishing a special regime for certain apparel and madeup products. The program, although not identical and less generous, is similar to the guaranteed access program in effect for the Caribbean Basin Initiative (CBI) beneficiary countries since 1986. Both programs cover foreign apparel assembled from fabrics formed and cut in the United States, and both programs have the same rigorous safeguards against fraud. In the CBI program, separate limitations known as Guaranteed Access Levels (GALs) are established for eligible imports, in addition to specific limits or designated consultation levels on regular imports. GALs are established at levels that cover current production, unused capacity, and committed expansion of these imports. In essence, the GALs provide for unlimited entry because they are automatically increased at the exporter's request, unless there is a threat of market disruption.

The special regime for Mexico covers categories in which a large percentage of exports from Mexico are apparel and madeup products produced from fabric formed and cut in the United States. It establishes high levels for imports that qualify as special regime imports because of this U.S. content and lower quotas for imports that do not qualify. The levels for the special regime are not as generous as those in the CBI, since they are not high enough to cover current and future capacity, nor does the regime provide for automatic increases during the period of the current bilateral arrangement other than the normal growth provided in the agreement. Quota levels for categories subject to the special regime are significantly higher than in previous agreements with Mexico.

The restraint levels do not correspond to the distinction between *maquiladora* and national industries. *Maquiladoras* assemble components cut in the United States, whether the fabric has been formed in the United States or in another country. However only apparel and madeup goods produced from the former components would enter under the more generous quotas. *Maquiladora* imports produced from the fabric not formed in the United States would enter under less generous quotas, even if cut in the United States and assembled in the *maquiladora*. They would have to share their quota with the production of Mexican national industry and any production from fabric cut in Mexico or in third countries.

In general under the special regime, access levels for products produced from fabric formed and cut in the United States were 200 percent to 500 percent higher than for apparel produced from fabric not formed and cut in the United States. Thus, the share of these quotas that can be filled by the production of the national industry is smaller than before the special regime was introduced.

The national Mexican industry argues that Mexican negotiators had to accept this to gain generous treatment for special regime categories. The Mexican negotiators argued that even though the allocations were smaller, they would not hurt the national industry, since the industry would not be able to fill even the reduced level. Today, they argue that this may have been a mistake because the national industry is recovering faster than expected and these limitations retard future investment. They do not believe they should have to pay for increased access under the special regime by stricter limitations in other areas, since U.S. mills and apparel producers benefit more from the special regime than Mexican producers.

Mexican Export Performance in the U.S. Market

The performance of Mexican textile exports in the U.S. market over the past few years has been mixed. *Maquiladora* exports have grown significantly, as have acrylic yarn and some fabric exports from the Mexican national industry. Between 1984 and 1988, Mexico more than doubled its exports of *maquiladora* apparel and made-up goods, from 70 million to 141 million square yards equivalent. But the *maquiladora* increase is not as significant as growth in apparel exports assembled from U.S. components in the Caribbean Basin. Although the percentage increase has been about the same, Caribbean increases have been greater by volume since their exports began at a much higher level. Between 1984 and 1988, U.S. imports from the Caribbean grew by 120 percent, for an increase of 273 million square yards equivalent. This was four times greater than the actual Mexican increase.

Table 6.24 lists those categories in which U.S. imports from Mexico exceeded $1 million or 1 million square meter equivalents in 1988 or 1989. Exports of apparel and most mill products produced by the national industry continued to perform poorly until 1989, when they experienced some recovery.

Sublimits of the special regime categories covering apparel from U.S.-formed and cut components were never more than 75 percent filled, and most were filled at lower levels. Two reasons were given for this. First, the higher and more flexible quota levels for such apparel under the CBI and the fact that they have been available for many years, led to a shortage of eligible components for processing in Mexico. Second, given the tightness of the other allocations within this

TABLE 6.24 U.S. Textile and Apparel Imports from Mexico (quantity and value units[a] in millions)

		1988		1989	
		Quan.	Value	Quan.	Value
Cat.	Description	(sme)	($)	(sme)	($)
201	Cotton/manmade fiber other yarn, cordage	1.7	1.0	1.6	2.1
219	Cotton/manmade fabric, duck	3.4	3.7	2.2	1.7
223	Cotton/manmade, non-woven fabric	12.1	2.7	5.9	1.2
224	Cotton/manmade pile and tufted fabric	0.2	0.6	0.5	1.5
229	Cotton/manmade fiber special purpose fabric	7.0	2.6	6.9	3.6
237	Cotton/manmade fiber playsuits, sunsuits, etc.	0.6	1.1	0.5`	1.2
239	Cotton/manmade fiber baby wear	0.2	0.4	2.8	5.7
300	Carded (uncombed) cotton yarn	19.5	5.3	14.1	4.2
301	Combed cotton yarn	11.8	5.0	14.5	6.1
313	Cotton fabric, sheeting	4.0	2.5	15.8	8.5
334	Men & boys' cotton other coats	1.8	5.8	0.5	1.5
335	Women & girls' cotton coats	2.3	7.2	0.8	2.3
336	Cotton dresses	3.5	6.2	3.6	6.5
338	Men & boys' cotton knit shirts	0.7	4.0	0.6	3.1
339	Women & girls' cotton knit shirts, blouses	2.1	11.8	1.7	10.2
340	Men & boys' cotton woven shirts	4.2	13.9	4.2	15.2
341	Women & girls' cotton woven shirts, blouses	3.8	12.3	3.0	10.4
342	Cotton skirts	1.9	7.0	1.2	4.3
347	Men & boys' cotton trousers, breeches, shorts	20.8	80.4	26.4	109.4
348	Women & girls' cotton trousers, breeches, shorts	11.7	46.3	16.6	67.7
350	Cotton dressing gowns	0.2	0.6	0.5	1.5
351	Cotton nightwear and pajamas	1.3	2.0	0.9	1.6
352	Cotton underwear	5.3	6.1	6.3	5.8
359	Cotton other apparel	6.7	9.0	6.5	8.3
363	Cotton towels, terry and other pile	1.2	3.4	0.7	3.3
369	Cotton other manufactures n.e.s.[b]	4.4	5.5	13.1	10.7
410	Wool fabric, other fiber fabric containing wool	0.3	1.8	0.1	0.8
433	Men & boys' wool suit-type coats	0.3	4.3	0.2	3.2
435	Women & girls' wool coats	0.3	1.6	0.2	1.4
443	Men & boys' wool suits	0.2	3.1	0.4	6.8
447	Men & boys' wool trousers, breeches, shorts	0.1	1.7	0.0	0.5
465	Wool floor coverings	0.1	1.3	0.2	1.5
600	Manmade fiber yarn of textured filament	40.0	13.1	49.6	18.6
604	Manmade fiber yarn of synthetic staple	7.1	3.0	9.3	4.2
606	Manmade fiber yarn of non-textured filament	63.2	9.2	34.9	6.4
607	Manmade fiber, other staple yarn	10.2	6.7	8.4	5.2
621	Manmade fiber fabric, impression	1.3	1.6	0.0	0.2
624	Manmade fiber fabric, 15% to 36% wool	0.2	0.5	0.4	1.3
632	Manmade fiber hosiery	1.1	1.2	1.1	1.0
633	Men & boys' manmade fiber suit type coats	1.9	12.4	2.1	15.4
634	Men & boys' manmade fiber other coats	1.1	2.7	0.5	1.9
635	Women & girls' manmade fiber coats	2.3	7.3	1.9	7.0
636	Manmade fiber dresses	2.4	5.2	2.2	5.2

(continues)

TABLE 6.24 (*continued*)

		1988		1989	
		Quan.	Value	Quan.	Value
Cat.	Description	(sme)	($)	(sme)	($)
638	Men & boys' manmade fiber knit shirts	0.6	1.0	1.1	1.3
639	Women & girls' manmade fiber knit shirts, blouses	1.1	2.6	2.0	6.3
640	Men & boys' manmade fiber woven shirts	1.1	3.1	1.0	2.9
641	Women & girls' manmade fiber woven shirts, blouses	5.7	20.6	5.4	22.1
642	Manmade fiber skirts	1.7	5.9	1.0	3.6
647	Men & boys' manmade fiber trousers, breeches, shorts	14.8	63.2	11.7	57.8
648	Women & girls' manmade fiber trousers, breeches, shorts	2.4	6.7	3.3	10.3
649	Manmade fiber brassieres & body support garments	5.8	35.1	6.4	41.4
650	Manmade fiber dressing gowns	0.9	1.3	1.2	1.8
651	Manmade fiber nightwear and pajamas	9.5	7.4	10.8	9.3
652	Manmade fiber underwear	22.3	17.3	24.4	22.2
659	Manmade fiber other apparel	13.8	13.9	21.6	19.5
665	Manmade fiber floor coverings	1.6	10.9	1.6	10.5
666	Manmade fiber other home furnishings	36.3	16.3	40.2	15.7
669	Manmade fiber other manufactures n.e.s.[b]	13.2	4.4	13.8	5.3
670	Manmade fiber flatgoods, handbags, luggage	6.0	17.5	8.3	25.1
810	Silk blend, non-cotton vegetable fiber fabric	1.3	1.2	1.2	1.1
899	Silk blend non-cotton vegetable fiber, other manufactures n.e.s.[b]	13.0	0.6	5.2	0.2

[a]Categories with values less than $1 million or fewer than 1 million square meters in both years are omitted.

[b]Not elsewhere specified.

Source: Adapted from International Development Systems, Inc., compiled from U.S. Bureau of the Census data.

category for non-U.S. components and the desire to maintain a quota record in these categories, many exports eligible for the larger quotas were still shipped under the more restrictive quotas.

The Mexican national industry appears to have filled only one quota, that of acrylic yarn. Wool suits have been largely filled, but many of these suits were from *maquiladora* operations and the overall quota was very small. The non-U.S. component subsector of the quota for manmade fiber and cotton trousers was completely filled, but this was principally by *maquiladora* operations. *Maquiladora* exports make up most of this saturated pants subquota.

Despite the devaluation and the surge in many manufactured exports, Mexico has not been able to fill most existing quotas for Mexican-made fabric and apparel. Mexico tried for many years to encourage exports from the national industry. Before the special regime was implemented in 1989, the quota could be filled by either chapter 98 or full Mexican production. The government encouraged national producers to fill the quotas and, in fact, told *maquiladora* producers that they would receive allocations above minimum levels only if quotas were not filled by the national industry. This was a legitimate objective, since full Mexican production contained much more Mexican value added and provided a yarn and fabric market. Yet national production often represented less than 10 percent of apparel exports.

This occurred in part because the protected Mexican market was more lucrative and attractive to domestic producers than competing in export markets. The subsequent opening of the Mexican market should have reduced, if not eliminated, any price differential between global and domestic markets. However, exports from the national industry were not officially encouraged even after Mexican import barriers were reduced. The Mexican government was reportedly concerned that increased exports would create domestic shortages and inflation, and did not object strenuously to the small quota share allotted to many national production categories under the special regime. Given the national industry's limited export capacity, it may have been easy for Mexico to accept low limits in these products in exchange for expansion of *maquiladora* quotas.

The national industry also faced a shortage of foreign exchange which made it difficult to modernize. This lack of capital may have also contributed to inferior levels of quality and workmanship that do not meet international standards.

The exception to the uninspiring export performance of the Mexican national industry has been in filament or acrylic yarn. Despite the imposition of dumping and countervailing duties on these products, Mexico exceeded its quota for this item over most of this decade, prompting the embargo of some shipments. In 1989, Mexico filled almost all of its acrylic yarn quota, exporting more than 2 million square meters equivalent.

Mexican Exports and U.S. Textile Politics

The U.S. textile and apparel industry has focused its political campaign on capping increases in textile imports to a level equal to or below increases in U.S. textile consumption. To achieve this objective, the industry formed the Fiber, Fabric and Apparel Coalition for Trade. The coalition has 26 members, including industry associations and unions such as the Cotton, Wool and Manmade Fiber Producers, the American Textile Manufacturers Institute, the American Apparel

Manufacturers Association, the International Ladies Garment Workers Union, and the Amalgamated Clothing and Textiles Workers Union.

The coalition's objective is to secure passage of legislation that would tie the growth of imports to the growth of the U.S. market. The argument is that without a new restraint program, the textile import program will continue to allow unacceptable import increases. They are opposed to the following practices under current procedures:

1. Extending large increases in import levels when bilateral agreements are renewed.
2. The ability of some countries to carry over unused quotas and to shift unused quotas from one category into another.
3. The ability of new entrants to build up trade before the U.S. government requests limits.
4. The migration of production from countries in which categories are limited to countries in which categories are not limited.
5. The establishment of new quotas at levels much higher than the minimum level stipulated by the MFA.
6. Shoddy enforcement that allows countries to violate their agreements with transshipments, mislabeling, and other procedures.

The industry was successful in both 1985–1986 and 1987–1988 in gaining congressional passage of legislation to establish global ceilings. However, both bills were vetoed by President Reagan. Textile industry supporters in Congress introduced new bills in 1989–1990, but none became law.

The major political obstacle to improving the terms of the special regime quotas for Mexico is the ability of the industry coalition to maintain unity among diverse members. Thus, many members of the coalition who would benefit from improved access for Mexican *maquiladora* production do not lobby hard for it. U.S. apparel workers fear the loss of jobs to Mexican assembly operations. The unions, particularly the International Ladies Garment Workers Union, have considerable influence with urban Democrats and have also enlisted the support of the powerful AFL-CIO. Mills in the South, which have strong ties to Republicans and conservative Democrats, do not want to anger the unions, thereby threatening the unity of the coalition. They reluctantly support union opposition to special treatment for Mexico unless it is accompanied by offsetting reductions in access from other suppliers. The Bush administration opposes such offsets on the grounds that they are GATT illegal and contrary to the MFA.

Apparel manufacturers, on the other hand, are too dispersed to have significant political power. They are also divided between those who rely on foreign operations and those relying on domestic production. Additionally, companies that rely on Far Eastern imports oppose special treatment for Mexico because it might lead to offsetting reductions from these suppliers or put them at a competitive disadvantage. They prefer an evenhanded global policy.

Political opposition to increased imports of apparel assembled from U.S. components was most recently exemplified in the debate on legislation to enhance the CBI. Much of the political dynamic evident in the debate would be applicable to Mexico as well. The major provision of this legislation would have provided duty-free entry and statutorily guaranteed access for this type of apparel from the CBI. The current special access program for the Caribbean is an administrative program which can be ended at any time. Apparel workers convinced the AFL-CIO to actively oppose the provisions. Not surprisingly, the Bush administration opposed the offset desired by the unions because it would have established an implicit global ceiling. Apparel importers and retailers remained largely neutral in this effort. Eventually, the textile provisions were dropped from the legislation.

This experience shows that special treatment is more successful when implemented through administrative actions than through congressional legislation. The only exception might be if such proposals formed part of a broader bilateral free trade agreement. This is because the special rules for Congressional consideration of trade agreements limit the influence of special interest groups. Under these fast-track procedures, Congress must vote these agreements up or down within a specific time period. Dilatory parliamentary maneuvers, including long speeches, tabling, committee delays, and destructive amendments, are not permitted. It would be difficult for the textile industry to muster enough votes to defeat such an initiative, particularly if related to Mexico, which currently enjoys great popularity in the U.S. Congress.

Due to GATT commitments, it is difficult to envision special tariff treatment for Mexico, as opposed to quantitative measures, without a free trade agreement. Since Mexico is not a principal supplier of any important textile and apparel product, the nation cannot negotiate duty reductions and there would be strong domestic opposition to duty reduction affecting all suppliers.

The United States and Mexico will decide in 1991 whether to formally pursue bilateral free trade negotiations. In the interim, duty-free treatment could be provided for apparel imports produced from

U.S.-formed and cut components from all sources. In that case, the CBI and Mexico would be the primary beneficiaries of the duty reduction.

At least one constraint on special treatment for Mexico appears to have disappeared. U.S. policy was based on the premise that any special treatment for Mexico should be less generous than that provided to beneficiary nations under the CBI. It was felt that, with a contiguous border, lower wage rates, a better-trained labor force, greater political stability, and a longer history of sewing operations, Mexico already had a competitive advantage over the CBI beneficiaries in apparel trade.

This attitude appears to be changing. In the U.S. textile industry there is increasing recognition that the future depends on both the CBI beneficiaries and Mexico as complementary, not competing sources. Second, while Far Eastern investment is increasing in the Caribbean, it is only modest in Mexico. Therefore, increased imports from Mexico should not face U.S. industry opposition arising from fears of transshipment from Far Eastern companies. Recent indications that Far Eastern investment may be increasing in Mexico's apparel sector could change this perception.

While the Caribbean and Central America were the favored regions of the Reagan administration, the Bush administration has shifted attention to Mexico. Differences in attitudes toward Central America were a source of divisiveness between the United States and Mexico during the Reagan and de la Madrid administrations. Both countries have recently played down this issue. Following a bipartisan agreement on Central America reached early in the Bush administration, there is less focus on Central American policy, and, in any case, events in Eastern Europe and the Middle East have overshadowed Central American developments. This was not changed by the intensification of the conflict in El Salvador at the end of 1989.

It remains to be seen whether this improvement in bilateral relations will be translated into more favorable U.S. import treatment for Mexican mill products and apparel, as opposed to *maquiladora* products. If the issue is framed so that Mexico's access is increased as Far Eastern exports are reduced, there is greater chance for success. Imports from Mexican national industry are seen as less threatening to U.S. producers than those from the Far East or from Far Eastern-controlled facilities in third countries. Far Eastern producers do not market through U.S. apparel companies, but often sell directly to retailers or to contractors in the United States. In contrast, Mexican producers are more likely to use normal U.S. distribution channels, including U.S. apparel companies.

Future Trade Policy Prospects

There is reason to be optimistic about the possibilities for deeper integration between the U.S. and Mexican textile and apparel industries, both for *maquiladora* and for national production.

Maquiladora operations in apparel will expand. Such operations are increasingly justified on an economic basis. Exchange rate relationships will continue to favor labor-intensive operations in Mexico and the Caribbean over traditional Far Eastern sources. Revised Mexican laws increasing the geographic scope for *maquiladora* operations and permitting increased sales in Mexico should aid *maquiladora* development. Substantial liberalization is likely to be granted to *maquiladora* production in the renewed 1992 agreement.

Although more difficult to achieve, the complete elimination of duties on special regime imports during bilateral tariff negotiations in the context of the Uruguay Round should not be ruled out. President Bush has authority to reduce or completely eliminate duties that are subject to fast-track congressional approval.

The more difficult question is whether U.S. access can be increased for mill products and apparel of entirely Mexican origin. Existing quotas are not now the major constraint on increased Mexican exports, except in one or two categories, although this situation may be changing as Mexican exports increase. It is possible than the current interim discussions may correct this problem.

The major constraint is the lack of competitiveness of the Mexican industry. Foreign investment will help improve the industry's productivity, quality control, and range of products. Joint ventures can improve the ability of Mexican producers to carry out a larger number of close tolerance operations, introduce technologically advanced machinery, produce better-quality items, and establish more flexible production runs. Additionally, some of the automated production methods used in U.S. production could be incorporated into the Mexican production process. Joint ventures with U.S. apparel manufacturers would not only assure more efficient production but would also assure integration into the U.S. distribution network.

One form of integration may be to assemble components made from Mexican-formed and cut fabric in existing *maquiladoras*. This would relieve the pressure of the shortage of U.S. fabric on these *maquiladora* industries, compensate Mexico for its opening of its borders to *maquiladora* imports, and increase the Mexican value added component of these operations. If such a transformation occurs, then the question of improved U.S. access for Mexican mill products and apparel will have to be addressed. The domestic industry would be less opposed to providing favorable treatment to these exports if such treatment is offset by reductions in access for imports from other regions.

Three issues must be addressed in free trade negotiations for this sector. First is the schedule for textile and apparel duty reductions. Second is the potential effect of a free trade agreement on the bilateral restraints. The negotiators must decide whether restraints should be completely lifted, liberalized, or dealt with outside the context of free trade negotiations. The third issue centers on rules of origin and whether they will allow Far Eastern components sewn in Mexico to benefit from the agreement.

Integration of the U.S. and Mexican industries will help both countries meet competitive challenges in the next century. The liberalization of textiles trade, if accomplished as part of the Uruguay Round, will force both countries to produce at world competitive levels to meet Far Eastern competition. U.S. trade experts expect exports from China, India, Pakistan, Bangladesh, Indonesia, and other competitive Far Eastern countries to be the main beneficiaries of sectoral reintegration into GATT, since exports from these countries are internationally competitive.

Joint ventures in *maquiladora* production, combining U.S. mills and Mexican sewing operations, have already demonstrated competitiveness. U.S. and Mexican competitiveness will be enhanced when their national industries are more fully integrated. Liberalization under the free trade agreement will encourage these developments.

SEVEN

Computers

Computers:
The U.S.-Mexican Relationship

Donald R. Lyman

Mexico's computer industry is highly integrated with that of the United States. Integration has been shaped mainly by the Mexican government's sectoral program in electronics. If the sectoral program disappears, integration will decrease or continue in a different form. The international computer industry is rapidly changing and increasingly competitive. Without the Mexican sectoral program, these forces will work against continuation of the current model for integration with the United States.

Despite impressive export and production statistics, the Mexican industry is still relatively undeveloped and uncompetitive. Only a few Mexican computer products are truly competitive internationally. The Mexican labor force has not developed strong computer manufacturing skills, except in a few multinational companies, and even those will be hard put to meet the demands of rapid technological change. Moreover, multinational corporations are increasingly limiting sourcing to one or two locations to lessen managerial burdens, with competition forcing the choice of the lowest cost production sites.

The speed of change and intensity of competition in the international computer industry also presents opportunities for Mexico. Rapid change often leaves niches temporarily unfilled or filled with unsatisfactory or expensive products. Mexico should choose its niches, ones in which it has a good chance to obtain a competitive advantage, even if these are in product areas that have not received government encouragement through the current sectoral program. Mexico is already competitive in a few labor-intensive parts and subassemblies. This has happened despite the sectoral program's focus on production of high technology input and complete computers. With a focused and coordinated effort, and especially without a government program encouraging a different production focus, Mexico can be competitive in even more of these products. With time, Mexico must learn to integrate these labor-intensive inputs, first with higher technology components manufactured elsewhere, and, eventually, in Mexico. Others will seize this opportunity if Mexico does not.

Industry Integration with the United States

The Mexican government's unpublished electronics sectoral program has shaped the computer industry and determined the level of integration with the United States. The sectoral program began as a draft decree in 1981 a precursor of what is now the Secretaría de Comercio y Fomento Industrial (SECOFI). Because of diplomatic pressure and domestic industry criticism, the decree was never published, but its detailed performance requirements—local content, exports, balance of trade, balance of payments, technology transfer features—became the basis for subsequent sectoral regulation.

To sell computers in Mexico, foreign companies have been required to conform to the general outlines of the sectoral program. The details have been negotiated on a company-by-company, product-by-product basis with SECOFI. SECOFI has sought the local manufacture of mini and microcomputers, with an increasing amount of local production of parts and subassemblies, as well as a neutral or positive trade balance. Market access to the mini or microcomputer area for products not produced in Mexico has required local production of other products in the same product areas. To import mainframe computers, local manufacturing of other computer-related products is required, as is compensation for mainframe imports with exports of computers or other goods.

Since 1986, multinationals meeting stiff performance requirements have been allowed, on a case-by-case basis, to hold complete equity in local manufacturing ventures for personal computers. Some of the larger U.S. computer companies have chosen this route. Smaller U.S., Asian, and European companies have chosen to license their technology or to take a minority position in joint ventures.

Production statistics seem to indicate the Mexican government's policy has succeeded. Production of minicomputers rose from $44 million in 1982 to $152 million in 1987. Microcomputer production rose from $26 million in 1982 to $210 million in 1987. Production of peripherals rose from $105 million in 1982 to $295 million in 1987. Production of subassemblies and parts has also increased.[1]

Export results are similarly impressive. Exports of computer systems and peripherals rose from $5 million in 1982 to $148 million in 1987 to well over $300 million in 1988. Export of subassemblies and parts has increased, if more slowly. Most of the exports have been by U.S. companies, but have gone more often to other Latin American countries and to the Far East than to the United States.[2]

Imports have grown, too, with the composition changing over time. Components and parts imports for manufacture have increased sharply, while import of computers has fallen. Total imports have increased from $149 million in 1982 to approximately $200 million in 1987 and $325 million in 1988.[3] Over 80 percent of the computers and computer parts have come from the United States, as have 75 percent of the peripherals and peripheral parts.[4] The growth of component and parts imports indicates increased local assembly and some increase in local value added. The trade balance shifted from a negative $103 million in 1982 to a $2 million positive balance in 1987.[5]

Employment generation has also been impressive, with direct employment rising from 3,000 or 4,000 in 1985 to 12,000 in 1988, with many more employed indirectly by the industry.[6]

Most of the investment in the manufacture of mini and microcomputers under the sectoral decree has been by U.S. companies, which have also accounted for the majority of exports. The major manufacturers of minicomputers include IBM, Hewlett Packard, NCR, DEC, and Honeywell, all U.S. companies. The major manufacturers of microcomputers include IBM, Hewlett Packard, Unisys, and Tandy, all U.S. companies; and Printaform, Electra, Televideo, Denki Corona, and Sigma, using licensed Taiwanese and Japanese technology. Unisys manufactures in a joint venture with Banamex, one of the largest Mexican banks. Most of the U.S. companies produce state-of-the art personal computers, while the others produce small, old technology machines for home or entertainment use. Exports, mainly of up-to-date machines, go all over the world, but the major emphasis has been on exports to Latin America and to Asia.[7]

Most foreign investment in manufacturing has been to gain access to the Mexican market, as required by the sectoral program. Computer production in Mexico has not offered a strong competitive advantage, except for certain labor-intensive parts and subassemblies, which do not weigh heavily in the final cost of mini or microcomputers.

The size of the Mexican market has not been sufficient to justify sizeable investment in the absence of real cost advantages. Most U.S. companies, however, because of the enormous potential of the Mexican market, have sought to obtain market access. They also have had other strategic imperatives, such as establishing an alternative to Brazil's market reserve, which has no production or importation of minis or micros by non-Brazilian companies, and obtaining duty preferences under the Latin American Integration Agreement . Finally, once they have obtained access, they have been competing in a protected or semi-protected market. But protection has not been absolute with such a long, relatively porous border between the United States and Mexico.

Although the sectoral program has not left Mexico lastingly competitive in computer exports, the sectoral program has done better from a domestic standpoint. Computers made in Mexico sell there at a much smaller differential to U.S. prices than computers anywhere else in Latin America or compared with imported computers. The Mexican government sets price limits, generally 10 percent to 20 percent above U.S. list prices, as part of its sectoral program. The large border with the United States, of course, exerts a downward pressure on prices, as does the absence of tariffs on imported computer parts, which lessens the price of locally manufactured or assembled computers compared with the prices of imported computers.

In parts and subassemblies, U.S., Japanese, and Mexican companies have invested in manufacturing. Much investment has been at the initiative of large computer manufacturers as they sought to increase their local content under the sectoral program. The weighted local content formula utilized by SECOFI gives more weight to high technology parts and subassemblies than to labor-intensive ones. These large manufacturers have provided technology transfer, equity capital, and equipment to move their suppliers into these high technology processes. For example, Adtec is a joint venture of U.S.-based SCI and Mexican-based Elamex. Adtec makes circuit boards for IBM and Hewlett Packard, exporting a large percentage of its production. Adtec is moving into surface mounted technology, as is Compubur, the joint venture of Unisys and Banamex. Compubur has begun the manufacture of multi-layered cards. IBM has provided technical assistance and equipment to Adtec.

Most of the local parts manufacturing activities, however, are of lower technology, more labor-intensive products. Most of the production is for the local market. Some, however, has been for export under the *maquiladora* program. For example, Unisys makes wire harnesses, cables, and disk heads in Guadalajara for export.

In the manufacture of peripherals, there has been more investment, proportionally, by Mexican companies. These companies often use technology licensed from the United States or Japan. Mexican companies have been especially active in printers and terminals, while in storage devices, multinational companies have made greater investments. Mexican printer manufacturers locally produce all components except the printing head, for which they do assembly and precision adjustment. There have been few exports, except by multinationals, mainly Hewlett Packard, which manufactures disk and tape storage units in Mexico for export to Canada, Australia, and Latin America. As part of its international cost-cutting efforts, Unisys recently closed a *maquila* plant in Nogales that had assembled disk drives and disk subassemblies.

Mexico's impressive performance still leaves open many questions about the computer industry's future there. Does the Mexican computer industry, as a whole or in part, have a comparative advantage that will allow it to continue to be integrated, still playing a significant role, with its United States counterpart? If not, can it hope to play such a role in the future? Has the country's work force obtained enough education, training, and experience to be truly competitive in the computer industry?

Computers made in Mexico by some multinationals have become internationally competitive in quality and price, but this is not a permanent advantage, nor one without hidden costs. There has been a large initial cost to transfer the necessary technology to in-house manufacturing employees and to part and subassembly suppliers, especially for higher technology, less labor-intensive subassemblies.

For parts and subassembly suppliers, the story is nevertheless slightly more positive than for computer manufacturers. Low technology suppliers, for example, those producing metal or plastic parts (covers, frames) or electric subassemblies or parts (power supplies, cables) have had lower initial costs to the companies they supply, while being more price and quality competitive than high technology suppliers. A few Mexican high-technology suppliers have become competitive with time, but barely so. But even the position of the strongest suppliers is only temporary. As technology evolves rapidly, large investments will be necessary to keep high technology suppliers and in-house manufacturing employees competitive. Local skills for producing very high technology subassemblies are still insufficient to keep up with the United States, Europe, and the Far East.

In peripherals, local skills are greater than in computers or computer parts and subassemblies, but, ironically, competition worldwide is much more intense. Mexican production is slightly behind in quality and price what is being produced in Asia.

Despite ambitious programs by some multinationals and by the Mexican government, Mexico does not have sufficient skilled professionals in manufacturing, materials science, computer science, and related fields to build a competitive computer industry. Crucial electrical engineering professionals are in especially short supply. Multinational and Mexican companies are justifiably proud of what they have accomplished in training their own people and in developing the skills of their vendors and business partners. But the scale of what they have done has not been enough to transform the Mexican industry into one with the broad-based infrastructure necessary to compete internationally. Technology transfer by multinationals has been done on a surprisingly large scale, considering the limited human infrastructure, but has not been enough to transform the industry into a permanently competitive one. Much of the production of computers by local companies has been merely "screwdriver" assembly, with little value added. This type of work has not increased local skills or developed the local infrastructure, except perhaps in distribution and customer support.

Even where Mexico has a small, temporary competitive advantage, it will be difficult to maintain production there. The trend within the computer industry is toward single or double sourcing of final products whenever possible, with production concentrated in the larger markets—the United States, Canada, Europe, Asia. Even for labor-intensive products, the difficulties of managing numerous manufacturing plants might negate the advantage gained by Mexico's low labor costs. Finally, producing low-cost, high-quality, labor-intensive inputs will only be a short-term solution because purchasers will look toward suppliers capable of integrating labor-intensive inputs with more sophisticated, high technology components and subassemblies.

The Future

The future of the Mexican computer industry and its integration with the United States depend upon Mexican government policy decisions on the future of the sectoral program and on policy steps once that decision is taken.

The Mexican government has talked publicly about removing the sectoral program. It has not yet established a timetable for doing so. The electronics, pharmaceutical, and auto industries are the only industries all or partially under programs of sectoral regulation, and the auto program has been substantially modified. Since Mexico signed a bilateral subsidies agreement in 1985 and entered the General Agreement on Tariffs and Trade (GATT) in 1986, Mexico has been aggressively liberalizing its trade regime. This liberalization continued with increased momentum under the Salinas administration.

The Mexican and U.S. governments agreed in 1987 to include the computer industry in talks under the bilateral framework agreement for investment and trade. Talks to date have only been exploratory. An agreement signed by both governments in October 1989, mentions product area negotiations to facilitate trade and investment. Perhaps the computer sector will be included in such negotiations. The possibility also exists that Mexico will unilaterally deregulate the computer sector.

Because the sectoral program has shaped integration with the United States computer industry, its dismantling would have a dramatic effect on future integration. Companies from all over the world, many previously kept out by the sectoral program, will enter the market, mainly selling their products. Those large international companies that have long been involved in Mexico will probably maintain some sort of manufacturing presence, if perhaps different from their current activities. Given Mexico's comparative advantage in labor-intensive subassemblies and parts, most multinational production can be expected to focus there first.

The long-term extent of integration would depend heavily, however, upon Mexico developing the skills and the infrastructure to combine these labor-intensive parts and subassemblies with more high technology parts and subassemblies, with at least some of the latter manufactured in Mexico. Mexico will need to have local architecture and design capabilities for these subassemblies to be competitive.

Policy Issues

Key policy issues involved in the future of the Mexican computer industry and its integration with the United States computer industry are:

If Mexico deregulates the computer industry, how should the short-term pressures on a suboptimized domestic industry based on a protected market be balanced against the benefits to the Mexican economy of a free trade regime?

What role, if any, does Mexico want to play in the international computer industry? Does Mexico have, or can it develop a true comparative advantage?

Should free market forces and private sector initiatives alone be allowed to shape the future of the Mexican computer industry and its integration with the U.S. industry or should the Mexican and/or the U.S. government play a role?

Recommendations

Mexico should deregulate its computer industry in a manner that will not punish those companies that have made enormous investments based on operating in a partially protected market. Import restrictions should be steadily phased out, first for those product areas in which there is no local manufacturing, then for minis and finally for micros. This should be completed under a fixed timetable, with no delays, exceptions, or departures from the schedule.

The U.S. and Mexican governments should work together with the private sectors in both countries to help the Mexicans decide where the best future opportunities in the computer industry might be. Then, they should jointly develop an education and training program, perhaps funded initially by international lending institutions such as the World Bank and the Inter-American Development Bank, to help Mexico pursue these opportunities. The emphasis would not be on distorting market forces or developing a false competitive advantage, but in understanding market forces and discovering where a true comparative advantage might lie. Once the program had begun to show results, private capital would be expected to bear the funding burden.

Both governments should increase the level of technology and scientific exchange, hoping to build a stronger scientific and technological infrastructure in Mexico that will allow market forces to increase Mexico's comparative advantage over time within the computer industry. Tax incentives should be created for private efforts in this area.

Specific computer industry infrastructure projects should be developed in the most promising areas. Initial efforts should be by governments or international lending institutions to show a record of success that will in turn attract private capital. In these project areas, there should be skills development in relevant basic sciences and in key applied science areas. Mexican subassembly architecture and design capabilities should be developed and encouraged, giving Mexico the base to expand its local content contribution.

Notes

1. Wallace y Associados, "Profile of Mini and Micro Computer Systems Market," for the U.S. Embassy, Mexico, June 1988, pp. 124-125. There are numerous and conflicting statistics for the Mexican computer industry. This occurs because there are many different ways of counting and classifying computer products, as well as problems with the gray market and smuggling during various periods. I won't debate the merits of the various statistics, but

instead utilize them to discuss the general trends they seem to indicate. If there is a major contradiction among statistics that seems to make conclusions difficult, I will mention that constraint. My focus will be on computer hardware. Software is a key area, but one that deserves discussion in a separate paper.

2. Wallace, "Profile," p. 70.

3. Author's estimate for 1987. The 1988 figure is based on industry studies. The 1982 statistics are based on Wallace, "Profile," p. 132. Imports of components have gone up more sharply than imports of finished goods, from $18 million in 1982 to $285 million in 1988.

4. Wallace, "Profile," pp. 132-133.

5. There is much debate about these trade figures, and the differences among the available numbers are substantial and difficult to resolve. Nevertheless, there is no doubt that Mexico's trade balance in the computer industry has improved dramatically since 1982.

6. William Cline, *Informatics and Development: Trade and Industrial Policy in Argentina, Brazil, and Mexico* (Washington, D.C.: Economics International, Inc., 1987), p. 91; United States Trade Center, Mexico, *Market Research Report*, 1989.

7. Wallace, "Profile," pp. 60-63.

EIGHT

Food

Food: U.S. Perspective

Lloyd E. Slater

To gain realistic perspective on present and potential integration between the food industries of the United States and Mexico, the scope of what constitutes a food industry must be established. Can one realistically limit our view of the industry in the United States and Mexico simply to factories that process and sell food?

Societal needs as well as search for profits must also be factored into the analysis and speculation. Can one realistically isolate market dynamics from influences such as food security and public health?

In recent years, agriculture, industrial processing, and global distribution of food products, formerly separate endeavors, have become closely intertwined. This is especially true in the United States, Western Europe and Japan, where giant multinational corporations control farm production. They process and store an increasing array of foods, often as trading commodities as well as consumer products, own many of the marketing outlets, and even operate large restaurant chains.

Figure 8.1 conceptualizes this enlarged view of a nation's modern food industry, perhaps better described as a "food system." While it shows the linkages between the growing, processing, and distribution of food, it also reveals the many optional pathways and opportunities for maximizing production given a nation's limits in natural resources, funds, and technology.[1]

Another recent development has been a gradual integration of each nation's food production and requirements (its supply and demand) into an evolving world food system. This materialized following World War II, when rapid population growth, severe climatic events, and failing agricultural systems created national food shortages that necessitated massive imports of grain. The impact of unpredictable

FIGURE 8.1 Elements in a Developed Nation Food System

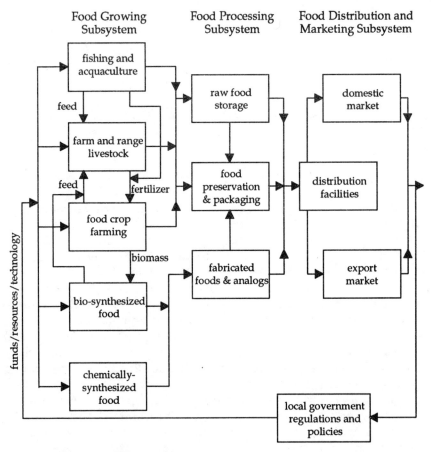

Source: L.E. Slater, 1978

weather, skewed national development priorities, and varied measures in population control have proven major forces within this global system.

Professor Donella Meadows of Dartmouth College has analyzed the emerging global food system. In studying the mechanisms which influence present and future availability of food, she developed the Composite Model of the World Food System shown in Figure 8.2. She augmented the basic Western economic supply-demand model with demographic influences constrained by environmental and population factors, as well as unequal distribution of social benefits.[2]

Figure 8.2 A Composite Model of the World Food System

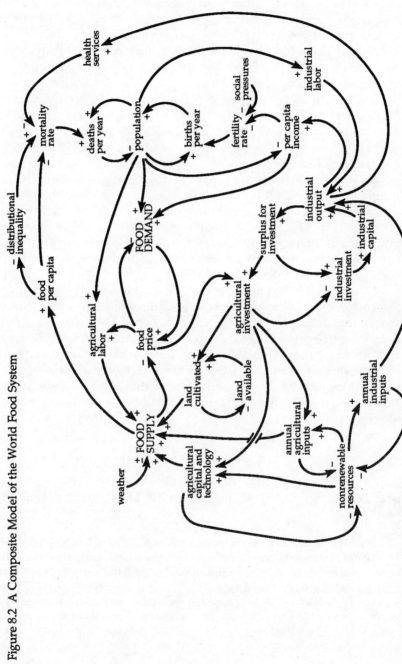

Source: Donella Meadows, 1975.

Professor Meadows' macro-perspective of forces at work in world food availability has a micro-perspective counterpart in a United Nations Research Institute for Social Development (UNRISD) program in Mexico called "Food Systems and Society." Its leader, Professor Rolando García of the Universidad Autónoma Metropolitana–Xochimilco, through complex systems analysis, has studied a transition from growing food crops to animal feed in the Bajío, a change which has led to increasing need for imported beans and corn, the staples of Mexico's poor. The work has revealed the astonishing number of forces—physical, social, economic, political—in the transition. It offers food policy decision makers rare insight into the roots of a national problem.[3]

While the task here is to appraise the relationship between food industries of the United States and Mexico, it is clear that such an examination cannot be targeted simply on analysis of production indices or economic indicators. Our enlarged perspective requires viewing the industries as interacting systems, sensitive in their performance to both countries' economies and societal needs, as well as to other forces at both national and international levels.

My approach is first to depict the U.S. food industry by describing its dimensions, character and trends for future developments. Next, to assess the potential for integration between the two industries, I examine the resource base for Mexican food production and how far and well it has been exploited. Then a survey of past and present integrative efforts between U.S. and Mexican food enterprises explores relevant policy issues. Finally, some thoughts on future closer relationships and suggestions for mutually beneficial initiatives are offered.

The U.S. Food Behemoth

Jim Hightower, Texas' former agriculture commissioner, offered this overview of the U.S. food industry in his 1975 book, *Eat Your Heart Out:*

There are 32,000 food manufacturing firms in the U.S. Fifty of these account for three-fourths of the industry's profits. A handful own most of the processed, heavily advertised brands. Eighty-nine percent of soft drink sales are controlled by Coca Cola, Pepsico, Seven-Up and Royal Crown. Borden, National Dairy and Carnation control 60-70 percent of dairy products. Three national firms produce 50 percent of the beer sold in the U.S. Kellogg, General Mills, General Foods and Quaker Oats account for 91 percent of breakfast cereal sales. The four top vegetable canners sell 60 percent of fruit cocktails, 57 percent of apple sauce, 82 percent of canned figs, 52 percent of sweet corn, 58 percent of tomato paste, 53 percent of canned peas, 72 percent of tomato sauce. Six multinational grain companies now handle 90 percent of all the grain shipped in the entire world.[4]

Commissioner Hightower's 1975 view of industry trends holds up fairly well today, although there have been some remarkable changes among its principal players. As Table 8.1 indicates, it is a huge industry. The nine main product branches listed accounted for 73 percent of the value of all food and beverage shipments in 1988, for an estimated total of more than $468 billion. This makes the food industry second only to health and medical services ($558.7 billion in 1988) among the largest industries in America. The industry contributes about 10 percent to the gross national product. Not factored into the table (the missing 27 percent) are the vast non-processed exports of U.S. corn, wheat, and soybeans, as well as internal sales of fresh farm produce.

Table 8.1 also reveals the U.S. food industry as home-market oriented, exporting less than 4 percent of its production. Thus, it apparently differs from many other developed countries that export 10 percent to 70 percent of domestic food production. This view is grossly misleading, since today's major U.S. food companies now secure a large portion of their earnings from foreign plants that often produce U.S. brand products for local sale.

TABLE 8.1 U.S. Processed Food Produce Statistics 1988 (billions of U.S. dollars)

Product Category	U.S. Production	U.S. Exported	U.S. Imported
Meat and poultry	75.6	3.925	3.647
Dairy products	44.4	0.487	0.736
Fruit and vegetables	41.0	1.241	2.175
Grain mill products	41.6	2.943	0.342
Baker products	23.2	0.062	0.317
Sugar and confections	18.6	0.649	1.333
Fats and oils	17.5	3.295	0.861
Beverages	50.0	0.609	3.478
Misc. foods	29.8	2.709	6.305
Total value	341.7	15.920	19.154

Source: U.S. Department of Commerce, *Industrial Outlook 1989.*

The United States suffers a trade deficit in processed foods because of a general practice of exporting low value-added products, such as fats and oils, meat, poultry and breakfast cereals. Spending about $1,340 per capita on food in 1987, the U.S. consumer increasingly went for high value-added imported items such as confections, cheese, cookies, and alcoholic beverages. The U.S. Department of Commerce estimated that personal consumption of food grew 3.1 percent in 1988 to $513 billion, with meals at home taking up $339 billion and restaurant dining the remainder.[5]

Food Supercorporations Emerge

Jim Hightower's alarm over dominance of the U.S. food industry by a few giant corporations must be at fever pitch today. In 1975, a remarkable consolidation of the industry was just under way, when a few dozen of the larger, wealthier firms started to buy up smaller competitors to achieve brand name dominance, acquire other product lines to enter a full-spectrum market, and move toward the control of supplies as well as market outlets.

A study completed in 1979 by Corporate Data Exchange Inc. confirmed this industry trend. Its *Stock Ownership Directory* (Agribusiness) profiled 222 companies that formed the backbone of the U.S. food system. Of $250 billion in revenues, nearly 75 percent was produced by only 73 corporations. The corporate move toward the consumption end of the system was evident. These firms had acquired and were operating 1,390 restaurants, 8,703 fast-food outlets, and 1,925 retail food and drug stores.

By the late 1980s, a few dozen multi-billion dollar corporations, enlarged by buying up others rather than internal growth, dominated the food industry. Most of the top 10, shown in Table 8.2, moved from single product categories—dairy, meat, cereals, baking, etc.—to full spectrum activities. Only the three listed beverage firms stayed mainly in their field, eliminating hundreds of smaller breweries and soft drink brands in the growth process. One newcomer, RJR, the tobacco products giant, moved into the food big leagues in 1979 by taking in front-ranking Del Monte (sales $1.56 billion in 1978) and even larger Nabisco in 1985. RJR's entry was a harbinger of similar wealthy non-food product firms buying into the stable and steadily growing food market.

By the late 1980s, food company expansion activities seemed almost frenzied as sensible mergers often become hostile takeovers. Some of the deals defied any growth rationale other than possible capital gain benefits. A typical example of the action involves three

TABLE 8.2 Sales of Ten Largest U.S. Food Companies in 1988 (billions of U.S. dollars)

Company	Sales
Philip Morris/General Foods	31.742
RJR Nabisco	17.000
Kraft Inc. (1987 information)	9.876
Anheuser-Busch Inc.	9.706
Conagra Inc.	9.474
Occidental Petroleum/BP	9.066
Coca-Cola Co.	8.337
Mars Inc.	7.500
Pepsico (1987 information)	7.301
Borden Inc.	7.244

Source: *Food Engineering International*, September 1989. Reprinted by permission.

multinationals. In 1987 RJR/Nabisco, then the largest food conglomerate, added Almaden Vineyards to its Hueblein Wine Division for about $130 million, making it No. 2 in the United States as a table wine source. But shortly thereafter, in 1988, Hueblein itself was sold off for about $1.3 billion to Britain's Grand Met (Smirnoff Vodka and other liquors) making it the world's largest wine and spirits vendor.

As Table 8.3 shows, many of these food industry takeovers were billion-dollar transactions—some of the most sizeable recorded in the United States. Philip Morris' $13.1 billion buyout of Kraft, the second largest takeover on record, more than doubled sales for its General

TABLE 8.3 Recent Billion-Dollar Takeovers Involving the U.S. Food Industry

Year	Companies Involved
1984	Nestle S.A. (Swiss) acquired Carnation Corp. for $3 billion
1985	RJR became RJR/Nabisco by taking on Nabisco for $4.9 billion
1987	Bond Corp. (Australia) gained Heileman B.C. for $1.1 billion
1988	Grand Met (U.K.) got RJR/Nabisco's Heublein for $1.3 billion
1988	Philip Morris purchased General Foods Corp. for $5.6 billion
1988	Philip Morris then acquired Kraft for $13.1 billion
1989	Grand Met's prolonged takeover of Pillsbury for $5.5 billion
1989	Management buyout of RJR/Nabisco made final for $25 billion

Source: Compiled by author using *Food Engineering Magazine* data.

Foods Division. Philip Morris thus became, in 1988, the top U.S. food company. On the other hand, RJR/Nabisco, its main rival as largest food conglomerate, built food sales up to $9.4 billion and in late 1988, went private in an estimated $25 billion leveraged buyout—the biggest business deal in U.S. history! Its new management has been steadily selling off food entities to pay off the debt.

Expansion by the Multinationals

Long before this past decade of industry consolidation, many of the larger U.S. food companies sought growth and a competitive edge through overseas initiatives. In 1974, *Food Engineering Magazine's* survey of the leading 75 companies found 60 owning or joint-venturing food plants in 46 different countries. Some of the large firms, Beatrice Foods, Coca Cola, Borden Co., Del Monte, were operating in more than half of these foreign lands. At that time, U.S. food industry investments abroad were $60 billion and were expected to reach $200 billion by 1980. During the same period, the value of world trade in food products was predicted to rise from $275 billion to about $1.5 trillion.[6]

In January 1989, *Food Engineering Magazine* took another look at international outreach by U.S. food companies. It cited a study by the U.S. Department of Agriculture's Economic Research Service of 57 major U.S. food processors whose 1987 sales were $147 billion, or 48 percent of the U.S. total. The survey found the 57 firms were operating 2,503 processing plants, with 26 percent of these abroad. Table 8.4 lists those with 20 or more overseas factories. Sales by these foreign subsidiaries accounted for 30 percent to 50 percent of total corporate sales volume. Table 8.5 shows foreign acquisition strategies of a few of the large food multinationals in 1987.

Tables 8.4 and 8.5, however, offer just a glimmer of the worldwide presence of U.S. food processors. Most, when reporting foreign sales, fail to include income from joint-venture and licensing operations. Many, especially the beverage firms, avoid the costs of setting up subsidiaries abroad by licensing foreign operators to produce their brands for the local market. Others, seeking virgin markets, undertook required joint ventures in socialist and communist nations. For example, Heinz and RJR/Nabisco recently had established joint ventures in China before the Tiananmen Square episode.

Global expansion by U.S. food processors intensified with the anticipated access to a unified European Community market of 320 million people in 1992. H.J. Heinz chairman and CEO, Tony O'Reilly, gave his views on this to shareholders at the 1988 annual meeting.

TABLE 8.4 U.S. Food Firms Owning 20 or More Processing Plants in Foreign Countries

Firm	Total Plants	United States	Percent of Total	Foreign	Percent of Total
CPC International	112	29	26	83	74
Ralston Purina	123	57	46	66	54
RJR/Nabisco	170	123	72	47	28
Kraft	96	52	54	44	46
Philip Morris (GF)	103	60	58	43	42
Heinz	63	25	40	38	60
Quaker Oats	65	31	48	34	52
Campbell Soup	87	59	68	28	32
Borden	153	127	83	26	17
Pepsico	115	91	79	24	21
Conagra	150	127	85	23	15
Int'l Multifoods	45	24	53	21	47
Sara Lee	67	47	70	20	30
McCormick	52	32	62	20	38
TOTAL	1,401	884	63	517	37

Source: Food Engineering Magazine, January 1989. Reprinted by permission.

Justifying recent acquisitions of Orlando S.A. in Spain (see Table 8.5) and Marie Elisabeth (fish canning) in Portugal, as well as earlier development of an ultra-modern tomato concentrate factory in Portugal, O'Reilly said:

> It is not inconceivable to think that in the mega-market of post-1992 all our ketchup in Europe could be sourced from a single location - perhaps Spain or Portugal. It is also not inconceivable that we will develop one single seafood location for the European market.

Heinz, the world's largest ketchup maker, started its foreign prospecting by looking for new farmlands to satisfy its gargantuan appetite for tomatoes. Today, tomato concentrate, aseptically stored in large silos, moves like grain and sugar as a world food commodity.

Foreign food multinationals, spurred by a weak dollar, have also been actively buying up large chunks of the U.S. food industry. In the mid-1980s, British, Canadian, French, and German companies acquired brand-name baking subsidiaries in the United States. Kirin, Japan's leading beer producer, bought five New England-based cola franchise plants. And as seen in Table 8.3, two of the largest multi-billion dollar

TABLE 8.5 Some 1987 Foreign Acquisitions/Investments by U.S. Food Firms

U.S. Firm	Acquisition/ Investment	Country	Products
Borden, Inc.	Kuntzle Group	Germany	Retail bakery chain
	Karl Jaus & Son	Germany	Bakery products
	Albadora Spa	Italy	Pasta
	Patty S.A.	Brazil	Pasta
CPC	Garrick Foods	U.K.	Flavors, seasonings
International	Nutrial S.A.	France	Breakfast foods
	Sun-Co S.A.	Brazil	Corn starch products
	Seasoned	Columbia	Spices, colors
	Ubena Co.	Germany	Spices, herbs
H.J. Heinz	Orlando S.A. (major interest)	Spain	Tomato products
	Pro Pastries	Canada	Bakery products
	Vin-Chance Foods	Thailand	Baby foods
RJR/Nabisco	Interbake Foods	Canada	Cookies, crackers
	Iracem Ind. Caju	Brazil	Cashews
Pilgrim Pride	3 process plants	Mexico	Poultry

Source: *Food Engineering Magazine*, January 1989. Reprinted by permission.

takeovers in the U.S. were by foreign giants: Nestlé gaining Carnation and Grand Met enfolding Pillsbury. The latter deal gave the British conglomerate major presence on the shelves of American supermarkets. Minneapolis-based Pillsbury, originally a flour miller, had itself acquired Green Giant vegetables, Häagen Dazs ice cream, Totino's Italian frozen foods, Jeno's pizza, Hungry Jack eateries and Burger King's 5,800 restaurants.

As Table 8.6 reveals, from 1984 through 1987, foreign investment in the U.S. food industry actually surpassed U.S. investment abroad by $3.6 billion. But U.S. firms earned a better return on their overseas investments, generating 1987 income of $2.79 billion, versus $878 million for foreign companies operating in the United States. Even after deducting for currency translations, income for U.S. firms in 1987 totaled $1.96 billion.

Big Is Beautiful?

Is this feverish trend towards a few dominant, global food supercorporations a healthy one? Multinational managers claim the trend is not only healthy, but inevitable. They argue that their global food conglomerates minimize the impact of periodic climatic disasters

TABLE 8.6 U.S. Investment in Foreign Food Industry versus Foreign
Investment in U.S. Food Industry (millions of U.S. dollars)

United States	1983	1984	1985	1986	1987
Direct investment	7,661	8,156	9,252	10,968	12,643
Capital outflow	25	478	1,196	1,469	1,630
Income	687	683	1,619	2,091	2,784
Foreign	1983	1984	1985	1986	1987
Direct investment	7,447	8,270	10,710	12,147	16,004
Capital outflow	798	818	2,538	1,337	3,832
Income	553	726	4,411	797	878

Source: U.S. Department of Commerce, various reports.

and political upheavals on the crucial flow of affordable food
worldwide. Citing the 1988 North American drought as an example,
they claim its impact on processed food prices was slight, despite
highly escalated commodity costs. This price stability results from the
global companies stockpiling during abundant harvest years as well as
hedging their commodity purchases in futures markets when spot prices
are low. They also enjoy quick and easy access to successful harvests
elsewhere in the world when major regional crop failures occur.

While this justification for voracious food multinationals seems
valid as well as virtuous, to shareholders the compelling reason for
such growth is profit. There are obviously other reasons why the food
giants manage to stay profitable despite climate/economic fluctuations.
For example, demand for food products is relatively inelastic. It is easy
to raise prices and pass along any higher costs in primary food supplies.
It is also easy to avoid lowering prices when such costs go down.

The food multinationals stress product diversity. Today's complex
food products contain a variety of fruits, vegetables, grains and oils.
Since prices for these do not move in unison, a big cost rise in one usually
has minimum impact on profits.

Food multinationals also stress brand name dominance.
Sophisticated marketing and advertising techniques have encouraged
brand loyalty among consumers worldwide. Strong brands can increase
prices without significant loss of customers.

Through their vast marketing outlets, the food multinationals are
best able to successfully introduce new moneymaking products. In 1988
there were 7,236 new food products introduced. Four of the leading food
firms accounted for more than half of them.

A less often stated reason behind omnipresent profits is that the food itself (the primary unprocessed material) usually represents a modest fraction of the cost of bringing processed products to market. Table 8.7 shows U.S. Commerce Department estimates of what a consumer food dollar paid for in 1987.

The share of advertising—4.5 percent of the food dollar—seems modest. But costly TV commercials are devoted exclusively to the brand-name packaged products of the dominant food companies. About 40 percent of their production is branded, 25 percent is sold to other food processors and to supermarket chains for their own name identity, and the remainder to food service operations. The cost of such advertising to a big brand processor can exceed $1 billion per year and consume over 12 percent of its total sales income (see Table 8.8).

Policies That Protect and Constrain

Governmental policies and associated regulations directed toward the U.S. food industry have served to both protect and constrain its remarkable development. The U.S. Department of Agriculture imposes rigorous standards for inspecting and grading farm products, assuring a safe, quality supply to the processor. The Occupational Safety and Health Administration (OSHA) monitors and assures safe and clean factory operations. The Food and Drug Administration tests and approves safety of ingredients added to foods.

While many in the industry find fault with and contest the policies and rulings of these agencies, the U.S.-based food industry, given the

TABLE 8.7 1987 U.S. Consumer Food Dollar Uses (percentages)

Uses	Percentage
Labor and salaries	34.0
Farm value	25.0
Packaging	8.6
Transport	4.5
Advertising	4.5
Depreciation	4.0
Fuel	3.5
Rent	3.0
Interest	2.0
Repairs	1.5
Average before-tax profits	3.0

Source: U.S. Department of Commerce, 1988.

TABLE 8.8 1988 Advertising Outlays by Major Food Firms

Firm	Sales (in millions)	Percent of Sales Spent on Advertising
Philip Morris	1,451.2	12.1
RJR/Nabisco	894.2	12.7
Pepsico	641.5	12.3
Anheuser Busch	643.9	no account
General Mills	550.4	no account
Pillsbury	498.2	11.1
Kellogg	371.4	6

Source: Author's compilation.

astronomical number of individual items it dispenses, has a remarkable product safety record. Its regulatory agencies set the standard in developing national food systems throughout the world.

A few recent laws and rulings on food processing in the United States have stirred up considerable anguish in the industry. One is the Delaney amendment, a prohibition of food additives found to induce cancer in laboratory animals. Many economically and technically important additives, such as those required for food preservation, coloration or taste enhancement, have been banned after long use, or kept from new applications. For example, the exceedingly promising technology of atomic particle irradiation of food to destroy surface micro-organisms and inhibit decay was interpreted, under the Delaney amendment, as a food additive. Although the United States pioneered this technology in the 1950s and it has long been used profitably in Europe and Japan, it took Reagan's regulation relaxation policy in 1984 to have its use condoned in the United States.

U.S. government policy has long been deeply involved with the nation's food production. It started out with the Morrill Act of 1862, which authorized grants for agricultural colleges and experiment stations. Since then, policy has reached almost all areas of the food system. Today, about 65 percent of all food-related research in the United States—a $1 billion plus activity—is carried out by federal and state institutions. Private industry itself accounts for little more than 30 percent.

A more controversial area of federal government food policy has to do with its efforts to stabilize the price of foods by controlling oversupply. The government has done this by paying farmers to not grow certain crops and compensating them for land removed from

production. It also has a policy of accumulating huge surpluses of
storable foods as redemption for loans made to farmers when their crops
fail to achieve a predetermined parity price.   The cost to U.S.
taxpayers for such farm programs has averaged between $3 billion and
$4 billion each year.

For many years, milk and sugar price support programs have had a
strong impact on U.S. food processors. Dairy farmers, successful in
lobbying against limits on milk production, have their surplus bought
by the government at a guaranteed price, but in the storable form of
butter, cheese and nonfat milk. In recent years, the huge government
inventories of these dairy products have been whittled down through
free distribution. However, growing opposition in Congress to this
dairy program caused a 50 percent decrease in support, down to a $1.2
billion outlay in 1988.

The U.S. sugar industry has been protected by import quotas and
grower price supports. The quotas restricted imports to 1.25 million tons
in 1989, less than 8 percent of the 16.5 million tons consumed by
Americans.   And the U.S. sugar growers, largely the refiners
themselves, get a support price for sugar that amounts to 22 cents a
pound—twice the price on the world market. Growing pressure by U.S.
confectioners and opposition among the members of the General
Agreement on Tariffs and Trade is causing the Bush administration to
reexamine the way domestic sugar producers are protected.

Perhaps the most contested area of U.S. food policy has been when
the government withholds commodities from world trade for political
reasons. Usually such actions prove counterproductive. When the
Carter administration reneged on contracts for vast shipments of grain
to the Soviet Union as a response to its Afghanistan invasion, this
trade was quickly picked up by Argentina and Australia. Earlier, when
the Nixon administration decided to limit its soybean shipments to
Japan, its best customer, that country undertook a vigorous program to
assist Brazil, Jamaica and other locations in soybean production to
supply its import needs. Needless to say, the American farmer was
hardly pleased with either result.[7]

Forces and Technologies for Change

While consolidation and growth of multi-product, multinational
corporations outwardly characterize today's U.S. food system, there
are other forces at work that are causing or should cause significant
changes in the way food is grown, processed, and sold. One such force is
the increasing sophistication of the U.S. consumer, who demands
responses from the food processor that are often rigorous and costly.

Proper nutrition and weight control have become consumer issues. The demand for nutrition motivated the industry to analyze its products and display a nutritional breakdown on its packaging. Informed health-oriented buyers sought products low in calories and saturated fats and high in important amino acids and vitamins. So-called light products were introduced, causing a dramatic shift in consumer preference. In 1975, for example, newly introduced light beer accounted for 2.8 percent of sales. By 1987 almost half of all beer quaffed in the United States was low in calories. An even greater market shift went to diet, non-alcoholic beverages.

Diet and nutrition consciousness are having some influence on the world food system. Tropical cooking oils high in cholesterol and saturated fat, such as palm and coconut oil, are losing markets to less encumbered safflower and corn oil grown in temperate zones. Sugar, also a mainstay Third World export, is being supplanted by low calorie artificial sweeteners such as Monsanto's Nutra Sweet (Aspartame). When Aspartame's patent runs out in 1992, its price is expected to drop from a present 30 cents per pound to 10 cents per pound, causing a major shift away from presently used sugar and corn syrup.

Some recently introduced technology is also reshaping the way food is processed and marketed. Food irradiation, previously mentioned, is expected to make packaged fresh foods available everywhere by greatly extending the safe shelf life of fish, meats, fruits, and vegetables.

Home microwave ovens, now commonplace in U.S. households, have spurred a convenience foods trend, causing processors to develop techniques for large scale production of chef-quality, precooked frozen meals.

Engineered or analog food products with rapidly increasing market acceptance are being developed. An example is the fabrication of normally high-cost shrimp and lobster from the minced, deboned meat (surimi) of underutilized fish species such as Alaska pollack, which has an estimated sustainable yield of 5.5 million metric tons per year.

Aseptic processing systems for fresh food liquids (milk, fruit juices, etc.) as well as concentrates (tomato, grape, beer mash, etc.) are making it possible to bulk ship them worldwide without spoilage and to decouple processing plants from harvest surges. The technology is also introducing fresh flavor qualities in non-refrigerated, packaged food products.

Versatile plastic packaging is used for 18 percent of all U.S. food and is expected to rise to 50 percent by the year 2000. Intensive work is now underway to make such packaging biodegradable, thus eliminating a vast and serious solid waste disposal problem.

Mexico's Food Industry Evolves

To gain understanding of Mexico's food industry and its potential for integrating with its counterpart in the United States, one should first assess the country's natural resource base for growing and harvesting food (see Table 8.9).

The data suggest Mexico's climatic constraints on food crop production. At least 70 percent of the country is classified as semi-arid. Rainfall is erratic, ranging from an average 8 cm per year in some parts of the northwest to more than 440 cm per year in the tropical south. Periodic droughts severely affect most of the arable land.

Most of Mexico's land considered arable is now under cultivation. Government financed irrigation, which defeats drought and often permits double-crop harvests, has reached only 40 percent of a potential 15 million hectares. The bulk of land with irrigation potential is in the southeast. Mexico's vast coastline indicates its large potential for cultivating and harvesting seafood.[8]

Transformation of a Society

Mexico's food industry has evolved under the enormous pressures and expectations of a society that has been transformed from rural to industrial in just a few decades. Table 8.10 reveals what has happened.

A United Nations study showed Mexico's agricultural production increased 100 percent between 1946 and 1965, due mainly to large public investment in irrigation systems, while population also doubled from 21 million to 42 million. But despite continuing large increases in public

TABLE 8.9 Mexico's Natural Resource Base

Resource	Size
Land area	192 million hectares
Arable land	30 million hectares
Cultivated land (1986)	25 million hectares
Irrigated land (1986)	6 million hectares
Range	74 million hectares
Forests	44 million hectares
Land too steep, dry or wet	44 million hectares
Seacoast	9,300 kilometers

Source: Banco de México, various reports.

TABLE 8.10 Key Indicators of Mexican Population

Indicator	1940	1980
Population	19,640,000	67,406,000
Male life expectancy	40.4	63.5
Female life expectancy	42.5	66.5
Literacy	42	81
Urban/rural distribution	65/35	34/66
Per capita income	not available	$1,800 (U.S. dollars)

Source: Banco de México, various reports.

spending on agriculture from 9.2 percent of the national budget in 1940 to 18.2 percent of a vastly larger 1985 budget, by 1970 formerly self-sufficient Mexico became a net importer of food.

Mexico's postwar population surge, with its massive move to urban centers of industrial development, created a dichotomy in the society which greatly influenced its food policies and the subsequent character of its emerging food system. On the one hand, the country now had a growing middle class in its large cities, demanding and able to buy the products of a modern food industry. On the other hand, a Nutrition Institute study in 1983 revealed that 66 percent of Mexico's people consumed less than a required minimum of 2,000 calories per day. Two-thirds of these undernourished were peasant migrants living in urban slums. Many had been persuaded by advertising to replace their traditional and subsidized diet of tortillas and beans with more costly, nutritionally inadequate products such as sodas, snack foods, and cookies. Mexico became the world's second largest market for cola drinks.

Social responsibility and avidness for development have often been in conflict in Mexico's postwar governments. While sincerely devoted to helping peasants stay on the land and furnishing affordable food to the poor, Mexico's leaders at the same time have fostered agricultural policies almost contrary to such dedication. Keen on export income, particularly during economic crisis periods, the government has perhaps inadvertently sponsored the decline of its subsistence crops, maize and beans, which has led to their massive import from the United States and to their subsidized distribution to poor consumers. In essence, official state actions, mainly encouraging large commercial farms in irrigated areas, caused peasants to abandon crops for human use, converting production to grains for feeding animals for export and to fruits and vegetables for the U.S. winter market.[9]

Politicized Food Systems

Concern about Mexico's food dependency and loss of peasant farming led President José López Portillo to announce in 1980 a Mexican Food System program (SAM). Its aim was to achieve self-sufficiency in corn and beans by 1982, and most other grains and oilseeds by 1985. Its main actions were to guarantee prices to grain producers and to increase technical support to peasant farmers through subsidized and improved seeds, fertilizer, crop insurance and credit—all requiring a huge outlay of government funds. The best rainy season in six years helped SAM show good results in 1981. But in 1982, SAM's two key variables—weather and money—both failed, and in 1983 grain imports from the United States rose to a record 8.5 million tons.

While good summer rains in 1983 and 1984 helped produce bumper crops of corn and beans and reduced need for imports, this bounty failed to eliminate a $1 billion annual subsidy for tortillas, beans, and cooking oil. SAM was dismantled by President Miguel de la Madrid in 1982, who then announced his National Food Program (PRONAL). Unfortunately, Mexico's severe economic crisis at that time caused PRONAL to be a SAM without money. It focused on food distribution rather than on improved production.

Mexico's attempts to boost peasant farmer productivity began long before SAM and PRONAL. Mexico started breaking up the vast estates or *latifundios* in 1934, and by 1958 about 33 million hectares had been turned over to two million landless peasants. The *ejido* system allows subsistence-level farmers, working cooperatively, to till communal land surrounding a village.

While well intended, the *ejido* system has failed to move most peasants into the cash crop economy—an estimated 80 percent of *ejidos* consume all the food they produce—or stem their migration to cities. Much land has been taken over by more affluent commercial farmers who have access to modern agri-technology and the know-how to take advantage of government subsidized credit, fertilizer, and fuel, as well as nearby cheap labor. They also have had the political clout to gain irrigation benefits. Such private landholders now exert powerful influence on food policy in Mexico. On just 20 percent of the nation's farmland, they produce 70 percent of all marketable food.

Mexico has not given up on its *ejidos*. Collective *ejidos* on irrigated land in the Yaqui and Mayo Valleys of Sonora, using the same technology as commercial farmers, have achieved comparable productivity. This potential has been recognized by the Inter-American Development Bank with $500,000 in support for a program in

Chihuahua. It furnishes farm credit to 250 *ejido* landholders and provides training and technical assistance for producing both traditional and non-traditional crops.[10]

Food Industry Development

The trend to push Mexico's small subsistence farms into large commercial ventures has been stimulated not only by a lucrative nearby export market, but also by a fast-growing middle class market in the big cities. Demand for processed foods by these urban dwellers has led to the full spectrum of food manufacturing facilities previously described in the United States. A good share of the country's best farmland now provides the primary food materials for this industry.

While a major part of Mexico's food industry development resulted from joint ventures which built modern U.S.-style factories near Mexico City in the Bajío's rich farming region, a surprisingly large number of locally originated and owned food plants have appeared. Consider the countdown in Table 8.11 on food plants in the state of Jalisco that serve the Guadalajara market.

While most of these food plants are relatively small and typical of the U.S. industry 50 years ago, some of the large ones use world-class technology and two Guadalajara brewers supply most of the Mexican market as well as a booming export trade. One export brand, Corona Extra, was introduced in 1983 and is now the second largest imported beer in the lucrative U.S. market (Heineken still leads).

Fishery activity in Mexico has prospered and is the fastest-growing unit in its food system. Between 1968–1987, Mexico's fishing fleet increased almost 4.5 times to over 65,000 vessels, and its shrimp exports are now third largest in the world. There are other similar success stories in Mexico's export of food products, and most have involved interaction with the United States.

TABLE 8.11 Food Plants in the Mexican State of Jalisco

Type	Number
Bakeries	415 (16 large)
Breweries	4 (all large)
Candy making	60 (14 medium)
Cheese and butter	26 (all large)
Ice cream	390 (12 large)
Milk	197 (54 large)
Meat	543 (5 large)

Source: U.S. Embassy, Mexico City, 1988.

Parastatal Food Businesses

Mexico's government processes basic food products and distributes them through the National Company for Popular Subsistence (CONASUPO), the third largest publicly owned industry in Mexico. CONASUPO has four divisions, including Iconsa, which supplies about 36 percent of the domestic market for corn flour and 18 percent for oils and fats; Liconsa, which supplies milk products, with 10 gathering centers, 651 small dairies and 20 major plants; Miconsa, which operates five plants to produce corn flour; and Triconsa, which operates mills, storage facilities and distribution centers for wheat and flour.

CONASUPO supplies over 1,900 affiliates, many in rural areas, with 130 different food products. With its large subsidies to assure affordable basic foods for the poor, it does not compete with the commercial food industry in profit making but surely does capture a significant share of the latter's potential market.

U.S.-Mexico Food Industry Interaction

A modern food industry started emerging in Mexico after World War II when major U.S. processors, eager to participate in a new and fast-growing urban middle class market, crossed the border to set up factories. Earlier food interactions between the countries had been mainly as traditional trading partners, where some primary food items such as cane sugar and beef on the hoof moved north while a variety of U.S.-preserved foods went south to a modest number of well-off consumers. There were a few pre-1940 exceptions. In 1929, Libby pioneered one of the first big transnational food factories in Mexico in the Querétaro region north of Mexico City. Many years later Heinz bought the plant and operates it today.

Besides the interesting new market, another magnet attracted the U.S. food companies. This was the prospect of locating their processing plants near bumper crops from Mexico's best farmland in the Bajío valley, and within convenient distance of what would soon be the world's largest urban area. In *Food Engineering*'s 1975 survey of foreign activities of the 75 top U.S. food corporations, 26 had plants in Mexico. Latin American food specialist William Paddock, in revisiting the formerly pastoral Bajío in 1967, was astonished as he drove the four-lane turnpike from Mexico City to Querétaro: "Along the new superhighway the factories of today's corporate elite were lined up like a guard of honor," he said.[11] Included in his list were Gerber Baby

Foods, Carnation Milk, Kellogg's Breakfast Food, Ralston Purina and what he called "that old capitalistic pioneer," Coca Cola.

Paddock identified Del Monte's big cannery in nearby Irapuato as a laudable venture. Productos Del Monte started operations in 1963 as a wholly owned subsidiary canning tomato products and chili. Within a few seasons, it was operating at a good profit and contracting produce from 5,000 acres. By 1970, the plant had expanded several times and was packing over 50 different products for the Mexican market. Its success led to a second cannery at Culiacan in 1975.

But Paddock had a less laudable story to tell about the Campbell Soup plant in the Bajío. Campbell contracted for its tomatoes from 20 to 30 growers on about 1,000 acres. It paid them $22 to $24 a ton, compared to $30 to $36 a ton to its New Jersey growers, and sold its soup for 40 percent more in Mexico than the United States, 23 cents per can versus 16 cents. Yet Paddock found the plant losing money in Mexico and operating at only half capacity.[12]

When Luis Echeverría became president in 1970, he found 75 percent of foreign investments in Mexico were from the United States, and two-thirds of its trade was with its northern neighbor. He vowed to lessen this "economic and cultural dependency" and lambasted the transnational corporations as "betraying Mexico's needs."[13] His landmark law of 1973 required all new business ventures to have a majority of Mexican ownership and local management control. The law also established more stringent regulations on licensing and patenting agreements. His administration also increased the number of state-owned corporations from 86 to 740.

Obviously, this policy shift by Echeverría put a damper on the enthusiastic flow of food multinationals to Mexico. But the big emerging market was still there and an aggressive indigenous Mexican food industry developed to meet it. Today, many distinctly Mexican name brand products, such as Maribel baked good, Darel dairy items, Carta Mo cooking oil, Zwan meats, and Modelo beer, compete on TV with the U.S. superbrands.

Cooperative Food Technology Development

While the multinational invasion was not wholly appreciated, many cooperative ventures in food development between U.S. institutions and Mexico have found favor and contributed importantly to Mexico's food system. The most famous was the work supported by the Rockefeller Foundation between 1945–1960 on high yield wheat and maize. Norman Borlaug led this work and was recognized in 1970 with a "Green Revolution" Nobel Prize.

In 1967, Borlaug's success fostered the Puebla Project, a Rockefeller Foundation-funded experiment between the International Maize and Wheat Improvement Center and the National Agrarian University of Chapingo. Some 43,000 families, farming about 116,000 hectares of unirrigated land, were trained in the new technology. Between 1968 and 1972, the average yield of maize in the Puebla Valley increased by 30 percent and farmer income rose 45 percent.[14]

This time, official policy favored a U.S.-originated food initiative. In 1976, newly elected President López Portillo appropriated public funds to operate Plan Puebla and build a training center. The project was taken over by a government agency in 1976, and its trainee graduates subsequently moved out to 36 regional programs.

A more recent and equally far-reaching example of U.S.-Mexico food technology development began in the late 1970s when the University of Arizona's Environmental Research Laboratory (ERL) started experiments growing food crops irrigated with seawater at Puerto Penasco in Sonora. Several promising species of halophytes (salt-tolerant plants) were found and the project was moved to a 50-acre farm on the sandy shore of Kino Bay to become a cooperative venture between Genesis S.A., a Mexican corporation, and Oasis Systems International, a commercial spinoff of the university laboratory. In 1987, after successful harvest of an oilseed halophyte named SOS-7, irrigated only with seawater, calculations showed that a 2,000 hectare farm would produce vegetable oil for 120,000 people, seed meal for 77,000 chickens and forage for 14,000 cattle.[15]

If expectations prove out, the contributions to Sonora and to the world's many arid seacoast areas could be enormous. At a press unveiling in September 1987, the Mexican government told investors it was offering logistical and financial support in a 500-acre site in Puerto Penasco to bring the experimental effort to prototype stage. There the ERL, working with Sonoran associates, hopes to implement a plan where the pumped seawater will irrigate landscape halophytes in town parks and then be routed through greenbank lagoons and a recreational lake. Then, enriched with detoxified town effluent, the flow will irrigate the 500-acre oilseed crop and furnish nutrients to an aquaculture facility and algae farm.[16]

Ten years earlier the ERL, collaborating with the University of Sonora, undertook a somewhat similar high-tech scheme at Puerto Penasco in a Coca Cola-funded project. Shrimp were grown in a closed system where seawater, exiting from closely controlled feedlots and enriched with detritus, was used to irrigate a halophyte crop which fed the growing shrimp. The system yields were phenomenal: 3,500 kilograms of high-quality shrimp per hectare of surface water per year or about 50 tons per acre per year. Given shrimp's high market value, this was a greater return per hectare than any other foodstuff cultivated. It gave more shrimp from one acre than four local boats caught in a season. Unfortunately, this reality may have caused the project's termination and the erection of barriers against the technology's use in Mexico.[17]

Uneasy Food Trading Partners

By far the most active and often troublesome area of U.S.-Mexico food interaction is the trade passing over the border. Mexico is a major market for U.S. exported processed foods—it buys around 9 percent of total U.S. food exports. Each year, Mexico also acquires from the United States an average 15 percent of its corn, 25 percent of its wheat, and 45 percent of its soybeans, even as successive Mexican leaders agonize over and implement policies for self-sufficiency in these crops.

But the food products flowing from Mexico into the U.S. market are even more significant. In 1987, while it imported about $1.5 billion in foodstuffs, mainly from the United States, Mexico's food exports to the United States were valued at over $2 billion. Mexican firms process 85 percent of all the frozen food products imported by the United States. They provide 43 percent of the broccoli, 31 percent of the strawberries and 21 percent of the cauliflower Americans consume. In 1988, Mexican growers shipped an estimated $250 million worth of tomatoes and an equal amount of other fresh produce over the border. One half-million metric tons of good Mexican beer went north that year to thirsty Americans. And 733,480 Mexican cattle and calves ended up with U.S. meat processors.

There is an interesting twist in Mexico's food export development. It has become a valid binational effort, rather than the usual expansion of capital flowing north to south. True, it began that way after World War II, when the pioneer Americans with capital went to Sinaloa to benefit from favorable labor costs and government-subsidized irrigated land. But they rapidly integrated into local society, gaining Mexican wives and citizenship in the process. Then their steady financial success led to a forward integration, where the Sinaloa producers, seeking ways to eliminate middlemen, set up their own distributors in Nogales. Today about half the Arizona distributorships are controlled by Mexican producers.

Governmental policies on both sides of the border provided significant help for the highly successful Mexican food export system. Eager for trade dollars, Mexican public policy literally helped finance the new industry. Sinaloa received 22 percent of total government investment in irrigation. In the 1950s, it modernized the crucial railroad linking Culiacan to Nogales, Arizona. Official sources also made available medium-term credit for producers to plant crops and build packing houses.

David R. Mares says the Mexican government helped to create a new and often contrary power base in the northwest, an economically and politically potent Sinaloan rural bourgeoisie.[18] Their enterprises, located around Culiacan, now exhibit the independence and clout of transnational corporations. They bargain for foreign capital, gain support from U.S. domestic growers, and lobby effectively in Washington and state capitals.

The U.S. government gave great impetus to Sinaloan food exports with its trade embargo on Cuba in 1961. Cuba's significant share of the U.S. winter produce market was eagerly appropriated by Florida, California and Mexico. Then, in 1964, termination of the *bracero* program, which provided cheap labor for harvests, caused California to move out of this market. The stage was thus set for a Florida-Mexico rivalry that erupted in the so-called tomato wars of 1969 and 1978.

Mexican Versus Florida Tomatoes

Mexican tomatoes surged into the United States when a disastrous freeze hit the Florida crop in 1957–1958, causing a 15-year crisis in U.S. production. By 1968, the Florida producers, facing a tripled Mexican import from 105,000 metric tons in 1961 to 294,000 in 1968, prepared for a trade war by organizing the Federal Trade Commission's Florida Tomato Committee. A year later, the FTC successfully convinced the U.S. Department of Agriculture to implement regulations which technically discriminated against the vine-ripened Mexican fruit because Florida tomatoes were machine-harvested green. This restrictive device was in effect for three seasons, causing a large drop in Mexican production and profits. In 1975, the Department of Agriculture and Arizona distributors representing the Sinaloan growers reached a truce in court.

In 1978, the tomato war flared up again when the FTC filed a petition with the U.S. Treasury Department claiming Mexican violations of the Anti-Dumping Act of 1921. Five products—tomatoes, cucumbers, bell peppers, eggplant, and squash—were alleged to have been sold below cost during the 1977–1978 season. The FTC effort, taken on its own initiative, created an embarrassing as well as complicated situation because the U.S. government at that time took a friendlier view of trade relations with Mexico. A sophisticated study using regression analysis, commissioned by the Sinaloan growers and Arizona distributors, showed no statistical support for the dumping accusation.

The U.S. Department of Commerce confirmed the study's results and Treasury rejected the FTC petition. In 1980, the Florida producers filed suit in U.S. Customs Court against Treasury and Commerce without success.[19]

This is an oversimplified account of a very complicated food trade dispute. Normally, the Mexican government allows the Sinaloan Growers Association to set its own export policy. But during the tomato wars, Mexico's Agriculture Minister stepped in and set quotas well below Sinaloan expectations. Mexico's official policy toward the United States is that trade between the two nations is complementary, not competitive. This requires restraints on exports during such crisis events.

Policies in Transition

Recent trade and investment policy shifts are bound to accelerate interactions between Mexican and U.S. food industries. After Mexico joined the GATT in mid-1986, import duties were subsequently reduced across the board to a maximum of 20 percent, and most prior import license requirements were eliminated. While restrictions covering the strategic and priority sector of agriculture still remain, those lifted on importing food processing technology should be a boon for modernizing Mexico's food industry.

President Salinas' 1989 decision to liberalize controls on foreign investments, allowing complete ownership of corporations instead of minority positions, should revive the stream of multinational food companies into Mexico. Other Salinas austerity measures to restrain inflation and reduce the national debt, such as privatization of food parastatals and reduction in food price supports, should also energize Mexico's processed food sector. One result should be more authentic Mexican cuisine exports to the United States' fast-growing market for this ethnic food.

U.S. trade policy, which might affect the binational food system, is very much in a state of flux. In the medium-term, the United States may emulate with Mexico the pact it recently made with Canada eliminating trade and investment barriers over the next ten years. While the U.S.-Canada agreement liberates many U.S. food and beverage products from tariffs, Canadian brewers managed to retain their protective barrier. On the other hand, the menacing U.S. trade deficit keeps fanning prospects for protectionism, which could conceivably extend to Mexico and threaten the food products that are a significant part of its favorable trade balance.

Finally, realists must also remember the open-ended U.S. appetite for Mexican oil. Some economists believe trade agreements that tie this appetite to an equally avid U.S. desire to reciprocate with vast shipments of corn, wheat, and soybeans to Mexico should be an enduring link between the two nations' food systems.

Future Integration

Although the U.S. and Mexican food processing sectors are conventionally viewed as a food industry, activities and policies at the agricultural and distribution ends of each food system profoundly influence food processing. Thus, to speculate on prospects for future integration between the industries requires a broader food system perspective.

Mexico's developing food system lacks the autonomy and clout of its big-business-dominated northern counterpart. How it develops or recedes through interactions with the U.S. system could be very much determined by societal issues in Mexico itself. Some major problems could be influenced by interplay between the two food systems. For example, the acute nationwide problem of undernutrition in Mexico could be lessened through food product development interactions; the flow of people to the big cities could be stemmed through rural binational consortia food industries; and the national debt could be diminished through expanded export of jointly created, uniquely Mexican food products.

Examples of cooperative initiatives abound. The U.S.-Mexico program that led to new corn and wheat-growing technology, however, has not been one of them. But the recent effort of U.S. and Mexican private sector firms to develop, with government support, seawater-irrigated oilseed production shows great promise for producing lower cost, basic food. Possibilities also exist for a similar approach using U.S. technology and Mexican capital to exploit Mexico's subtropical climate, ready rural labor, and competent infrastructure in projects yielding low-cost protein through biomass fermentation and aquaculture.

As Figure 8.1 suggests, there are many ways for often isolated elements within the food system to integrate and maximize efficiency and profits thorough closely coupled energy and food byproduct utilization. Rural food industrialization schemes work well on this principle. The area's agricultural production feeds an integrated system of processing plants where product wastes from one furnish energy or raw materials for another. A consortium of U.S. and Mexican food corporations, working cooperatively with government incentives, could design and implement the endeavor. Business associations in the United States, such as the Agribusiness Council, have provided incentives for such projects in Third World locations. Besides providing needed cash crops for farmers, they create factory and service jobs in formerly subsistence areas. When successful, they bring many city migrants back to rural origins.[20]

A pertinent development is the worldwide popularity of Mexican foods. They are now the fastest-selling ethnic variety in U.S. supermarkets. Mexican entrees showed a 12.5 percent growth in 1988 with annual sales at more than $245 million. Yet most of these distinctive products were made by domestic Hispanic divisions of U.S. food giants. Mexico could boost its present 9 percent share of the big U.S. food import market with products featuring its popular cuisine. It could also encourage joint ventures with U.S. firms to apply new technology, like high-vacuum concentration, aseptic containerizing, to potentially large tropical fruit crops of wet and needy southern Mexico.

Integration Incentives

While Mexico's food industry can benefit by acquiring needed technology and distribution skills, what are the incentives for integration as seen from the U.S. side? In this case, we are dealing with a fully mature industry, much less coupled to government, and dominated by very large multinational corporations. Adding confusion is the fact that a growing number of the corporations controlling large chunks of the U.S. food system are managed and owned by shareholders in other nations.

So as we consider prospects for integration between Mexican and U.S. food industries, we seem to be dealing with an illusion. Certainly, Mexico's developing industry is indeed an entity, well fenced into its food system by national policies and social imperatives. On the other hand, the food industry sector of the United States is much more nebulous, much less constrained by government and society. Many claim that its motivation and guidance is increasingly in the hands of global corporations that are the governing force in a fast-surfacing world food system.

What compels the U. S.-based food multinationals to move into or cooperate with Mexico's food system? Obvious incentives are new markets for their products and lower production costs. Less obvious is the multinational's increasing need for primary food to supply its processing plants and meet an expanding world market for its branded product. The Heinz outreach towards Mexico's great tomato crop is an example and Mexican tomatoes probably supply the ketchup on Fiji hamburgers. When the processing plant is jointly owned, technicians and managers are locals, and the plant yields a valuable export, Mexico's food system profits.

Another subtle incentive for food multinationals to establish in Mexico is to avoid U.S. policy constraints. For example, it seems reasonable that the Mexican government, keen on stimulating exports, would encourage a U.S.-owned subsidiary to trade with Cuba despite the United State's economic embargo. Thus far there has been no outcry about this and similar possibilities.

If the U.S. proposal for reform of agricultural trade is adopted and taken seriously by the 97 members of GATT, by the year 2000 there could be a phasing out of all subsidies—direct or indirect—that affect agricultural trade. This would surely further linkages between the U.S. and Mexican food systems and food industry sectors through food crop interdependency based on least-cost production.

Should the United States fail in its goals for a non-subsidized world trade in agriculture, another antipodal pressure could arise to foster closer coupling between the two industries. It is possible the European Community may choose to protect its great market from imported food products after 1992. A hypothetical response could be the emergence of a North American common market, with strong integration among the food industries and food systems of the United States, Mexico, and Canada.

Political developments within the two nations could affect the industrial bonding. Mexico's new political pluralism and the possibility of future changes in government policy could restrict the activities of food multinationals. In the United States, an inability to redress the balance of trade could lead to new demands for protectionism. The political challenges facing both nations are formidable.

Notes

1. For more details on the food system diagram, see "The Interaction of Food, Climate, and Population" by Walter Orr Roberts and Lloyd E. Slater in the 1980 Woodlands Conference book, *The Management of Sustainable Growth*, Harlan Cleveland, editor (New York: Pergamon Press, 1981), pp. 246-247 and pp. 262-263.

2. Donella Meadows' comprehensive discussion of her composite model of the world food system is in *Alternatives to Growth-1*, Dennis L. Meadows, editor (Cambridge: Ballinger Publishing, 1977), pp. 11-33. The book is a product of the 1975 Woodlands Conference.

3. The planning and analytical techniques used by Rolando García in Mexico are the contents of a 1984 monograph, "Food Systems and Society—A Conceptual and Methodological Challenge" (Geneva: United Nations, RISD Report No. 83.5), pp. 73.

4. Jim Hightower's book is *Eat Your Heart Out* (New York: Vantage Books, 1975), pp. 11-19.

5. A remarkable collection of data on yearly performance of the U.S. industry is available from the Department of Commerce in its massive publication *U.S. Industrial Outlook*, issued each January.

6. The 1974 survey of the 75 leading food corporations is in *Food Engineering*, 1975 (January), pp. 45-53. The analysis of U.S. food companies' foreign activities is in *Food Engineering*, 1989 (January), pp. 53-72. Available from Chilton Co., Radnor, PA.

7. Almost all of the numbers cited (and accompanying insight) on the U.S. food industry were gleaned from recent monthly "Industry Reports" of *Food Engineering* and the Commerce Department "Outlook" series.

8. A cogent discussion of Mexico's natural resources and climate is in *Mexico* (New York: Time-Life Publishing Co., 1985).

9. Much of my comments on Mexico's transformation is based on material in Alan Riding's thoughtful book, *Distant Neighbors* (New York: Alfred A. Knopf, 1985).

10. A comprehensive discussion and analysis of Mexican agricultural development and the *ejido* system is offered by Gustavo del Castillo and Rosario Barajas de Vega in "U.S.-Mexican Agricultural Relations: The Upper Limits of Linkage Formation," in *World Food Policies Towards Agricultural Interdependence*, W. Browne and D. Hadwiger, editors (Boulder, CO: Lynne Reiner Publishing, 1986), pp. 153-178.

11. William and Elizabeth Paddock's report on food industry developments in the Bajío in 1967 can be found in *We Don't Know How* (Ames, IA: Iowa State University Press, 1973), pp. 195-230. The Paddocks include a critique of achievements of the Rockefeller Foundation agri-development program.

12. See Note 11.

13. See Note 9.

14. A more positive view of the Rockefeller Foundation-sponsored programs in agricultural development in Mexico, including the Puebla Project, is presented in Sterling Wortman and Ralph Cummings, Jr.'s *To Feed This World* (Baltimore: Johns Hopkins University Press, 1978), pp. 198-203 and pp. 220-224.

15. The Kino Bay halophyte project was well described in the September 28, 1988, issue of *El Imparcial*, the Hermosillo, Sonora newspaper.

16. The University of Arizona's Environmental Research Laboratory has a brochure, "Desert Seacoasts: An Integrated Vision of Community Productivity and Stability," which depicts and details the research and the technology behind the Puerto Penasco plan. The brochure is available at 2601 E. Airport Drive, Tucson, AZ 85706.

17. ERL Director, Carl Hodges, describes the shrimp culture project and early work with halophytes in his chapter "New Options for Climate-Defensive Food Production," in *Climate's Impact on Food Supplies*, L. E. Slater and S. K. Levin, editors (Boulder, CO: Westview Press, AAAS Selected Symposium 62, 1981), pp. 181-205.

18. David R. Mares has written a fascinating and detailed account of Sinaloan "rural Bourgeoisie" and the tomato wars in his chapter, "Agricultural Trade: Domestic Interests and Transnational Relations," in *Mexico's Political Economy: Challenges at Home and Abroad*, Jorge I. Dominguez, editor (Beverly Hills, CA: Sage Publications, 1982), pp. 79-132.

19. See note 18.

20. In the late 1970s, the Agribusiness Council, a trade association of internationally-minded U.S. food corporations was the coordinator for member groups organized as consortia to engage in food system development projects in the Third World. Its address is 345 East 46th Street, New York, NY 10017.

Food: Mexican Perspective

José Carlos Alvarez Rivero
Herbert Weinstein

This analysis will offer a limited view of some key issues that Mexican food producers and processors confront in the process of industrial integration with the United States. These issues include the strong competition that Mexican manufacturers face from U.S. multinationals, the cultural barriers to breaking into the potential markets of Mexico, and the growing ethnic food market generated by Latin Americans living in the United States.

We will also discuss the non-trade barriers to agricultural integration with the United States. Related to this is the problem of food sanitation and the continuing controversy over the use of pesticides in agriculture.

Because the Mexican food industry is virtually unregulated and there are few reliable statistics on it, many aspects of integration are hard to predict. Obstacles to integration do exist, but evidence also indicates that the Mexican and U.S. food industries can contribute much to joint ventures capable of exploiting both Mexican and U.S. food markets.

Industry Structure

Multinationals are important actors in the Mexican food industry, and they advertise so heavily that the public identifies these firms largely with the production of processed foods. Multinationals also maintain a strong presence in self-service stores, where companies like Kellogg, Pepsico, Kraft General Foods, Nestle, Corn Products (CPC) Unilever, Pillsbury, Heinz, Campbell's, Gerber, Danone, and others market their products.

Nevertheless, a variety of agricultural and food processing industries are run by Mexican entrepreneurs, who use a blend of self-made technologies and traditional food preparation methods. Some Mexican-owned food firms are capable of sophisticated marketing operations. Among these is the Bimbo Group, which includes the vertically integrated firms of Marinela, Barcel, Panificación, Tía Rosa, and Ricolino. The strength and presence of these firms lie not only in the manufacture of high-quality products, but also in efficient and sophisticated marketing distribution systems.

Regional tastes in Mexico vary, and thus the levels of sweeteners, aromatic flavors, chiles, citric fruits, and other ingredients used will vary by region. International firms sometimes alter their product recipes in Mexico to adapt to these local tastes.

Mexico's food industry is primarily supplied by domestic raw and packing materials. However, with the opening of the economy under the General Agreement on Tariffs and Trade (GATT), supply changes are taking place.

The food industry employs the largest work force in Mexico, giving it substantial economic weight.

Access to Markets

Global agricultural markets should be thriving. A significant portion of the world's population is hungry and malnourished, and world population is growing quickly. By the year 2000, the world population will be an estimated 6.1 billion, and by 2025 it will have grown to 8.2 billion. About 75 percent of this population will be in developing countries, which will experience estimated annual growth rates of 2.1 percent, compared to 0.6 percent in developed countries.

Despite this phenomenal population growth, Mexico's ability to sell agricultural products is thwarted because world markets are flooded with such products. Mexico is most successful in exporting staples like corn, sorghum, soybeans, and wheat, as Table 8.12 indicates. Corn exports have recently dropped in tonnage, but the rapid rise of wheat exports more than compensates for the drop in corn exports.

Mexico's inability to exploit world markets is due primarily to poor food distribution systems. GATT should provide Mexico with access to certain export markets, but in some instances, such as vegetable exports to the United States, Mexico finds itself the victim of non-tariff trade restrictions.

Sanitation and product safety rules also pose trade barriers for Mexico, particularly as they relate to the use of pesticides, authorized waste in agricultural production, and the use of filth tests for handling

TABLE 8.12 Selected Mexican Exports, 1987–1988 (tons)

Export	1987	1988
Coffee beans	212,252	154,743
Fresh legumes and vegetables	787,318	848,180
Tomatoes	516,445	466,544
Melons and watermelon	295,561	299,535
Fresh fruit	298,433	304,906
Sesame almonds	22,877	31,144
Fresh strawberries	14,508	21,012
Frozen shrimp	35,416	28,450
Beer	581,975	505,490
Sugar	510,143	869,248
Legumes and canned fruit	168,004	179,168
Orange juice	32,013	48,274
Frozen tuna	47,118	52,317
Roasted coffee	10,781	14,444
Cocoa butter	7,018	6,535
Frozen strawberries	42,051	32,344
Tomato sauce or tomato juice	19,853	26,997
Fruit juices	15,538	18,596
Corn	3,602,890	3,302,574
Soybeans	1,062,260	1,097,857
Sorghum	751,929	1,147,288
Wheat	434,580	1,191,717
Oilseeds	417,540	327,660
Fresh vegetables	36,131	32,991

Source: Authors' compilation.

and processing foods. Mexico must also observe many quality control rules for labeling, brand identification, and product size. In contrast, the domestic Mexican food industry thrives as a cottage industry with few sanitation controls, product regulations, or taxes.

The United States stringently enforces its agricultural rules. And, even though the Mexican industry rules are different, overly enthusiastic U.S. enforcement sometimes hides protectionism, such as when sanitary concerns unnecessarily delay product approval for fresh vegetables.

Many of the agricultural products that Mexico attempts to export to the United States are rejected because of the use of non-authorized pesticides. These pesticides are manufactured and marketed by small U.S. enterprises established in Mexico. In many cases, these companies use the same trade names that multinationals use, and manufacture their products even though company executives are aware that the pesticides are prohibited in the United States. They manufacture these products under other names, but the products nevertheless have the same active ingredients. These products are then sold to farmers, who pay for them and use them in good faith, without realizing that border authorities will return these agricultural products as unfit for human consumption. For example, the U.S. Food and Drug Administration (FDA) recently rejected several cargos of peanut-based products because they contained more than 20 parts per million of aflatoxines, a carcinogen. But the peanuts used in the rejected food were supplied by a Mexican factory in the United States. These peanuts, therefore, were cultivated, harvested, and stored in the United States. The aflatoxines levels present in the rejected peanut products were 16 to 33.2 times higher than the aflatoxines levels of products exported from Mexico.

The canned foods of low and moderate acidity exported to the United States come from factories registered by the FDA. They are run by Mexican technicians who have taken special training courses in the United States, Puerto Rico, and Mexico City. The processed canned products exported from Mexico to the United States, even though they come from authorized factories, must meet special, rigorous technical and sanitary regulations. The majority of these products returned to Mexico are rejected not because they are unsanitary or badly packaged, but because they are not labeled properly.

Industry Integration

The proximity of the United States to Mexico leads to an easy integration of food products. This integration is facilitated by mass media and tourism. Thus, Häagen Dazs ice cream is known in Mexico as a high-quality U.S. product. At the same time, tacos and other Mexican ethnic products are served frequently at U.S. restaurants that do not specialize in Mexican food. For example, nachos appear in the menus of cafeterias such as Denny's, Big Boy, and sports concessions.

Processed foods—those sold in commercial packings—have undergone a technological process that prolongs their shelf life while reducing their sanitary risks. These include canned products, cookies, candies, and sweets. From a technical viewpoint, there is little difference between the products canned in the United States and the equivalent products canned in Mexico. Both products must meet the technical, legal, and packing requirements of each country. For example, peaches must be a specific size and packaged in specified units—requirements that must be met when the sale is finalized. The rules and regulations of world organizations like Codex Alimentarius apply only if Codex quality is agreed upon when the commercial transaction is carried out. Otherwise, only the rules and regulations pertaining to the buyer's country apply.

Mexican processed foods should generate a commercial boom in the United States, given the large number of Mexicans living in cities like Los Angeles, Houston, and Chicago. In fact, 63 percent of the Latin American population living in the United States are of Mexican origin. When Mexican products first entered U.S. markets, they were frequently smuggled in by U.S. travelers returning from Mexico with four or five cans. Later, these products were exported to self-service chains with special sections of ethnic foods. Today, self-service chains provide specialized services in Spanish. Ethnic products manufactured in the United States are similar to those manufactured in Mexico and consumed by the middle and low-middle classes. But the U.S. manufacturers also cater to distinctly U.S. tastes by marketing Mexican-style products like nachos, which are not actually sold in Mexico. These products generally carry labels in both Spanish and English that indicate how spicy the product is. Many Mexicans living in the United States frequently buy these Mexican-style U.S. products out of a sense of nostalgia.

To fully exploit the Latin American markets in the United States, the food industry needs more information on this ethnic population. The dangers of advertising in a little-known ethnic market were perhaps best exemplified by a Braniff campaign to promote leather seats by inviting the public to "viajar en cuero" (to travel in leather). In some Spanish speaking countries this phrase actually means "to travel naked." In the same vein, Tropical once advertised orange juice as "jugo de china," even though "china" means orange only in Puerto Rico and the Dominican Republic. Jack in the Box showed a group of Mexican mariachis (popular music characteristic of the state of Jalisco in Mexico) in a television commercial dancing the flamenco—a dance style of the Andalusian gypsies in Spain.

Americans frequently confuse Mexicans with other people of Latin American origin in the United States. U.S. residents of Latin American origin now total 19 million people—a figure that is growing rapidly. From 1980 to the present, the U.S. Latin American population grew four times faster than did other populations, and by 2015, an estimated 40 million people of Latin American origin will live in the United States, making it the nation's largest minority.

To advertise successfully to this large and growing market, the food industry must take into account language and cultural differences. For example, a corn oil company recently captured two-thirds of its share in the U.S. Latin American market by launching an advertising campaign in Spanish and promoting what these consumers wanted: good flavor, regardless of the cholesterol level.

This market can be reached with relatively modest advertising expenditures. A 30-second spot on *Sabado Gigante*, the top-rated Univisión program for Latin American audiences in the United States, costs $11,500, while a 30-second spot on the Cosby Show costs $360,000.

Many companies have avoided the Latin American market because it is considered too poor to be economically attractive, even though the annual median income per Latin American family is an estimated $22,900, compared to the national median family income of $32,800. Such purchasing power should not be disregarded, since Latin Americans tend to spend a significant portion of their income on goods and services that can be consumed immediately.

This U.S. Latin American market is also durable because Latin Americans maintain strong bonds with their original culture for several generations. When compared to European immigrants, the Latin community's assimilation into the U.S. way of life is neither quick nor easy. About 90 percent of the Latin community lives in nine U.S. states, and 80 percent of them marry within the same community. The chuppies (Chicano professionals), and the yucas (Cuban-American young people from well-to-do families), constitute the best example of U.S. residents who maintain dual cultural ties. These groups drive U.S. cars and watch television programs in English. But they also eat Mexican and Cuban food and listen to Spanish music.

As in television ads, the use of Spanish in other promotions and in descriptive product labels provides manufacturers better access to the market. More than two million U.S. adults speak Spanish only. Many surveys indicate that more than 70 percent of the Latin American community speaks Spanish at home and 96 percent attempt to teach it to their children. Many people of Latin American origin keep their accent when speaking in English, even after the first generation in the United States.

More than $490 million was spent on advertising to Latin Americans in 1987. This was more than twice the amount spent five years previously, but represented only a small portion of the $110 billion in advertising spent each year in the United States. *Hispanic Business* has noted that U.S. companies spend less than 1 percent on advertising to attract the Spanish-language market, which represents 8 percent of the U.S. population.

Advertising campaigns in Mexico must consider the unique characteristics of that society. Since the opening of the Mexican economy, a considerable number of foreign confectionery products like chocolate and chewing gum have entered the Mexican market. At first, these products were commercially successful, but these same products are now considered too expensive and no longer new or exotic.

When Webber Farms from Kentucky introduced a line of sauces into the Latin American market, it met with lukewarm response because the products had too few spices. Mars, after conducting meticulous research, decided to bag rice instead of boxing it, and promoted a successful ten-pound product in the Latin American market. Pepsicola changed its advertising commercials targeted for Latin Americans from images of space trips to that of a Latin American youngster dreaming of becoming a rock star. McDonald's promoted its 15th anniversary in Latin American communities, where the fast-food chain is well-known.

Ethnic Restaurant Food

Today's adults are the first generation to routinely consume fast food, food to go, and home-delivered food. The number of adults who both dine out and consume fast food will continue to increase each year. Already, Americans dine out for one out of every three meals and spend over 40 percent of their food budget on food prepared outside their homes. That is significantly higher than the 26 percent they spent in 1960.

Restaurants and food delivery services are increasingly popular for U.S. families in which both parents work and prefer to relax in the evening instead of cooking. In 1987, U.S. fast food restaurants generated an estimated $60 billion in sales. Of these, $2.6 billion were sales of Mexican food. Taco Bell contributed $1.5 billion of these sales. The chain was particularly successful because it introduced new menu items, opened a number of restaurants in strategic areas like commercial centers, and offered its customers low-cost items.

Overall, Pepsico is the fast food leader with more than 16,500 restaurants in the United States. These include Kentucky Fried Chicken, leader of the U.S. chicken market, with estimated annual sales of $6.1 billion; Pizza Hut, leader of the U.S. pizza market, with estimated annual sales of $2.5 billion; and Taco Bell. Kentucky Fried Chicken and Pizza Hut are established in Mexico, but Taco Bell is not. Other U.S. chains like McDonald's, Tom Boy, and Burger Boy have been established in Mexico. Together, these U.S. chains are achieving a cultural exchange through foods. They are, in effect, exchanging tacos for hamburgers.

Food Sanitation

The concept of safe restaurant food has changed significantly over time, and restaurants now need technical experts who specialize in food and service management as well as a professional public relations staff to combine tasteful food presentation with food safety. Years ago, the concept of safety was limited to the search for pesticides in foods. Today, the definition of food safety is much broader. It extends to issues involving a variety of microorganisms in food products. For example, the FDA and the National Marine Fish Reserves in early 1989 warned the food industry about the presence of a new microorganism, *lysteria monocitogenes,* in cooked seafood. This microorganism originally appeared in milk products. Despite the risk, seafood consumption has increased 25 percent during the last five years, according to the National Fishery Services. This trend is likely to continue; by the turn of the century seafood consumption is expected to be 24 pounds per person per year — double the 1987 consumption rate.

The safety of seafood, which is served in more than 80 percent of Mexican ethnic restaurants, varies by fishing area. Some fishing areas are polluted with lead, mercury, cadmium, and other chemicals. Seafood can also become contaminated through unsafe fishing methods, improper refrigeration on fishing ships, lengthy transportation time, certain commercialization practices, and by improper handling or preparation at restaurants where it is served.

The shellfish products that Mexico exports to the United States come from areas which have been analyzed and certified as safe by U.S. officials. Such certification is important because improper handling of seafood products can result in diseases. An April 1988 survey supported by the Institute of Food Technologists said that between 69 million and 275 million diarrhea cases were generated by food consumption in the United States, resulting in medical and lost productivity costs of between $5 billion and $17 billion annually. Of the cases of food poisoning reported to the U.S. Centers for Disease Control during one five-year period, 77 percent were attributed to restaurant foods, 20 percent to food prepared at home, and 3 percent to food manufactured in industrial plants.

These figures point to the need to improve sanitary conditions for food preparation in restaurants. The food industry needs corrective and preventive educational programs, adequate thermal procedures, procedures to eliminate the contamination of foods, utensils and equipment, and adequate cleaning and maintenance of food preparation surfaces and equipment.

Trends

Recent studies on merchandise marketing indicate that only 20 percent of the products now sold at large U.S. self-service stores will continue to be marketed in the year 2000. Continuing advances in science and technology that allow for creativity and innovation, combined with demographic studies and research on behavior patterns, will make segmented marketing possible.

Globalization will propel the food industry toward a scientific system based on exotic chemical compositions that will yield highly developed inventions that will be placed in the hands of consumers by means of sophisticated communication devices.

In self-service stores and restaurants, consumers with different values, needs, and lifestyles, will demand products with longer shelf lives. Store managers will need to recover investments faster, despite complex food regulations on world markets.

The technological changes in the food industry will be plentiful. These include the use of genetic therapies, white line, simulated foods, genetic engineering, hydroponics, aquaculture, robots, dispatch machines, packages that control temperature, environmentally safe and aseptic packaging, irradiation, and other applied sciences. The success or failure of the food industry hinges on the development of such new products.

The trend toward specialization may turn Mexico into a supplier of partially prepared foods that otherwise demand a great deal of labor. This activity may be complementary to other highly industrialized procedures. These may result in U.S.-Mexican joint ventures. Such joint ventures could manufacture some of the convenience foods that are becoming popular, such as a frozen meal consisting of a vegetable salad, fruit salad, and a piece of meat cooked in a cheese-and-mushroom sauce that only needs to be heated in a microwave oven before serving.

Mexican and U.S. food producers can benefit from the opening of Mexico's economy, from its inexpensive transportation costs, and from its competitively priced labor. Food trade can be one link in creating a North American trade grouping capable of responding to the competition that will be forthcoming as the European Community breaks down its border restrictions in 1992.

The Latin American population residing in the United States is increasing every day, thereby increasing the potential for ethnic foods in the growing field of partially processed products.

Technology is an important element in the achievement of these goals. Technological changes must work in harmony with the modification of legal barriers, so that food sanitation is protected without restricting international commerce.

Bibliography

"Agriculture in the GATT," *Foreign Trade,* 38 (10), 1988.
Ethnic Foods," *Food Technology,* 43 (2), 1989.
"Food Safety in Ethnic Groups," *Dairy and Food Sanitation,* 8 (12), 1988.
"International Foods," *Food Technology,* 41 (9), 1987.
"Main Exported and Imported Products," *Foreign Trade,* 38 (10), 1988.
"Statistics Seminar," *Foreign Trade,* 39 (4), 1989.
"Survey on Food Expenses," *Foreign Trade,* 39 (1), 1989.
"The Latin Market in the United States," *Marketing News* 1 (1), 1989.
"The World Food Prize," *Winrock International Project Profile,* 1989.

NINE

Environment

Environment: Mexican Perspective

Roberto A. Sánchez

Mexicans have not yet agreed on the benefits and risks of a free trade agreement. Some groups fear that such an agreement will jeopardize domestic industries, the economy as a whole, and national sovereignty. The federal government sees the agreement as a means of obtaining badly needed resources for investment and for revitalizing the domestic economy. Neither side has considered the possible environmental effects of such an agreement.

This chapter deals with some of the environmental impacts that a free trade agreement would have on the border region. It analyzes the impact of border growth that could be expected with free trade, particularly the increased demand for water resources. The problem of hazardous wastes in the *maquiladora* industry and the possible implications for regulating these wastes under the free trade agreement are also analyzed. Finally, the potential ramifications of the trade agreement on the transboundary movement of hazardous wastes and the impact of free trade on global warming are discussed.

Border Region Water Resources

In terms of environmental impact, the transition to free trade on Mexico's northern border should pose few new problems because the region has been essentially a free trade zone for decades, one marked by intense daily interactions with neighboring U.S. communities. Nevertheless, a free trade agreement is likely to worsen problems in the border economy in three ways: from greater growth in manufacturing, services, and trade.

As the border further develops, as is likely under free trade because of its proximity to the United States, this could result in a selective migration to the region, although not necessarily to the United States. This migration would be likely to include professionals and skilled labor attracted by a revitalized border economy, as is already noticeable in Tijuana. This trend can be expected to spread to other border cities as their images and economies improve.

A free trade agreement also will increase the relocation of foreign industry to Mexico.[1] Although a number of the new plants will probably locate to the interior, some industry will still be attracted to Mexico's northern border, which has already grown dramatically through the *maquiladora* industry. Currently, *maquiladoras* employ about 11 percent of all the industrial labor in Mexico, about 470,000 workers, which is expected to jump to about 25 percent, or between 1.7 million and 2.25 million workers, by the year 2000.[2] Labor shortages over the next decade will probably force a slowdown in *maquiladora* growth to about 10 percent per year, a significant reduction when compared to the average *maquiladora* growth of 20 percent per year over the last five years. The *maquiladoras* will continue to be the leading sector in the border economy and, therefore, border growth will continue to be tied to this industry.

A strengthened border economy will encourage more rapid growth in the border cities. Although population is also growing fast in the U.S. border communities, the highest growth is expected on the Mexican side (see Table 9.1).

The estimated population increase contrasts negatively with scarce border water resources, since most of the border region is arid, with very little water. The two main surface water sources, the Colorado River and the Rio Grande (Rio Bravo), are severely strained on both sides of the border, and they face increasing pollution. The smaller border rivers—the Tijuana River in Baja California, and the San Pedro and Santa Cruz Rivers in Sonora—face similar threats.

The water in these rivers was appropriated under the 1906 and 1944 binational treaties. But the treaties did not contemplate changes in water use requirements on either side of the border. The population estimates outlined in Table 9.1 help to explain the limitations of the binational treaties in satisfying current water needs and those anticipated over the next decade.[3] Although it is difficult to anticipate the new parameters that might be established by a free trade agreement, it is plausible that the 1906 and 1944 bilateral water treaties will be redefined.

The groundwater situation is no better. Groundwater is pumped unilaterally on both sides of the border in the absence of any binational agreement to regulate its usage. Border residents are alarmed at the

TABLE 9.1 U.S.-Mexican Border Population

County	1960	1970	1980	1990[a]	2000[a]
			Year		
Tijuana	165,690	340,583	461,257	898,453	1,444,724
San Diego	1,033,011	1,357,854	1,861,846	2,553,764	3,502,820
Mexicali	281,333	396,324	510,664	761,333	1,034,910
Imperial	72,105	74,492	92,110	113,862	140,750
Nogales	39,812	53,494	68,076	99,897	126,108
Sta Cruz	10,808	13,966	20,459	29,977	43,922
Ciudad Juárez	276,995	424,135	567,365	961,131	1,432,406
El Paso	314,070	359,291	479,899	640,709	855,406
Piedras Negras	48,408	46,698	80,290	79,956	92,616
Maverick	14,508	18,093	31,398	54,475	94,514
Nuevo Laredo	96,043	151,253	203,286	297,745	414,568
Webb	64,791	72,859	99,258	135,196	184,145
Reynosa	134,869	150,786	211,412	282,888	391,917
Hidalgo	180,904	181,535	283,229	441,976	689,699
Matamoros	143,043	186,146	238,840	304,396	387,231
Cameron	151,098	140,368	209,727	313,502	468,627

[a]1990–2000: Population estimates.

Source: Mexican and U.S. population census figures, various years.

rapid use of aquifer reserves and are increasingly concerned about the potential for hazardous waste pollution.

The most critical water shortage along the border is at El Paso-Cuidad Juárez. Each city obtains more than 90 percent of its drinking water from the Bolson del Hueco, and each is pumping water out of it as fast as it can. Under present usage, the aquifer is expected to last no more than 10 years.[4] Recent allegations of illegal dumping of hazardous waste from the *maquiladoras* or its improper storage near the plants has also raised alarms about water quality. At present, there are no reliable data on water quality in the aquifer, but because hazardous wastes from the *maquiladora* are not controlled, fear of pollution is growing substantially. The threat would likely be greatest in the El Paso-Cuidad Juárez area, which is the largest *maquiladora* center in Mexico, and thus likely to be the most important generator of hazardous wastes.

Evidence of water shortages is growing in most other Mexican border communities as well. About 40 percent of the inhabitants in these communities depend on irregular and unhealthy sources to satisfy their water needs.

Wastewater treatment is also a problem. About 50 percent of the border inhabitants have no municipal sewage system. This is not only a water availability problem, but also a problem of water supply. Distribution networks along the border are old and insufficient to cope with today's demands. Most sewage systems in border communities need costly repairs and upgrading, particularly to treat raw sewage. Cities with acute sewage treatment problems include Tijuana, Mexicali, Ciudad Juárez, Pedras Negras, Nuevo Laredo and Matamoros.

The greenhouse effect and its implications for climatic change may also have an effect on the border water supply. Although existing models on the greenhouse effect are not widely recognized for accuracy, some of them forecast lower precipitation rates for the central United States.[5] This could affect water supply at least at the western edge of the border, mainly in the Colorado River watershed, thus aggravating an already bitter water dispute among upper and lower Colorado River users, and between residents of California and Arizona, Northern and Southern California, and between Mexico and the United States.

The Canadian-U.S. experience shows us what to expect when the United States and Mexico negotiate a trade agreement. The United States and Canada did not include environmental issues in their trade agreement, but left open the possibility that such issues will be negotiated in the future. Canadians are sensitive about allowing free or even regulated access to their natural resources. In fact, many of them see it as a threat to national sovereignty. Thus, any arrangement that the United States and Canada make on the use of natural resources is not likely to surface until the later stages of their free trade agreement some time over the next ten years.

When the United States and Mexico negotiate trade issues, they should discuss the allocation of border water resources. They must find a method of allocating water that reconciles different water consumption patterns on each side of the border. Currently, water consumption is two-to-three times higher on the U.S. side than on the Mexican side of the border.

The pressure of rapid urban growth that will result from a free trade agreement between Mexico and the United States is likely to force additional deterioration of an already strained urban infrastructure, including housing, communications, roads, green areas, and health services. This deterioration in infrastructure will present an important obstacle to future border industrialization and economic growth. In fact, *maquiladora* growth is already taking place outside the border area because of the lack of urban services and a border labor shortage.

This problem can be solved in part with U.S. investment in the border infrastructure, as some groups have proposed. The *Cabeza Foundation*,[6] and California Republican state Sen. Kenneth Maddy,[7] have generated infrastructure financing proposals for Baja California, which focus on the creation of entities that would serve the *maquiladoras*. Similar initiatives have been proposed in Arizona.[8] Although most of these initiatives are still in the planning stage, it would be interesting to see what role they would play in a free trade agreement.

The Mexican legislation establishing debt-for-nature swaps to promote border economic development and environmental preservation was an important precedent for the initiatives now under study, including U.S. House Resolution 3146, introduced by Rep. Jim Bates of California to the first session of the 101st Congress. A similar plan sponsored by U.S. Senators Lloyd Bentsen (D-Texas), Dennis DeConcini (D-Arizona), and Jeff Bingaman (D-New Mexico) became an amendment to the Clean Air Act. The amendment frees up financial resources for urbanization projects in Mexico's border communities in order to improve air quality in the U.S. border cities. This type of cooperation could be strengthened and expanded under a free trade agreement.

Environmental and Health Risks in the *Maquiladora* Industry

The environmental and health risks associated with the operation of the *maquiladoras* have received increased attention over the past several years. These risks are created by multinational corporations that use lower occupational health standards for their Third World workers than they do for workers in the United States.[9] These corporations are also subject to very lax controls on hazardous waste emissions. These lower occupational health and environmental standards have the potential to allow catastrophic environmental damage.[10] The operation of *maquiladoras* carry three basic risks: 1) in the work place (occupational health); 2) to the inhabitants of neighborhoods near the *maquiladoras*; and 3) to the environment.

The public health risk is primarily due to the common practice of storing hazardous materials and wastes in the *maquiladora* plants for years with inadequate security measures. This can produce major catastrophes. In fact, accidents involving hazardous materials are becoming more frequent at the border. In July 1990, for example, a tank containing sulfuric acid, a highly toxic substance, was involved in an accident in Mexicali. More than 1,500 people had to be evacuated from the area. Equally as frightening as the potential spills of hazardous chemicals is the absence of emergency training in border communities to handle such disasters.

One of the longest standing criticisms of the *maquiladoras* is the risk to worker health. Since the *maquiladoras* were established in the 1960s, they have been criticized for allowing "sweat shop" labor conditions to proliferate. However, most of the studies on occupational health have faced fierce opposition from the industry and have, therefore, failed to provide sufficient epidemiological data to determine the threat to workers. Researchers attempting to carry out a study on the health of female *maquiladora* workers in Tijuana in 1986 ran into this opposition.[11] Last year, Dick Kamp, writing in the Sierra Vista Herald, stated that when he attempted to investigate allegations of health threats to workers in Nogales, Sonora, he ran into strong opposition from plant operators. In his column, Kamp concluded:

> The government of Mexico should be persuaded that concerned citizens in both countries (but particularly in the United States), who are encouraging resolution of twin plant social issues are not doing so to drive them out of the country.[12]

Although Mexican law (the *Ley Federal del Trabajo* and the *Ley General de Salud*) have established measures to protect workers, in practice these laws are largely unenforced. Mexican agencies lack the budget or staff to monitor the 1,700 *maquiladora* plants in Mexico.

The law requires that health and security squads be established in each plant; this provision has been enforced since 1985. Many of the standards established to control workers' exposure to hazardous and toxic materials are similar to those established by the U.S. Occupational Safety and Health Administration. Medical facilities for treating emergencies are supposed to be established in each plant; workers are obligated to wear safety equipment, and employers are supposed to provide information to the workers about hazardous materials in the work place.[13]

Little data exist on occupational diseases in the *maquiladoras* because of scarce government resources, few controls, and alleged corruption within the government agencies empowered with occupational health. Under these circumstances, it is difficult to reliably estimate the social cost that can be linked to occupational diseases in this industrial sector. But mounting evidence of intense use of hazardous materials in the *maquiladoras* and documentation of deficient safety measures used in the plants point to the gravity of these concerns.[14]

Hazardous wastes also pose a risk to public health and the environment. Mexican environmental law and Annex 3 of the 1983

Binational Agreement for the Protection of the Border Environment require the export of all hazardous waste generated by *maquiladora* manufacturers in Mexico, but compliance with the law and the agreement have been lax.[15]   According to records of the U.S. Environmental Protection Agency, no more than 20 *maquiladora* plants out of more than 1,200 operating in 1987 returned their hazardous waste to the United States.[16]

The Mexican government allows the *maquiladoras* to recycle part of their waste in Mexico using authorized companies. But Mexico has few facilities for managing hazardous wastes. Only six recycling firms exist in Mexico, and only two of them are located at the border. The Secretaría de Desarrollo Urbano y Ecología (SEDUE), the Mexican agency charged with controlling the generation of hazardous waste both from domestic and *maquiladora* industries, has authorized only five landfills in Mexico, of which two are located in border communities. Most of these facilities began operating only recently, and only a small portion of the *maquiladoras* (around 200) contract for their services.

SEDUE itself is severely understaffed and underbudgeted. SEDUE, for example, lacks national, regional, or local inventories of hazardous waste emissions from the *maquiladoras* or the domestic industry, and it lacks control over the final destination of the waste. Thus, hazardous wastes are sometimes dumped illegally into municipal sewage systems or landfills.[17] They are also recycled by unauthorized companies, and these improper handling procedures threaten the future growth of the border region by threatening its water resources.

Under the provisions of the 1983 binational agreement, EPA and SEDUE established a cooperative effort to jointly address the use of unequal environmental health standards in Mexico and the United States. So far, the effort has generated two binational conferences and only a handful of visits to *maquiladora* plants. EPA and SEDUE have issued a bilingual edition of the two agencies' regulations for handling hazardous waste in Mexico and the United States. But stronger cooperation is critical, if any significant joint actions are ever to take place.

Perhaps this cooperation could be formalized within the framework of a free trade agreement. We must determine to what extent the agreement will encourage additional relocation of polluting industries to Mexico. New evidence indicates that certain industries, particularly those affected by stricter U.S. environmental regulations, such as furniture manufacturing, chroming, and certain types of electronics manufacturing in Southern California, are relocating part or all of their operations to the U.S.-Mexican border.

Chemical companies are already advocating provisions in the free trade agreement that would allow U.S. chemical plants to relocate to Mexico. Dow Corning recently said they view Mexico as a potential worldwide source of methanol, and Occidental Chemical is reportedly considering a chlor-alkali plant in Mexico.[18] Most of these plants pose high risks to health and environment, and they should be carefully regulated.

About 10 percent of the *maquiladoras* surveyed in a recent study cited environmental regulations as a primary factor in the decision to leave the United States, and 17 percent considered environmental regulations to be an important factor. Almost 13 percent said weaker environmental controls in Mexico were a primary factor in relocating to the border, and another 13 percent said lax Mexican enforcement was an important factor.[19] Other questions need to be addressed. What type of controls must be included in a free trade agreement to hinder unsafe industrialization? How can health and safety standards be normalized for both *maquiladoras* and other U.S. corporations operating in Mexico? Should the agreement impose a moral code on U.S. corporations operating in Mexico? Or should other types of controls be incorporated within the framework of the agreement?

The least controversial solution would be to incorporate a voluntary moral code of operation. Support for this type of *maquiladora* control has grown in Mexico and the United States over the past year. Attention in both the Mexican and U.S. media,[20] together with SEDUE's limited but increasing enforcement of Mexican environmental laws, has generated support for voluntary controls among the members of some *maquiladora* associations like the Border Trade Alliance and the Asociación Nacional de Maquiladoras. As a result, some of the more outspoken *maquiladora* supporters in the U.S. Congress have also asked for voluntary controls.[21] SEDUE, confronted by a lack of technical, economic, and material resources, signed a voluntary environmental control agreement with the Associación Nacional de Maquiladoras in November 1989.

Unfortunately, voluntary industrial compliance to environmental regulations has had limited success, and it is questionable whether voluntary compliance can be effective in Mexico or whether it should be considered as part of a free trade agreement. Even in the United States, the use of voluntary compliance.

In my opinion, a more strict approach is needed to avoid the discrepancies between U.S. and Mexican environmental, occupational, and health standards. Laws and regulations should be standardized both for the *maquiladoras* as well as for U.S. manufacturing companies that locate outside the border region.

A more suitable framework has already been established within the U.S. Foreign Corrupt Practices Act. The act could be amended to force U.S. corporations to comply with U.S. environmental standards in their Mexican operations. A recent proposal by Alan Neff for a U.S. Foreign Environmental Practices Act, modeled after the Foreign Corrupt Practices Act, goes in this direction in controlling U.S. businesses operating overseas.[22] The design and statutory provisions of such an act would be similar to the Foreign Corrupt Practices Act. Neff assumes that this new statute would be enacted as an amendment to the Securities Exchange Act of 1934.

Neff's proposal aims to equalize the standards that U.S. corporations use for domestic and overseas operations. The law would subject U.S. corporations to criminal prosecution and civil suits by public officials and private citizens in U.S. courts for violation of host nations' environmental laws or for violating U.S. environmental standards. This law would establish adequate protection for Mexico's environment and for public health, but its scope should be expanded to include occupational health standards to avoid loopholes in the legal framework.

It will be an enormous challenge to include environmental and health regulations for U.S. manufacturers as part of free trade negotiations. However, one factor that will help to simplify negotiations is the fact that, as written, U.S. and Mexican environmental and occupational health laws are already similar. The environmental and occupational health standards established by the EPA and OSHA are generally the same as those used by SEDUE and the Secretaría del Trabajo in Mexico.[23] The primary difference is that U.S. standards cover a broader range of hazardous materials and risks than do Mexican standards.

I do not expect environmental standards to be as difficult to negotiate as occupational health standards, primarily because industry is more willing to participate in environmental protection programs than in worker health programs. Environmental protection, in general, does not represent an immediate threat to industrial production. But many manufacturers are fearful that informing workers of workplace risks will prompt some workers to leave or to demand higher salaries. For many industries, including the *maquiladoras*, this signifies difficulties in maintaining a labor force, and therefore productive capacity. Tied to this is the fact that environmental issues have received a great deal of media attention, and the public has begun to exert pressure on corporations in this area. The problems of worker health, however, have received less media attention, and are not seen as a formidable public threat.

Although traditionally neglected, however, occupational health issues should be addressed to assure millions of Mexican workers at least minimal levels of protection. By the year 2000, the *maquiladora* industry, or its successor along the border, will employ an estimated two million workers. And, under a free trade arrangement, increasing numbers of Mexican workers will be employed by U.S. corporations in other industrial fields.

The Transboundary Movement of Hazardous Waste

The transboundary movement of hazardous waste is already a critical environmental issue in the binational relationship between Mexico and the United States. Mexico is increasingly concerned about both illegal and legal exports of hazardous waste from the United States into Mexico. These concerns center on several trends: 1) the continuous growth in hazardous waste generation in the United States; 2) the increasing cost of hazardous waste management; and 3) the growing community pressures against all kinds of waste handling facilities (the "not in my backyard" or nimby syndrome). These three trends encourage the U.S. export of waste as an inexpensive, easy, and relatively uncomplicated solution to waste disposal. In fact, the 2,000 miles of common border with the United States have become an irresistible temptation to many hazardous waste brokers and generators, particularly those operating in two of the largest U.S. generators of hazardous waste—Texas and California. Direct, illegal exports of hazardous waste from the United States to Mexico were documented as early as 1979. However, the largest documented increases of illegal exports took place after 1984. Although illegal hazardous waste exports have been discovered as far inland as Mexico City, most of the documented cases have been traced to the western border area around Tijuana.

According to SEDUE, in 1987–1988, Mexico received petitions to import 260,000 tons of hazardous wastes.[24] Only about 10 percent of these wastes actually were imported legally as recyclable material. Mexico bans hazardous waste imports that are to be dumped or incinerated in Mexico, but allows imported wastes to be recycled in Mexico when the waste is not a major hazard and when the importing party meets security standards. Imported wastes are not allowed to be transported to a third country.[25]

Annex 3 of the 1983 binational agreement regulates legal and illegal transboundary movements of hazardous wastes between Mexico and the United States. Although Annex 3 has been enforced since 1986, the United States does not always honor the agreement, thus aggravating

Mexico's problems in controlling the transboundary movement of hazardous waste. In one 1987 case, Mexico discovered an illegal shipment of 377 barrels of hazardous waste from California near Mexico City. Following the procedures outlined in Annex 3, SEDUE asked EPA to take legal action against the exporting party and to guarantee the shipment of the barrels back to California. After years of negotiations, EPA has still not removed the wastes, nor have the responsible parties been prosecuted. In another 1990 case, under strong pressure from Mexico, the EPA finally agreed to remove 84 barrels of hazardous waste found in a Tijuana neighborhood warehouse. The FBI is currently investigating a California company in connection with this case.

The hazardous waste problem is aggravated by several factors, including the inability of customs personnel from both countries to detect shipments of hazardous waste. Also lacking is a common code, preferably an international harmonized code, to keep track of hazardous materials and waste imports, as well as sufficient communications and statistical information sharing between customs agents in the two countries. A computerized retrieval system for storing and exchanging data would be ideal for better record keeping. On the Mexican side, SEDUE also lacks manpower and financial resources to strictly control hazardous waste imports or to oversee hazardous waste management within the *maquiladora* industry.

Enormous pressure is building in the United States for the export of hazardous wastes, but Third World countries are increasingly reluctant to accept such exports. Thus, it is possible that those special interests most affected by public opinion on hazardous wastes will seek to ease the export of hazardous waste into Mexico within the framework of the free trade agreement. This could take the form of pressure to allow within Mexico the construction of landfills, incinerators, and recycling facilities to handle U.S. hazardous wastes.

For now and in the near future, Mexico is ill-prepared to guarantee the safe operation of such sophisticated waste facilities. If already precarious controls are relaxed, Mexico would be faced with tremendous environmental and health setbacks. It is entirely possible that such relaxation could, for example, prompt an increase in the export to Mexico of hazardous materials banned in the United States but still manufactured for export. These materials are currently regulated by Annex 3. Rather than relaxing environmental and health standards, the free trade agreement should strengthen existing provisions of Annex 3 by embracing the provisions of the proposed Foreign Environmental Practices Act.

Global Warming

Future negotiations on global warming are a major challenge to the international community. Any regulations to control global warming will affect the national economies of developed and developing countries alike. Third World countries fear that they will be forced to accept a disproportionate share of the total cost of saving the environment in the absence of a fair proposal to distribute the economic and social costs between industrialized and Third World countries. The distribution of social and economic costs must be based on each country's historic and present pollution record.

The distribution of costs among nations must not overlook the role of transnational capital in the global economy and its responsibility for and contribution to the deterioration of the global environment. Pollution can be generated in Third World countries by transnational corporations, but at present the country and not the corporation is held responsible internationally for those emissions. By targeting countries rather than corporations for punitive action, the international community unfairly distributes costs among those groups that received fewer economic benefits from the industrial activities that caused environmental degradation.

The free trade agreement could be structured in a way that allows the easy relocation to Mexico of those industries that produce significant quantities of those chemicals closely associated with global warming—carbon dioxide, methane, and chlorofluorocarbons. If such industries do move into Mexico, the free trade agreement should contain provisions that require those industries to be internationally accountable for their emissions.

Conclusion

The structural changes to the Mexican economy that are likely to occur as a result of the free trade agreement will have a significant impact on the country's environment and public health. The key issue for Mexico is how to minimize this impact. Mexico can seek to include protections within the free trade agreement negotiations, but such protections will require a strong commitment from the nation's federal government. It is unclear how far President Carlos Salinas de Gortari is willing or able to push these issues during trade negotiations. Environmental protection has been prominent in the Salinas administration's political agenda, but has not resulted in any significant funding increase for SEDUE or other Mexican agencies in charge of environmental protection.

Mexico cannot allow itself to repeat costly past mistakes, particularly the environmental mistakes made in the *maquiladora* program. The environmental and social repercussions of Mexico's management of the oil boom provide a similar example.

Notes

1. See "Capital Internacional y Relocalización Industrial en la Frontera Norte de México," by Alejandro Mercado, José Negrete and Roberto Sánchez, El Colegio de la Frontera Norte, mimeo, 1989.

2. See "Perspectivas Estructurales de la Industria Maquiladora," by Bernardo González-Aréchiga and José Carlos Ramírez, a conference paper presented at La Industria Maquiladora en México, sponsored by El Colegio de México, El Colegio de la Frontera Norte and La Fundación Friedrich Ebert, Federal District, Mexico, June 7, 1989.

3. On future water needs at the border see "Anticipating Transboundary Water Needs and Issues in the Mexico-U.S. Border Region in the Rio Grande Basin," by E. Neal Armstrong, in *The U.S.-Mexico Border Region: Anticipating Resource Needs and Issues to the Year 2000*, edited by César Sepúlveda and Albert Utton, 1982, Texas Western Press, University of Texas at El Paso.

4. See Armstrong; and "Water—Its Role From Now to the Year 2000," by T. Ernest Smerdon and "Surface Water Quality in the Border Between El Paso and the Gulf of Mexico," by A. Gerard Rohlich, both in *The U.S.-Mexico Border Region: Anticipating Resource Needs and Issues to the Year 2000* (see Note 3).

5. For a discussion on the greenhouse effect on climatic change in the United States, see *The Greenhouse Effect, Climate Change, and U.S. Forests*, E. William Shands and John S. Hoffman, editors, The Conservation Foundation, Washington, D.C., 1987; and *Climate Change and Society*, by W. William Kellogg and Robert Schware, Westview Press, 1981.

6. See "*Cabeza*: Financing the Future of the Border Region, an Opportunity for the United States and Mexico," 1989, *Cabeza* mimeo; and "California and Baja California Enterprise Zone Foundation," March 6, 1989, *Cabeza* mimeo.

7. See "California and Baja California Enterprise Zone Authority," SB 961, introduced by Sen. Kenneth Maddy to the California State Legislature, March 6, 1989.

8. See "Arizona and Northern Mexico: Building a Golden Age," by Jim Kolbe, paper presented to the Arizona Academy of Public Affairs, Grand Canyon, Arizona, Oct. 26, 1987; and "McCain, Kolbe Urge Twin Plants to Provide Workers with Housing," by Mark Turner, *Tucson Daily Star*, June 7, 1987.

9. See "U.S. Plants Turn Mexico's Border into a Toxic Dump," by Jane Juffer, *Sacramento Bee*, Sept. 25, 1988; "Border Boom Feeding Hazardous Waste Ills," by Patrick McDonnell, *Los Angeles Times*, San Diego County Edition, Sept. 10, 1989; "Hazardous Waste in the *Maquiladora*: The Case of Mexicali," *Natural Resources Journal*, by Roberto Sánchez, University of New Mexico, Vol. 30, Winter, 1990; "Hazardous Material Inventory of Aqua Prieta, Sonora Maquiladoras, with Recommendations for U.S.-Mexico Transboundary

Regulation," by Dick Kamp and Michael Gregory, Border Ecology Project mimeo, 1988.

10. For a broader discussion see "Multinational Corporations in Developing Countries," *Multinational Corporations, Environment, and Third World Business Matters*, by Barry Castleman, Duke University Press, Durham, 1987; "Industrial Relocation and Pollution Havens," (also in *Multinational Corporations*), by Charles Pearson; and "The Lessons from Bophal," by M. Fergus Bordewich, *The Atlantic*, March, 1987.

11. "La Salud y la Mujer Obrera en las Plantas Maquiladoras: El Caso de Tijuana," by Jorge Carrillo and Monica Jasis, Cefnomex mimeo, Mexico City, March 1984.

12. "Maquiladora Peril to Workers' Health?" by Ruben Hernandez, *Tucson Citizen*, June 6, 1989; "Health, Safety Checks of Twin Plants Difficult," Dick Kamp, *Sierra Vista Herald*, Sept. 13, 1987.

13. See "Contaminación de la Industria Fronteriza: Riesgos Para La Salud y el Medio Ambiente," Las Maquiladoras: Ajuste Estructural," by Roberto Sánchez, edited by Bernardo González-Aréchiga and Rocío Barajas, Colegio de la Frontera Norte, 1988; also Kamp and Gregory (see note 9); and "Salud de Obreras de la Maquiladora: El Caso de Nogales, Sonora," a paper presented to the Conference on Survival Strategies, Demand Satisfaction, and Urban Social Movements, Chapala, Jalisco, Feb. 29-March 2, 1988.

14. See "Mujer y Trabajo en la Industria Maquiladora de Exportación," in the *Cuadernos de Trabajo* series, by Rocío Barajas and Carmen Rodríguez, Fundación Friedrich Ebert, Mexico City, 1989; "Derechos Laborales y Humanos en la Maquila (testimony of Zenith workers in Reynosa)," by Sorjuana Loera and Cruz Chavez Reynoso, paper presented at The *Maquiladora* Industry in Mexico Conference, sponsored by El Colegio de México, El Colegio de la Frontera Norte and La Fundación Friedrich Ebert, Federal District, Mexico, June 7, 1989; *Sangre Joven. La Maquiladora por Dentro*, by Sandra Arenal, Editorial Nuestro Tiempo, Mexico City, 1986; "La Flor Más Bella de la Maquiladora," by Norma Iglesias, Cefnomex mimeo, 1985; "Mujeres Fronterizas en la Industria Maquiladora," by Jorge Carrillo and Alberto Hernández, Cefnomex mimeo, Mexico City, 1985; "Mallory Plant is Long Gone; Some Say It Left a Grim Legacy," by Michael Beebe, *Buffalo News*, March 11, 1987.

On the living conditions of the *maquiladora* workers see "Boom and Despair. Mexican border towns are a Magnet for Foreign Factories, Workers and Abysmal Living Conditions," by Sonia Nazario, *Wall Street Journal*, Sept. 22, 1989; Barajas and Rodríguez (see note 13); and "La Frontera. Land of Opportunity or Place of Broken Dreams," Sandy Tolan, *Tucson Weekly*, Oct. 18-24, 1989.

15. These include La Ley General del Equilibrio Ecológico y Protección al Ambiente (1987) and the Reglamento Para el Control de Residuos Peligrosos (1988).

16. See "The *Maquiladora* Industries: Hazardous Waste Management," from the U.S./Mexico Hazardous Waste Working Group, EPA-SEDUE, 1st edition, November 1989, distributed by the Border Trade Alliance and the Asociación Nacional de la Industria Maquiladora.

17. See "Contaminación Industrial en la Frontera Norte: Perspectivas para la Decada de los Años 1990," *Estudios Sociológicos*, by Roberto Sánchez, El Colegio de México, June-August, 1990.

18. "What Mexico has to Offer and What it Needs," by Leslie Ann Layton, Peter Coombes, and David Hunter, *Chemical Week*, June 6, 1990.

19. See "*Capital Internacional y Relocalización Industrial en la Frontera Norte de México*," by Alejandro Mercado, José Negrete and Roberto Sánchez, El Colegio de la Frontera Norte, mimeo, 1989.

20. See "The Border Boom. Hope and Heartbreak," *New York Times Magazine*, July 1, 1990; "EPA Opposes Funding Clean-Air Effort Along Mexican Border," by Jennifer Dixon, *The Arizona Daily Star*, March 28, 1990; and "Senate Agrees to Seek Cleaner Air Along Border," by Anne Hazard, *The Arizona Daily Star*, March 23, 1990.

21. See Kolbe, note 8.

22. See "Not in Their Backyards Either: A Proposal for a Foreign Environmental Practices Act," by Alan Neff, submitted for publication to *Ecology Law Quarterly*, 1989, University of California at Berkeley

23. See "Ley Federal del Equilibrio Ecológico y Protección al Ambiente," Diario Oficial, Jan. 7, 1988; "Reglamento Para el Manejo de Residuos Peligrosos," *Diario Oficial, Nov. 27, 1988;* "Brigadas de Salud y Securidad, Recomendaciones, Programa de Salud y Seguridad Para los Trabajadores de la Empresas," by El Congreso Del Trabajo, STPS, IMSS, Federal District, Mexico, 1985; and "Acuerdo por el que se reforman y adicionan diversas disposiciones del instructivo número 10 relativo a las condiciones de seguridad e higiene en los centros de trabajo donde se produzcan, almacenen o manejen sustancias químicas capaces de generar contaminación en el ambiente laboral," *Diario Oficial*, May 31, 1989.

24. See *El Comercio International de Desechos: Inventario de Greenpeace*, by Jim Vallette, Greenpeace, 4th edition, 1989.

25. See the "Decreto relativo a la importación o exportación de materiales peligrosos o residuos peligrosos que por su naturaleza pueden causar daños al medio ambiente o a la propiedad o constituyen un riesgo a la salud o el bienestar público," *Diario Oficial*, Jan. 19, 1987.

Environment: U.S. Perspective

C. Richard Bath

The United States and Mexico share a 2,000-mile border that generates numerous resource and environmental issues. Historically, the major concern for the borderlands, largely a semi-arid desert region, has been water availability. Water supplies are dependent, in part, on two major river systems, the Colorado and Rio Grande (Rio Bravo in Mexico).

Treaties in 1906 and 1944 allocated the water in these river systems between Mexico and the United States, and among the affected U.S. states. Nevertheless, two of the most contentious issues in bilateral relations have involved these two river systems. The Chamizal dispute involving the Rio Grande at El Paso was settled in 1964 after years of bitter negotiations.[1] Another dispute involving the Wellton-Mohawk irrigation project in the United States, which increased the salinity of the Colorado River as it flowed into Mexico, was resolved in 1974 with an order signed by the International Boundary and Water Commission (IBWC). The IBWC, which celebrated its 100th anniversary in 1989, has proved to be successful in managing riparian water disputes between the two countries.

Groundwater, which accumulates in large underground aquifers or bolsons, is important to a large section of the U.S.-Mexico border, but is especially critical for El Paso-Ciudad Juárez, which is dependent on its aquifers for drinking water. The shortage of groundwater has forced El Paso to seek sources other than the Hueco Bolson. In 1980, the city applied for drilling rights in the Mesilla Bolson, located primarily in New Mexico. New Mexico rejected the application, and since 1982 the case has been in court. The U.S. Supreme Court will likely give the final decision in the case.

The Mexican government is standing on the sidelines, carefully watching the New Mexico water case. Mexico shares the Hueco and Mesilla Bolsons with the United States, but the portion that it will receive from the aquifers is unclear, since no international agreement exists on aquifer sharing.[2] Since water is essential to economic growth, Mexico is obviously concerned about the potential loss of this resource. If consumption patterns continue to increase in the desert region of the border, a water shortage may be the single largest constraint to regional industrialization. Currently, much of the border industry uses relatively little water and that is likely to persist, but if the population continues to increase and water consumption rates, particularly in Mexico, continue to increase, there will be a shortage of water from El Paso to San Diego.

Increasingly, water quality is becoming a major issue all along the border. In the Lower Rio Grande Valley, municipal and agricultural wastes present pollution problems. The major concern is the potential damage to estuaries and coastal zones of the Gulf of Mexico, which could greatly threaten marine resources. One major problem that has attracted the attention of Sen. Lloyd Bentsen, D-Texas, has been Nuevo Laredo's dumping of millions of gallons of raw sewage into the Rio Grande. This untreated sewage is a threat to the public health of residents living downstream, and Bentsen wants a bilateral agency to handle the problem.

In October 1989, the U.S. Department of Justice filed suit against the city of El Paso for failure to meet water emission standards established under the Clean Water Act. The city could be fined up to $2 million for failing to take adequate measures to handle industrial wastes discharged into the city's treatment plants. The industries involved were a blue jeans stone washing plant and a metal plating plant. The case could eventually have some impact on the types of industries that can locate along the border.

Another serious pollution case involves the New River in Calexico-Mexicali. The New River rises in the United States, flows into Mexico, and then returns to the United States, where it provides irrigation for California crops in the Imperial Valley. On the Mexican side, the river has become the recipient of increasing amounts of raw sewage, but even more threatening are huge amounts of hazardous and toxic substances that pour into it. These substances threaten the health of anyone who comes into contact with river water, and may well affect crops produced in the region. This pollution is the direct result of the rapid rate of industrialization in the Mexicali area.

Untreated sewage is a major problem all along the border. Perhaps the most celebrated case of water pollution is in the San Diego-Tijuana area where untreated sewage flows north from Tijuana onto the beaches of San Diego.[3] The problem is incredibly complex, and resulted in one of the first bilateral agreements under the umbrella of the binational environmental agreement signed in La Paz, Baja California. Tijuana and Mexicali have treatment plants, but they are inadequate. Ciudad Juárez, a city of more than one million people, has no water treatment facilities at all. El Paso does have treatment facilities, but they often break down and wastes are dumped into the river. Perhaps the major success story is in Nogales, where a unique method of financing prompted construction of a plant treating sewage from both sides of the border.[4]

The untreated sewage problem in the San Diego-Tijuana region remains the most serious environmental threat. Over 12 million gallons of untreated sewage flow into the Tijuana River each day, and the river contains substantial amounts of highly toxic chemicals. The river flows into the Pacific Ocean, and then dumps wastes onto Imperial Beach in the United States. The beach has been closed for ten years, and a valued estuary is threatened by the pollution. Public health officials attribute diseases such as amoebic dysentery, vibrio cholera, staphylococcal disease, hepatitis, encephalitis, and even malaria to the *agua negra* in the river. Worse, polio agents have also been found. Clearly, the situation requires immediate attention and, hopefully, a recent agreement will help.

Air Quality

With increased population and industrialization, air pollution has also proved to be an increasing problem in the borderlands, particularly in the copper-producing region of Sonora and Arizona.[5] A new smelter would have contributed enormous amounts of air pollutants flowing into the Douglas, Arizona region, a problem that was addressed by an annex to the La Paz agreement.[6] The San Diego-Tijuana region also has air pollution problems but, fortunately, they are not as severe as they could be because of prevailing coastal winds.

The area with the most severe air pollution problem is El Paso-Ciudad Juárez.[7] The region is characterized by winter inversions that trap the pollutants against the surrounding mountains. As a result, El Paso exceeds federal emission standards for total suspended particulates, carbon monoxide, and ozone. The area also has high levels of sulfur oxides, lead, and heavy metals. The nature of air pollution in the El Paso-Ciudad Juárez region is also changing, from suspended particulates to vehicular emissions, giving the area the same type of photochemical smog found in Los Angeles.[8]

Regulating these pollutants is extremely difficult because they come from so many sources. In Ciudad Juárez, for example, most of the streets in the city are unpaved, which contributes substantially to suspended particulate pollution. Dust and smoke are also generated by open burning, particularly during winter months, and the proliferation of small factories in the area. Periodic fires in city dump sites and the operation of a large cement plant also contribute to particulate pollution.

As Ciudad Juárez develops economically, many of the sources of particulates will disappear. That has already happened in El Paso, which itself was characterized by dirt streets and open burning 50 years ago. Today, El Paso streets are paved and home heating is provided largely by relatively clean natural gas. Meanwhile, the pollution from Ciudad Juárez is visible, making it easy for U.S. officials to blame Mexico for the pollution.

The most difficult present and future problem is vehicular emissions. The international boundary is itself responsible for violation of federal standards. The highest concentrations of carbon monoxide and ozone are found at the boundary as a direct result of the time it takes to clear U.S. Customs. Cars waiting in line for an average time of 30 minutes leave their engines running, thus contributing to pollution. In recent years, the problem has been exacerbated by the increase in trucks transporting goods for the *maquiladora* industry. For example, in the summer of 1989, 300 to 400 trucks waited in line for 12 to 16 hours to cross the international bridge, and pollution increased accordingly. That problem may have been eased by recent changes in Customs hours and staffing.

Aside from the Customs lines, the increasing number of cars also contributes to air pollution. Ten years ago, the number of El Paso vehicles was roughly twice that of Ciudad Juárez. Now the number is rapidly equalizing. Ciudad Juárez traffic has increased as a result of a relaxation of import regulations, which allows for the entry of older vehicles without the restrictive import tax of previous years. As a result, Ciudad Juárez has become a living grave for older vehicles from the United States. These are the types of vehicles most likely to contribute the heaviest amounts of pollutants.

Traffic patterns do not help. In Ciudad Juárez, there are few freeways but plenty of stop-and-go traffic, which aggravates pollution. In El Paso, the public transportation system serves very few, and the automobile remains the chief means of individual transportation. In neither city does there appear to be any plans for mass transit or for joint planning to handle international traffic.

Hazardous Materials and Wastes

Hazardous materials and wastes pose a new and complex issue in bilateral relations. The issue, which involves the creation of new chemicals for which there are no clear methods of use or disposal, has been the subject of a host of conferences in the last two years. No effort will be made here to give a comprehensive view of the hazardous waste problem.[9]

Mexico and the United States must face the issue of importing and exporting banned substances. The United States may ban a chemical, but permit it to be exported to Mexico where it can be used on a product like tomatoes that will be exported to the United States. Examples of this dilemma abound.

There is also genuine concern, especially in the Lower Rio Grande Valley, that farm workers have suffered severe health problems from pesticide spraying in the fields where they work. Jim Hightower, former Texas agriculture commissioner, created a political storm by insisting on protecting the health of these workers. But the nature of farm labor on the border will make it difficult to track the actual impact on health of the workers. In El Paso, the workers may be picked up in the morning at the border, work all day in the fields, then return to Mexico. If they get sick, no one tracks them down and, in any case, medical practices in Mexico do not include looking for pesticide poisoning.

Border environmental specialists are particularly concerned about the hazardous wastes generated by the border *maquiladora* industry. No one seems to know where the waste is going—there is little record of what eventually happens to that waste. Under Mexican law, this waste should be returned to the United States, if that was its point of origin, but existing evidence suggests that very little is actually returning. New Mexican regulations implemented in May 1989 have focused attention on the problem of wastes generated within Mexico, and we may know more in the near future.

An even more serious problem is the illegal dumping in Mexico of hazardous wastes from the United States. There are recorded instances of such dumping, and the practice may become more prevalent in the future as new waste regulations become effective in the United States. The costs of disposal continue to escalate. They are exacerbated by the land ban against hazardous-waste dumping that took effect in 1990, as well as by increasing regulation of landfills and incinerators. These factors make illegal disposal outside the country more attractive, and Mexico is an obvious target.

A recent example illustrates the nature of the problem. In October 1989, 175 barrels of PCBs were found abandoned on four trucks in an El Paso neighborhood. The barrels were leaking and presented a definite health threat to residents. The trucks belonged to Adán Sigala, a Mexican national from Chihuahua City. He had apparently picked up the barrels in Denver and was in the process of transporting them to Chihuahua. When the barrels were discovered, Sigala fled into Mexico.

Sigala is the state leader of a Marxist-oriented political party representing the residents of *colonias*—poor squatters. *El Diario de Juárez* questioned Sigala about his involvement in the shipment of PCBs, and his answers were frightening.[10] He called the chemicals "totally inoffensive," and added, "this substance has curative properties and, therefore, it is not the first time I have brought them to Chihuahua. It is very good for rheumatism, and those who suffer from it greatly benefit from the PCBs."

Reporters went into the Mexican *colonias* and found PCB barrels used for water storage and garbage. Such usage is also found in *colonias* on the U.S. side of the border. One environmental engineer, in fact, commented that Chihuahua was becoming the chemical cemetery of the United States.

This brief review of water, air, and hazardous waste problems by no means exhausts the range of environmental issues in bilateral relations. With increasing population and urbanization along the border, environmental issues will become more evident and, most assuredly, more controversial. With economic growth and industrialization, these problems will require far more governmental attention than in the past.

Regulatory Framework

Environmental policy in the U.S.-Mexico borderlands is determined by three regulatory frameworks: those of the United States, Mexico, and bilateral or international law. These three entities are greatly affected by rapid population increases along the border and the relative poverty of the region.

Population and urbanization began to increase during World War II when military bases expanded significantly along the border. Many of the key decision makers in Washington served at Fort Bliss, or the San Diego Naval Station or the Laredo Air Base, and their memories of sleepy border towns are hard to overcome.

On the Mexican side, the *bracero* program bringing farm workers to U.S. fields during the war also stimulated population increases. Today, partially because of migration and higher birth rates, the entire border is a population leader for both countries. El Paso and San Diego are two of the fastest growing cities in the Sunbelt, and other border cities are not far behind. But growth on the U.S. side is low compared with the growth of border communities in Mexico. Both Ciudad Juárez and Tijuana have populations of more than one million; 30 years ago both had less than 200,000, giving them a population growth rate of more than 300 percent over the last 25 years.[11] Mexicali, a city of 60,000 in 1960, now has more than 650,000 inhabitants.

Although the border growth rate has slowed in recent years, the border still attracts new residents. The primary attraction, aside from proximity to the United States, is the jobs generated by the *maquiladora* industry.

The impact of this population increase on border resources is quite evident. Indeed, rapid urbanization is essentially responsible for both environmental deterioration and resource depletion. Increased resource consumption rates threaten water supplies all along the border. Air pollution directly results from an increased number of vehicles. Those cities along the border that do have sewage treatment facilities are hard-pressed to respond to the demand from a growing population. Both Mexicali and Tijuana have built sewage facilities in recent years, but are unable to build them fast enough. As conditions in the *colonias* indicate, the more developed United States has a similar problem.

The second border characteristic that affects the policy framework is poverty.[12] On the U.S. side, with the exception of San Diego, which some argue is too distant to be a border community, all border communities are characterized by poverty. The Texas border communities of El Paso, Laredo, Brownsville, and McAllen are all ranked at the very bottom of U.S. metropolitan areas in terms of wealth and income. These cities also have unemployment rates above the state and federal unemployment levels.

This poverty has important consequences for successful resource and environmental management. Environmental policy is widely considered to be a quality-of-life concern for the middle class,[13] but on the U.S. side of the border, the middle class is sadly lacking. This is evident in the lack of significant environmental policy groups. Other problems take priority over environmental ones. Employment, housing, education, nutrition, health, and the basic requisites of life are far more likely to receive attention than quality-of-life issues like the environment. It is difficult to get excited about air pollution when you are starving.

If the U.S. side of the border is poor, the Mexican side is even poorer. Ironically, however, most of the border region is much better off economically than the interior of Mexico, and so the border still attracts people. The disparity of wealth between the U.S. and Mexican sides of the border complicates the implementation of binational environmental and resource policies. Given the low level of economic development, Mexico, until recently, tended to forego environmental management in favor of economic growth. Additionally, Mexicans tend to view U.S. intentions within a framework of dependency and to be extraordinarily suspicious of U.S. actions, which complicates the ability of both countries to address the costs of mutual policy efforts. Tied to this is Mexico's economic crisis since 1982, which has widened the economic disparity between the two countries. To put it bluntly, little money is available to support effective environmental policy.

Mexican government agencies operate on modest budgets that pay salaries and little more. Until the economy rebounds, there is little possibility that the public sector can find the funds necessary for environmental protection. International financial requirements brought on by foreign debt also prevent such expenditures.

The most important resource loss along the border is the terrible loss of human capital. Human capital is essential for economic growth and industrialization, but we may be losing the very people we need to sustain development. On both sides of the border, polluted water is a major cause of intestinal disease. The obvious target is children. How many children die from drinking poor quality water? We know that intestinal disease is the major cause of death on the Mexican side of the border.[14]

On the U.S. side, disease is rampant in the *colonias*.[15] In one El Paso *colonia* children spend an average of only nine years in school. Many of these children may be dropping out of school because they are too sick from drinking contaminated water to keep up with their work. In turn, their lack of education will condemn them to the lowest paying jobs. Society loses productive workers who cannot pay the higher taxes that would help alleviate the problems of poverty. Perhaps environmental management should be weighed in terms of losses in human capital.

An outstanding characteristic of the U.S. regulatory framework is federalism. The national government may pass environmental laws but leaves enforcement to the states. Often states leave actual enforcement to local governments. This loose chain of command results in problems. State and local governments sometimes lack the resources or political will for effective enforcement. This appears to be the case for air pollution policy in Texas. The state has shown no enthusiasm for effective air pollution control.[16] In fact, efforts to implement federal laws led to a virtual war between the U.S. Environmental Protection

Agency and the Texas Air Control Board, which left the state with no policy for many years.

Federalism may also lead to great discrepancy among states over policy implementation. Pesticide use, for instance, is strongly regulated in California but, until recently, was barely regulated in Texas. Federalism may also contribute to confusion about policy responsibility, that is, the agency responsible for handling a given problem. A plethora of laws may be contributing to confusion over responsibility for regulating hazardous materials and wastes.

Federalism also affects water policy. Water policy in the United States is essentially left to the states, unless it involves one of the big river systems, like the Colorado or Rio Grande. In these cases the federal government plays the role of water developer and allocator by interstate compact.[17] But in the case of groundwater, there is no federal policy. Eventually the courts may have to resolve this issue, but at present there is no legal way to divide groundwater among states, thus throwing doubts on the legal basis for international divisions.

Federalism also creates confusion for Mexico. Mexicans do not understand the U.S. federal system. States in Mexico rarely act independently of the central government in Mexico City, making it difficult for Mexicans to understand state powers in the United States. In the Mexican system, the president can direct policy, often without concern for either state or municipal governments or for special interest groups. The president of the United States has no such powers, especially for border issues that generally have separate policy groups and government agencies to address each issue. Thus, Mexico often is prepared to trade one issue for another, but such trade-offs are usually impossible in the U.S. system.

A major problem in Mexican environmental management is the degree to which Mexico is serious about effective regulation.[18] Mexico jumped on the environmental bandwagon early in the 1970s, passing new laws and creating a government agency, the Subsecretaría de Mejoramiento del Ambiente, to handle environmental policy. From the start, however, there was a real question about how much the government would do because of a perceived conflict between environmental policy and economic growth. Mexico regarded environmental policy as being in conflict with rapid industrialization. As a result, industrialization took precedence over any concern for the environment, especially in the heartland of industrialization, Mexico City. The Mexican government took no serious interest in environmental policy until the middle class, primarily in Mexico City, became concerned with quality-of-life issues.

Miguel de la Madrid, who took office in 1982, was the first president to put environmental issues on the federal agenda. Unfortunately, concern for the environment grew at the very time the government lacked resources. De la Madrid created a new cabinet-level agency, the Secretaría de Desarrollo Urbano y Ecología (SEDUE), to handle environmental policy, but from the outset the agency was handicapped by lack of funds. Funds are still lacking for basic equipment or technical training for environmental purposes. This economic problem should ease in time.

Surprisingly, in spite of the weak policy framework found within each nation, the binational policy framework has enjoyed some success in recent years. Since 1973, government representatives, scholars, and other interested parties have met on environmental issues, and conferences that address a variety of bilateral relations will normally have a section on environmental problems.[19] Environmental issues are also part of the working agenda for the U.S.-Mexico Border Public Health Association, which operates under the auspices of the Pan American Health Organization. As a result, a sizeable community of environmental interests has developed that keeps these issues on the bilateral agenda. In fact, environmental issues are periodically discussed by the U.S. and Mexican presidents when they meet.

Presidents Jimmy Carter and José Lopez Portillo signed an agreement making environmental problems part of the bilateral agenda in 1981. In 1983, Presidents Ronald Reagan and Miguel de la Madrid signed what may be the most significant binational environmental agreement at La Paz, Baja California.

The La Paz agreement is highly important for several reasons. First, it designates agencies to handle border environmental issues—EPA in the United States and SEDUE in Mexico. Previously, confusion existed over which government agencies should be responsible for binational environmental issues. The IBWC can still interfere on policy issues because its two sections are attached to the U.S. Department of State and the Mexican Ministry of Foreign Relations. The La Paz agreement draws into the negotiating process state and local officials, who traditionally have been ignored. Local officials should be consulted since they are better informed on most border issues.

The agreement also defines the environmental management region as extending 100 kilometers on either side of the boundary. Such a definition acknowledges the fact that many environmental problems do not originate at the boundary.

The La Paz agreement also calls for coordination of national programs, scientific and educational exchanges, environmental monitoring, environmental impact assessment, and periodic exchanges of information and data. The provision for sharing information is important because Mexican officials are often very reluctant to release any accumulated data. One provision in the La Paz agreement calls for special financing for the training of personnel, equipment transfers and the construction of installations. Such a provision could help sidestep the issue of Mexico's scarce resources.

Under the La Paz agreement, three major working groups were established to deal with water, air, and hazardous substances. Smaller groups under these three working groups can handle local problems. The two governments are also signing annexes to the La Paz agreement to deal with specific problems. To date, five have been signed. Annex 1 deals with the problem of sewage in the Tijuana-San Diego region. This problem reportedly will be the subject of Annex 6 as well.[20] Early in October 1989, Presidents George Bush and Carlos Salinas de Gortari signed an agreement calling for a joint treatment plant on the Tijuana River. Interestingly, the United States agreed to pay about half the cost of the plant. However, the plan is complicated by a suit filed by the EPA against the City of San Diego over the operation of its Point Loma treatment plant.

The working group on air quality focused initially on the problems in the Douglas-Nacozari-Cananea region. Eventually, Annex 4 addressed the problem, although it is by no means fully resolved, and is likely to remain controversial in the future. In 1986, an El Paso-Ciudad Juárez air quality task force was established to deal with air pollution in the region. The group has generated more cooperation among federal, state and local officials on regional air quality issues. EPA has sponsored four major training sessions for SEDUE personnel, giving a boost to cooperation on the international level. Some U.S. assistance has also been provided to Mexican officials for an inventory of pollutants, and to initiate a vehicle inspection and maintenance program on the Mexican side of the border.[21]

In October 1989, Presidents Bush and Salinas de Gortari signed Annex 5 to the La Paz agreement. Annex 5 is a general agreement dealing with air pollution along the border. It provides a legal framework for handling the problem. An appendix to the annex targets the El Paso-Ciudad Juárez region as an immediate area of concern. Each nation is obligated to identify the magnitude, type, and source of each pollutant within their respective territories. Each country agreed to identify needed controls for stationary pollution sources and to bring these sources into compliance with federal emission standards. And, each nation is obligated to monitor pollutants, to analyze them with state-of-the-art mathematical air modeling, and to harmonize air pollution control standards, when possible.

Annex 5 covers only stationary sources and does not attempt to address the problem of vehicular emissions. This means the primary pollutant will be particulates, and perhaps sulfur oxides and other emissions associated with industrial sources.

Ciudad Juárez does not have the technical means to monitor pollution; the city is dependent on the United States for a monitoring inventory. Therefore, the U.S. Congress allocated funds for the monitoring and, in a recent meeting, EPA officials adopted a monitoring plan. But bureaucracy remains a major stumbling block to successful implementation of Annex 5, mainly because of the conflicts between EPA and SEDUE and their respective foreign ministries.

Annex 5 had been scheduled for signing in October 1988, but was delayed a year by opposition within the State Department. Next, the agreement was reportedly held up in the Mexican Ministry of Foreign Relations. This exemplifies the problems associated with bureaucratic turf battles.

The hazardous materials and waste management working group has addressed important issues under its rubric. Annex 2 called for a joint contingency plan to handle spills of hazardous materials, primarily to prevent environmental threats similar to the blowout of the Ixtoc I oil well in the Gulf of Mexico in 1979. A pilot program was established in Calexico-Mexicali under Annex 2. A joint response team was formed to inventory hazardous materials and wastes along the border. This work could be greatly enhanced if the local emergency planning committees outlined under the U.S. Emergency Planning and Community Right to Know Act were actually functional on the border. These committees are in the incipient stage and do not appear to be very effective bodies.

Annex 3 on the transboundary shipment of hazardous materials and wastes was signed in November 1986. The agreement was prompted, in part, by the EPA's concern that hazardous material exports were not effectively controlled under provisions of the Hazardous and Solid Waste Amendments of 1984. In November 1986, just a few days before Annex 3 was signed, the EPA enacted new regulations to cover these exports. The new regulations stipulated that EPA had to be notified of the intent to export within 60 days; and that the receiving government give written, prior consent before shipment. These amendments to the Resource Conservation and Recovery Act (RCRA) were intended to provide "cradle to grave" tracking of hazardous materials.

As part of the closed loop system, EPA inaugurated a licensing procedure for disposal sites and incinerators. Only about 20 percent of both sites and incinerators were licensed. When the land ban becomes effective this year, it will put tremendous pressure on those dealing with hazardous materials to dispose of them effectively. But at the same time, the costs of legal disposal will escalate, making illegal disposal in Mexico far more likely.

The handling of hazardous materials and wastes is complicated by the puzzling bureaucratic responsibility for their oversight.[22] Hazardous wastes fall under the provisions of RCRA, but toxic chemicals are covered by the Toxic Substance Control Act (TSCA), and pesticides are under the Federal Insecticide, Fungicide and Rodenticide Act (FIFRA). Thus, the reporting and tracking of chemicals is exceedingly complex. For example, the EPA, the Department of Transportation, and U.S. Customs must be notified of any exported materials. As a practical matter, a truck carrying hazardous materials at an El Paso border crossing deposits a manifest in a mailbox just before crossing the border. U.S. Customs then picks up the manifest and sends it to the Department of Commerce in Washington D.C. But, as in the case of the recently discovered PCB barrels, the procedures for hazardous wastes are different. They go through the EPA back to the Texas Water Commission, which is responsible for RCRA enforcement. The FBI becomes involved in cases of illegal shipment in interstate commerce.

The situation is not much better on the Mexican side. Annex 3 defined hazardous waste as any waste defined by national policy, which, if improperly dealt with, could result in damage to health or the environment. Hazardous substances are defined as any substance, including chemicals or pesticides, which can harm public health, property or the environment. These included banned chemicals or those severely restricted. Each nation pledges to apply its domestic laws to any transboundary shipment of such materials, and obligates itself to cooperate in monitoring and spot-checking transboundary shipments of hazardous wastes and materials. In 1989, a common computer tracking system was scheduled to be adopted by the customs agencies on both sides of the border.

Under Annex 3, notification requirements are somewhat different from the requirements under RCRA, but the annex does call for specific information about the shipper, the material, and the destination. The recipient country has 45 days to reject the material after notification of its intended shipment. Each country must notify the other if it bans or severely restricts the use of a hazardous material. One provision explicitly deals with the *maquila* industry. It states that any hazardous waste generated from imported raw materials used in production, manufacturing, processing, or repair, must be returned to the country of origin.

Mexican officials believe one of the most important provisions of the annex is Article 14, which covers damages. When a violation is discovered, the annex stipulates that the "country of export shall take all practicable measures and initiate and carry out all pertinent legal actions." The hazardous waste or material is to be returned to the country of export; the affected ecosystem is to be returned to its previous state, to the extent possible; and compensation is to be given to repair the damages caused to people, property, or the environment. The country of export must also report to the affected country all measures and legal actions taken.

It is difficult to determine the effect of Annex 3 on regulation of hazardous materials and wastes for the border community. Before 1989, the annex appears to have had little impact. A study performed by the border Ecology Project in Agua Prieta-Douglas, Arizona revealed that few of the *maquila* managers even knew Annex 3 existed, and they were also blissfully ignorant of Mexican laws regulating hazardous materials.

It is doubtful that much of the material is returning to the United States. Any returning material must be registered with the EPA, but a spokeswoman for Region 9 covering California and Arizona admitted the agency had received only ten such requests from 1983 through 1987.[23] A spokesperson for the AFL-CIO, a harsher critic of the *maquiladora* industry, looked into available records of Region 9 and found that out of 100 *maquiladoras* in Mexicali, only two filed notices of intent to send hazardous materials back into the United States.[24] In data obtained from the Texas Water Commission for the 400 *maquiladoras* operating along the Texas border, only 11 returned waste to the United States in 1987. In 1988, a total of 90 companies returned material. Two privately owned disposal firms in El Paso contend that they disposed of wastes from 110 of the 362 *maquiladoras* operating in the El Paso region in 1988. But officially there were only 262 *maquiladoras* in Ciudad Juárez. The interesting question is what happened to the rest of the hazardous waste? No one really knows.

Mexico promulgated the General Law of Ecological Equilibrium and Environmental Protection in March 1988. While ostensibly a comprehensive law, funds are lacking for effective enforcement. In June 1988, new rules for hazardous materials were published in the *Diario Oficial*.[25] Additional regulations were announced in November 1988, and all generators of hazardous wastes were to achieve compliance with the regulations by May 26, 1989. It was that deadline that sparked interest in the maquiladora industry.

Under Mexican law, each facility must register with SEDUE and list the chemicals generated and used in the plant. Each facility must have a detailed plan for either recycling wastes or effectively disposing of them. All *maquiladoras* must maintain accurate records and report twice yearly to SEDUE on the volume and type of hazardous wastes generated. Wastes can be recycled by transferring them to a third party within Mexico. However, if the chemicals are imported, they must be returned to their country of origin. This provision may prove to fit very well within the framework established by Annex 3 of the La Paz agreement.

The new regulations should have a profound effect on the entire *maquiladora* industry. For example, the classification of hazardous materials under the new regulations includes wastewater treatment sludges from electroplating operations, solvents used as cleaners, and acids and bases used in etching baths—all of which are prominently found in the *maquiladora* industry. Thus, the regulations are likely to stimulate the growth of the Mexican waste management industry. In fact, new companies are already being established. The regulations may also encourage the production of chemicals within Mexico. The entire *maquiladora* industry seems to be moving toward local, rather than imported, supplies. If this trend continues, Mexico will have to handle waste management largely by itself.

Currently, recycling and hazardous waste disposal is practically nonexistent in Mexico. Few qualified recyclers exist, and those that do are primarily small operations. Mexican law appears to prevent the *maquiladoras* from recycling, although *maquiladora* wastes can be turned over to Mexican firms. This situation could prompt unscrupulous entrepreneurs to form companies without the necessary expertise to adequately recycle or dispose of wastes. Disposal is complicated by the lack of sites along the border. Wastes have to be transported to an existing site in Mexico City, and a second site will soon begin operation near Monterrey. The lack of disposal sites, coupled with a lack of transport facilities, makes midnight dumping appear all the more attractive.

The *maquiladora* industry also encounters problems in attempting to transport hazardous wastes back to the United States. Each state has different rules relating to hazardous wastes, and disposal sites are lacking. California has no sites and Texas has only one licensed site. To send wastes back, the *maquiladora* must locate a Mexican transporter, a U.S. transporter, and a U.S. disposal company. To complicate matters, Mexican truckers are not guaranteed passage onto U.S. roads, unless they can meet U.S. safety standards. All of these measures can greatly increase the costs of disposal for the entire industry.

SEDUE's ability to regulate hazardous wastes has been frequently questioned. Mexico has few people trained in the handling and assessment of hazardous materials and wastes, and SEDUE is greatly understaffed. The agency has only five employees to regulate almost 300 *maquiladoras* as well as other environmental problems in Ciudad

Juárez. These staffers would have to work long, hard days just to visit all the plants. SEDUE has just begun to train its personnel in the United States through the auspices of the EPA, but it will be a long time before the agency's staffing needs are filled.

In October 1989, Rosa Manuela Salas, who heads the Ciudad Juárez office of SEDUE, told the *El Paso Times* that 30 percent of the city's *maquila* plants were complying with the new regulations.[26] She said the percentage would be greater by counting the number who had complied but had not filled out the necessary paperwork. For short-term regulation, she said, SEDUE would rely on surprise plant inspections to be carried out by four inspectors.

Notes

1. Alan C. Lamborn and Stephen P. Mumme, *Statecraft, Domestic Politics, and Foreign Policy Making: The El Chamizal Dispute* (Boulder: Westview Press, 1988).

2. Stephen P. Mumme, *Apportioning Groundwater Beneath the U.S.-Mexican Border* (San Diego: Center for U.S. Mexican Studies, University of California at San Diego, 1988); also *Natural Resources Journal*, 22, 4, October 1982; and *Natural Resources Journal*, 25, 3, July 1985.

3. Stephen P. Mumme and Joseph Nalven, "National Perspectives on Managing Transboundary Environmental Hazards: The U.S.-Mexico Border Region," *Journal of Borderlands Studies*, 3, 1, Spring 1988, pp. 39-68.

4. Ibid, pp. 59-60; and Joseph Nalven, "Transboundary Environmental Problem Solving: Social Process, Cultural Perception," *Natural Resources Journal*, 26, 4, Fall 1986, pp. 793-818.

5. Stephen P. Mumme, "The Cananea Copper Controversy: Lessons for Environmental Diplomacy," *Inter-American Economic Affairs*, 38, Summer 1984, pp. 3-22.

6. Richard Kamp, "The Smelter Triangle: An Overview of U.S.-Mexican Negotiations." Testimony before the U.S. Senate Committee on Environment and Public Works, Denver, Colorado, August 12, 1985.

7. See Howard G. Applegate and C. Richard Bath, "Air Pollution in a Transboundary Setting: The Case of El Paso, Texas and Ciudad Juárez, Chihuahua," in C. Flinterman, B. Kwiatkowska, and J.G. Lammers (eds.), *Transboundary Air Pollution* (The Hague: M. Nijhoff, 1986), pp. 95-116; also C. Richard Bath and Victoria E. Rodriguez, "Comparative and Binational Air Pollution Policy in El Paso, Texas and Ciudad Juárez, Chihuahua," *The Borderlands Journal*, 6, 4, Spring 1983, pp. 171-197.

8. Robert Gray, et al., *Vehicular Traffic and Air Pollution in El Paso-Ciudad Juárez* (El Paso: Texas Western Press, 1989).

9. Howard G. Applegate and C. Richard Bath, "Hazardous and Toxic Substances as a Part of United States-Mexico Relations," in Lay James Gibson and Alfonso Corona Renteria (eds.), *The U.S. and Mexico: Borderland*

Development and the National Economies (Boulder: Westview Press, 1985), pp. 226-242.

10. *Diario de Juárez*, October 25, 1989.

11. Niles Hansen, *The Border Economy*, (Austin: University of Texas Press, 1981).

12. Ellwyn R. Stoddard and John Hedderson, *Patterns of Poverty Along the U.S.-Mexico Border* (Las Cruces: Joint Border Research Institute, 1987).

13. See Robert Cameron Mitchell, "Public Opinion and Environmental Politics in the 1970s and 1980s," in Normal J. Vig and Mitchell E. Kraft (eds.), *Environmental Policy in the 1980s: Reagan's New Agenda* (Washington: Congressional Quarterly, 1984), pp. 51-74.

14. C. Richard Bath, "Health and Environmental Problems: The Role of the Border in El Paso-Ciudad Juárez Coordination," *Journal of Inter-American and World Affairs*, 24, 3, August 1982, pp. 373-392.

15. See U.S. General Accounting Office, *Health Care Availability in the Texas-Mexico Border Area* (Washington: GAO, October 1988); also Hearings Before the Subcommittee on Water Resources of the Committee on Public Works and Transportation, U.S. House of Representatives, *Inadequate Water Supply and Sewage Disposal Facilities Associated with "Colonias" Along the United States and Mexican Border*, 100th Congress, Second Session (Washington, D.C. GPO, 1988).

16. Texas House Study Group, *Air Pollution Control in Texas* (Austin: Texas House of Representatives, Group Report No. 65, 1981).

17. Norris Hundley, *Dividing the Waters* (Berkeley: University of Calfornia Press, 1966); also Marc Reisner, *Cadillac Desert* (New York: Penguin, 1986).

18. Stephen P. Mumme, C. Richard Bath and Valerie J. Assetto, "Political Development and Environmental Policy in Mexico," *Latin American Research Review*, 23, 1, 1988, pp. 7-34.

19. Papers from these various conferences are published in the following volumes: Howard G. Applegate and C. Richard Bath (eds.), *Air Pollution Along the United States-Mexico Border* (El Paso: Texas Western Press, 1974); Stanley R. Ross (ed.), *Ecology and Development of the Border Region*, Mexico: Mexico City, ANUIES/PROFMEX, 1983); and César Sepulveda and Albert E. Utton (eds.), *The U.S.-Mexico Border Region: Anticipating Resource Needs and Issues to the Year 2000* (El Paso: Texas Western Press, 1984).

20. Clifton G. Metzner Jr., *Water Quality Issues of the San Diego-Tijuana Border Region* (San Diego: San Diego State University, Institute for Regional Studies of the Californias, 1989).

21. Howard G. Applegate and C. Richard Bath, "Air Pollution in the El Paso-Ciudad Juárez Region," *Transboundary Resources Report*, 3, 1, spring 1989, pp. 1-2.

22. A good description of the U.S. and Mexican legal and bureaucratic framework is in Dick Kamp and Michael Gregory's *Hazardous Material Inventory of Agua Prieta, Sonora Maquiladoras with Recommendations for*

U.S.-Mexico Transboundary Regulations (Naco, Arizona: Border Ecology Project, 1988).

23. Kathleen Shimmer, Conference on Hazardous Waste Management, Tijuana, Mexico, November 15, 1988.

24. Leslie Kochan, *The Maquiladoras and Toxics: The Hidden Costs of Production South of the Border* (AFL-CIO, No. 186, February 1989).

25. Recently, lawyers seem to have taken over analysis of the impact of Mexican laws on the *maquiladora* industry. One example is Douglas W. Alexander, co-author of "Hazardous Waste Regulation of the Maquiladora Industry: Legal Framework and Practical Guidelines for Compliance," *Twin Plant News*, February 1989; and the *Lormal Letter* published by the law firm of Gray, Cary, Ames, and Frye, San Diego, Fall 1989.

26. *El Paso Times*, October 29, 1989.

About the Contributors

Contributors to this book come from a variety of backgrounds and cities throughout the United States and Mexico. All have unique expertise in U.S.-Mexican trade relations. The following is an alphabetical listing of their names and a brief summary of their backgrounds.

José Carlos Alvarez Rivero is director of the Centro de Control Total de Calidad, an organization that he founded. He is a former director general of food and beverages of the Mexican Secretaría de Salubridad y Asistencia. Alvarez Rivero graduated from the Universidad Iberoamericana with a chemical engineering degree. He earned a Master of Arts degree in food technology from Reading University in England and a second Master of Arts in food sciences from the University of California at Davis.

C. Richard Bath is a professor in the Department of Political Science at the University of Texas at El Paso. He is a member of the U.S.-Mexico Border Health Association, PROFMEX, and the Rocky Mountain Council on Latin American Studies Executive Council. His research focuses on Latin American-U.S. environmental and natural resource issues. He has taught at Lamar University, the Universidad de San Simón in Bolivia, and the University of Arizona's summer program in Guadalajara, Mexico. He earned his B.A. from the University of Nevada at Reno and his graduate degrees from Tulane University.

Ovidio Botella C. recently joined Cia. Mexicana de Aviación, S.A., as a project manager. Before joining the aviation company in 1990, he was project director and commercial and information service director of Texel, S.A., where he was responsible for commercial and strategic planning, marketing research, the budget, and project administration. From 1981 to 1986, Botella was project coordinator and marine and marketing manager of Gilsa Bienes de Capital, S.A. Before moving to Gilsa, he was general manager of Técnicos Asociados, S.A. He holds a

B.S. degree in engineering from the Universidad Nacional Autónoma de México.

Benito Bucay F. is adjunct director of Industrias Resistol, S.A. He is the former general director of Fenoquimia, S.A., director of the chemical and petrochemical division of the Sociedad de Fomento Industrial, director general of the Grupo Sabre, S.A., and president of the Consejo del Grupo Pliana. He received a chemical engineering degree from the Universidad Nacional Autónoma de México, and has studied finance and accounting, personnel administration, project administration, engineering, and business at Oklahoma University, the University of Chicago, and the University of California at Los Angeles.

Enrique García C. is general director of Texel, S.A., where he formerly served as sales and marketing director. From 1963 to 1974 he worked in textile chemical sales and marketing for Ciba-Geigy in Mexico, Switzerland, Spain, and Australia. He has a B.S. degree in chemistry from the Universidad Nacional Autónoma de México.

José Giral B. is a chemical engineer and head of the Study Group on Technology in the Division of Graduate Studies at the Universidad Nacional Autónoma de México. Before joining the UNAM faculty, he worked for 20 years at DuPont, serving in various technical and operational functions. From 1983 to 1988, he was responsible for the rescue of Pliana, one of the food sector enterprises adversely affected by Mexico's financial crisis. Pliana now operates successfully as Texel. In 1988, he became director general of XABRE, a consortium of 200 companies. He was the 1985 recipient of a national award from the Mexican chemical industry.

Enrique Gruner Kronheim is advisor to the Mexican Secretaría de Comercio y Fomento Industrial and represents his country at international meetings dealing with the manufacture of pharmaceutical products. He has worked in production, engineering, maintenance, chemical product manufacture, design, and plant installation for Syntex, S.A., Diosynth, S.A., L.B. Russell Chemicals de México, S.A., Productos Esteroides, S.A., Quiñonas de México, S.A., and Desc, S.A. He is an original member of the Mexican Institute of Chemical Engineers, and a member of the Chemical Society of Mexico and the American Chemical Society. Gruner also has served as a pharmaceutical consultant for SELA, UNIDO, UNESCO, and other international organizations.

Alan D. Jones was the conference director for the 1989 Woodlands Conference, *U.S.-Mexico Industrial Integration: Today and Tomorrow*, which led to the publication of this volume. He is the associate director of the Center for Growth Studies of the Houston Advanced

Research Center, an independent, nonprofit research corporation. The Center for Growth Studies conducts policy research on global environmental and natural resource issues, including the relationship between environmental protection and economic development. Jones worked with the U.S. Environmental Protection Agency in Washington, D.C. and Science Applications International Corporation in McLean, Virgina. He has a Master of Public Affairs degree from the Lyndon B. Johnson School of Public Affairs at the University of Texas at Austin.

Stephen L. Lande is president of Manchester Trade, Inc. and an international trade expert and professional negotiator. He is also adjunct professor for international trade in the Karl F. Landegger Program in International Business Diplomacy at Georgetown University. He has formerly served in the Office of the U.S. Trade Representative and as a Foreign Service officer in the Office of General Commercial Policy and the Office of Textiles. He received a B.A. degree in economics from Colgate University and an Master of Arts in international affairs from Johns Hopkins University's School of Advanced International Studies.

Florencio López-de-Silanes is a researcher at Harvard University, where he is completing a Ph.D. in economics. He formerly served as a Department of Economics faculty member at the Instituto Tecnológico Autónomo de México in Mexico City. He is the author of numerous publications on Mexican trade and industrial policy.

Donald R. Lyman is PS2 project manager for IBM Latin America in Boca Raton, Florida. Before joining IBM in 1984, Mr. Lyman was a U.S. Foreign Service officer in Bogotá, Columbia; Washington, D.C.; and Mexico. In Mexico he was executive assistant to the U.S. Ambassador and acting deputy chief of mission. He has written numerous articles and chapters on U.S.-Mexican and U.S.-Latin American relations.

Marc E. Maartens is senior managing partner of Marc E. Maartens Associates, an international business counselor based in Birmingham, Michigan. Previously, he worked for Ford Motor Company as staff director of operations and business planning for Latin American Automotive Operations. He is a former chairman of the Latin American Affairs Committee of the Motor Vehicle Manufacturing Association of the United States, and former chairman of the Program Committee of the Council of the Americas. He is a graduate of the Amsterdam Lyceum College and has studied in France, Switzerland, England, and at other Dutch institutions.

Rina Quijada is responsible for expanding the Latin American marketplace for Chemical Market Associates, Inc., of Houston. Before joining CMAI, Quijada was with Petroquímica de Venezuela, where she worked throughout Latin America in the petrochemical and plastic markets. She is presently working on her dissertation for a Ph.D. in economics. She received a chemistry degree from W.J. Bryan College and then entered the American Graduate School of International Studies.

Rogelio Ramírez de la O is director general of ECANAL, S.A. de C.V. He is formerly an economist at the Center for Transnational Studies at the United Nations in New York. He received a B.A. in economics from the Universidad Nacional Autónoma de México and a Ph.D. in economics from Cambridge University in England.

Clark W. Reynolds is a professor of economics in Stanford University's Food Research Institute and director of the university's Americas Program. He is principal investigator for a U.S.-Mexico relations project that focuses on economic policy in Mexico since 1960. In his seven years on this project, Dr. Reynolds has examined the structure and growth of the Mexican economy and its implications for employment, income, and sector and regional development in the context of growing interdependence with the United States. He has consulted with private and government organizations in Brazil, Columbia, Argentina, Costa Rica, Peru, Mexico, Central America, and Jamaica, as well as with bilateral agencies and international financial institutions like the World Bank, the Inter-American Development Bank, the United Nations Development Program, and the Organization of American States.

Luis Rubio F. is director general of the Centro de Investigación para el Desarrollo, A.C., a Mexico City-based independent think tank devoted to the study of economic and policy issues. Dr. Rubio has edited and authored numerous publications on these issues, and has served as a member of the board of directors of Banco Obrero, a member of the Board of Jueves de Excelsior, and president of the Association of Political Risk Analysts. He has also served as planning director of Citibank, N.A., Mexico, and as advisor to the Mexican Secretary of the Treasury. He received his Masters of Arts in strategy and Latin American studies and a Ph.D. in political science from Brandeis University, and a Licenciatura in political science and public administration from the Universidad Iberoamericana.

Roberto A. Sánchez is director of the Department of Urban and Environmental Studies at the Colegio de la Frontera Norte in Tijuana, Baja California. He previously served as a professor of urban planning in the School of Architecture at the Universidad Nacional Autónoma de México. His research focuses on Mexican environmental issues, particularly the transboundary movement of hazardous waste, the impact of *maquiladora* plants on northern Mexico, border water resource management, and the impact of border urban growth. He is the author of numerous journal articles on these subjects, as well as *El Medio Ambiente como Fuente de Conflicto en la Relación Binacional México-Estados Unidos*. Sánchez has a Ph.D. in regional and urban planning from the University of Dortmund in Germany.

Robert M. Sherwood is an international business counselor who serves as counsel to the Brazil Ad Hoc Group on Intellectual Property, a U.S.-British industrial group focusing on the role of intellectual property in economic development. He also serves as counsel to a similar group in Mexico. He is chairman of the Licensing Executives Society Committee for Latin America, and has served as vice president of the advisory board for the Council of the Americas. Mr. Sherwood also has practiced law on Wall Street and served as a corporate attorney for several international companies. He is a graduate of Harvard College, Columbia University, and Harvard Law School.

Lloyd E. Slater is a consultant on food trade policy and the author of articles on automation, food science, and biomedical engineering in numerous scientific and technical journals. He was the executive director of the Academy of Independent Scholars and manager of the Food and Climate Forum, a project of the Aspen Institute for Humanistic Studies, before retiring in 1985. He is also the former head of the Institute of Social Technology and former editor of Food Engineering International. He also directed the Reston, Virginia Foundation for Community Development and was associate research director at Case Institute of Technology. He is a Cornell University graduate.

Sidney Weintraub is the Dean Rusk Professor at the Lyndon B. Johnson School of Public Affairs at the University of Texas at Austin and a distinguished visiting scholar at the Center for Strategic and International Studies in Washington, D.C. He is a former career diplomat, who served as assistant administrator of the Agency for International Development, deputy assistant secretary of state for economic affairs, and chief of the AID mission in Chile under the Alliance for Progress. He has also served as senior fellow at the Brookings Institution. Weintraub is also author and editor of numerous books on U.S.-Mexican economic, political and trade relations, and the author of numerous articles on similar topics. He has a Ph.D. in economics from American University, an M.A. in economics from Yale University, B.J. and M.A. degrees in journalism from the University of Missouri, and a B.B.A. in accounting from City College, New York.

Herbert Weinstein is corporate technical director for Grupo Quan in Mexico City. He is responsible for ice cream manufacturing, logistics, and technical functions dealing with product quality and development. Before joining Grupo Quan in 1989, he worked for General Foods Corporation. He was technical vice president for General Foods de

México, S.A. de C.V. from 1985 to 1989. He is a member of the Institute of Food Technologists, Asociación de Técnicos en Alimentos de México, and the Instituto Mexicano de Ingenieros Químicos. He graduated from the Massachusetts Institute of Technology with M.S. and Ph.D. degrees in food science and technology, and from the Universidad Nacional Autónoma de México with a chemical engineering degree.